BEYOND SURVIVAL

New Directions for the Disarmament Movement

BEYOND SURVIVAL

NEW DIRECTIONS FOR
THE DISARMAMENT MOVEMENT

Edited By

Michael Albert & David Dellinger

South End Press / Boston, Ma. 02116

TABLE OF CONTENTS

Introduction   1
    Michael Albert and David Dellinger
The Bread Is Rising   7
    David Dellinger
Lessons from the Sixties   43
    Michael Albert
Feminism and Militarism   81
    Leslie Cagan
Racism: Fuel for the War Machine   119
    Jack O'Dell
An Atoll, A Submarine and the U.S. Economy   155
    Alex Cockburn and James Ridgeway
Labor and Disarmament:
The Meeting of Social Movements   187
    Paula Rayman
Many Paths To War: Right, Center, and Left   205
    Holly Sklar
Which Way for the Disarmament Movement:
Interventionism and Nuclear War   247
    Noam Chomsky
What About The Soviet Threat?   311
    David Dellinger
Afterword   349
    Michael Albert and David Dellinger

INTRODUCTION

A perplexing problem confronts the disarmament movement. It must broaden and deepen at the same time, two tasks that appear contradictory. To succeed it must broaden its active constituency to include people who have traditionally viewed unconventional ideas and activist movements with suspicion, if not hostility. But it must also deepen its critique of a society that is spiritually and politically capable of threatening to use weapons that can destroy the human race.

We did not reach our present plight by accident. And we won't escape it without changing the beliefs and institutions that got us here. But many Americans have been conditioned to think that the beliefs and institutions that have to be changed are necessary features of a society that is both "free" and "democratic." Some of the economic, political and cultural conventions that are discussed in the following pages can be compared to earlier practices in large sections of the country that required blacks to sit in the back of busses, use separate toilet facilities and be excluded from "nice" restaurants. To change them is necessary but many people fear that to do so would be unnatural or even impossible. They have been shaken by the prospect of nuclear annihilation and are warily open to new ideas. But they have deep-seated resistances to the changes and methods (such as mass demonstrations and civil disobedience) that are required if we are to save ourselves and go beyond survival to the creation of a better society.

1

There is no easy solution to this dilemma. It calls for patience, sensitivity, and experimentation. It calls for a diversity of actors and actions and an open, respectful dialogue that does not sweep anyone's views under the rug of silence or contempt. In particular, it requires humility on the part of those of us who attempt to explain the linkages between the nuclear peril and other problems of society so as to facilitate the necessary changes.

We do not mean the false humility that is encouraged by a hierarchical society. That kind of humility leads people to trust "experts" and political insiders more than their own institutions and humanity. But it is a long series of insiders, both liberal and conservative, Democratic and Republican, together with their overlapping coteries of experts, who have gotten us into the current mess. And it has been some unaccustomed assertions of common sense by ordinary people who are not usually involved in national decision-making that has produced a dramatic explosion of anti-nuclear sentiment and activity at both the grassroots and national levels. These people have emerged as a dynamic factor in the country's politics because they are "naively" concerned with survival for themselves and their fellows. They must not now be coopted by sophisticated, personally ambitious office-seekers who say that they agree with the need for disarmament (which may even be true), but tell us that if we turn the problem over to them, they will get us as much "arms control" as is possible, given the "realities" of "practical politics" and the need for a strong military defense. Arms control is, by definition, a rejection of disarmament. Replacing a more belligerent set of lawmakers and executives with a less belligerent set who also accept the premise of nuclear deterrence but think that it can be secured less expensively and with more compassion for the poor, may win us some breathing space, but it will not solve the problem. It may slow down the tide carrying us to annihilation, but it will not stem it. Instead it will retard the flows of creative energy and citizenly involvement that have begun to resuscitate a population that has been too long intimidated and dormant.

This "normal" electoral response to our abnormal problem is particularly ironic because an important dynamic within the disarmament movement is concern for the dehumanizing effect—particularly on future generations—of living in a society that says there is no way to respond to serious international conflict except by preparing for nuclear war. Many adults have become active because of what they see happening to children who live with a knowledge we cannot keep from them; namely, that a terrifying death may envelop them and everyone they know at some unpredictable moment in the near future. We have graduated from a time when a superstitious society threatened its children with the fires of a distant hell, if they acted "badly," to a time when a society with new superstitions threatens our children with being engulfed without warning in a flaming inferno even while still alive, no matter how they act. How much worse is it for them if parents, teachers, and neighbors indicate by their passivity that there is nothing we can do about this, only pile up nuclear weapons (the right-wingers' solution) or hold onto them (liberals) so that we can kill our rivals and their children while they are killing us and our children. All the while, everyone knows, including the children, that faulty computers, itchy fingers, or a foolish bluff that is called, may cause one side or the other to initiate the dreaded event at any time.

The kind of humility we need comes hand in hand with the sense of empowerment we get from working with people of widely varying backgrounds and differing views in a common effort to prevent cosmic disaster. On occasions such as the massive disarmament demonstration in New York on June 12, 1982, the overwhelming sense of unity and strength was not undermined by the obvious diversities in lifestyle and viewpoints among the participants. In fact the knowledge of that diversity made the feelings of solidarity and hope stronger and more invigorating. Diversity becomes strength when we avoid the self-righteous organizational cannibalism and ideological dogmatism that sometimes goes with strong convictions, and engage instead in searching, non-manipulative dialogue. Such a dialogue is indispensable for the constantly improving politics the movement (and all of its various sections) requires and for the various forms of genuinely cooperative effort necessary for success.

It is not easy to live up to this understanding when planning new campaigns, debating old and new tactics, presenting our views at committee meetings or public events. Even with the unifying pressures generated by a common emergency, it is hard to put ideas that differ from our own into the perspective that comes from reminding ourselves of the changes we ourselves have gone through in the course of our life journey and from knowing that unpredictable changes lie ahead if we are not to stagnate.

As this book indicates, this spirit did not always prevail in the planning and organizing for June 12th. And it won't always prevail in the future. But combining struggle and solidarity, heterogeneity and unity, has to be the standard at which we aim and to which we keep returning. It is the standard by which we tried to organize this book, despite and because of the strong views held by the editors on the necessity for facing up to a range of injustices—economic, racial, sexual, political, and ecological— that we feel have contributed to creating the nuclear crisis.

We did not try to live up to this standard, however, by artificially including every possible viewpoint, which was a practical impossibility in any case. In fact we have purposely left out one tempting view that is sufficiently well publicized and promoted not to need repeating here. It is the view that every issue except the horror of nuclear weapons should be excluded from the agenda of the disarmament movement. Instead we invited writers with a more wholeistic attitude. They play influential roles in the broad mass movement for disarmament (whether as coalition leaders, researchers, speakers at teach-ins, authors, or journalists with a diverse and politically hetero-geneous readership) and are also in the forefront of other struggles that have an important identity of their own.

Leslie Cagan and Jack O'Dell worked in key positions on the staff of the coalition that organized the June 12th event and play equally significant roles in organizations devoted primarily to working for racial justice (O'Dell) and an end to patriarchal oppression and homophobia (Cagan). However, they are not partisans of other causes who jumped on disarmament, as believers in elitist "vanguard" groups often do. For besides their vital work in other areas, both have long histories of anti-war activity, including leadership roles in the movement to end U.S. aggression in Vietnam. They could no more be silent in the face of the nuclear peril than they could be misled by it into becoming quiescent concerning their own oppression or that of other members of an oppressed race, sex, or sexual preference group.

Alex Cockburn and James Ridgeway are imaginative and iconoclastic investigators and authors in the fields of ecology, the economy, the arms industry, Washington politics, and the media. Because of their mordant exposures of media hypocrisy and fatuity, it is widely rumored that editors and publishers at the *New York Times* and *Washington Post* have considered contracting with the Pentagon or CIA to remove them from the scene, or at least to do away with Cockburn's weekly column, "Pressclips" in the *Village Voice*.

For years Noam Chomsky has been providing the anti-war movement and others with scrupulously researched, devastating material on the philosophy and practices of U.S. imperialism— and its media mystification in Indochina, the Middle East, Timor (a ravaged country that most Americans had never heard of until Noam exposed what had been happening there) and all over the world.

Holly Sklar is an active feminist and opponent of nuclear power. She is known for her research and publications on the Trilateral Commission and is currently working as the director of a new radical media and education project of the Institute for New Communications.

In short all of our contributors have approached the subject of the nuclear threat and the road to disarmament from a background of active commitment to both the anti-war movement and other struggles for justice, dignity, and human fulfillment. They share the editors' conviction that all our problems are related and none can be solved in isolation from the others.

They also share our desire that the anti-nuclear movement both broaden its constituency and deepen its understanding of why a reputedly free and democratic country oppresses so many people and is governed by leaders who think that nuclear war is winnable.

1

THE BREAD IS RISiNG
By David Dellinger

Dave Dellinger is old enough to have become a veteran of quite a few struggles for social justice, peace, and human rights, beginning in the Great Depression of the Thirties. So he stresses the importance of Albert Camus' warning to "Beware of all veterans." He takes this to include veterans of anti-militarist and other positive struggles as well as war veterans.

Dellinger is an advocate and strugglng practitioner of nonviolent action as a way of life and method of liberation. Currently he is associated with Mobilization for Survival, War Resistors League, and a number of groups advocating self-determination for both Palestinians and Jews in the Middle East. (This includes opposition to U.S. supported Israeli expansionism and support for creation of a Palestinian state in the West Bank and Gaza, as initial steps toward more creative relationships). He also works with CISPES, the Vermont Coalition for Jobs, Peace and Justice, the North Country Coalition, Northern Lights Affinity Group, the Coalition for a People's Alternative and the Institute for New Communications.

A former editor of Liberation, Cooperative Living *and* Seven Days, *he is the author of* Revolutionary Nonviolence *(Bobbs-Merrill and Anchor Press/Doubleday),* More Power Than We Know *(Anchor Press/Doubleday and a nearly finished* Autobiography in the Form of a Novel. *(Or should it be* A Novel in the Form of an Autobiography?)

A failed poet, flawed feminist and convinced pantheist, Dellinger teaches social studies and creative writing in the Adult Degree Program of Vermont College.

It is a commonplace to decry the fact that history has a tendency to repeat itself—meaning, "the errors people make are often avoidable, if people would only learn from their experiences the first time around." David Dellinger makes fewer errors than most and, in addition, has learned from his experiences—over forty years worth of front-rank activism in peace, anti-racist, labor, ecology, and other movements for social change. In this essay he draws lessons from those experiences and applies them to understanding the current problems and possibilities confronting anti-nuclear activists.

I have known Dave for almost fifteen years, but only peripherally as co-participants in projects, events, and organizations. We would have a conversation, sometimes lengthy, sometimes very brief, maybe two or three times a year. The opportunity to co-edit this volume, working together on its conception and jointly writing its introduction and afterword, was a wonderful aspect of this project. I hope readers will benefit from Dave's contribution as much as I have from working with him, and will look forward as I do to the time when Dave will complete the book he interrupted work on to edit this volume. It is an autobiographical treatment of the history he has lived and the lessons he has drawn from it.

—M.A.

Growing up, I was taught that the instinct for survival is basic to all forms of life, and that no species could survive without it. Many times in the last sixty years I have thought that perhaps this instinct had become diluted as the human species evolved and became ever more separated from its roots in the natural universe.

Perhaps it survived in a twisted way, as an impulse in individuals that expresses itself in the competitive scramble for money and glory, privilege and power, that is so central to Western culture and is conventionally attributed to "human nature." Or in the patriotic fervor that grips countries in the face of external danger, sometimes real and sometimes invented by special interest groups for unpatriotic reasons: to promote highly profitable arms sales, to exalt the military with its pompous rituals and authoritarian ways; or provide foreign scapegoats for problems they themselves have brought upon us or exacerbated. If these were the ways the instinct survived in us, obviously it survived imperfectly.

How else to explain the wars we have engaged in, the ever more sophisticated weapons of mass annihilation we have developed, the poisoning of our food, soil, air, water and human relations in the pursuit of private profits? How else to interpret the establishment, bit by bit, of a monetary "bottom line" as the criterion for deciding the uses to which our natural resources and productive capital are put, and therefore the uses to which most of us must devote our energies of mind, body and soul if we are to survive, even in "peacetime"? This is in defiance of our once recognized mutual interdependence and our innate, never quite stifled, sense of community responsibility for one another, including "even the least" of our sisters and brothers.

The system that institutionalized our denial of the inter-dependence on which the survival of the race depends used to be called capitalism. Now its defenders prefer to call it the "free market economy." But it is privately owned capital, not freedom, that dominates the marketplace, workplace, elections, and arms industry. Capital is the common product of generations of labor and inventiveness joined with the riches of nature. But we have denied its communal origins and its sources in nature and have imagined that it could "belong" to individuals whose "owner-ship" gives them the right, with only the most minimal safeguards, to use it against the welfare (and now the survival) of the world community. Those who benefit from this deception claim that what is good for capital is good for everyone. The benefits, they say, will "trickle down" to the masses (like crumbs from the tables of the kings and barons whom we pride ourselves we no longer believe in).*

Now, as if out of nowhere (though we shall see that this is not really the case), the communal instinct for survival of the species is asserting itself in spectacular fashion. Wave after wave of public opposition to nuclear weapons sweeps over Western Europe and the United States. Millions march, pass resolutions and sign petitions. Millions of others who have not yet overcome their socially conditioned prejudices against such actions blurt out their concerns at neighborhood grocery stores and corner taverns, in union halls and at church suppers, at the cocktail parties of the rich and in the ghettoes of the poor. It's fast getting to be like the latter years of the Vietnam War, when no government sponsored event or other prestigious occasion was safe from having some entertainer or honored guest stand up and speak her or his mind in opposition to government policy. Despite the official assurances that the only way to save the human race is to be willing and able to destroy it, there is a groundswell of understanding that we will not survive, in either the short or long run, unless we take our money and energies out of the arms race and devote them to socially useful projects that benefit the human family.

---

*Capital has more power over our daily lives than anyone we elect to take the heat or sop up the glory. From late 1973 to early 1977, a lot of people were worried that neither the President (Ford) nor the Vice President (Rockefeller) had been elected. It would have made more sense to worry about Nelson's brother David, the Chairman of Chase Manhattan Bank, who wasn't elected either, at least not by the American people, but he had more power than either of the others and unlimited tenure of office.

Consider the following description of what happened in New York City on June 12, 1982. It is from a newspaper that is not noted for taking a sympathetic view of anti-war or disarmament protests, especially in its editorials. But its news columns often reflect the hopes and fears of ordinary people more accurately than more liberal (and elitist) papers, such as the *New York Times* and *Washington Post*.

> On the second Saturday in June, a critical mass began to move together in Manhattan. From all points of the compass, from dawn until late afternoon, they assembled.... The soldiers of this sudden army eluded classification. They were young and old, poor and privileged. They were radical and reactionary, recurrent activists and reluctant witnesses....It was apparently a common perception of danger that ran like a shudder from the remote refuge of New England to the tenements of the lower East Side. *Some animal instinct seemed to respond, as if a threat had entered the human forest.*[1] [Emphasis added]

In a later chapter, I will discuss some evidence that the same instinct is asserting itself in Eastern Europe and the Soviet Union, in opposition to the militarism of their governments and strengthened by news of our opposition to the militarism of our government. Here, I will just mention that on February 13, 1982, six thousand East Germans defied their government by demonstrating publicly in Dresden against the nuclear weapons and foreign policies of the Warsaw Pact and NATO countries. The same animal instinct is at work, like yeast, on both sides of the Cold War.

As Clergy and Laity Against the War in Vietnam used to say in the Sixties, "The Bread is Rising." The bread is indeed slowly rising all over the world because, for the first time in human history, humanity faces the possibility or even the probability that it will destroy itself. Not gradually, not by the hundreds, thousands or even millions, but at one fell swoop. Totally, irreversibly. And as a species we are beginning to react in self-defense, incomplete and imperfect as our understanding of the danger is or of how best to go about saving ourselves.

Optimism in High Places

Do I overstate the case? Possibly. There are those who tell us that destruction would not be total or final; that somehow, somewhere, sometime, some people would survive and some section of the earth's surface become habitable again. Meanwhile, whoever is technically correct this month, the United States and Soviet Union are extending the arms race into outer space and perfecting diabolical plagues and chemical potions to make sure that ultimately the direst predictions come true and absolutely no one survives.[2]

For more and more of us, the denials of total obliteration, the intended assurances and words of hope about the future, only add to our sense of peril. To our knowledge of the awesome, ultimately incalculable destructiveness of nuclear war, they add the knowledge that we suffer from insanity in high places. Something quite possibly more dangerous than conventional insanity in the decision-making circles where, until we get rid of the weapons and alter the power relationships of the society, the decision can be made to use them.

It is perhaps even more frightening to realize that this insanity does not exist in a vacuum. It cannot be dismissed as "them" versus the rest of us. As several chapters indicate, it is less an individual deviation than the culmination in our elected leaders and their appointees of a lot of collective "insanities" that have accumulated for years and are deep in the culture. They can be seen in our economy and in commonplace attitudes and practices toward people of color, women, homosexuals, members of the underclasses, non-achievers, Nature, ecology, the Third World, and socialist countries.[3]

Here is an example from the testimony of Eugene V. Rostow at the Senate Hearings that led to his confirmation as Director of the U.S. Arms Control and Disarmament Agency:

> Japan, after all, not only survived but flourished after
> the nuclear attack....Some predict that there would be

ten million casualties on one side and one hundred million on the other. But that is not the whole of the population.[4]

I am tempted to think that the incredible insensitivity of this statement would have made Hitler, Stalin, and Genghis Khan blush. More important, is this perhaps part of a calculated attempt to prepare the American people (or maybe Congress) for a forthcoming U.S. First Strike? So that "they" would lose the hundred million and "we" *only* ten million? If so, would the First Strike have taken place already if the anti-nuclear movement had not swept through Europe and the United States?

Did the predictions of the number of casualties come from a government document under discussion in the circles where, under present circumstances, the decision on whether or not to launch a sneak attack will be made? If so, did the decision-makers think that the American people could be persuaded, after the fact, to accept ten million casualties, provided the Great Communicator, the wryly smiling, deeply moral Ronald Reagan, explained the circumstances to the irradiated survivors, from his airborne Command Post? Have they told his speechwriters to include in his text the ludicrous estimates they have made of how many years it will take to get the country's gross national product back to normal after a nuclear war?

When I hear such "comforting" predictions of "acceptable" casualties from the present Republican administration, I remember a similar "optimism" that was expressed by the previous Democratic administration. President Carter announced in his State of the Union Address for 1980 that the United States was prepared to use "any means necessary, including military force," to protect our access to what for all practical purposes is considered as "our" oil in the Persian Gulf area. As Jonathan Schell has written:

> Since the United States clearly lacked the conventional power to repel a Soviet attack in a region near the borders of the Soviet Union, *"any means" could refer to nothing but nuclear arms.* The threat was spelled out explicitly shortly after the speech in a story in the

New York Times—thought to be a leak from the Administration—about a 1979 Defense Department "study" which, according to the *Times*, said that American conventional forces could not stop a Soviet thrust into northern Iran and that "to prevail in an Iranian scenario we might have to threaten or *make use of* tactical nuclear weapons."[5]

The politically unrealistic reference to *tactical* nuclear weapons was part of a public relations campaign to convince a worried public that the administration would be able to preside over a "limited" nuclear war without danger to the American people. This despite the fact that it couldn't get six helicopters in and out of an unguarded Iranian desert safely. Meanwhile, the official spokesman assigned to interpret the President's frightening announcement, William Dyess of the State Department, made the real nature of the threat clear:

"Q: In nuclear war are we committed not to make the first strike?
A: No sir.
Q: We could conceivably take the offensive...
A: We make no comment on that whatsoever, but the Soviets know that this terrible weapon has been dropped on human beings twice in human history, and it was an American President who dropped it both times."[6]

My second example from the current administration comes from Energy Secretary James B. Edwards, after he witnessed the test explosion of a nuclear bomb on the anniversary eve of the date the bomb was dropped on Hiroshima. He said he found the event "exciting," that President Truman was right in having the bombs dropped on Hiroshima and Nagasaki, that the Reagan administration would continue to manufacture and test nuclear bombs, and that under some circumstances these might include bombs outlawed by the limited test ban treaty of 1963. Speaking of the anti-nuclear movement, he said:

The thing they're talking about is the weapon that can preserve their ability for free discussion*....War is hell, but if we get into one, I want us to come out of it as number one, not number two.[7]

Daniel Ellsberg and other former "insiders" have provided information concerning a series of threats by American Presidents, including Truman, Eisenhower, Kennedy, Johnson, Nixon and Carter, to initiate nuclear warfare. Some of President Reagan's rhetoric may be more belligerent than that of some of his predecessors, and some of the statements by members of his administration less guarded. Some of his programs, such as trying to crush the Soviet Union economically, or developing the imagined capacity to fight even a "protracted" nuclear war and win, may be more reckless. But in the area we are discussing U.S. policy has remained basically the same from 1945 to the present, through liberal and conservative, Republican and Democratic administrations. It appears that until we bring into play other, non-electoral restraints and effect changes in the *de facto* power relationships within the country, any administration we will be able to elect will be willing to use nuclear warfare if it thinks it is "necessary" in order to preserve America's superpower status and protect the "vital interests" of America's corporate empire. In reality, of course, nuclear war cannot achieve these goals, not any longer. But the threat of launching such a war has gone a long way toward doing so. For this reason—and undoubtedly for

---

*As an example of the type of "free discussion" they might be having, for a while, I refer you to Robert J. Lifton's decription of "a scene conjured up by Herman Kahn. The bomb has fallen; one survivor who feels weak and complains of radiation effects has his individual radiation meter (everyone has one) read by another survivor: 'you look at his meter and say, 'You have only received ten roetgens, why are you vomiting? Pull your self together and get to work.''' [*Indefensible Weapons, The Political and Psychological Case Against Nuclearism* Robert J. Lifton and Richard Falk, Basic Books, Harper; 1982.] As I understand it, Kahn's example was intended to be reassuring. If everyone is equipped with a radiation meter, we will be able to respond to a nuclear attack and its disabling effects rationally, with courage and discipline.

"humanitarian" considerations as well, no matter how narrowly conceived—all nuclear-age presidents so far have preferred to achieve their geo-political aims by invoking the threat rather than by indulging in the reality. But this is a slim thread for the future of the human race to hang on. Who can tell when the dynamics of threat and counterthreat will get out of hand, in this country or some other, whether through mechanical accident, political miscalculation or the kind of insanity I have mentioned? As United States power gradually recedes throughout the world and our leaders find themselves unable to be "No. 1" any longer in the Superbowl of international economics and politics, the insanity itself may get out of hand. Some "born again" "patriotic" Samson may decide to pull the temple of human civilization down on everyone's heads rather than see the United States become, in the words of a former President, "a pitiful, helpless giant."

A Danger in the Anti-Nuclear Movement

Did I overstate the second half of my thesis? Does the current response to this insanity signal something more basic and hopeful than the rise of one more anti-war movement that is doomed to political impotence and eventual failure? Is there really a new factor at work this time that is capable of saving us?

Let us begin with some negative evidence that throws some doubt on this optimistic view. It is the existence of a serious danger in the current, relatively primitive stage of the anti-nuclear movement.

The danger I refer to is illustrated by the case of a man who was driving through a small town and suddenly found himself confronted by a huge truck that was barreling down the middle of the road. Unnerved by the prospect of a head-on collision, he swerved sharply to the side and mowed down six people on the sidewalk. In reacting to the nuclear peril, we must not lose sight of the overall context in which it exists. Otherwise we may do more harm than good and contribute to the coming of the very disaster we are trying to avoid.

Continued spread of information on the destructiveness of nuclear weapons is critical. It can wake us up to the urgency of our plight and sensitize us to the nature of a society that has brought such weapons into being and, unless altered, will use them. But it will not have this dual effect if we become so narrowly preoccupied with the prospects of a nuclear Armegeddon that we overlook the people of Third World countries who are already being mowed down at an alarming rate by so-called conventional weapons. These weapons range from bombs, helicopter gunships and intruments of torture to forms of violence that are just as deadly but not conventionally classified as weapons. In the latter category, consider the domination of Third World economies and governments, rape of their resources, pollution of their environments and murderous exploitation of their labor by U.S.-based transnational corporations backed by the CIA, the State Department, and the military.

Twelve million babies a year (more than thirty thousand a day) die in developing countries before their first birthday, while their resources are depleted by profit-seeking corporations and the demands of the U.S. arms industry and the Pentagon for strategic minerals and other raw materials. At home, the infant death rate of blacks is double that of whites, the maternal death rate triple. If only a thousand babies or women in labor were gathered in one place intentionally and blown up by a bomb they wouldn't be any more dead, but the anti-nuclear movement (and everyone else) would raise a storm of protest.

Between thirty-five and forty million people have died in the "limited" wars that have taken place since World War II and ninety-five percent of these wars have been fought in developing countries, with foreign powers intervening in most of them, and 79% of the interventions carried out by Western nations. This cannot and must not be ignored, yet the danger that it will be is great.

"Less Important Deaths"

I was thrilled by the numbers, spirit, music, signs, banners, and even most of the speeches at the June 12 Disarmament Rally in New York. But my joy was offset by knowledge that while the inspiring demonstration was taking place, Israeli planes were slaughtering Palestinian and Lebanese civilians with cluster bombs, phospherous and other obscene, non-nuclear weapons. These armaments were paid for by U.S. taxpayers and supplied free of charge to the Israeli invaders. To compound the tragedy, young Israelis brought up in the aftermath of the Nazi holocaust were being killed as they imposed a new holocaust on young Palestinians who were brought up in exile and longing for a homeland.

Yet there were some who argued, with the best of intentions, that it would disrupt the unity and mar our day of triumph to mention this "lesser" problem or these "lesser" deaths. In a follow-up meeting in my home state of Vermont, an anti-nuclear organizer warned that to include a speaker from the Committee in Solidarity with the People of El Salvador in a forthcoming rally might scare away those who favor a nuclear freeze but don't want to hear about other issues. In March of 1982, several traditional peace groups that concentrate on the need for a single-issue nuclear freeze movement stretched a little to endorse a national demonstration in favor of cutting off U.S. military aid to El Salvador, but objected to having speakers who would stress the connections with U.S. racism at home and abroad. As if failure to root out racist—and for that matter sexist—practices and attitudes were not one of the reasons "little" genocidal wars and oppressions get legitimized, or at least tolerated, and grow into big wars.

I respect the people who sincerely argue that the road to peace is to get out the largest possible numbers by avoiding "controversial" issues. But we cannot afford to overlook the institutional and psychological linkages that join these "other" wars and daily violations of human life and dignity to the nuclear horror. We cannot afford to underestimate the ability of the government to coopt a movement that does not make these connections, as it coopted the anti-bomb movement of the late Fifties and early Sixties by signing a limited test ban treaty. Nor can we predict with any degree of certainty in what internal area of the society or external area of the globe the next crisis will erupt, often with powerful implications for the issue on which we have been concentrating with single-minded passion.

Recent history is replete with examples. For a year or two before the ban on atmospheric testing was adopted, leaders of the anti-war movement made strenuous efforts to ban any references to Vietnam from the massive (for those days) marches and rallies against bomb testing, arguing that Vietnam was a minor confusing issue compared with the Bomb. At the Easter 1963 anti-bomb rally in New York, some demonstrators raised signs demanding "U.S. out of Vietnam" and "No U.S. Military in Vietnam." The M.C. ordered them to remove their signs from the demonstration and told the next speaker, who had counselled against the order, not to mention Vietnam in his talk. The next speaker happened to be me. I knew less about what was going on in Vietnam than I should have, but I knew that the presence of the U.S. military there was a danger. I spoke of the links between U.S. bomb testing, U.S. military presence all over the world, including Vietnam, and the drive of the U.S. military-industrial establishment for world-wide economic and political domination. For this I was told by the chairman of the event, an anti-bomb zealot whose sincerity I have never doubted but who still argues at coalition meetings for "keeping the issue simple," that I would never be allowed to speak at another coalition anti-war rally.

When the partial test ban was adopted, it shut off mass protests for several crucial years while the government proceeded full speed ahead toward the abyss, not only with production and deployment of nuclear weapons but with expansion of its military aggression in Vietnam. In addition to all the other horrors of the Vietnam war, the government under both Johnson and Nixon came perilously close to "testing" its nuclear weapons on their Vietnamese opponents.

An earlier example of a different kind from the anti-bomb movement involved efforts to exclude references to racism from the rallies and educational material of the Fifties. But it was the unexpected eruption of nonviolent black revolts in the South, beginning with the Montgomery Bus Boycott and the student sit-ins, that energized large sections of the country creating a new mood of hope that it was possible to "fight city hall" (and Washington), when human life and dignity were clearly at stake. This not only strengthened the anti-bomb movement but also added significantly to the pressures on the government to make concessions in either or both areas before, from its point of view, the growth of independent thinking and the spread of resistance activities got "out of hand." It also played an important role in the rise of the anti-Vietnam War movement. When the historic anti-war organizations were equivocating because of their traditional anti-communism and their fear that to call for U.S. withdrawal from Vietnam was to endorse the crimes of the Soviet Union and China, blacks from the Student Nonviolent Coordinating Committee and white youths who had been inspired by working with them in the South or by knowledge of their example helped fill the gap.

For a more recent example, it was only a few years ago that cautious leaders of the movement against nuclear power fought against linkages with opposition to nuclear weapons. Again the argument was that the people were not ready to accept a movement that went "too far," this time by calling into question the necessity for a strong military "defense" through nuclear weapons. The amazing, again unanticipated, rise of the anti-nuclear (weapons) movement gives some clue as to how unrealistic this fear was. Now the problem exists in reverse—to calm the fears of those who argue that to mention nuclear power plants at coalition events will frighten those who are worried about a nuclear holocaust. Apart from several other linkages, it shouldn't be that hard to point out that every nuclear power plant that is hit with even a conventional bomb becomes a nuclear bomb capable of immense destructiveness. Jonathan Schell ponts out that "attacks on the seventy-six nuclear power plants in the United States would produce fallout whose radiation [had] much greater longevity than that of the weapons alone."

Drawing on an article by M.I.T. physicist Dr. Kosta Tsipis and one of his students, Stephen Fetter, which calculates the damage from a one-megaton thermonuclear ground burst on a one-gigawatt nuclear power plant, Schell tells us that:

In such a ground burst, the facility's radioactive

contents would be vaporized along with everything nearby, and the remains would be carried up into the mushroom cloud from which they would ascend to the earth with the rest of the fallout...[T]he long-lived radiation that was produced both by the weapon and by the power plant could prevent anyone from living on a vast area of land for decades after it fell.... [I]n building nuclear power plants nations have opened themselves to catastrophic devastation and long-term contamination of their territories by enemies who manage to get hold of only a few nuclear weapons.[8]

The last sentence of this excerpt reminds us of another linkage that we ignore at our peril: The virtually uninhibited profit drive of major U.S. corporations, including General Electric, Westinghouse and Babcock and Wilcox, has already made it possible for a still growing number of countries other than the Soviet Union (most of them staunchly anti-communist) to "get hold of...a few nuclear weapons." They may turn out to be the ones that do everyone in.

Even before the multiplication of omnicidal nuclear weapons threatened to divert our attention from the reasons these and other weapons are made, the poet Kenneth Patchen spoke ruefully of the antiwar movement of his day: "The trouble is they want to get rid of war without getting rid of the causes of war."

We should never forget that small wars are apt to grow into big ones. The nuclear holocaust is more apt to result from a conflict over which superpower controls some Third World country's (or region's) natural resources, markets and labor than from a desire by either Cold War rival to take over the homeland of the other and rule its people. Besides, "limited" wars are not limited for the people who die in them, or their surviving children, parents or lovers. What would it say about the moral integrity of the peace movement (or for that matter its political astuteness) if after a timely concentration on the suicidal nature of nuclear war it settled into a position that ignored the deaths of thousands because they are not millions—or, to be more accurate, because they become millions little by little rather than in a few apocalyptic hours? Or worse, what if we accept, however sadly, the deaths of millions, so long as they do not include our own, or members of our country, race or culture? What is the difference between that and the willingness of certain North American policymakers to sacrifice Europe, if need be, in the supposed interests of the United States? Is it unconscious racism?

The institutions and attitudes that threaten us are already destroying large numbers of people in other parts of the globe with whom our lives are inextricably linked. Connections must be made between their plight and ours. Most Americans have been conditioned by the media and multi-million-dollar electoral campaigns posing as exercises in democracy to be suspicious of new political ideas. Anything outside the narrow range of conventional approaches that are debated with such fury by "our" leaders in Washington is considered either dangerous or utopian. Suspiciousness has been increased by the overblown rhetoric, narrow dogmatisms and lack of compassion of certain Left sects. So we need to be sensitive to people's fears and past negative political experiences as we probe the links. But at the heart of the grassroots upsurge of anti-nuclear sentiment are the beginnings of a readiness to think new thoughts, engage in previously deplored actions and search for new solutions. One way or another, our slowly awakening consciousness of the nuclear danger must be extended so that we understand its roots in other wars, whether they are carried out by overt military action or through other forms of violence and oppression.

We must not shortcircuit the process of awakening that is already going on by underestimating the power of people concerned for their own lives, their children's lives and the future of humanity, to embrace new ideas; especially if we go to them with a willingness to listen as well as to speak, to learn as well as to teach. Ironically, some of the groups that have new ideas that all of the rest of us need to reflect on and learn from are those who some of the movement's organizers want to push discreetly back into the closet—strong women, homosexuals, people with unconventional lifestyles, people of color, people lacking middle or upper-class attributes.

An Example from the Middle East

Two of the linkages between the nuclear danger and war in the Middle East were emphasized for me on a trip to Israel and

Lebanon in late 1979. The Israeli town of Metulla sits on the border which separates Israel from the "promised" land of Lebanon. At its outskirts is the strip of Lebanon that was already being held in escrow for the Israelis by Lebanese war lord Major Sa'ad Haddad and his "Christian" armies (later to be implicated in the massacres in the Shatila and Sabra camps of West Beirut.) In Metulla I interviewed both Major Haddad and Colonel Yoram Hamuzrahi, the Israeli officer in charge of liason between the Israeli armies and Haddad's forces. Apart from observing that Hamuzrahi gave the orders and a fawning Haddad jumped when he gave them, I learned that the salaries of Haddad's soldiers are paid and their weapons supplied by Israel. This means that both are paid by the United States. I also heard some chilling words from Colonel Hamuzrahi. They were spoken in anguish after hours of probing discussion, but with bottom-line cynicism and terrifying implications:

> When it comes to policy, every government in the world would sell their mother, their brother and their sister in order to advance their own interests. Why should Israel be any different?...*We are not going to yield an inch to the Arabs, even if it means atomic flames in New York.*

I realized a second connecton in West Beirut during an interview with Yassir Arafat. Another North American who was present asked Arafat if he was worried about the Jewish lobby in Washington. After carefully rephrasing the question to substitute the word Zionist for Jewish, Arafat replied, "I am not nearly so worried by the Zionist lobby in Washington as I am by the U.S. lobby in Israel."

I thought of this recently when I learned that Washington showed obvious foreknowledge of what Israel was planning to do four days *before* the long planned Israeli invasion and two days before the attempted assassination of the Israeli ambassador in London that served as a pretext. The U.S. Navy began at that time moving aircraft carriers and other ships to supporting positions off the coast of Lebanon and off the island of Crete (the U.S.S. Kennedy, the U.S.S. Eisenhower and their escorts and taskforces). Orders were issued prior to the invasion for U.S. Marines and other landing forces to assemble in Rota, Spain and prepare to proceed by sea toward Lebanon.[9]

Israeli General Matti Peled, hero of the 1967 Six Day War affirmed U.S. collusion when he spoke in New York, in October:

> The whole thing was in fact a joint American-Israeli venture. Israel could not allow itself a war like that without prior American consent...Israel got full backing from the U.S. all through the war. But has America achieved anything? Probably more than Israel.*

United States officials may complain from time to time, about the crude actions and blunt rhetoric of Israeli Prime Minister Menachem Begin, Defense Minister Ariel Sharon and Foreign Minister Yitzhak Shamir, much as they used to complain about some of the words and actions of Diem, Thieu and Ky in Saigon during the Vietnam war. High officials may even sincerely regret the "excesses" of these leaders, and try to replace them. (Diem was eventually assassinated either by the C.I.A. or at the instigation of the C.I.A.) But it has been U.S. policy, through a series of Republican and Democratic regimes, to build an overwhelming strike force in Israel, capable of monstrous blitzkriegs totally unrelated to the security of the Israeli people. The U.S. government has consistently supported racist, expansionist policies, not out of love for the Israeli people, not because Israeli actions benefit the American people, and certainly not in search of peace or justice. The morally offensive and politically counterproductive terrorist actions of embittered and desperate Palestinian refugees have not been the reason

---

*Village Voice, October 12, 1982. According to Peled, "We now know that by September—from what Sharon has said—the probable war was seriously discussed by both the Israeli and American governments. Apparently the turning point came when the Americans accepted the Israeli argument that the cease-fire agreement applied all over the world; thus some act against an Israeli institution or personality would suffice. In an interview Sharon gave after the invasion, he repeated that everything had been discussed with the American government, and that it had agreed that in the event of an act of terror, Israel had the right to attack.... It was clear right away that there was a tremendous disproportion between a goal of 40 kilometers and the number of Israeli forces involved.... [T]he

either, but the services Israel provides for the geopolitical ambitions of the U.S. military-industrial complex.

Three months after the invasion of Lebanon, the *New York Times* analyzed the results. The body of the article included some valuable information about the repressiveness of the new domestic regime. But the bold headline on the front page, which is the only information most people will read or remember and which provides the official framework of interpretation for those who do read further, was grossly misleading. It announced that "Christians Won Vast New Power In Lebanon." If the *Times* had headlined, more accurately, that "Phalangists Won Vast New Power In Lebanon," this would at least have indicated the fascist origin and philosophy of the *internal* forces that gained control of the government and most of the country and set about murdering Palestinians, leftists, Moslems and members of rival Christian sects. But even this would have been misleading. For the real information as to who won vast new power as a result of the Israeli invasion was printed on page 12, beginning on the 96th line of the story and surrounded by colorful material, some of which portrayed the oppressiveness of the new regime. There the persistent reader was finally told, in one short sentence, who the real victor was:

> ...it is expected to be an unabashedly pro-American era, aloof from the currents of Arab nationalism [even though the Lebanese are Arabs—D.D.] and governed by a conservative alliance dominated by Maronite Christians but also including Moslem privileged classes.[10]

This virtually hidden sentence explains why the United States backed the invasion from the outset, why its "peace-seeking" mediator concentrated his efforts on getting the PLO

forces mobilized for this war were greater than those used against the Egyptians in 1967.... So when the [Israeli] Labor Party endorsed the invasion, it knew that the army was going all the way to Beirut as discussed in plans circulating for months." And so, of course, did the Americans as well.

rather than the Israeli invaders to leave Lebanon,* and why the Israelis are so useful to the United States, despite some of their embarrassing ways and a persistent nationalism.**

To Israel's chagrin, the United States is currently engaged in the delicate process of gathering Egypt, Saudi Arabia and other feudal or semi-feudal Arab regimes as additional client states in the area and major customers for the U.S. arms industry. This so-called shift represents an expansion of the deadly policies of recent years, not a modification or turning away from them. Far from lessening the dangers, it compounds them. Does anyone think that Bechtel, the giant corporation whose directors shuttle back and forth from high U.S. government posts, puts the interests of the Arab people, the Israeli people, or world peace ahead of its drive for profits and power?

To ignore such realities, or to treat them as outside the province of the anti-nuclear movement is to increase the likelihood that atomic flames will burn in New York and throughout the world.

---

*The constant media reference to arranging the exodus of all foreign forces never mentioned that the Palestinians would be "foreigners" in every land they might go to except the homeland from which they were expelled and to which they are not allowed to return. It was clear from the beginning that Philip Habib, whose wartime services in the American Embassy in Saigon are never mentioned, was intent on getting just one group of foreigners out of Lebanon, the Palestinians.

**After this chapter had been set in type, retired Admiral Elmo R. Zumwalt Jr., a former Chief of Naval Operations and member of the Joint Chiefs of Staff confirmed this observation in fairly blunt language. Here are a few excerpts: "Within the Administration...there has been a recognition right from the start that Israel's strategic objectives in the war closely paralleled American interests." "...the sweeping victory opens the possibility of additional gains beyond Lebanon. Indeed while the political situation is static to deteriorating in much of the rest of the world, Lebanon is emerging as the one place where we can see a decisive gain for the West...." "A pro-Western regime is now being developed in Beirut. Lebanon thus will be added to Israel, Egypt and Turkey—a solid bloc of U.S. friends." "Israel has handed the United States its most dramatic victory since Anwar el-Sadat expelled the Russians from Egypt in 1972." "Considerable opportunities flowing directly from the Israeli operation are now open to America—if it has the courage...to work with our one reliable and effective ally in the region to press the advantage while we have it."

Is There Any Hope?

Are we to conclude from the dangerous ambivalences of the anti-nuclear movement and the mammoth tasks that confront it that the effort is hopeless? Did I indeed overstate the case when I proposed that the explosion of anti-nuclear sentiment expresses a deep-seated instinct for survival that transcends ordinary political movements and will not be satisfied until major changes are accomplished in the dominant attitudes and institutions that have produced the danger?

Here again, there are limits to what any of us can know with total certainty. But it seems useful to recall Antonio Gramsci's famous dictum, from prison in fascist Italy, that the times call for "pessimism of the intellect and optimism of the will." Don't misunderstand me! I am not saying that we should will ourselves into thinking that there is hope when there is not. Rather, I am saying that our experience of the governments of the world, our knowledge of the weapons at their disposal, and our awareness of our own limitations justify pessimism. But some mysterious factor deep in the human psyche has produced a countervailing conviction that educating, organizing, uniting, and acting will make a difference.

Unlike some other bleak periods in human history, the typical reaction of those most convinced of the apparent hopelessness of the situation is not Overeat, Get Drunk and Pretend You're Merry, for Tomorrow We Die. That phenomenon is more common among those who argue that the danger is not as great as we say it is, and use their false optimism as an excuse for clinging to the unsatisfying way of life that has produced it. Contrary to what one might normally expect, the almost total ominousness of our situation is producing not widespread resignation, apathy, anomie and despair, but activity and hope. And the greatest "optimism of the will" exists among those who are most aware of the suicidal impasse we are in. Despite all the gloomy statistics and descriptions of our plight that are heard on the loudspeakers or seen on the signs at rallies, the prevailing mood on such occasions is joy, even elation. Despite the known failings of the organizers and the divisions of opinion among planners, speakers, and other participants about causes and cures, the dominant impression most everyone goes home with is of empowerment through solidarity and action.

It is true that it is hard to sustain these feelings back in the everyday world. But once touched by them, few of us ever lose them completely. And for all our derelictions, they are having an effect on our everyday consciousness and the ways in which millions of people are beginning to view the world and approach its problems. As Susan Sontag has observed (in her book *Trip to Hanoi*), "Someone who has enjoyed...a reprieve, however brief, from the inhibition on love and trust our society enforces is never the same again."[11] And people who are not the same begin sooner or later to challenge institutions and practices that offend their new consciousness, whether they are nuclear power plants and weapons factories or practices particularly harmful to blacks, women, gays, people on welfare, and children.

Robert J. Lifton, research psychiatriast who won the National Book Award for his study *Death in Life: Survivors of Hiroshima* observes a phenomenon that I will call Life in Death or, more accurately, Life asserting itself in people confronted by the prospect of nuclear death. He writes:

> ...one becomes aware of the eagerness of audiences to be told, accurately and systematically, the bad news about nuclear weapons—along with the good news that one can become part of a worldwide struggle to get rid of the weapons. Indeed one can sense that hunger in people everywhere....Numbing ceases to work, more people become emboldened to articulate and receive the painful message and to reflect on the morality of extinguishing ourselves as a civilization, as a species. ...everywhere the quest is for real, not bogus, security; for life, not massive murder-suicide.
> And we are beginning to suspect that the struggle to get rid of the weapons ties in with the most profound collective values. If we address these problems seriously, with reasoned thought and appropriate passion, we find ourselves recovering certain qualities we had very nearly lost. Physicians become more genuine healers; universities become true centers of learning, inhabited by genuine teachers and students. We become

more genuine professionals, more genuine working
people, attuned to the central dilemma of our time.
...we find ourselves more in touch with what we care
most about in life—with love, sensuality, creative
realization, and the capacity for life projects that have
meaning and satisfaction for us.[12]

The test of the success of a mass demonstration is not how
soon we can hold another one with the same or even bigger
numbers. We need such events from time to time for our own
vision and courage and for the messages they send to the
government and to people afraid to believe in their own good
instincts. But their real success is measured by what we begin to
do with the knowledge of our numbers and strength that we gain
from them. Held too often and without having led to other
actions, both quiet shifts in our daily attitudes and relationships
and more militant forms of nonviolent direct action, they
become time-and-energy-consuming distractions from the work
that has to be done. They can even become dispiriting exercises
in futility that begin to draw fewer rather than greater numbers.

Nor is the most important test of success the number of
immediate steps taken by the government to pretend that they
are dealing realistically with the problem, such as Reagan's
partially changed rhetoric and newly found willingness to discuss
"arms control" with the Russians. (As Nobel Prize Winner
George Wald has pointed out, arms control not only is *not*
disarmament but is its opposite.) Or the mildly helpful but
essentially opportunistic resolutions introduced in Congress,
such as the Kennedy-Hatfield Amendment, and other gestures
by the Party out of power to persuade us to put our faith in them
(rather than in ourselves). Typically, the midterm convention of
the Democratic Party, held shortly after June 12, genuflected
toward the nuclear freeze, and got good media P.R. on that score,
but simultaneously called for "a steady, prudent buildup" of U.S.
military strength, including an expansion of conventional forces
in Europe. It also accepted Reagan's contention that we suffer
from "a window of vulnerability" vis-a-vis the Russians. Unani-
mously, Kennedy forces included, it supported Israel's invasion
of Lebanon.

Attempts by those in power, and by those ambitious for power, to pacify or coopt us serve as seismographs, giving us readings of the shock waves we have created. And occasionally they bring us useful, if temporary, benefits, such as cutting the arms budget to merely astronomical levels, restoring a few important cuts in social services or postponing introduction of the draft until, they think, they can change the mood of the country. But they leave the core of the problem and the central dynamics of the system intact, in a divisive political economy and culture based on competition and inequality rather than on cooperation and solidarity.

Only time will tell whether the unaccustomed feelings of unity, strength and purpose we gain at the mass rallies (and a growing number of us are experiencing in acts of aggressive nonviolent resistance as well) are based on an illusion or flow from some reality deep in the nature of things. I like to suggest that it is our Earth Mother, Nature, asserting herself. Or, given the self-serving cynicism of apologists for capitalism concerning "human nature," Human Nature coming into its own, what Buddhists call everyone's Buddha Nature.

During the Sixties, an earlier period when psychic changes and political activities were interacting with each other in a symbiotic relationship, Susan Sontag wrote,

> To describe what is promising, it's perhaps imprudent to invoke the promiscuous ideal of revolution. Still it would be a mistake to underestimate the amount of diffuse yearning for radical change pulsing through the society. Increasing numbers of people do realize that we must have a more generous, more humane way of dealing with each other; and great, probably convulsive social changes are needed to create these psychic changes. To prepare intelligently for radical change requires...getting more perspective on the human type that gradually became ascendant in the West from the time of the Reformation to the industrial revolution to modern post-industrial society. Almost everyone would agree that this isn't the only way human beings could

have evolved, but very few people in Europe and America really *believe* that there is any other way for a person to be or can *imagine* what they would be like.[13]

Today, under the pressure of our present situation, more and more people are beginning to realize that there *is* another way to be, and that a different kind of society is not only possible but necessary. We still cannot imagine what the forms of that society will be. But we will gradually find out as we work to eliminate the causes of war in our daily relationships.

It is not important that we use any particular words to refer to whatever it is that is responsible for the paradoxical optimism of the will that is energizing the disarmament movement and its many sister movements, making possible animating reprieves from the inhibitions on love and trust imposed by the present society. I don't care if some of our number call it Christ or Historical Materialism, The People Rising or Jehovah, The Great Spirit or The Force.* The significance of the present upsurge is that it is not monolithic, not directed or controlled by a vanguard party comitted to the unscientific and sectarian notion that there is a single correct line, or by any comparable tendency within any other section of the culture or movement. Like the natural universe, which does not limit its exuberant vitality to any single form or species, our surge of life is more impressive and stronger for its diversity. It transcends our differences in views and nomenclature. All are welcome so long as they are committed to the common purpose of ridding the world of the weapons and attitudes that threaten the continuation of life on earth. We need to probe and debate our differences, while marching or sitting in jail, at teach-ins or while talking at the supermarket, while working together in the new-life "projects that have meaning and satisfaction for us." But they are not as important as our solidarity and must not disrupt it.

*I am not arguing that the symbols we use to designate our most powerful experiences and awarenesses do not affect our daily lives and relationships. They often do, because of their historical overtones, past and present associations. But no symbol (or ideology) can adequately express the living reality and

Internal and External Difficulties

I have been arguing that there is a thrust within the explosion of anti-nuclear consciousness that is capable of changing the world we live in. I believe that millions of people are beginning to have small tastes of a new spirit that is born of necessity, or at least strengthened by it, and is capable of transforming us and our politics. Somewhere down the road, our gradually changing selves and politics will change the society. Either that or there will be no society.

But none of these changes will take place automatically. They will occur only if, as with every good thing, we respond intelligently, with our heads as well as our hearts, not to forget our ears as well as our voices. We need to draw on the feelings of elation and empowerment to strengthen ourselves for the difficulties ahead. We must not let them seduce us into minimizing the internal or external obstacles we face and expecting steady progress toward our goals. That way disillusionment and burnout lie.

In the Sixties, some of the people who expected too much too soon too easily matured and deepened in the struggle. Others began falling away, from the civil-rights movement as early as 1963 or 1964, from the anti-Vietnam war movement as early as 1967 or 1968. Especially in the anti-war movement, this phenomenon was not noticed generally, because for every hundred who dropped out several hundred or thousand flocked in to take their places. But their departure was known to those who had been involved from the early stages and missed them. Their departure was a loss for everyone, themselves included.

The irony was that some of the activities organized by those who left inspired the new people to come in and help build a

---

a lot of effort is sometimes wasted in trying to get people to fix on a particular set of symbols that may be quite natural to us but either not natural to someone else or even offensive. Being open to use different words in different situations to describe the same dynamic processes helps avoid the dangers of reification and fetishism and increases the possibilities for communication and solidarity. Of course it is important not to let this practice slip into opportunism, glossing over genuine differences that should be brought into the open and explored.

movement that helped end the U.S. aggression in Vietnam. But if they were looking for a different kind of success, quick reversals of basic government policy rather than sea-changes in the consciousness and activities of the population that would gradually lead to concessions and adjustments followed by more significant changes later, they became discouraged. If they expected a few petitions, demonstrations, arrests, beatings, tear-gassings, to change the leopard's spots, they dropped out after a year or a few years. Alternatively, some "dropped out" by abandoning the original spirit and taking the counterproductive path of small-scale violence now and organizing for serious armed struggle later.

One of my closest associates was a powerful organizer who used to rouse people to take part in a forthcoming action by saying "the next six weeks will determine the future of Western civilization." But he did not stay the course. Another argued that the emergency was so great that no one should start a family, go to college, take up music, read a novel. He is not active today. Many of those recruited by such methods are no longer with us either. Because the nuclear emergency is so great does not mean that it will not last a long time or does not require "whole" people to deal with it creatively and to fashion healthy alternatives.

There will be lulls and setbacks in the advance of our not-quite-so-sudden army of anti-nuclear activists. Disappointments and failures are inevitable, given the unabating pressures of daily life on its footsoldiers. We cannot avoid necessary (and potentially stimulating) disagreements on how far and fast to go. We cannot magically wash away the deep divisions within the country and therefore within the movement. Nor can we easily counteract the ability of the merchants of quick profits and permanent death to play on these disagreements and divisions.

How many of us can participate how often over how long a period of time in how many marches and rallies, let alone actions involving arrest? In a protracted struggle requiring masses of people and a range of activities, some sense of pace must be developed to avoid neglecting the children we are trying to save, the jobs on which our livelihoods depend, the other routines that hold life together for ourselves and our families or other intimates. Many of us will find that we change our jobs, alter our conceptions of what the "material necessities" are, shift from individualistic lifestyles to experiment with income-sharing and other ways of handling our responsibilities and obligations more cooperatively or communally. But there will still be only 24 hours in the day, and other positive, life-affirming necessities beyond meetings, demonstrations and protests. And even within a movement of people conscious of the historical necessity to embrace new ways of relating with each other, divisions of race, class, sex, sexual preference, age, lifestyle and temperament persist and must be dealt with. They are exacerbated by deeply engrained habits that we can outgrow only gradually. One culturally induced habit that keeps threatening our unity is the habit of competing for dominance or eminence: the triumph of our ideas, organization, tactics, leadership or claim to being the most enlightened or oppressed group. This attitude plagues us even when we want to cooperate, think we are cooperating, know we must cooperate in order to carry out a successful action today to survive tomorrow.

Cointelpro

As if we didn't cause ourselves enough troubles, anyone who has studied the Freedom of Information documents from the Sixties knows that the F.B.I., C.I.A., and other governmental agencies infiltrate our ranks with *agents provocateurs*. They add to our confusions, play on our rivalries and other worst impulses, even supply fictitious documents and real weapons to support their efforts to divide and discredit us. I will mention three examples from my own personal experience.

In January, 1969, when the Mobilization Committee to End the War in Vietnam was holding a protest demonstration in a huge circus tent in Washington D.C. on the eve of Nixon's inauguration, a badly wounded Vietnam veteran left his hospital bed, against doctor's orders, to address the protestors and add his voice to the sentiments for ending the war. His wounds had left him not only weak but badly disfigured, so it was a remarkable act of dedication and courage for him to do so. But when I introduced him from the platform, a group of "Veterans for Peace," led by a veteran who was a member of the Mobe's National Steering Committee, started a chant, "Cut the Bullshit and Into the Streets." Over and over they shouted it. They had bullhorns and it was only with the greatest of difficulty that some partial semblance of order was restored and the wounded veteran was allowed to speak. But the heckling continued. Apart from the cruelty involved, this was not the kind of incident that was apt to encourage most people to take part in future demonstrations.

Earlier, shortly before the August 1968 Democratic National Convention in Chicago, the member of our steering committee who led this chant and was the most persistent heckler, had offered to supply Rennie Davis, the project director, and myself gas balloons equipped with timing devices, to drop "heavy objects" (bombs?) on the roof of the convention hall while the sessions were in progress. So we already suspected him of being an agent and had warned key people to be on their guard. Sure enough, nine months after the Washington disruption he turned up at the trial of the Chicago Eight (later Seven) to testify (dishonestly) for the government. He identified himself to the Court as an employee of the Chicago Red Squad and the F.B.I.

At the 1972 Conventions of both the Republican and Democratic Parties in Miami, at least six people (four of whom were later revealed to be agents) tried persistently and specifically to persuade me and other demonstrators to let them supply us with guns, so that we could use them in "self-defense," in the event of a police riot, such as had taken place at the Chicago Convention. Among their arguments, they told us that they had secret information that Rennie Davis and I had been marked by the F.B.I. for assassination. Since Rennie and I had already been told this by movement lawyers who were in contact with a resigned employee of the F.B.I., it wasn't hard for us to believe them. But of course we knew that the worst thing we could do was to arm ourselves or resort to armed bodyguards.

The final incident I want to mention began when I received, during the Chicago trial, a letter from the Black United Front (of the time) in Washington D.C. It was addressed to me as chairman of the National Mobilization Committee that was organizing a mass mobilization and March Against Death to be held in Washington on November 15, 1969. The letter demanded that the Mobe pay the Front a dollar a head for every demonstrator that would come to Washington, beginning with an immediate downpayment of ten thousand dollars. This would, it said, compensate the Black community for the damage that it normally incurred when demonstrators came to town and the police took out their anger and frustration on the country's traditional scapegoats, out of sight of the press. Unless we complied, the letter said, members of the Front would meet arriving buses and break the kneecaps of demonstrators as they got off.

Four alarmed leaders of the Mobe went to Washington, joining a fifth who was already there, and met with the group. After the first few exchanges of threats and our attempts to explain why we neither would nor could comply, a leader of the group ostentatiously locked the door of the meeting room and told us that we would not get out in one piece unless we gave them the first check on the spot.

Fortunately, there were honorable members of the Front present, in addition to *agents provocateurs*. Little by little they and the Mobe representatives worked out a solution that was satisfactory to the Front and the Mobe. We promised to add another Black speaker to the program (to talk about D.C. Statehood) and to take a number of other steps to minimize the insensitivity of the demonstrators and the disruptions to the Black community by them or the police. With mostly good feelings on both sides, we left without payment and without bloodshed.

Incredible as it may seem, despite all our previous experiences of the F.B.I. at work, we were not convinced at the time that they had staged this confrontation. We knew that the Front's charge of what often happened to the Black community when hundreds of thousands of demonstrators came to town was only slightly exaggerated. And we knew that the racial insensitivities of many of the white participants in the mass mobilizations had added to the already deep and legitimate anger of many of our black counterparts. However, a few years later a disillusioned black member of the F.B.I. confessed that he and other F.B.I. personnel had set up the entire incident, typing the letter in the F.B.I. office and acting as chief instigators from beginning to end.

Naive as we clearly were, our approach was right and would have been right even if we had known that the F.B.I. was playing the role it did. It is almost always counter-productive to pass off other people's grievances or complaints as figments of the F.B.I.'s imagination (or those of similarly acting local Red Squad members). The only sound response is to examine our own words, actions and habits and do our best to remove any legitimate causes for complaint.

Responding sensitively in this manner is entirely different than what occasionally happens in coalitions. Sometimes, white people (or men or heterosexuals) automatically accept, for the moment, every complaint or demand made by Third World members (or women, or lesbians, or gay men) without honest discussion. To succumb to that temptation, whether in the interests of temporary harmony or in response to guilt-tripping (made more acute by our own consciousness of unresolved areas of insensitivity or prejudice) is a denial of respect for both them and ourselves. It undermines honest attempts to be equals. Yet in the absence of genuine equality, no coalition can survive for long in today's world or become a legitimate champion of "new ways of dealing with one another." Usually those who fall into this trap have bitter second thoughts after the meeting and make secret attempts to nullify the agreements that have been made. This in turn intensifies the distrust and whatever problems made it possible, or necessary, to have the confrontation in the first place.

The best way to prevent *agents provocateurs* from turning our differences into disasters is to deal openly with whatever grievances are raised by anyone. Of course coalition meetings are not held for the primary purpose of being therapy sessions, even if a lot of beneficial therapy for all of us takes place there, given the diversity of backgrounds and attitudes represented and the mutual commitment of most of those present to the creative solution of human conflicts. So care has to be taken not to let the programmatic and planning items on the agenda get crowded out in endless sessions of unresolved soul-searching. This can become as demoralizing as unattended conflicts. But a great deal of harm was done in the latter stages of the civil-rights and anti-war movements by people who started whispering campaigns that one or another of the participants was an agent and then used this as an excuse for shutting off the open dialogue that is one of our greatest strengths. This became particularly destructive when some of the leaders began to conceal or withhold their true positions on sensitive questions and then got together with their cronies and other leaders to make or change important decisions. It wasn't even a question of whether the decisions they made were intelligent or "correct," but of the harm that was done by bypassing the membership. Everyone, not least of all those in leadership positions, suffers from the absence of a functioning participatory democracy. No wonder a favorite tactic of the F.B.I. is to start rumors that meetings are infiltrated in an attempt to create paranoia and encourage resort to tactics that destroy the "love and trust" that should be a peace movement's distinguishing characteristics.

The worst possible response to knowledge that the F.B.I., C.I.A., and other agencies infiltrate our ranks is to become intimidated by them. Assassinations aside, they can't do anything to us that we don't do to ourselves. They can't capitalize indefinitely on the antagonisms they whip up if we do not allow them to fester and grow by refusing to face up, both in our own minds and in the give-and-take of open meetings, to the possibility that the complaints and arguments of those who differ with us may be true.

The Current Situation

I have no similar, provable stories of outside interference with the internal working of the organizing committee for the massive demonstration on June 12. But anyone familiar with the agonizing planning sessions during one long stretch of the campaign (or who was called in, as I was, to mediate some harrowing conflicts on the platform during the event), is aware of the severity of the controversies and the bitterness of some of the charges and countercharges that threatened to destroy the coalition and cripple the demonstration. They know that, sadly, few if any of the competing factions were completely innocent or lived up to their best intentions. They also suspect that, as usual, government agents were at work intensifying the conflicts.

Fortunately, reports kept coming in from all over the country of people's enthusiastic response to the initial calls for the action. Their determination to come to New York to take part in a mammoth demonstration on the designated date kept revivifying committee members who were disgusted or worn out by the internecine struggles. Since they were dedicated people and were, at a minimum, in agreement on the necessity for a huge rallying of forces against nuclear weapons and in favor of meeting human needs, (even though they differed on what these needs were and how to meet them), they managed to unite on these objectives and to agree that a wide variety of spokespersons from different tendencies would present their particular emphases on the questions on which there was not unanimity or consensus.

Of course nothing would have prevented people from showing up at the event with signs and banners proclaiming the linkages between nuclear weapons and the particular oppression or problem that most concerned them—racism, intervention in El Salvador, sexism, homophobia, unemployment, etc. But the gradual shift of the committee away from the early insistence of some of its leading members on an exclusively single-issue orientation was important to the numbers of such people who came and the positive, unifying mood with which they did so. The underlying reason that many of them came to this particular demonstration was their awareness not only that the nuclear danger is the culminating product of the attitudes and institutions that make their daily life difficult, but also that their daily oppressions have reached a terrifying climax in this danger.

The knowledge that we are threatened with extinction of the human race makes a profound difference in the period in which we live. It strengthens the possibilities for unity, or at least solidarity, among those whose differences would otherwise seem more major than they ultimately are. It also opens up the possibility of profound personal and political changes whose effects can not yet be measured in terms of people's daily lives or the society.

It was a pleasure to be able to quote from the media in support of my contention that there is a growing, "common perception of danger that [runs] like a shudder" from remote rural refuges to the tenements of our blighted urban areas, and that it is activating "some animal instinct" that can unite "young, and old, poor and privileged...radical and reactionary, recurrent activists and reluctant witnesses." It is at least a minor sign of the times that the New York *News* put aside its frequent charge that anti-war demonstrators are spoiled brats, unwashed hippies, Commie dupes, bleeding hearts, etc., to affirm this insight. Thanks!

We shall see how the *News* and other media react when this instinct and these witnesses take the anti-nuclear movement a step further and begin to insist on the changes in the power relationships of the society that will be necessary to eliminate the danger.

Given the magnitude of the "threat" that [has] entered the human forest" and the nature of the breakthrough that has begun, we can be certain that many, many individuals within the media and in every other institution, including other corporations, the military and the government, will grasp the necessity for the changes and join the struggle, whether reluctantly or not. Like the rest of us they will differ on details, but not on the need for fundamental changes. After a few disappointments, they will see the need for actions that go beyond the conventional castng of a ballot every two years.

We can even expect important defections within the tiny, male-dominated power centers of the huge corporations that own the instruments of mass information and communication— and especially from their children and wives. But we cannot expect the centers themselves to be transformed from within, or think that the media will welcome the changes or report fairly on the movement that presses for them.

We learned these things in the Sixties, when the consciousness of present disasters and imminent future perils was great, but not as great as now. That was the so-called decade (actually a period of nearly twenty years, from the Montgomery Alabama bus boycott in December, 1955 to the fall of Saigon, in 1975) when preparations for what is happening today first became widely visible. The preparations continued more quietly and less visibly (especially to the media and those blinded by a one-dimensional conception of social change), but on a surer footing, in the so-called Seventies. During that period they were immeasurably strengthened by the resurgence of the women's movement, the growth of the ecology movement, the coming out of the closet of the lesbian and gay movements. They gained new depth and vision through important turnings to the spiritual resources of the American Indian, Hispanic, African, and Eastern cultures, and through the slow and painful process of creating centers of revitalization among practitioners of the Jewish and Christian faiths.

What comes next? Will the Eighties combine the best discoveries of the Sixties and Seventies in a new synthesis? Will veterans of past struggles welcome the fresh insights of those newly joining the effort, and vice versa?

In my lifetime I have known three people who some have called saints: Dorothy Day, A.J. Muste and Martin Luther King Jr. Each was flawed in one way or another, at one time or another—as all human beings are. But each attained great heights when she or he sensed impending death. Knowledge of approaching death doesn't affect everyone that way, but it can, particularly if one doesn't have to struggle alone to make love and justice real, but can draw on the strengths and inspirations of others.

Since 1945, when the first primitive atom bomb was exploded, a sense of the impending death of the human race has been working like yeast in our society, with painful slowness at first, recently with increasing effect. Now it is becoming a collective phenomenon, enlightening and empowering people beyond their individual capacities for understanding and action.

What will we do with this phenomenon? Will we close ourselves to the possibilities of change it offers, believing those who say there is no liberation and no hope, only the possibility of mild reforms of what we have now? Do we really believe there is no alternative to genocidal armaments and superpower inter-ventions save their being more efficiently organized by "saner" leaders? Is there no substitute for private privilege and power that desecrates victors and leaves losers impoverished and powerless? Will we cling to divisive prejudices and deny connections between the approaching War to End War and the abuse of millions because of their race, sex, sexual preference, or age in a society dominated by the blindnesses of class arrogance?

Or is it possible that we will respond to our instinct for survival and develop a new reverence for life, everyone's life, all life? Will we begin the slow process of learning how to reshape our personal relationships and social institutions to express this reverence and the knowledge of unity that can flow from it?

Notes

1. James Stolz, *New York Sunday News*, August 8, 1982.
2. Anyone holding out hope that a nuclear war would be "winnable" and that the race would survive should read "A Republic of Insects" in Jonathan Schell's *The Fate of the Earth* (Avon: N.Y., 1982).
3. For a thoughtful treatment of the "insanity" of our approach to agriculture see *The Unsettling of America, Culture and Agriculture,* by Wendell Berry (Avon: New York). Howard Zinn's *The People's History of the United States* (Anchor: N.Y. 1980) provides a valuable, little known account of the less attractive, "undemocratic" aspects of our culture from its earliest beginnings: American history as experienced by its victims.
4. Quoted in a mailing by the Democratic Senatorial Campaign Committee "to launch the 1982 Democratic 'Anti-War' Chest."
5. Ibid. p. 30, emphasis added.
6. NBC TV, February 3, 1980. See "Call to Mutiny" by Daniel Ellsberg in *Protest and Survive* (Monthly Review Press: N.Y., 1981) for a detailed account of this incident in the administration that ran for office on an anti-nuclear platform.
7. *New York Times,* August 6, 1982.
8. Ibid. pp. 60, 61.
9. Claudia Wright, Pacific News Service, June 23, 1982.
10. *New York Times*, October 29, 1982.
11. Susan Sontag, *Trip to Hanoi,* (Farrar, Straus and Giroux: N.Y.) p. 90.
12. Richard Falk and Robert J. Lifton, *Indefensible Weapons, The Political and Psychological Case Against Nuclearism* (Basic Books: N.Y.) pp. 125, 126.
13. Ibid.

2

LESSONS FROM THE SIXTIES
By Michael Albert

As an undergraduate at MIT in the class of 1969, Michael turned from his love for physics to a life of political activism. He was deeply involved in the student and community movements of MIT, Cambridge, and Boston from 1967 through the early Seventies, and became involved in regional and national anti-war and coalition organizing in those years as well. In 1971 he wrote a book titled What Is To Be Undone *later published by Porter Sargent. In the mid-Seventies he went to U. Mass. Amherst in economics, taught there and in two Boston area prisons as well as at U. Mass. Boston.*

In the same period he also helped found South End Press where he still does his main political and life sustaining work. Since 1977 he has teamed with Robin Hahnel to co-author three books, Unorthodox Marxism, Marxism and Socialist Theory, *and* Socialism Today and Tomorrow *and a number of articles. Together Michael and Robin are now hard at work on a technical volume about welfare economics, a reformulation of their overall political framework, and a study of exactly how a participatory socialist economy could work in an industrialized country.*

Originally Mike Albert asked me to put together this book and promised that as the publisher's representative he would be available for whatever [anonymous] help he could provide. After a few consultations, I realized that his vision and understanding were at least as important to the project as any contribution I could make. So I asked him to become co-editor.

I asked him also because of his work in the late Sixties and early Seventies, when the best achievements of the New Left were being challenged by two opposite trends. One was toward a dehumanizing sectarianism that increasingly turned people into objects to be manipulated or trashed, always in the name of getting at the roots of war in an unjust society, certainly a necessary and laudable goal. The second was a de-politicizing tendency to exclude from the anti-war movement's agenda all serious critiques of the society that had produced the war and all tactics that would offend those who had helped initiate it, but now felt it was "the wrong war in the wrong place at the wrong time."

Appropriately, Albert writes of the lessons from this tumultuous period. Equally important, his writing is informed by his involvement in two important areas of work that continually further his insights. One is the publishing collective, South End Press. Like many endeavors the media overlooks when it tries to make us believe that the veterans of the Sixties are all safely "back in the system," the SEP collective attempts to carry the best of the Sixties into their everyday life and work, gaining new understandings as they do so. The other is Albert's ongoing study of social change and of alternatives to the societies that exist in the United States, Western Europe, the Soviet Union, China and Cuba. These are presented most recently in *Socialism Today and Tomorrow*, co-authored with Robin Hahnel.

—D.D.

I remember going to and from school, pertrified. I was in ninth grade and I worried that each day might be my last. It was Cuban missile crisis week and literally overnight we went from complacency to paranoia and, within a week or two, back to complacency. From background data to central fact of our lives, to background data again. So went our fear of nuclear war.

Years later I learned my paranoia had been justified. John Kennedy had bet the fate of humanity to defend the principle that the Soviets had no right to place missiles beyond their homeland, while the United States had a responsibility to place whatever we wanted wherever we wanted it. The Soviets were happy to remove their missiles from Cuba if we would remove ours from Turkey. Moreover, ours were obsolete, and already scheduled for removal anyhow, and the Soviets knew it. But Kennedy ignored their olive branch and risked the world to defend obsolete missiles he had already ordered removed. And this was his finest hour.[1]

The same evidence that convinced me we had been right being scared during the Cuban missile crisis also convinced me we were wrong not being scared all other times. For the world *is always* precariously balanced. Nuclear death *is always* only minutes away, and the triggers *are always* fingered by men certainly no wiser than Kennedy.[2] Each day could be the last day before a nuclear war.

It is a kind of common sense to ignore thoroughly disorienting, seemingly inexorable problems. If we can have little impact on nuclear policy-making, worrying is only depressing. But now a new kind of movement which can allow us to collectively decide our fates for ourselves is growing and it is no longer masochistic to address the problem of nuclear war head on.

Yet, as elated as I was at the mass awakening symbolized by the June 12th demonstration, I was also concerned. Motion is not victory and awakening from sleep should not be confused with attaining wisdom. Surging down the streets is necessary, but not sufficient. Having been through a round of awakening when the

New Left burst on the scene in the sixties, and knowing something about past errors, my hopes for the disarmament movement were tempered by fears that the new project might go astray. What if the disarmament movement repeated old errors? What if it started over at the bottom of the movement-building mountain, rather than at the highest plateau already reached? The new movement might be stillborn, die a very early death, or even strengthen the existing system of domination, a system whose nuclear bombs are but the most insane weapons in its arsenal of political, economic, and psychological compulsion.

Lessons From The New Left Experience

The New Left was a profound experiment in practical politics. Carried out by the relatively inexperienced, it made many mistakes and too often went down routes at odds with its best purposes. But by its accomplishments *and* its errors the New Left left a legacy of insights. It affected the mindset of the nation, helped create our present cultural and political context, and helped end the war in Indochina.[3] Here, then, are some New Left caricatures chosen to highlight weaknesses and strengths we need to understand.[4] They are not, by any means, mutually exclusive.

The Extremist Left

A young college sophomore is dislodged from his studies by the war. He has never been argumentative, just a nice guy with humane values. But the realization that his democratic, freedom-loving country is engaged in a vast crime against humanity challenges all his prior beliefs. The media images of war in Asia and his lurking awareness of racism and inequality at home combine with his personal distaste for plastic culture to turn him toward new ideas and involvements. Soon he feels solidarity with the victims of his country's bombs as strongly as he has felt anything before. He is at odds with his family and many of his teachers and friends. He goes to demonstrations and travels in new circles. Conversation focuses on U.S. criminality and the facts of death in Vietnam are daily hammered home. His anger grows, as does his sense of outrage at all those implicated. It is obvious to him that if only the truth of the war's costs could be brought to everyone's attention, then the war would stop. Once enough teach-ins open everyone's eyes, even people at the top will see the futility and ugliness of the war and end it.

Guided by this analysis he dedicates himself to leafletting, teaching-in, and demonstrating. He becomes an anti-war activist, an outsider who has broken laws and, even worse, betrayed his parents' trust. Where is his diploma? Why is he so critical of everything? Why can't he dress and talk properly? He has broken not only with his parents' values but even with his own past self-image. Yet the war drags on.

There were a number of possible outcomes for committed but insecure activists of this type. Some felt if one level of protest didn't work, the next would. They continually "upped the level of struggle," often more vigorously as the required behavioral jump was less in tune with their prior experiences. Their identities became wrapped up in a willingness to take "movement logic" to absolute extremes. To defend themselves against criticism *and* their own doubts these activists needed something more solid than flexible commitment, something more akin to "religious faith." The resulting mixture of extremism and ideological sectarianism was too potent for most to handle. Ultimately, at the apex of this trajectory, the Weathermen entered a kind of fantasy-world of their own creation. Envision, for example, three Weatherpeople slinking into an apartment to plead for "sanctuary" even though they were actually in no danger at all. Before drifting off to sleep, they whisper, "we are the Vietcong," and next morning they are off to practice guerrilla fighting for the coming "civil war at home," or to seek new recruits by provoking brawls in neighborhood parks to prove to working class youth they are courageous and deserve respect.

By a similar self-propelling dynamic, martyrs also emerged. Perhaps they had a better sense of what activities were reasonable, but they nonetheless lost touch with their own capacities and needs. They equated self-sacrifice with commitment. Working till there was nothing left to give, they faded away, either physically or emotionally burned out. I remember the Juche, "make do with what you have," collective. They lived up to their name by working herculean hours with little sustenance or rest. Proud, courageous, before long they were also wasted. Like the distance runner who, but for lack of pacing, might have had a record, these activists too accomplished far less than they might have.

Finally, there were those who built their political identity on fierce negativity toward anyone who disagreed with them. We couldn't engage in intelligent conversation about controversial issues because we denied that anyone else had anything worth saying. We got our identity from our theories and so any threats to these theories also threatened our integrity as activists. Intellectual debate took on the tenor of a battle to the death. No need to listen, only to squash.

What is most important about this litany of caricatures is that before turning ultra leftward many of these activists were among the most sensitive members of their generation. They were insightful people trying to do their best in difficult circumstances, who nonetheless drifted into extremism. Disarmament activists will not avoid these failings by dint of some superior character structure or greater knowledge. No one is easily immune to this type of dissolution.

And that these descriptions aren't about underlying economic contradictions or subtle analyses of the state doesn't make them less relevant. Movements need clarity about where they wish to go, but they need internal health as well. And the two, as we shall see, are intimately related.

The Myopic Left

Not everyone went directly to dogmatic leftism, either to burn-out or burn-out others. Most progressed with greater attention to understanding what they were trying to do. The most familiar instance was a steady growth in awareness about the causes of the war itself. Many activists moved from understanding the horrors of Vietnam to analyzing the policy-making which had led to Vietnam. Then, in turn, we became aware of an international system which subjugated many countries to the will of a few. This system became recognized as an international horror, a structure which ensured disease, starvation, cultural denial, and political subservience. "Imperialism" thus replaced "Vietnam" as the focus of attention for certain activists. The war was now a symptom of something larger.[5]

We came to understand why revelation didn't always change some people's minds about the war, especially the minds of businessmen and politicians. For a whole interconnected international system and supporting mythology about the role and place of the U.S. in the world was at stake. Huge corporations had a vast stake in an international alignment which made a subset of the world "free" for their exploitation. And plundering resources and labor couldn't be accomplished without buying off local ruling elites, providing military aid so they could subdue their own citizenry, supplying back-up threats of military intervention, and evolving elaborate rationales stressing "development" and "democracy." The latter, indeed, were particularly important for giving the looting an aura of legitimation necessary for the consciences of the looters themselves, and for justifying the activities to the broad population at large. All this was at stake in Indochina, as well as the specific benefits of neocolonial dominance in Southeast Asia itself.[6] So imperialism became the hideous sun around which the lives of these activists revolved, a hot sphere dripping in violence, corruption, deceit, and death. It was a heavy load to carry, much like that borne by disarmament activists concerned for the future of human civilization. Other problems were understood peripherally, only as they affected the fight against imperialism. Anti-imperialist activists sustained themselves by feeling that they had reached the nucleus of all oppression, mastered its dynamic, and rightly poised themselves as specialized surgeons ready to excise the malady. At the extreme, we saw Che Guevara in our own mirrors and viewed the U.S. as if it were the Sierra

Maestra. For those on this path, any challenges to our own extremism were as dangerous as the real enemy. An awareness of imperialism, which should have been a positive enrichment of anti-war consciousness, degenerated into an obstacle to clear thinking.

In time other left tendencies also emerged. We re-discovered Marxism and the working class. The domestic capitalist economy has built into its very definition an inexorable inclination toward inequality, alienation, continuous economic instability, and international expansionism.[7] There *are* capitalists who own means of production and workers who own only their ability to do work and who must sell that, generally for low wages, and work at jobs whose character, timing, and products are all geared to increasing profit, not human well-being. Class struggle, therefore, *is* an on-going central reality of life in capitalist societies. But these rightful insights and many more were again grist for sectarian exaggeration. "*All* problems are produced by an economy geared to the pursuit of profit," some urged, and another powerful insight degenerated into a partial obstacle. People rushed to explain everything with the familiar rigor of a science lab. Imperialism itself was deemed a simple outgrowth of the dialectical workings of capitalism. Many movement members went from traditional work, family, or student roles to unquestioning espousal of Marxist Leninist ideology. Overnight we became American Lenins, Maos, Castros, or even Enver Hoxhas—and the distinction was considered crucial. In retrospect personal identity was clearly at the forefront as class-focused activists adopted a new intellectual perspective and often a favorite infallible country emblematic of their reason for being—be it Vietnam, China, Cuba, or even Albania.

However mechanical it often was, the drift to incorporate Marxist insights was undeniably an intellectual step forward. But the follow-through to Leninism, the romantization of the working class—usually by other than working class people—and the development of sectarian party commitments were a debacle for the left. They insured that even the useful insights of

Marxist thought would be swamped by absurd formulations.[8] "The working class this, the working class that...the vanguard us..." many preached, until finally, at the bottom of the sectarian pit the Progressive Labor Party newspaper declared that sex must be put off limits since it impedes cadres' capacities for evolving correct "working class lines" at the same time as Weatherman orgies were initiated to "crush the basis of the monogamous patriarchal family." Naturally, neither was an effective rallying call, but they exemplify the extremes to which "movement logic" was sometimes pushed.

So evolved the less rational extremes of the otherwise reasonable debate between those who would approach anti-war work with an eye solely on Vietnam, those who would have their attention keyed to the entire imperial system, and those whose main attention was pegged to an abstract image of capitalist economic dynamics. Indeed, these conflicts were serious, often reaching the point of fist-fights, and sometimes—with help from police infiltrators—escalating to free-for-alls involving clubs and broken bottles. Yet the people involved in these debates and fights were often the most astute of their generation, those most in tune with the critical realities of their time and most committed to fighting injustice. But these virtues didn't place activists above confusion and error then and they won't now either. Something more is needed.

However, as the anti-war movement and New Left evolved, another perspective also emerged, this time not so much from a further analysis of the dynamics of the war, as from a growing insight into the internal dynamics of the movement itself. For it was in their roles *within* the movement that activist women first discovered their own oppression and became feminists.[9] They did the cleaning, the organizing, the filing. They provided the nurturance and often the strength and continuity of the movement. But men made the decisions, played starring roles, and took credit for successes. At first sexism was viewed simply as an obstacle to be addressed in the context of broader struggles. But before long women discovered a way to organize and understand reality which discerned a new sun—different from the war, imperialism, or the economy—around which all else orbits. Gender definitions themselves were correctly perceived as social creations. We were not biologically determined, but socially bent and shaped. The division between men and women which propelled the former, on average, to domineering social roles and the later, on average, to passive nurturing and caretaking roles, was a social construct women called "patriarchy." The accompanying array of violent physical and psychological behaviors—rape, wife beating, sexual objectification, denial of intelligence, etc.—served to perpetuate male dominance and advantage by keeping women dependent, fearful, and insecure. Moreover, the associated personality implications for women and men—the definition of feminine and masculine—tended to texture all other characteristics of daily life. Not only was there a role division pervading all society, but macho and feminine ways of perceiving, thinking, feeling, and interrelating pervaded whole institutions, bodies of learning, and ways of conducting affairs.[11]

Should "the woman question" be addressed at the anti-war rally? Peripherally or centrally? What about women holding leadership positions? And are "personal problems" grist for political debate? The rediscovery of feminism was a major insight, just as the rediscovery of Marxism had been. Women had to find a new identity and feminism rightly helped them to do so at the same time that it shed light on countless social phenomena. But regrettably, for some women adopting the new perspective demanded denial of the legitimacy of all other perspectives. For these women *only* feminism was a workable viewpoint. One should oppose the war and imperialism, but *only* as manifestations of patriarchy. The women's movement was pivotal to enlightening the whole left to the importance of many of the problems this essay enumerates and to their solutions as well. But, nonetheless, women weren't immune to activist pressures and pitfalls. It wasn't only the "male left" that suffered holier-than-thou sectarian strife.[12] It isn't only men who grow up subject to the distorted pressures of a society premised on the reproduction of many interlocked forms of oppression.

In any case, there were now three possible foci, three "big bangs" from which everything else was seen to emanate— imperialism, the economy, and patriarchy. The intellectual arena was crowded with contenders.

And, what's more, a final legitimate challenger for the ideological crown had already emerged from the Civil Rights movement even before the anti-war movement appeared.[13] Indeed, the Civil Rights movement had marked the birth of the New Left and contributed many of its most profound insights and methods. The rebirth of Nationalism as the Black Power movement led to the view that all problems derive from oppresive racial relationships and the ills of caucasian culture. Race, too, was a social creation, a biological myth created to justify the subjugation of some communities by others. Whether this subjugation took the form of slavery, cultural imperialism, apartheid, or "separate-but-equal" institutional hierarchy, it required ideological justification. The dominating community brands its victim inferior and the interface becomes a constant battle-zone. The culture of both communities is affected: the one by the need to overemphasize defense and survival, the other by the multiple diseases of perception and personality that stem from treating other people inhumanely. The racism which affects roles, mentalities, and material relations projects a field of influence that reaches into all sides of life. Regarding international relations, for example, as sexism propels a macho/militarist orientation to "diplomacy," racism cheapens our view of life, makes the opponent appear sub-human, and thus simultaneously propels and rationalizes militaristic behavior of all kinds.[14] Given these new insights held by a part of the left, would the anti-racist dimension which had been a key part of the anti-war movement in the late fifties and early sixties now be restored to a central position? Would teach-ins address the demands of local black political movements? Would the whole movement defend blacks under police attack? How would demonstration dates be determined, and who would get the best ones? With what right did the white-dominated movements get all the money? Yet, again, as these questions were debated, the infusion of a perspective that might only have enriched the movement also led to the most acrimonious battles. Nationalists often took their valid insights to sectarian extremes denying the validity of other insights, and, vice versa, whites often denied that the nationalist argument had any merit at all.[15]

The irony of many intellectual insights of the period was that they frequently led activists toward narrow, all-consuming views of what *everyone* on the left must think and do lest he or she be "part of the problem rather than part of the solution." In its worst extreme, the dignity and rights of the individual are lost in the shuffle of political right and wrong and, as a result, what hopes to be the solution duplicates the problems. Whatever the multiplicity of their causes, these tendencies toward narrow-mindedness were everpresent obstacles to creating a politics commensurate with solving the problems of the day. Each viewpoint improved our understanding of one aspect of society and shed some critical light on our understanding of the whole. But no two viewpoints ever really fully transcended a sectarian attitude toward one another.

Should our demonstration against the war have a single focus or many foci, one demand or many? Should we try for the largest possible audience or for a more committed involvement from fewer people? Should we obey laws, use civil disobediance, or engage in violence? How should demonstration dates and resources be allotted to the various movements? How should each movement relate to the others? A few examples might help relate the flavor of New Left struggles around these issues

1. A very critical anti-war demonstration planning meeting is interrupted by the entrance of a great many women, perhaps a quarter the number of people already at the meeting itself. They march in, take the podium, and present a list of demands for fifty percent membership in leadership committees, fifty percent women speakers at all events, and a women's veto over all male-conceived, "macho-informed" ideas. They are organized, disciplined, and vow not to allow demonstrations to proceed unless their demands are met. The meeting's 120 or so attendees enter a realm of chaos and for the next few days we debate the women's demands and behavior. Ultimately, to the

lasting credit of the Boston area anti-war movement, these women from an organization called "Bread and Roses" win.

2. Imagine a national meeting of campus activists from all over the country debating possible alternative demonstration/teach-in/demand scenarios for a national student anti-war offensive. The anti-imperialism, anti-this-war, and anti-capitalism factions are all present pursuing their own perfect proposals. The debate is heated with no end in sight. Suddenly, Rennie Davis—then an anti-war honcho, later a devoted supporter of Guru Maharaji—enters with "a direct communication from the Vietnamese." Naturally, it favors his proposals and they are quickly accepted by voice vote. Apparently the Vietnamese halfway around the globe and knowing very little about our specific situation, realized the correct path for us to follow. Perhaps we were lucky the "message bearer" wasn't a devotee of the Albanians.

3. At still another of the many difficult interfaces of new left struggle, an undercurrent of racism often pervaded movement debates. Sometimes whites assumed blacks, whoever they were, couldn't possibly know the intricacies of this or that sophisticated analysis. This likely explained the occasion when Fred Hampton, perhaps the most capable of all Panther organizers, flattened SDSer/Weatherleader Mark Rudd with a short right to the face. Ironically, the same whites would also often uncritically accept black commentary and criticism as if it were gospel. For example, occasionally a Black Student Union would criticize an SDS chapter organizing around the war. Even if these blacks had no history of participation in campus organizing, their word would be sanctified and will enacted.

Fights over focus, resources, strategies, and theories. Support, but often partly out of guilt or opportunism. This was the worst, to be sure, but it was prevalent enough to have severe effects. Directly these faults impeded cooperation and clear thought and made the movement a less effective place to work. Indirectly, they gave the movement's enemies many targets for criticism or, in the case of infiltrators, ammunition to create dissension and hatred.[16]

Each competing perspective—nationalism, anti-imperial-ism, feminism, and Marxism—was rich, powerful, highly tex-tured, and under attack by established ways of thinking *as well as* by competing viewpoints on the left. Each perspective viewed the others suspiciously, as a threatening competitor for activists and resources. Each angle of analysis added to the store of insight of the left and each spoke to real feelings and events. None would disappear in the heat of battle, and one can be quite certain that every time radical activism reaches substantial levels all these perspectives will emerge anew. How then can we avoid the sectarianism of the past? More importantly, how can we insure that an analysis stressing the intersections of various oppresions advances?

The Elitist And Coopted Lefts

Some people in the New Left had a remarkable aptitude for distancing themselves from the potential activists they so desired to recruit. If our cries that the war was inhumane gained ground, we battered listeners with slogans that went further, for example extolling the Vietnamese National Liberation Front. If we made headway with an audience about the ills of sexism, we would demand the immediate demise of the nuclear family. In the most absurd variant I encountered, demonstrations at college mixers menacingly snake-danced through the crowds to "smash monogamous couples"—usually people who had only just met.

It wasn't that people escalated slogans just to push themselves out of range of anyone nearing their turf. We often extended movement recognitions to new levels, but frequently flaunted our insights in aggressive slogans as if others were dummies for not understanding immediately. As a result, "exclusivists" were always more informed, more correct, more principled—and more disruptive of efforts to reach new people. Our myopia was an inability to see the way political ideas evolve differently for different people and the harm that comes from packaging new ideas in alienating ways.

At the opposite extreme were those whose eagerness to address the largest possible audience overwhelmed their memory of why, indeed, they had sought to communicate in the first place. These were the people who would argue against any formulation or tactic which would alienate any potential consti- tuency, the media, liberal legislators, etc. This group too sometimes became quite elitist about their pursuit of support from exactly those sectors of society that welcomed the oppor- tunity to coopt activists away from their politics and toward a meaningless fling with mass media visibility. The "coopt-left" saw itself as the only serious activists forebearing "moral perfection" in the name of real progress. Often, in fact, the coopt left and the elitist left would bait each other into ever more polarized stances while the majority's desire for a principled, meaningful political analysis and program projected as far and as accessibly as possible was lost in the shuffle. How, in the disarmament movement, can we avoid the allure of Kennedy- type cooptation at the same time that we refrain from losing sight of the initially cautious attitudes of most potential constituents?

Another type of elitist left came about because many leftists sought maximum efficiency by extolling the virtues of expertise and experience. We enshrined a few people with only relatively greater experience or expertise as leaders. Our movements would then come to reflect the new leaders' attitudes, ideas, mannerisms and even ways of talking. You could quickly identify members of different segments of the left by their vocabularies and accents, for these weren't geographic, but idiosyncratic. They were variations on the often weird linguistic styles of one or two leaders. Most fascinating was when leadership changed and the more scientifically minded could calculate the spread of new mannerisms through the subgroup, almost like a wave of influenza.

But the worst by-product of top-down movements was more subtle. The "efficiency attitude" characteristic of Soviet Leninism (after the famous revolutionary) and American Ford- ism (after the famous industrialist), was coupled with a taste for professionalism. This caused these movements to resemble upper middle class, "professional/managerial" think tanks.

They talked, debated, played, and even walked like fledgling academics/lawyers/managers. The potential campus student body president became a movement leader. The taste in movies, sports, dance, and music within the movement was determined by a relatively few trend-setters with greater verbal expertise, confidence, or ability to fund or fund raise. This cultural exclusivism caused the mood of the left to grow foreign to just the people the movement needed to address.[17] How can we extend our insights and yet retain touch with the pulse of the communities of people we seek to address? How can we make our movements powerful and take maximum advantage of our skills without creating hierarchy and stifling participation and diversity?

The Goodbye Left

To eliminate the danger of nuclear holocaust or end a war like Vietnam, we must not only convince new people but also create a movement which can retain and nurture their allegiance. To have a revolving door through which old members leave as fast as new members enter is obviously pointless.

Yet one characteristic of the Vietnam anti-war movement was its alarmingly high turnover rate. The reasons had less to do with weak committment or "incorrect lines," than with the debilitating effects of movement life.

For example, people who entered the movement rebelling against society's authoritarianism often found the same phenomena in movement organizations. People who had been alienated by society's instrumentalism, found little different in many parts of the movement. And people who suffered the movement's debilitating personal affects often left. People who didn't want to be leaders or led, when both roles implied insensitive behavior, left.

Women who came to understand sexism and were maliciously rebuffed in their efforts to prevent the movement from reproducing it, frequently left. Blacks, Hispanics, and Asians, became sick of racism and paternalism, and left. Working people who couldn't find images of themselves in a movement defined by people of middle class background, left.

Countless people joined the movement against the war out of profound feelings of shame, horror, and anger about the war itself. But latent concerns about commodity culture, lying politicians, discrimination, and poverty were also quickly activated by the liberating context that arises whenever people rebel against injustice. And the same will be true in the disarmament movement. Awareness of daily oppression increases as one enters the movement, and because so much is expected, movement weaknesses are themselves intimately scrutinized and when the movement for a new society seems to replicate old oppressive patterns, people leave.

It does no good to know the enemy, have the correct line and right analysis, but the wrong mood. The basketball team with most talent but bad morale won't win the championship. The volleyball team with a star who gets steadily better while her teammates' skills atrophy doesn't win the trophy. No matter how skilled or knowledgeable a team may be, to win, an internal ingredient is essential. And, in the "game" of trying to change society, whether it be to end genocide in a distant part of the world or to prevent nuclear holocaust, winning *is* essential. How do we create a movement culture and mentality that can sustain "good vibes" and support commitments based on other than debilitating self-sacrifice at the same time that we put our all into righting social injustices?

Is The Disarmament Movement So Different?

These weaknesses I have briefly characterized partially crippled the New Left, preventing us from accomplishing more than we did. Will similar weaknesses diminish contemporary successes? In the disarmament movement, haven't some people already become "macho-anti-nukers," totally dedicated till personal dissolution? Aren't others so caught up in the importance of preventing armegeddon that they ignore all other problems? Can't we hear people saying, "on this stage only 'no nukes' is allowed, not 'no racism,' not 'no war in El Salvador.'" We needn't use imagination to see conflicts over the proper interface between anti-nuclear and anti-racist organizing; over who will speak at rallies, when they will be held, how they will be publicized, what their demands will be, or how funds will be allotted; over whether coalitions will stay together or dissolve. And regarding disarmament culture and decision-making—do people with funds, degrees, and speaking experience have more say than their admittedly important contributions warrant?

Nor do we need imagination to see women playing pivotal roles only to become alienated by the disarmament movement's sexism. And haven't strands of the movement already found more "systemic roots" to the disarmament problem, to the point of overemphasizing economics, for example, and forgetting other factors?

Haven't there already been great tensions over whether the Israeli invasion of Lebanon is a rightful topic for disarmament discussion? Over whether issues of sexism within the movement are worth the time and energy women want to give them? Over whether supporting blacks, Chicanos, and workers is worthwhile even if it alienates some middle class citizens, newspaper reporters, or financiers? Are fights over leadership sending people sensitive to authoritarianism out a new revolving door? Are some activists becoming cynical about movement prospects, or uselessly militaristic in their frustration and anger? The real question is not whether the past is relevant, but whether we will learn enough from it to avoid reproducing all its errors. We needn't ask whether there will be interrelations between disarmament, economic, racial, gender, and other social movements. The question is whether these interrelations will be mutually enriching or disenchanting.

I have emphasized many failings of the New Left in hopes that by assessing their causes we can learn to avoid them in the future. But before analyzing their causes, we should remember what these movements were confronting. Contrasting movement weaknesses to inequities in the rest of society shows them in a different light. Movement people weren't always as sensitive or steadfast as we might wish. But in daily life far worse interpersonal dynamics go unquestioned only because they are the normal order of affairs. In any case, the tendencies of many activists to various kinds of extremism and sectarianism and the inhospitable cultural and behavioral characteristics of the New Left *were* significant failings which *did* lessen the movement's effectiveness. Understanding some of the structural roots of these weaknesses should help contemporary efforts to strengthen the disarmament movement.

The Causes of New Left Weaknesses

First, it is critical to realize that most negative trends within the movement had a head start because of the socialization people brought with them to their movement work. We all have dispositions to perpetrate or accept sexist, racist, classist, and authoritarian behavior to one degree or another. We all tend to personalize and polarize every difference into antagonistic extremes. In effect, the negative trends in New Left history were already built into our personalities, at least to a degree. If we can find other causes that were built into the ideologies and structures of the movement, we will have explained why some people succumbed. After all, it wasn't that everyone slid into the extreme dissolutions described above. Overall, most people in the New Left had positive styles and attitudes only partially influenced by negative aspects. But when you combine the pervasive influence of prior socialization with the impact of internal movement pressures you get a movement which displays the failings we have talked about in spite of the insights and efforts of most of its members.

The Importance of Analysis, Strategy, and Vision

One principal underpinning to counter-productive scenarios is a failure to develop adequate analysis, strategy, and vision. Everyone knows you need analysis to help determine how events are interrelated and what movement activities will have desirable effects. But for a young movement won't a relatively simple analysis suffice? After all, at the outset, given its small size and limited resources, the movement's tactical options are meager and a limited analysis would seem sufficient.

Yet this logic is misleading. We need to understand society broadly if we are to know how our initial efforts in a restricted context will eventually relate to a full program for change. Without a comprehensive analysis we may know what acts to undertake first—for example, demonstrations, teach-ins, or civil disobedience—yet have little comprehension of how many repetitions will be needed before there is discernable response, or what other follow-up acts will be essential to solidify gains, or what efforts in other areas will be necessary to win the day.

To have a proper timeline and reasonably estimate the worth of one's efforts, some theoretical knowledge of the whole system is essential. For example, in the anti-war movement hundreds of thousands of people participated in marches and rallies. Most were organized by slogans and leaflets calling them to "end the war, now," "stop the warmakers," and the like. But after a few such demonstrations many participants became disillusioned. They saw no progress because they only looked at bombing rates and troop counts, ignoring more subtle indicators like demonstration turn-outs, changes in newspaper coverage and social discourse, and, most important, the initiation of growing numbers of local organizing projects reaching ever-widening constituencies. And now, how many participants in the June 12th demonstration feel they had no effect because they look to the silos for evidence? How likely are they to demonstrate again?

Analysis is also critical because it helps tell what the eventual scope of our activity must be. For example, if the war in Vietnam were solely a product of political dynamics, a movement attentive only to government policy might be successful. But if the war was partially determined by economic factors broader programs would be necessary. And if responses to the war were influenced by culture or sexism, a serious anti-war movement would need to address these factors as well. At least a rudimentary analysis of society as a whole must complement a more detailed analysis of war to help us understand what is necessary to end war. The structures of the system and the system itself are the problem.

Analogously, a disarmament movement focused entirely on the irrationality of creating multiple means of total destruction might succeed if the sole determinant of opposition to "war-making policy" were the desire to rationally mediate international conflicts between super powers. But what if imperial conflicts with Third World countries, and domestic economic pressures, cultural norms, and sexist ideological and behavioral assumptions also influence nuclear policies and popular attitudes toward them? Imagine the frustrations of a nuclear activist who doesn't understand the dimensions of the problem or of the required response. At a minimum, serious disarmament activists must address the multiplicity of possible answers to the two questions "what propels arms production?" and "what increases the likelihood of nuclear war?" Finding such answers as a) geopolitics and the pressures of capitalist accumulation propel arms production, and b) wars of imperial design, and racist//sexist machinations which devalue life and promote militaristic mindsets, increase the liklihood of nuclear war, the activist will have to explore the roots of these additional causal factors and consider programs aimed to address them, too.

Similarly, everyone knows that strategy should inform action, but nonetheless many of the New Left's problems came about because it operated with no strategy, vague strategy, strategies known only by a few, or inflexible strategies based on outdated theories repeatedly employed regardless of results. It wasn't that New Leftists didn't know better, but we didn't feel the need for strategic advances as keenly as we felt the war was wrong and the need to protest. Clear strategy allows continual reassessment and adjustment of methods. It helps us measure our efforts against a trajectory of real possibilities so we can realize what is and what is not being accomplished. Do a legislative freeze initiative, teach-ins, and an occassional demonstration constitute a coordinated strategy for increasing the size, strength, and breadth of focus of the disarmament movement?

Will they produce a steady sequence of reductions in the likelihood that nuclear war will occur? Do they even address all the factors determining the likelihood of nuclear war? How must they be augmented if we are to have a comprehensive approach?

Vision with a global and local component, that is both political and personal, and that is rooted in daily experience, also sustains activists against the ups and downs of organizing. It provides a positive identity and tone to the movement. Obvious as this is, it is very hard to keep in mind under the pressure of daily movement needs.

For example, parents, friends, news commentators, as well as enemies would ask New Leftists over and over, "but what do you want?" And it was a threatening question because New Leftists also experienced the nagging doubt: "What if there is no real alternative? What if our criticisms of the U.S. are accurate but no better social arrangement is possible?" And with reason many people didn't turn to activism despite their agreement with New Left criticisms, precisely because they were unable to subordinate their fear that no better alternative existed.

For anyone unprepared to be moved solely out of anger, vision must underlie allegiance. In the absence of a compelling movement vision, those activists who required more than anger to sustain their commitment idealized "revolutionary" countries and movements abroad. They clung to myths religiously, often despite compelling counter-evidence. It was only a very unusual few who could sustain their commitment on the basis of hope or will alone without allowing these to become sectarian.

In this light, how many June 12th demonstrators can answer the question "what would you propose to make the danger less" even to their own satisfaction? If one naively believes the only issue is not producing a tool that is self-destructive, it is easy to answer, "destroy the missiles." But what do we say to the critic who argues unilateral disarmament might disrupt the balance of terror thereby making war more likely? Or to the critic who reasons that bilateral disarmament could reduce the fear of holocaust, thereby increasing rather than decreasing the chance of war? Or to the critic who responds that economic pressures insure no reduction in arms spending, so if the nuclear budget is reduced without a change in the economy, then the conventional budget will be increased with the result that there will be more deaths now, and greater likelihood of nuclear war in the future? And how do we answer the aerospace worker fearful for his or her job? To answer these questions we need a vision of a solution to the threat of nuclear war that is compatible with solutions to all other social problems as well. Otherwise, support for disarmament will be tenuous and confined to certain narrow sectors of the population

Finally, as activists begin to realize the interconnections between the existence of nuclear weapons and the type of economy, polity, culture, and sexuality that prevail in our society, how will they address the average citizen's cynicism about protest? How will they counter the view that "societies will always be this way"? It won't suffice to dramatically repeat casualty figures for a nuclear war. To last beyond the initial fervor of discovery, any movement must successfully answer the challenges "you can't fight city hall," and "show me something better before you risk what we have." The disarmament movement will ultimately feel this need for vision even more than the New Left since the threat the disarmament movement addresses is more abstract than T.V. reports of massacre in Vietnam, readily visible poverty in downtown ghettos, rising unemployment and rape counts, and palpable fear on the streets. In the absence of reasonable goals of a broad type many disarmament activists will succumb either to resignation or to the temptation to swear allegiance to some existing "ideal" society, however limiting, sectarian, ignorant, and self-defeating such allegiance may be.

Reductionism

When the New Left did create analysis, strategy, and visionary ideas, regrettably our efforts were often crippled by our reductionist tendency to relate all causes to one cause, all methods to variations on one method, and all aims to outgrowths of one aim. In theory-building, reductionism is the search for the "primary contradiction" which ultimately dominates all others. It is an *a priori* assumption that sufficiently diligent research can unearth a single defining feature of society clarifying all other features we care about. It leads groups to espouse an exclusively class, culture, gender, or power analysis as the only correct basis for all social theorizing, and to denounce adherents of other perspectives for having confused priorities that threaten to divide the left. The reductionist mode denies the obvious possibility that more than one dynamic, one cause, and one aim can have a priority impact on everything we care about.[18]

The ways this theoretical narrowness hurt the left are multiple. The difference between good and bad theory is rarely that one is more logical or consistent than the other. Rather, social theory with any claim on people's allegiance will most often be internally consistent and logical. Weakness will lie in incorrect assumptions about what the theory should address and what comprises the whole it is assessing. No theory can enumerate all attributes of all individuals, groups, or institutions. A good theory for a particular purpose addresses the whole relevant subject matter and probes each aspect to a required level of detail. An inferior theory ignores or misinterprets important factors. In a world in which events and processes *are* all highly interconnected, if each loyal purveyor of a partial view wishes to maintain allegiance, he or she will have to censor contradictory evidence. Then each reductionist activist will also aggressively defend his or her line precisely because his or her identity will come to depend on its correctness.

Reductionism is not confined to theorizing, however. Our daily experience in a society which stresses a simplistic idea of science and allows little serious debate about social issues teaches there is "one right way to do things." As a result, movement debates are invariably reduced to conflicts over whether this *or* that approach should be undertaken—for example, assembly and dispersal at every demonstration *or* assembly followed by civil disobedience every time; aiming exclusively for a national audience *or* building at the grassroots level to the neglect of national demonstrations; having a single *or* a multiple focus.

Whatever the reasons for resisting the possibility that different courses of action might be complementary, this behavior prevents us from developing an integrated strategy involving a variety of different levels and types of activity designed to mutually support and build upon one another. Instead, a variety of activities do occur, but each is isolated from the others and all organizers worry that someone else's efforts will upstage or undercut theirs. In the anti-war movement, for example, there was an almost continuous competition between local and national, legal and extra-legal, single-issue and multi-issue approaches. One national coalition emerged around the need for single-issue (anti-war), single-tactic (legal peaceful) demonstrations. Another loose amalgam of sects always argued for near military tactics and shotgun focuses on every social ailment imaginable. More or less in the middle, however, there emerged the People's Coalition for Peace and Justice, an only partially successful effort to pursue a multi-faceted strategy emphasizing diverse issues and tactical orientations. Despite this coalition's efforts, most discussions assumed, regrettably, there was a *limited* quantity of energy to be used which had to be allotted only to this *or* that approach. Activists failed to realize that how much energy we had actually depended on what approaches we chose, and that not all energy was equally applicable to every approach.

Single issue demonstrations or movements are often important stop-overs for people entering activism by way of concerns about one particular social problem. But multi-issue approaches are critical if demonstrators are to progress from concern or outrage to a compelling understanding of the linkages between social problems and if movements are ultimately to develop broad-based support. The two orientations can constitute a whole or compete antagonistically, one with the other. Similarly, the legal peaceful demonstration is meant in part to educate and organize, and in part to put pressure on authorities to yield to specific limited demands. In essence the message is, "we will continue to assemble, protest, and thus raise the social cost of your war (or armament) policies, till you change them."

But, in fact, the real cost policy-makers are loathe to pay is not the occasional presence of even large numbers of single-issue legal demonstrators. Instead, the feared prospect is that these demonstrators will continue to move left, becoming an opposition willing to disrupt via civil disobedience and geared to act around many issues. Again, rather than the legal peaceful and civil disobedience approaches being at odds, understood more flexibly they are complements, each enhancing the power of the other. What we needed to understand then and need to understand now is that simultaneously pursuing a variety of different options can increase available energy and apportion it more effectively, thereby enhancing the viability of all projects.

Finally, reductionism can also extend to the level of vision. Often movements will transcend their inability to espouse any positive image, but only in a limited way. We want "a non-sexist/non-racist society," "a world without poverty and war," "a nuclear free planet," or "socialization of the means of production." These visions survive in reductionist form because they are rarely drawn out and often ignore important institutional and social/psychological factors. Each movement and sub-movement is so fixated on its own priorities that it generally fails to realize that many prospective members will doubt the likelihood of a "partial millenium." Indeed, before losing track of the interconnectedness of all social life by adopting a reductionist ideological framework, we all intuitively sense that everything fits together and that you can't expect piecemeal solutions to big problems. This doesn't say a movement can't have a priority focus, but it does say that to be effective movements should see themselves as part of broader processes with more comprehensive aims.[19]

Reductionism is a way of thinking that takes its adherents out of reasoned discourse into sectarian competition. Since most people realize there is a powerful tie between global social problems and the personal failure of being unable to converse with an open mind, when sectarian behavior corrupts the practice of movements trying to create a better world, it puts the lie to their slogans of deliverance.

Movement Process

This leads us to the last cause of movement weakness we will address. Most movements direct their intellectual and practical energies against enemies and toward potential allies (often narrowly conceived). They do *not*, however, often attend to their own internal structure and process. Left theories haven't labelled this an important focus. But in the absence of sensitivity to what we are creating in our own movement, by habit we will naturally create something very akin to the systems of the society we are most used to. Most movements reduce the problem of winning to the problem of overcoming an adversary—the state, a corporation, advocates of discrimination—without realizing that another opponent always lies within our own structures and attitudes. A few activists on the other hand, reverse the error, never noticing the world beyond and fixating instead entirely on movement flaws and interpersonal relations, exaggerating them, and holding utopian ideas about how easily we can become other than who we have been taught to be.

In either case, if a movement is to persevere it has both to develop understanding and strategy directed outward, and to integrate these with honest appraisals of inward potentials and weaknesses. Yet these inward characteristics, especially the weaknesses, are indicated not by insight but by testimony. They are noticeable because they engender complaint, distress, fear, or anger in movement members. The usual attitude of those established and comfortable in the movement is that the ones complaining just aren't serious or strong enough to hack it. But this is a sure prescription for progressive deterioration. There is no simple-minded right and wrong when one is trying to build a movement which can sustain itself, create an internal environment attractive to outsiders, and maximally increase and employ people's talents. What people *do* feel is what's important, not what someone else says they should feel. Of course, like any other, this insight can be taken too far, allowing individuals with slight commitment to complain the movement into paralysis. But if activists are collectively self-conscious, the danger of time-wasting is much less than the danger of non-self-conscious activists creating dynamics unattractive to outsiders and incapable of extending people's insights and skills or putting them to best use. Closing meetings with "criticism self-criticism" sessions in which people collectively try to evaluate weaknesses and strengths to improve, not to compete or place blame, is one practical way of combatting this weakness.

One example might be helpful. A mindset fixated solely on relations to the outside usually yields the attitude that once an individual has some experience in a particular kind of activity—organizing against rape, public speaking, writing leaflets, organizing tenants, fund raising, chairing meetings, etc.—then that experience should be exploited by the person's continued intense employment in that task. No one else can do quite as well, and the gap widens daily. Why waste this accumulated insight and skill? Put it to use where it is most effective and let other people do other things.

With serious attention to the *inside* of the movement, however, this analysis falls to pieces. The perpetual pursuit of a single activity is usually debilitating to the person involved, often distorting their view of reality and making them unreliable participants in movement decision-making. It can even jaundice their specialized talents, disassociating them from changing conditions in other parts of the movement's program or environment. Additionally, exploiting temporary differentials in experience to create lasting ones tends to create hierarchies of skill and responsibility which consign new movement activists to lowly, not very responsible tasks. The oldtimers may stick around, feeling a sense of self-worth, but the new recruits will come and go, not overly enamored of their peripheral participation in movement life. Hierarchies of power and influence will emerge in parallel with established divisions of access to knowledge and different types of daily activity. Guided by familiar instrumentalist mentalities, needless to say, the emerging structure will come to resemble the anti-participatory institutions we are confronting.

This may seem obvious but history shows it is neither easy to understand nor to act on. For example, at which rally is the best speaker going to be replaced by one who is less experienced? If never, then there will always be few reliable speakers and they may become progressively disassociated from broader concerns. But if room is created, a movement can develop many speakers to talk more widely without risk of each becoming disassociated from other activities or accruing undo influence. Moreover, the same type of analysis applies to dealing with problems of racism, sexism, or classism within the movement. Some will argue, "look, we are trying to end the war (or eliminate nuclear weapons...), we can't do everything at once. To worry about whether there are as many women as men on the speaker's platform when we have more men ready to speak, is a mistake. It weakens our presentation for a peripheral aim of immediate importance only to a few people in the movement." But process affects everyone in the movement and ultimately, as a result, everyone outside as well. It is centrally related to the movement's coherence, strength, integrity, and capacity to reach out. To have good process demands attention to more than the immediate moment and more than a single simple-minded criterion of efficiency or success. More, these arguments extend beyond quotas for speakers to our styles at meetings, our modes of interaction, our attention to issues of mutual respect, our forms of leadership and decision-making, and to all types of division of movement labor.

New Left Strengths

In my experience the best of the New Left paid careful attention to the issues outlined above. Fairly early a sensitivity to process emerged, to be greatly enhanced by the development of the women's movement. Elements of the New Left with this attitude sometimes described their efforts as "prefigurative," meaning they were trying to embody the values they envisioned for a new society in their own present practice. Prefigurative activists thought that positive evidence that people could behave differently was needed to overcome cynicism. They challenged traditional ideas about how labor should be divided and emphasized rotation of tedious tasks as well as the prevention of sexual, racial, or class-inspired differences in decision-making power. They designed tasks to insure that as many people as possible would gain the skills and insights necessary to participate equally in all facets of movement work. Theirs was also the part of the left—especially in the women's movement—that pioneered "consciousness-raising groups," designed so people could express their feelings about society, the movement, and their own lives. It was also this subset of activists who urged the value of political education sessions *not* for an elite to show off their knowledge or force-feed followers an immutable line, but so everyone could develop a theoretical and strategic literacy commensurate to participating equally in movement decision-making. For these prefigurative activists knew their efforts to create participatory democracy would be sterile without widely shared preparedness achieved through participation at every level. Finally, these activists also emphasized small "affinity groups" so even at massive gatherings people would be able to express themselves and seek support in a manageable environment.

None of these experiments was perfect, by any means, but the intuition and motivation behind them was certainly valid, and hopefully it will be resurrected before new movements make unneccessary procedural errors.

There was also a subset of the New Left that fought hard and long against the tendency to reductionism. They recognized the centrality of perspectives associated with problems of class, race, sex, and power, and sought to keep them all in the forefront of attention. Rosa Luxemburg SDS in Cambridge, Massachusetts, for example, had specific guidelines that in most circumstances whatever the principal focus of a teach-in or rally there would have to be speakers linking the main topic (say the war) to other related topics. Leaflets would usually reflect this balance, and whenever possible so would demands. Discussions of aims would reflect an awareness that people's immediate concerns didn't exhaust their intents or desires.

When attempts to create more comprehensive theory like socialist-feminism and anarcho-Marxism led to new strategic attitudes, people began talking about a totality of oppressions that required a corresponding totality of responses on the part of the left. People with this view were convinced of the need for *autonomous movements* each with its own priority, but also convinced that these movements had to develop *ties* to one another and respect one another as partners in an encompassing process of social change. The success of each movement would depend on the strength of the others *and* on a sharing of orientations. Society was seen as a system of mutually entwined social networks each significantly influencing how we live. It was felt that each kind of oppression the left addressed—economic exploitation, racism, sexism, and authoritarianism—was connected with the others in a single mosaic. Ultimately to understand fully and alter any one, all would have to be addressed. We knew different movements would emerge out of the interstices of each kind of oppressive system and that each of these movements would rightfully focus its energies principally on the social relations responsible for its birth—a women's movement confronting patriarchy, a rank-and-file worker's movement confronting capitalist class relations, etc. But we also knew that for any one movement to succeed, it would have to incorporate many of the lessons about oppression and struggle learned by other movements, and other movements would have to succeed as well. How then could we combine the need for autonomy with the need for solidarity through sharing lessons, coordinating strategy, and developing compatible ultimate aims? This was the central question articulated by the New Left, perhaps its most original contribution.

This question led to two innovations relevant to the present. On the one hand, we recognized that in any sharply focused movement, if reductionism was to be avoided, room would have to be made for alternative perspectives to express themselves and exert influence. The rationale for caucuses *within* a movement was honed. The anti-war organization in a particular city would have a women's caucus and a black caucus which would use their special perspectives to enrich the organization's approaches and guard against internal oppressions. In this way movements could maintain their integrity while simultaneously benefiting from contributions by people from diverse perspectives.

On the other hand, though never fully articulated in practice, there was also an original approach to *inter-movement* relations. The idea was that movements with different principal aims should be allied with one another in ways that would preserve the integrity of each and yet allow them all to appraise one another, provide each other insights, pool resources, allocate calendar dates, and collaborate on demonstrations, teach-ins, rallies and other projects with multiple focuses. It was hoped that each movement would benefit from coalitions of this type without jeopardizing any of their own particular priorities. Each movement would try to accommodate the others to make the whole more than the simple sum of its parts. No movement would have to adopt all the demands and aims of every other in the coalition, but each would have to respect certain bottom-line principles of agreement and be open to at least discussing all issues of concern to other coalition members. In the period of the New Left, this vision was never carried through to its full potential, partly due to the weakness of each strand of the left, and partly due to the far greater size, wealth, and immediacy of the anti-war part of the left. But, in any case, the impetus was valid and should be remembered and learned from.[21]

Do We Dare to Win?

Our discussion of New Left weaknesses and strengths has many implications for disarmament activists. It will be necessary, for example, to guard against many different kinds of internal movement-building weakness and to put a priority on developing analyses, strategy, and vision that can sustain movement organizing. Even more important, means will have to be found to explore the various linkages between disarmament and peace organizing on the one hand, and movement work directed toward more day-to-day concerns on the other. It will be necessary to create alliances or coalitions of a type that can preserve the integrity of each member organization and yet foster their cooperation and create a climate in which each can learn and benefit from association with the others. Perhaps what is called for is an effort to examine the lessons of the New Left experience in light of contemporary disarmament needs and aims.

In any case, there is one last insight I would like to try to convey. In the New Left there were a host of different slogans adopted to succinctly communicate aims and feelings. Sometimes this led to greatly oversimplified messages but other times a surprising degree of wisdom could be packed into a very brief phrase. For example New Leftists were fond of calling for "power to the people," a phrase which still very neatly expresses what has to be a central desire of any movement worthy of support from sensitive and freedom-seeking people. Another slogan, however, was borrowed from its Chinese creators—"dare to win." This one has a much less obvious content, that is, however, at least as important. Of course everyone wants to win, don't they? Why do we need to "dare to" do something we all desire?

The specter of winning is actually quite frightening to people. It is quite beyond the horizon of possibilities most of us organize our thoughts and actions around. Yet the effort to substantially change our society is going to be long and difficult. Our achievements will be met with the most resolute and often violent opposition. To meet this day-in and day-out and to attain the level of commitment essential to accomplishing desired ends, perhaps more than anything else a social movement must really desire to win, really believe it can win, and really be willing to accept the responsibility of winning.

The New Left was an interlude on the way to creating a better society. It came and went. The halls of power are still distant from the wills of the populace. Production still goes to useless or destructive ends. Inequalities in income grow. Racism and sexism, never overcome, are on the ascendency anew. Our culture is in decay. And maniacs finger nuclear triggers bragging that they refuse to succumb to the temptations of peace.

We must soon embark upon a struggle that will not end until we win. We must not confine our aims to short-term goals, to narrow goals, nor even only to being moral, right, or in tune with our own values. We must address ourselves to winning a new way of life—*that* mindset is the first prerequisite to developing good analysis, serious strategy, meaningful vision, worthy process, and every other kind of ability, structure, or insight we need.

We cannot successfully fight for disarmament with an attitude that maybe we might just barely be able to eke out some changes. We cannot successfully struggle against sexism or racism or classism with an attitude that our efforts are just a holding action, or that all we can accomplish are some minor adjustments in an inexorably despicable system. We cannot give only lip service to winning, while really, deep-down, we go through each event, each strategic calculation, each visionary discussion, with no real hope of victory.

And we cannot forego feelings of outrage and anger. These emotions are a part of being civilized in a world that threatens to put an end to our species. The New Left had many excesses and made many errors, but for many people it also uncovered the truth about our society in a way which went beyond theories and analyses to produce a desire for change unquenchable short of complete victory. This desire needn't convert people into mindless militants or "intellectualizing" automatons. Indeed, if it is sincerely and rationally felt it will have a very different effect. It will make us into committed, patient, but determined revolutionaries. It is a very regrettable but unavoidable fact that nothing less is going to reverse the slide of humanity toward barbarism and deliver a more human future.

Notes

1. For an eye-opening account of the Cuban missile crisis deliberations see, Arthur Schlesinger, *Robert Kennedy and His Times* (Ballantine: 1980).
2. Daniel Ellsberg's "Introduction", to *Protest and Survive* (Monthly Review Press: N.Y., 1982) provides a relevant accounting.
3. There are many histories of the New Left or of specific parts of it. Here are a few references for people who wish to read further on the subject. Greg Calvert and Carole Neiman, *A Disrupted History* (Random House: N.Y., 1971); Stokely Carmichael and Charles Hamilton, *Black Power* (Vintage: N.Y., 1969); Dick Cluster, *They Should Have Served That Cup of Coffee* (South End Press: Boston, 1981); Dave Dellinger, *More Power Than We Know* (Doubleday: N.Y. 1975); Sara Evans, *Personal Politics* (Vintage: N.Y., 1970); Dan Georgakis and Marvin Surkin, *Detroit: I Do Mind Dying* (St. Martin's: N.Y., 1975); Robin Morgan, *Sisterhood Is Powerful* (Vintage: N.Y., 1970); Sheila Rowbotham, *Beyond the Fragments* (Carrier Pigeon: Boston, 1982); Kirkpatrick Sale, *SDS* (Vintage: N.Y., 1073); Bobby Seale, *Seize the Time* (Vintage: N.Y. 1970); Cleveland Sellers, *River of No Return* (Morrow: N.Y. 1972); and Daniel Singer, *Prelude to Revolution* (Hill and Wang: N.Y., 1976).
4. The examples I give are real and not even the most extreme instances populating my own personal memories. Nonetheless, they are caricatures in that a) they were the exception, not the rule, and their importance derives not from their prevalence but from their disproportionate impact, and, b) much of the texture of the conditions and desires leading to negative trends are left out of the presentation, in particular the debilitating effects of police and FBI disruption, repression, etc. I would like to emphasize, however, that I do not in any way wish to contribute to the sometimes fashionable (on the left) practice of dumping on the New Left as a childish or immature period, nor to the prevalent mainstram effort to rewrite the period's history in ugly shades. I report weaknesses not to belittle the New Left but so we might do better in the future. As will become clear I feel that despite its failings, the New Left was a powerful and insightful movement whose testimony about our society and lessons about activism must be heard and remembered. If the history of progressive struggles is long and broad, surely the decade and a half of New Left activism marks one of its most creative and effective periods.
5. There are many excellent books explaining the dynamics of imperialism and detailing its existence and effects. Two which were particularly important during the rise of the New Left were Carl Ogelsby and Richard Shaull's *Containment and Change* (MacMillan: N.Y., 1971) and Harry Magdoff's *Age of Imperialism* (Monthly Review: N.Y., 1969). More recently the two volume set by Noam Chomksy and Edward Herman, *The Political Economy of Human Rights*, as well as Edward Herman's own

The Real Terror Network, all published by South End Press, Boston, 1980 and 1982, respectively, provide a very detailed account.

6. The books mentioned in note five above, by Chomsky and Herman also go into great detail regarding the media and intellectual community's obfuscation of the reality and magnitude of imperialism, as does almost the entire corpus of Chomsky's writing, including, most recently, *The New Cold War* (Pantheon: N.Y., 1982).

7. The most important book for introducing leftists in the U.S. to Marxist economic thought was by all accounts Paul Sweezy's *The Theory of Capitalist Development* (Monthly Review: N.Y., 1942). A more recent work which applies Marxist theory to analyze the contemporary economic scene in great detail and in a very understandable and accessible fashion is The Institute for Labor Education's *What's Wrong With The U.S. Economy* (South End Press: Boston, 1982).

8. Two early criticisms of the use of Marxist theory in ways detrimental to the left were Murray Bookchin's "Listen Marxist" in his *Post Scarcity Anarchism,* Ramparts Press, and my own *What Is To Be Undone* (Porter Sargent Publisher: Boston, 1974). More recently Robin Hahnel and I have written three volumes which address this and many related issues: *Unorthodox Marxism* (1978), *Marxism and Socialist Theory* (1981), and *Socialism Today and Tomorrow* (1981), all published by South End Press, Boston.

9. We still don't have a really good history of the FBI's involvement—and that of other agencies as well—in disrupting, repressing, assassinating, and otherwise terrorizing the New Left. Seale's biography, mentioned above does give some insight and more can be garnered from the recently published volume on the railroading of Leonard Peltier of the American Indian Movement—Jim Messerschmidt's *The Trial of Leonard Peltier* (South End Press: Boston, 1983).

10. *Personal Politics,* mentioned in note three, makes these points in detail and with great clarity and insight.

11. The resurgence or Second Wave of the feminist movement in the past decade and a half has produced a library of important volumes. Some central ones are: Shulamyth Firestone, *The Dialectics of Sex* (William Morrow: N.Y., 1970); Robin Morgan, *Sisterhood Is Powerful* (Vintage: N.Y., 1970); Dorothy Dinnerstein, *The Mermaid and the Minotaur* (Harper Colophon: N.Y., 1977); Zillah Eisenstein, *Capitalist Patriarchy and the Case for Socialist Feminism* (Monthly Review: N.Y., 1979) Barbara Ehrenreich and Deirdre English, *For Her Own Good* (Doubleday: N.Y., 1978); and Lydia Sargent, *Women and Revolution,* South End Press: Boston, 1981).

12. *Personal Politics,* op. cit. note three, is again invaluable, though this history has yet to be fully written.

13. Howard Zinn's history of SNCC, The Student Non-Violent Coordinating Committee, is a good addition to the books listed in note three, (Beacon Press: Boston, 1969).

14. An interesting attempt to understand imperialism and colonialism in a way that gives a priority position to issues of culture as well as class is Mansour Farhang's *U.S. Imperialism.* (South End Press: Boston, 1980).

15. Useful volumes for information and analysis of the causes and implications of these dynamics include Robert Allen's *Reluctant Reformers* (Doubleday: N.Y., 1979); Harold Cruse's *Rebellion and Revolution* (Apollo: N.Y., 1968); Manning Marable's *From the Grassroots* (1980) and *How Capitalism Underdeveloped Black America* (1982) both (South End Press: Boston) and chapter six of Albert and Hahnel's *Marxism and Socialist Theory,* op. cit. note eight.

16. See note nine.

17. Barbara and John Ehrenreich's "The Professional-Managerial Class" and especially Sandy Carter's "Class Conflict: The Human Dimension," both in Pat Walker's collection, *Between Labor and Capital* (South End Press: Boston, 1979) address these issues.

18. There are surprisingly few books which deal with socialist or other favorable visions written in the contemporary period. The most informative include a brief book by Cornelius Castoriadis, *Workers' Councils and the Economics of a Self-Managed Society,* put out by Root and Branch pamphlets, Paul Sweezy and Charles Bettleheim's, *The Transition to Socialism* (Monthly Review: N.Y., 1971), Ursula LeGuin's novel *The Dispossessed* (Harper Colophon: N.Y., 1974), all dealing primarily with economic issues; Marge Piercy, *Women At the Edge of Time* (Fawcett: N.Y., 1980) dealing with issues of feminism; and Steven Shalom's collection, *Socialist Visions* (1983) and Albert and Hahnel's *Socialism Today and Tomorrow* (1981) both from South End Press and both dealing with issues of culture, race, gender, class, *and* politics.

19. These issues are treated in more detail in *Marxism and Socialist Theory,* op. cit. note three.

20. For related strategic discussions see Sheila Rowbotham's *Beyond the Fragments,* op. cit. note three, and all three Albert/Hahnel volumes, op. cit. note three, as well as, of course, the other essays in this volume.

3

FEMINISM AND MILITARISM
By Leslie Cagan

When President Nixon announced the mining of Haiphong and Hanoi harbors Leslie was part of a small group who took over a decommissioned mine sweeper on the Mississippi River; a gesture of solidarity with the Vietnamese, a people Leslie learned about struggle from. Leslie graduated from college in 1968, influenced by the activism of the new left, the anti-war movement and student struggles. In the late 60's Leslie became involved in the women's liberation movement, expanding the definition of her politics. From 1970-72 she lived in St. Louis working on the McDonnell-Douglas project, an anti-lead-poisoning effort and a women's radio program. In 1972 Leslie moved to Boston to a community that encouraged her feminism to grow. Coming out in the early 70's, she took up new work in the Lesbian/gay liberation movement. Over the past seventeen years Leslie has helped organize literally hundreds of events and projects. She has worked in efforts ranging from support for Black Panthers to reproductive rights, from producing concerts to organizing the Venceremous Brigades to Cuba, from lesbian/gay pride marches to anti-nuclear actions. Since the spring of 1980 Leslie worked as a staff co-coordinator for the June 12th Disarmament Rally in New York City. Leslie defines herself as a socialist-feminist.

Leslie Cagan begins her chapter with a personal
remembrance of experiencing the nuclear threat as a
grade schooler who was given a dog tag so that her
charred body could be identified in the event of a
nuclear holocaust. Along with this early warning of
adult insanity she was given the triumphant message
that "the whole world lay open before us." The
following essay examines what it means to be an active
feminist who believes that the "cornerstone of feminist
process rests...in respect for each individual," and an
energetic opponent of nuclear weapons.

Drawing on her experience as Staff Coordinator for
the massive June 12 demonstration, Cagan points out
the importance of bringing larger numbers of people
into the process of change and says: "I believe that it
would have been impossible to turn out so many
people if in fact June 12 had been solely a freeze
action." She indicates, further, that "people stay
plugged into the struggle when the struggle is connected to their daily lives."

Leslie's ideas flow from a remarkable ability to understand the complex interactions involved in political
work, the recognition that different people will inevitably form different judgments of how to proceed and
the importance of struggling through this reality to
unity. She champions a unity that is made stronger by
our differences rather than weaker because it sur-
mounts our disagreements not by hiding them but by
dealing with them openly and respectfully.

—D.D. & M.A.

Born, in the postwar baby boom, I grew up in America in the fifties and early sixties. From a very early age I knew there was a bomb that could cause great havoc and that if it dropped near me I would die. It didn't matter that I knew nothing about radiation, or thermal blasts, or ICBMs, or plutonium. My teacher had explained that we were wearing those metal dog tags around our necks so that if our bodies were burned beyond recognition (after the bomb dropped) they could identify us for our parents. That was all I had to know: it was possible to die very quickly in a very horrible death.

I was in the New York City public school system, and along with literally hundreds of thousands of other young people I wore that tag until the Board of Education was forced by parental pressure to remove them. We were part of the first generation to grow up with the ever-present threat of nuclear annihilation. We don't know just what effect this had on each of us, but it would be a terrible mistake to think that it had no impact. Dog-tags, fall-out shelters, the Rosenberg trial and execution, nuclear weapons testing and the struggle to stop it (at least above ground), and strontium-90 in our milk were all part of the America we grew up in.

Those of us who were white and middle class (we or at least our families were moving into the middle class) also grew up in a climate and culture that told us we could control our own lives: we could be whoever we wanted; we could do whatever work we liked. We would be free adults living in a country that served the world. If we happened to be girls, a suburban home with all the newest appliances and a family with 2.4 children would be included in the package American dream.

On the one hand we learned that our lives could end very suddenly; on the other hand we were told that the whole world lay open before us and we could be whatever we wanted to be when we grew up (especially if we wanted to be what we were expected to be!).

In many ways the Kennedy years dramatized all of this still further. The Cuban missile crisis probably brought the world as close to the nuclear brink as any other event has. At the same time, Kennedy encouraged the nation's youth to serve in the interest of the world's poor people (the Peace Corps, etc.). And in the early sixties, some new opportunities for education, training and even jobs did open up for our generation.

Through this same period, black people, who were confronted with racism in all aspects of life, initiated an effort that would eventually burst the bubble of the American dream and uncover the truth about freedom and democracy in this country. The civil-rights movement, born on the day Rosa Parks refused to move to the back of the bus in Montgomery, Alabama, touched the fabric of American life from coast to coast. As a young white person I heard the message of black people and saw that this was *not* the land of equal opportunity and justice for all.

By the mid-sixties many of my generation were activists. We worked in both the South and the North against racism in all its institutional and individual expressions. We watched the war in Vietnam on our tv screens and we learned about U.S. foreign policy. Through the civil-rights movement (and later the black and other Third World liberation struggles) and the anti-war movement, many recognized the deep problems our country faced. It was not long before the second wave of feminism hit this nation. Within a few short years many women had realized that we were not only treated differently than men, we were in fact regarded as less important.

Coming of age in the fifties and sixties meant that we could not escape the mushroom shadow of nuclear technology. But it also meant that we had to confront other issues such as U.S. foreign policy, racism in every aspect of our lives, and a deeply entrenched sexism. Our youthful belief that America was destined to be good for the world and that as free adults we would live in harmony with others and control our own lives was shattered in the cluster bombs and napalm of Vietnam, in the racist murders of people of color and in the violence of sexism.

The sixties brought new understandings and with them new forms of action. In so doing, those years laid the groundwork for much of what we do today and the types of changes we work for. The mass media would have us believe that today's mass movement has nothing to do with the decade of protest we now call "the sixties." In fact, today's work for disarmament is very connected to that period, just as it is tied to the struggles of the seventies. It was during this past decade that feminist and anti-racist work shed new light on the powers that control and dominate our lives. It was in the seventies that the anti-nuclear-power movement re-awakened us to the nuclear nightmare. It was also the time when the right wing strengthened itself ideologically and organizationally, intensifying its own struggle for political, social and economic power in this country. All of this history, indeed a great deal more, would have to be examined for a comprehensive exploration of the present disarmament movement in America. It is not within the scope of this piece to take that on, although it is worthwhile to remind ourselves of the importance of such a task.

*   *   *

For most of us nuclear weapons are an abstraction. It is impossible to comprehend what a nuclear exchange would really mean. Aside from testing, only twice in history have those horrific weapons been used: the bombings of Hiroshima and Nagasaki. And yet we know enough to be sure that we never again want to see those weapons used. A long list of books, articles, slide shows and films thoroughly documents the dangers of nuclear weapons. While much of this information has been available for the past three decades, it is only recently that large numbers of people have begun to address this issue openly and articulate their fears and concerns.

The present administration in Washington talks about using nuclear weapons in a way that no other administration ever has. There is discussion of limited nuclear war, winning a nuclear war, civil-defense plans (even plans to deliver the mail after the bombs have dropped!), and closing our so-called "window of vulnerability." Beyond talk there is a commitment to spending 1.5 trillion dollars over the next five years to strengthen what is already the strongest armed force in the world's history. While only a fraction of military expenditures are nuclear, there are plans on the drawing boards and work already in progress for new nuclear capabilities.

At the same time, U.S. foreign policy is more and more belligerent. Reagan has revived cold war attitudes toward the Soviet Union (and in today's version of cold war ideology our "enemies" include Cuba and Nicaragua). His administration, filled with ideologues of the New Right, sees the fight against communism as central to the maintenance of our "national security" and our "national interests."

Our government supports right-wing military dictatorships and repressive regimes throughout the world, and, in all too many instances, our country is involved in military solutions to political, economic, and social problems or conflicts. Our government promotes war.

The combination of increased militarism and expanded nuclear capabilities has provoked a new fear in this country and around the world, the fear that we might actually chose to use those nuclear weapons. It is clear to many that the notion of nuclear superiority as a deterrence to nuclear war has given way to serious talk and actual planning for fighting a nuclear war.

As is true with any mass social movement, it is virtually impossible to offer a description that accurately reflects all parts of today's disarmament movement. The very fact that we call it a *movement* implies that there is a flow of people, activities and of political content. Nonetheless, there are characteristics of the movement we can identify, indicating its strengths and weaknesses.

The disarmament movement has surfaced as a truly majority movement in this country. (In the fall of 1981 the tremendous demonstrations in Europe helped Americans become aware of the movement there.) That fact that one million people marched and rallied on June 12 in New York City is but one indication of just how large the movement is. The call for a bilateral nuclear weapons freeze has generated over 2.5 million signatures, and in 752 city councils and town meetings, 56 county councils and 11 state legislatures freeze resolutions have already been passed. Eight states passed landslide voter referenda in favor of the freeze on November 2. Indeed, the freeze campaign has grown massive enough that even politicians and elected officials are scurrying for ways they can use the movement to further their own advantage. (Of course there are some politicians who do sincerely want a freeze, and who are genuinely commited to disarmament.) New organizations, very often professionally-based groups like Physicians for Social Responsibility, Educators for Social Responsibility, Lawyers' Alliance for Nuclear Arms Control, etc., have gathered great support across the nation. In addition, more and more Americans see the connections between increased military spending and the cuts in social spending on which the Reagan Administration is building its economic "recovery."

Given today's realities and the level of potential nuclear destruction that already exists in the world's nuclear arsenals, it makes sense that people are scared. What is interesting is that people are translating that fear into action. For many, this is the first time they have acted in such a public way. What is it that people are organizing for? What are the political demands or goals of this movement? The mass media would have us believe that a freeze on nuclear weapons would satisfy the movement: that our end and only goal is the proposal laid out in the freeze campaign. In fact, even those people most active in the freeze effort believe that this is just a first step. The real issue is what is the freeze a first step toward? The answer to that question is as controversial as any inside this movement.

For many, the freeze campaign is the first step toward the goal of securing *nuclear disarmament*. Numerous people and organizations feel the disarmament movement today is and should be about nuclear weapons/nuclear disarmament. The media always does whatever it can to portray our struggles in limited, simplistic ways. But that is not all that is going on here. For many people, the perception of the danger of nuclear annihilation leads to a belief that we must focus our attention and our energies narrowly on the nuclear issue.

In some ways I understand this sort of focus. For one thing, even a limited definition of the problem of nuclear weapons implies a tremendous task. If we can't change everything at once, and the problems of nuclear weapons are so big and important, why not just address nuclear weapons? We certainly cannot deny how critical the nuclear issue really is. With enough nuclear weapons in the world to kill every single human being forty times over we can be assured of the death of the human race in a full nuclear exchange. It might not be that everyone would die from the bomb blasts or from direct exposure to radiation. But over time, with the contamination of the planet's water and food systems, everyone would be touched by the poison.

Jonathan Schell's *Fate of the Earth* dramatically and eloquently paints the picture of mass destruction from a nuclear exchange. As he also points out, we are talking not solely about our own deaths but also about the end to the human race as we know it, as well as the potential destruction of the ecosystems which function on this planet.

We cannot take the issue of nuclear weapons lightly. They do stand in a league by themselves and present a horror unmatched in human history. Nonetheless, our definition of disarmament must go further. Nuclear weapons do not exist in a vacuum. To dismantle the nuclear arsenals requires that we understand where they come from and what role they play. This means a closer look at military and foreign policy, at conventional weapons and the arms race in general. I will even argue that our task is to broaden our understanding of disarmament still further than this, and that feminism helps us in such a process.

While disarmament work today is generally presented as focusing on the freeze and on nuclear weapons exclusively, there are strong groupings within the movement that go much further in their analysis and work.

There is a growing consciousness that it is not enough to examine nuclear weapons from the point of view of the medical and environmental problems they cause, that to fully understand nuclear weapons we have to look at political and economic relations also. It is of course possible that a nuclear exchange could start by accident (either human or mechanical error), or that one nation might go berserk and start dropping bombs. In all likelihood though, the use of nuclear weapons would happen in the context of an already ongoing military conflict. And there are real wars, wars that people are dying in, going on right now. Since Reagan became President wars have begun or continued in the Middle East, Southeast Asia, Southern and Northern Africa, Afganistan, the Malvinas/Falklands, and throughout Central America. (The United States has played, or continues to play, some role in each of these situations: as arms supplier, as ally, as supporter of oppressive regimes, as "negotiator," etc.) The point is that in less than two years there have been at least a dozen times when political differences erupted into military conflict. Any military conflict runs a risk of escalating, and any escalation runs the risk that one side or the other will resort to nuclear weapons. Our present economic and military systems, so closely tied to each other, take this country into virtually every corner of the world. This combined with the stance and policies of the present administration must all be considered when we talk about disarmament. The world is too small and the weapons systems too fast and accurate for us to be unconcerned with wars that seem distant from our shores.

There is an expanding awareness that we must link foreign and military policy to domestic issues and realities. Reagan again has played a role in moving people to such an awareness. His budget shifts (for after all the total expenditures of the federal government are not being cut but shifted from one area to another) take much needed monies away from social spending while increasing military spending. The facts speak quite clearly.

— The $1.4 billion it costs to build one Trident Nuclear Missile submarine could save the $1.1 billion of proposed cuts in Title 1 education assistance to poor and disadvantaged children.
— The $2.0 billion it will cost to buy 776 over-cost M-1 tanks could save the $2.2 billion in proposed cuts in jobs training programs.

— The $800 million added to the Department of Energy funding for nuclear weapons programs could save the $900 million cut from Department of Energy sponsored research on solar energy and energy conservation.

— The $13 billion needed over ten years to outfit just one of the two new aircraft carrier battle groups with escort ships and aircraft could provide the funds needed to rehabilitate New York City's transit ($6.8 billion) and sewer ($5.1 billion) systems.

— The 3.0 billion for 84 F-18 Navy fighters could save 90% of the cuts in Food Stamps ($2.3 billion) and AFDC ($1,1 billion).*

The June 12th march and rally has predictably been called a freeze demonstration, ignoring the fact that it was built on a call for a freeze *and* reduction of all nuclear weapons *and* the transfer of money from military spending to social spending. I believe that it would have been impossible to turn out so many people if in fact June 12 has been solely a freeze action. The June 12 coalition articulated a connection between nuclear weapons and military spending, between military spending and cuts in social spending. This link was the backbone of the call to June 12th. Making those connections increased the turn-out whereas a narrower political call would have limited the size. By making some (and it was certainly just some, not all) of the political and economic connections, June 12th organizers were able to build the largest demonstration in U.S. history. Just as important, June 12th was able to bring together people from diverse and often separate constituencies and communities, no small feat in a society as segregated, compartmentalized and alienating as ours. The long term success of June 12th will be measured by the ability of the disarmament movement to broaden the definition of its own struggle. Is the winning of a nuclear freeze only a first step toward nuclear disarmament, or will it be the first step toward a much more total view of disarmament?

The struggle for disarmament must encompass nuclear and conventional forces. It must address the use of militarism to

*Figures from the Coalition for a New Foreign Military Policy.

resolve disputes. The disarmament movement has to embrace a clearer economic analysis and we must address the issue of intervention.

Taking all of this one step further, the disarmament movement also has to start thinking about the issue in domestic terms that go beyond the obvious economic concerns. Not only has our economy become militarized but so many of our institutions have become militaristic. Every level of government has armed forces capable of using extreme forms of violence to maintain the status quo. Black and other Third World communities are often the first to experience unchecked police violence. The fact that 36 states have death penalty legislation, with several other states presently engaged in legislative battle around this issue means that state governments claim the right to kill.

It is not just the actions of uniformed enforcers of the status quo that reflect the depth of militarism in our culture. We see it in movies and on tv every day, in films and programs showing the "good guys" as the strongest ones, the ones most able to subdue others physically. There is the increasing problem of random violence played out on the streets of our cities: muggings, thefts, arson, and even killings for no apparent reason. Of course, much that is identified as random violence is in reality the violent expression of racism and woman-hating. Rape, for example, is not merely an act of violence; it is a direct expression of male domination and the oppression of women. Likewise, so-called random attacks on black people can not be separated out from the racism which teaches white people that their lives are somehow worth more than the lives of people of color. Black and Third World people daily experience the violence of racism. Racism has infected every institution and level of reality in this nation, but I am talking here specifically about lynchings, beatings, and fire-bombings—organized violence directed by white racists against people of color only because they are people of color. It is one more instance of the use of force and violence to maintain a system of oppression.

There is a parallel system of oppression that maintains the power of men over women, a system called sexism. It too requires the use and threat of violence (rape, wife-beating, etc.) to sustain its power.

To be strong enough to be a positive force for change, the disarmament movement would do well to look more closely at the insights and understandings of both the anti-racist and the feminist struggles. These social struggles and mass movements reveal many critically important levels of the dynamics of power relations and control. Many people in the disarmament movement today are moving beyond a narrow focus on nuclear weapons and making connections to foreign and military policy issues, as well as to economic concerns. In the long run, to bring lasting changes, we must open up our definition of the struggle for disarmament to include more of peoples' daily realities and not less of them. Our movement will be stronger, not weaker, when we incorporate the lessons of anti-racist and feminist struggles.

*   *   *

All of what I have said so far is actually just a backdrop to the central point of this chapter: the feminist perspectives that the disarmament movement needs to take up and how the disarmament movement addresses the concerns surfaced by feminism.

Feminism is built on the experience of women. Specifically, the oppression that more than one half the population lives with because we are female. In the late sixties a second major wave of feminist thought and practice swept this country almost overnight. (The first wave culminated in 1926 after decades of struggle that included not only the right to vote but the right to birth control, jobs and education.)

While a full discussion of the roots of the second wave of feminism is not possible in this chapter, it is worthwhile to note that much of the energy and enthusiasm was born in the civil-rights and anti-war efforts of the sixties. For one thing, those struggles raised serious and fundamental questions about the nature of equality, justice and the American dream. Along with other things, black people challenged this nation to re-think and re-examine the ways we interact with one another. The Vietnam

War taught us much about the foreign and domestic policies of our government and the ruling class. Indeed, through these events we learned that power was more than government, and that control came from more than money and weapons. In such a context it was inevitable that women would also raise questions about how control and power was exercised in and over our own lives.

Such questioning first occured within and was heightened by the dynamics within the great social movements of the sixties. We found that we were treated as second-class citizens inside the movements which called for equality, justice and peace. Women did the typing while men made the speeches, women served the coffee while men discussed strategies. Women were often the backbone of organizing drives while men were found at the head of the marches. Perhaps the clearest expression of this dynamic was in the anti-draft movement. Women were told that because they did not face the draft as men did they could not speak at meetings, in effect that their ideas and creativity were not even to be considered. It wasn't long before women started to meet and talk together, without men. In those initial discussions and consciousness raising groups (groups that sprung up all across this country within a matter of months) women found that there was more to learn than we had ever imagined.

Through sharing our own experiences we realized that the problems ran very deep indeed. As we examined each institution and social structure, we discovered that women are viewed and treated differently than men, that men have power over women's lives, and that women are systematically denied the right to achieve full potential as human beings. Years of thinking that our problems were personal, that somehow we had "fucked up" individually, had to be undone. We were able to identify the system that oppressed women because of their sex as sexism. It was an important breakthrough for the women's movement to name that system and to begin the work of building a feminist political perspective that understands sexism as fundamental to the present human experience, and the challenge to sexism as critical to the liberation of all people.

Feminism is a political perspective that demands an end to the oppression of people because of their gender, and an end to the institutional and individual structures that define men as more valuable than women. Feminism rests on a belief that we can live in a world without hierarchies of control and domination, that people can exercise control over their own lives and live in harmony with others, and that women and men can share equality of opportunity and freedom. It was hard to break out of the conditioning we all grow up with, a conditioning that stresses differences between men and women and insists that one gender is stronger, smarter, better than the other. It was painful to learn that we, as women, could not lead our lives as we wanted because of this oppression. But we started to learn, began to break out of the conditioning and built a movement.

I assume that it is not necessary here to offer a detailed argument about women's oppression. There are ample facts and figures that clearly make the point: wage differentials, job and educational discrimination, exclusion of women from decision-making structures in virtually every area of work, the lack of women's control over their own bodies, etc. It does make sense though to look more closely at the specific issue of violence against women, especially as we seek to tie the insights of feminism to our disarmament work.

— Once every eighteen seconds a woman is beaten in her home. (FBI estimate)
— One in every three women in this country will be raped or sexually molested in her lifetime.
— A majority of rapes are pre-meditated, and in over 80% of the cases the victim knows the rapist.
— One out of every four girls will be sexually abused by the time she is eighteen, probably by a family member.
— According to surveys conducted by Working Women United, Redbook Magazine, and the United Nations, the majority of working women have experienced or are aware of sexual harassment at the workplace*

*These statistics come from the Rape Crisis Center in Cambridge and the Alliance Against Sexual Coercion of Boston.

Physical violence against women does not stand apart from other expressions of woman-hating and sexism. It is central to the maintenance of the control that men have over women. Whether or not she has actually been raped virtually every woman in America has felt the impact of rape. The threat of such violence keeps women home at night, off the streets, away from deserted places, and even more profoundly, tied to men (for "protection"). The fact and fear of such a brutal act limits the mobility of most women, at least at some time in their lives. Violence against women stands as a cornerstone of the oppression of women. It is part and parcel of a sexist system of domination, and as such, a parallel might be drawn with other forms of violence and the role they play in keeping mechanisms of control functioning. The ever-present possibility of rape parallels the threat of military intervention strong nations use against weaker ones. Stay in line or you will get hurt. Play by the rules or the most brutal force will bear down on you. In both cases a broader and more subtle system of ever-present inequalty lies behind and is defended by the more overt form of coercion.

The women's, gay and lesbian liberation movements have taught us that oppression functions on many levels and runs very deeply in all the social, political and economic structures of our society. We can no longer identify a single area of human activity untouched by sexism. It functions not merely in the workplace, *or* on the streets, *or* in the schools. To some degree every institution and every individual is shaped by sexist ideas and history. Indeed, our so-called personal or private lives are arenas in which sex, race and class power dynamics are all played out.

In the early days of the second wave of feminism there was an expression that was frequently used—the personal is political. Captured in that phrase was a dual understanding a)that "political" struggle reflects the dynamic between one group that has control or power and another that seeks it, and b)that even in interpersonal interactions there also exists political dynamics of power and control. If we live in a world that defines men as superior to women, and a man and a woman are in some relationship to each other, then there must be an inevitable playing out either of the power dynamic already in place or of a struggle to alter that dynamic. The way we live our lives, and our interactions with other people (be they of the opposite sex or not) are reflections of political realities and tensions. There *is* such a thing as sexual politics.

Approaching from another angle, the exploration of our private lives sheds light on larger political dynamics and realities. There are things to learn about how groups of people interact by examining how two people interact. And there are things to learn about how nations interact by looking at how groups of people interact. Nothing functions in isolation from the dynamics and realities around it. For instance, the ways we express our sexuality do not occur separated out from the rest of our interactions with people. Even sex, often viewed as the most personal of acts, reflects social realities. It is in this context that the struggle to insure sexual freedom takes on a political dimension.

Feminism rests on an understanding that many systems are all connected to one another, that the fragmentation we feel in our lives only masks the interconnections that exist. Just as our personal lives are connected to political dynamics, we can draw the connections between economic hierarchies and the domination of one gender over the other. Feminism argues for the necessity of understanding how things, including systems of oppression, are tied together and reinforce each other, rather than pulling out any one experience from all the rest, as if they are all separable, independent, abstract.

There are two specific issues that perhaps lend greater clarity to this view and how it is important to disarmament activists. The first is the economic relationship between women and militarism; the second is the issue of women and children vis-a-vis the disarmament struggle.

Marion Anderson has published a telling report on women's employment and military spending, *Neither Jobs Nor Security: Women's Unemployment and the Pentagon Budget.* Her research clearly indicates that increased military spending means fewer jobs for women. Of course, it means fewer jobs for men too, but given the types of jobs that are available to women, the effect on us is even sharper. "American women's jobs," she reports, "are heavily concentrated in manufacturing, services and state and local governments. These are the hardest hit categories of the economy when military spending is high." It is not a coincidence that women hold these jobs. Rather, it is a reflection of the sexist bias about women's work and role in society. Many of the jobs we think of as "women's work" are extensions of the idea that women are best suited to be mothers, homemakers and wives. Women are defined as support systems for other people—their husbands or lovers, their children, their bosses, even strangers. Women are regularly defined in relation to *other*, therefore not in relation to self. (One of the reasons lesbians are so frightening to so many men is because they are a living challenge to this notion since their lives are not tied to men in the traditional way.) The fact that women's unemployment runs high when military spending is high speaks both to the economic problems of military spending and to the very nature of women's job opportunities. Women's work options are limited not by capability but rather by a set of sexist stereotypes intrinsic to the system of sexism. That is, for men to function as the controlling, dominating force means that some things must be done by women. It is not an accident that women's employment rates are so adversely affected by military spending. It is another expression of the depth and power of sexism.

A related but different economic concern is that of social spending. Reagan's federal budget and his spending priorities have made it clear that military spending is more important to the people with real power than providing the most basic social programs. Dramatic cuts in food stamps, day care centers, health care facilities, mass transit and public education all indicate that meeting the needs of people is not deemed important by the government. Women are hardest hit by such topsy-turvy spending priorities. In terms of race, class, age and other social distinctions, black and other Third World people, the poor, the elderly and the physically disabled suffer greatly from the cuts in social spending. But within each of these categories it is women who suffer most.

Again, this is not an accident but a reflection of the institutionalized and enforced differences between men and women. It is sexist ideology that would have us believe that women's place is in the home, raising children and providing for their every need. It is not only ideology; the social and economic institutions of this society keep women in this position, making it difficult at best to break away from home life. Statistically, women make more visits to doctors (both for themselves and because they take their children), they have more contact with the educational system, they use day care facilities, etc.

While it is critical to work for a reversal of spending priorities away from the military and into meeting human needs, we should not fall into the trap of thinking that it is only a problem of militarism. I can't help wondering whether, if the flow of money into the Pentagon could be stopped, that would automatically mean the money would go to socially useful spending. We must remember who has power in this country and that their interests are in expanding profits and insuring their own monopoly in garnering the benefits of profit, not in meeting basic human needs. How they make their profits is not solely a function of class but is also directly shaped by sexism and racism. Along with the fact that military production is highly profitable we also have to understand that the powers that be do not *want* women or minorities to be economically strong or politically viable. The ideas and the institutions of sexism and racism are as central as class relations in setting the terms of human behavior and interaction in this culture.

There is often an assumption that children, and the relationships that women have to children, are the cutting edge of women's connection to disarmament work. It is unfortunate that in some instances it is women themselves who project this idea. For example, Helen Caldicott argues with great conviction that women as child-bearers, or potential child-bearers, are connected to the life-giving process in a way that men are not, and therefore have a tie to the earth and its processes which gives us a particular responsibility to insure its continuation, hence to take up the struggle against nuclear weapons specifically.

Her argument rests on a biological fact: women have the physiological capability to bear children. But it is this same biological fact that has served as a justification for literally centuries of women's oppression. It almost doesn't matter what role biology played in the origin of women's oppression. What is important is that a biological fact has been translated into a social dynamic. While there is no reason on earth that men cannot participate equally in the social work of raising children, in this culture, this activity has been viewed as women's work. For centuries, a biological reality has defined women's destinies. Women are still portrayed as home-makers and child rearers today. This is the very same reason that women come into greater social contact with social agencies and programs. When a school system is closed down, who is "supposed" to be at home with the kids? When a child gets sick, who is "supposed" to take her/him to the doctor?

We have fought hard to break out of the limiting definition of women as mothers, not in the biological but in the nurturing sense. Why can't men mother? Why can't people who spend part of their time mothering have an identity transcending motherhood? The definition of woman as mother ties our identity to the *other*, in this case the child. The woman's movement insists that women and men must be able to give whatever definition to their lives they want. There must not be assumptions that any one biological fact maps out the parameters of our whole lives. The rigid equation that woman = mother can no longer stand. This of course is not to say that women do not want to have children. Far from it. Women, and men as well, in many instances want children, and they want children to be a central part of their lives. But this does not mean either a) that their lives and personhood are completely and solely defined as mothers, or b) that there are not some women who do not want to have children, or c) that there is some natural distinction between women and men regarding raising and caring for children. The differences that presently exist are social. The bottom line must be that women have the right to decide for themselves whether, when, and how to have children, and that women and men must be free to determine the relationship of the mothering they do to other aspects of their lives. Just as women should not allow governments or religious or social structures to limit them to being baby-makers, we also shall not allow the disarmament movement to interpret our relationship to its struggle solely vis-a-vis our assumed relation to children.

At the same time, it is true that women and men *are* biologically different. Our bodies are different; we have different roles in the child-bearing process; we express our sexuality differently (not that our sexual feelings or needs are necessarily different); the bone and muscle structures are just not the same. The problem we face is that because of the reality of sexism (in all its forms) it is impossible to know which differences between men and women are solely biological and which are defined by the social limitations of our oppression. If we lived in a world of equality (not sameness but equality) and justice, in a world where all people were free and respected, in a world based on mutual trust and the dignity of each human being, then perhaps we could identify any innate differences between the sexes. But even naming such differences does not necessitate hierarchies of control and domination. Things and people can be different without one being better. And there is no reason on earth to assume that biological structure should define limitations and denials for half the human race.

Having said all of this, I also know that in almost all instances today women do have a different relationship to children than men. Our socialization has shaped that difference, encouraging women to be sensitive, to care for and about others, to solve problems without resorting to violence, to express emotions and feelings. In an ironic twist, the same sexist ideas that serve to limit who we are have allowed us to strengthen several human characteristics that men are trained to repress. In our struggle against sexism we do not aim to be more like men, but rather we seek to redefine the relation between the sexes, indeed between people. There are parts of what it means to be a woman in today's world that we want to expand and deepen, parts that we hope men will learn from and incorporte into who they are and how they interact with others.

To sum up, we cannot simply say that women are interested in disarmament because we bear children. At the same time, we cannot lightly dismiss the differences that might inherently exist between women and men. As I have said before, one of the foundations of a feminist political perspective is that connections exist where we have been taught they don't, and that systems function in relation to one another. It would be a gross error to ignore the biological system in the final analysis of human behavior and interaction. And it is equally important not to give undue weight to biological facts, given what we know about the impact of social, economic and political structures and dynamics in human experiences.

* * *

As the feminist movement grew in this country it not only developed insights about social dynamics and systems of control, but also about "political process" itself. Indeed, the oppressive internal dynamic of so much of the movement of the sixties served as one catalyst for the women's liberation movement. It was striking and upsetting to realize that so many of the dynamics of the society at large, dynamics the movement was determined to change, were being duplicated within our own efforts. Just as feminism identified the personal as political it also identified the fact that process is political.

In some ways, many contemporary movements have tried to incorporate new understanding about process into their work. Often this means only the most token gestures. Women are perhaps called upon more in meetings, and women are more often emcees or even speakers at public events. (Although the disarmament movement today is noticeably weak on the inclusion of women as speakers at its events.) In the most enlightened groups you can even find men taking the minutes or sharing in the housekeeping functions. By and large, the traditional sexist breakdown of work still exists and feminist insights about process have not been incorporated into daily practice. Most movement structures still have the tone and tenor of a men's institution. While there might be cases of some women in leadership positions, most movement groups are still sexist in their basic structures and character. A feminist attention to process must incorporate awareness of divisions of physical *and* emotional labor, interpersonally *and* organizationally. Feminist process means that we must take the work of mediating power relations and nurturing seriously, and that we pay attention to who does these tasks. The point is to not duplicate the traditional division of labor in these areas either. It is how people interrelate, what is valued and what is not, a group's style, language, level of mutual supportiveness, and even thinking patterns that are at issue.

The cornerstone of feminist process rests not in females holding certain positions, although that is a necessary step, to be sure, but in respect for each individual. Through the experience of the consciousness raising groups of the late sixties and early seventies women learned that no one of us has the full story. Only as many women spoke did we begin to have enough information to put things together, to articulate the systematic oppression all women face. Understanding a system (be it social, economic, political, or whatever) means knowing all of its parts. As complex human beings we interact not only with other complex human beings but also with the institutions and structures created by centuries of human life. It is nothing less than all of this which must be understood and then changed. No single person can grasp it all. The male tendency (sometimes masquerading as "scientific") to leap to conclusions based on isolated thinking and isolated perceptions is unlikely to yield the type of insights we all need. The whole seems overwhelming— in its size and its complexity. But the solution isn't to ignore most of the whole and rush to judgement with simplistic answers. We must re-structure it *all*, for without such fundamental, deep and hopefully lasting changes we will continually face the horror of nuclear annihilation.

Feminism argues that a good place to start is with the individual. Each individual manifests (sic) an expression of the systems of oppression, and our interactions (both in small, one-to-one exchanges and as large social units) are the playing out of those dynamics. The personal is political, and the individual is critical to the political process.

There are several important implications in all of this. First, a part of our job must be to incorporate larger numbers of people into the process of change. Second, the reason for this is not solely to have more warm bodies on our side but because each new person brings new insights and strengths to our efforts. Third, the way we treat one another inside our own organizations and structures will influence the extent to which people are able to make their contributions, and sooner or later will determine whether they continue to work with us.

The present structures of our lives put limits on the changes each of us can make. Yet it is still possible for each of us to change to some degree. As we change, we pressure the structures around us to become different (hopefully we are becoming more self-conscious about this and also better at it). As they change, the limits of our options, choices and actions also alter. Needless to say, there are some structures that we can have a greater impact on—including our organizations and communities of protest and social activism. Let us at least start with them.

The women's movement has translated all of this into a few immediately practicable ideas. While a large scale social movement is the backbone of lasting social change, small units of people are an important component. It is in the smaller group that people have the chance to interact on a more human level. We get to know each other better and it is easier to give support. After all, all of the other places in our lives are not designed to give us support (work, school, etc.).*

*There are those who argue that the family is the one social institution designed specifically for support. But again we must remember that the division of work within the family that most frequently is referred to reflects a sexist hierarchy of male domination and control. While the family often still does provide some support (especially for children) we can not ignore the oppressive features of contemporary American family life. Also, we cannot forget the fact that most people in this country do not even live in the family as described by right wing ideologues: a wage-earning husband with a non-wage-earning wife and several children. There are more single-parent heads of households than ever before and most of them are headed by women. The truth of the matter is that people live and love in all different sorts of ways.

Each individual must be encouraged to participate in as full a way as s/he wants to. Sometimes this means the teaching and sharing of skills. Again, we have to remember that we have all grown up in a society that systematically teaches boys certain skills and denies those skills to women. If women's place is in the home, and men address affairs of state, problems of war and peace, economic and political issues, then men but not women must learn how to speak in public. The very act of speaking in political groups, let alone at public meetings or huge rallies, is a departure from what we are taught women are supposed to be like. The fact that more women are doing it in the disarmament movement and other struggles is an important step forward but as yet only a tiny beginning. Many more women need to learn a whole range of skills, and women need the support to test those skills not only in the women's movement but also in the disarmament movement and other struggles.

As I've said several times already, feminism is a political perspective that calls for uncovering interconnections. The women's movement has found that it is possible to find the connections between people's daily "personal" reality and the issues that seem so far away. The disarmament movement must take this seriously. While so many people have shown their concern about nuclear weapons and the idea that militarism is the way to solve the world's problems, these issues can still seem distant and hard to grasp. It is hard for people to allow them to be ever-present, just because they are so frightening. There is an interrelated tendency, taught by society, to rely on experts to deal with such matters. Of course women are also assumed to be incapable of even understanding the most basic scientific information. People stay plugged into struggle when struggle is connected to their lives. Yes, for a while you can move some people into activity even if they don't see or don't want to see its connection to their own, daily experience. But for the sustained activism that securing disarmament demands, it is essential that we find the direct ties to people's daily concerns. I am saying what I have said before in other ways—we must link our work for disarmament to the daily economic and social realities of people in this country.

There is another piece of what has become known as feminist process that the disarmament movement needs to incorporate into its own work. That is, a commitment to confront sexist, racist, and class-biased behavior inside our own movement, and whatever other forms of interaction are based on hierarchies of domination. Time and again women have been told that while our concerns might be valid and our struggles important, there were "bigger issues" that must be addressed first. The disarmament movement, especially when it narrowly focuses on nuclear weapons, often repeats this linear and "stage" notion of change. Feminists argue that it makes no sense to ignore the concerns of racism and sexism, for without confronting those dynamics we will never learn about power and how to challenge it. To be strong enough to overcome the military and industrial forces that have brought us so close to the nuclear brink we must confront the structures and attitudes which keep us divided and weak. If we seek to build a broad movement, representing the diversity of the nation, then we cannot ignore the factors that keep us separated. It is not in raising feminist concerns that we divide ourselves. Rather, it is the relegation of women's issues to secondary importance that denies women full participation in this movement.

Perhaps even more importantly, there is, again, the issue of "interconnections." In our society many alterations can occur piecemeal, linearly, in stages. When we start to discuss major changes like disarmament, ending sexism, putting needs before profits, eliminating racism, or really extending democracy we leave the realm in which piecemeal alterations can be lasting and effective. Instead, at these socially defining levels, society is too entwined to try usefully to change one main aspect in isolation from the rest. The disarmament movement must pay attention to the lessons of feminist and other movements because ultimately its success is directly correlated to the success or failure of those other movements, just as the social problems each movement addresses are entwined with those addressed by other movements.

To sum up, feminist and anti-sexist struggles have articulated several ideas about process which would serve the disarmament movement well.

a) respect for each individual
b) the need for people to work in small groups
c) skills sharing and support
d) the importance of connecting people's daily experiences with the "larger" issues our movement takes up
e) the importance of acknowledging sexist, racist and other oppressive dynamics when they surface within our own organizations and communities and struggling against them

*   *   *

So far I have been arguing that it is important for the disarmament movement to learn from and incorporate the insights of feminism into the body of its thought and practice. But there is also the question of the relationship between these two movements. In the past twelve years the women's movement and struggles around sexual politics have become part of the fabric of political life in this country. The disarmament movement does not function in a vacuum; there are other social and political forces which help to set the stage for the work we have undertaken. In such a context, it makes sense that the disarmament movement should address the issue of its relationship to the women's movement, and to feminism.

On the most obvious level there are practical considerations. If the disarmament movement addresses other issues, that is, issues not immediately seen by many as connected to disarmament, will it weaken or dilute its strength? Given the critical nature of the nuclear problem, it is often argued that our first and foremost task must be to unite all those who oppose nuclear weapons (and sometimes militarism is included), regardless of our differences on other issues. There is certainly a logic in this approach, given the range of options and feelings on virtually all issues on the political, social and economic agenda before us today. If we could all agree to disarm the world's nuclear arsenals that would of course be a terrific achievment, to say nothing of its being a powerful step in the process of securing global disarmament. So why "rock the boat" with other issues, especially issues we know there are disagreements about?

There is not an easy answer to this question. We all know there are basic principles that none of us will or should compromise on. While we of course want everyone to be against nuclear weapons, would we allow an avowed racist to speak for our movement? No, I am not suggesting political credential-checking as we build the disarmament movement. I am suggesting that it is valuable and necessary to explore our relationship to other social movements. It is the same issue—interconnections—in still another guise. The relationship implies a two-way dynamic, a give and take. If we seek the involvement of those now struggling for racial and economic justice in disarmament work, does it not make sense that they would ask what we will do to secure their goals? And in the same manner, if we seek to expand women's participation in the disarmament movement, does it not make sense that women would ask what we are willing to do to aid their efforts? If one of our goals is to incorporate more people into this work then it makes sense for us to seek further clarification of the ways seemingly distant issues are actually connected.

People come together when they see and feel the need to come together. We will not pull diverse groupings of people together into *sustained* political activity around disarmament (be it a limited notion of nuclear disarmament or a more comprehensive definition) unless they see how such an effort is directly tied to other pressing issues in their lives. While it is true that a nuclear bomb kills regardless of race, sex or economic status, we will be unable to build a unified and long-lasting movement solely on this argument. For nuclear weapons and the threat of nuclear war, even in the present world context, remain an abstraction, while the suffering of peoples throughout this country and around the world are felt every single day. The connection between today's immediate experiences and the possibilities of nuclear holocaust in the future can and must be drawn out.

What does all this mean about the specific relationship between the disarmament movement and the struggles of both the women's movement and the gay/lesbian movement? (I link those together in this instance because both movements address issues of sexual politics and power relationships based on gender and sexuality.) There is already some awareness of the importance of relating to these movements—when outreach lists are drawn up feminist and gay groups are now included, speakers representing either the women's movement and/or the gay and lesbian communities are sometimes even included in disarmament programs. But a fundamental problem still exists. The kinds of political insights I spoke of earlier have yet to be integrated directly into the political perspective of the disarmament movement and therefore the links to struggles around sexual politics have not been seriously addressed. First steps have been taken, but more is required. There is a parallel with the anti-racist movement. While people of color are encouraged to come to disarmament activities there still seems to be a resistance to taking a clear stand against racism in all its forms and to help activists in that struggle.

To make the practical connections among these issues clearer, it would be useful to take a moment to look at the New Right and its rise to power in this country. The 1980 electoral victory of Ronald Reagan is perhaps the clearest example of the kind of power that the right has gathered, but it is certainly not the sole expression of the impact of right wing ideas and practices. There are a few critical elements of right wing ideology in America today, and if we are to understand the right's rise to power we have to acknowledge each of these components, and recognize that they form an interrelated whole. Very briefly, they are:

a) Racism. There has been a tremendous rise in racist violence (beatings, cross-burnings, fire-bombings, etc.) directed against people of color for no reason except that they are not white. Affirmative action programs both in the workplace and in institutions of higher learning are challenged in the courts. School desegregation plans (even in their most liberal forms) are fought against and delayed and then used to drive wedges between communities. There is of course the nationwide revival of the KKK.

b) Anti-big-government. It is argued that it is not the proper role of the federal government to support social programs and that the individual states should handle such matters. The concern over a balanced budget is a thinly veiled attempt to cut spending which meets human needs as opposed to bringing in big profits. The right wing argues that the role of the federal government is to insure each American (sic) the right to participate in the "free" enterprise system. Washington's job is to fight against any "enemy" that threatens the "American way of life."

c) Militarism. They say that America is strong when we are well armed, that this country can't let itself be "pushed around" by other nations, that we have the right to protect our so-called vital interests even if it means military intervention in the Third World, and that the only way to "stop the Russians" is to have the biggest, fastest, most accurate nuclear weapons systems we can develop.

d) Sexism. The campaigns against the Equal Rights Amendment, against the most basic civil rights for lesbians and gay men, against reproductive rights for women (including birth control, sex education programs, family planning centers, day care facilities, etc.) are all based on traditional sexist ideas that keep women in the home while men rule the world. (The most sweeping statement of right wing ideas is included in the proposed Family Protection Act, legislation that would have a negative impact on women, children, gay people, minority groups, and many others.)

e) An economic package that combines union busting, plant closings, the highest unemployment since the Great Depression and spending priorities that are inflationary while social spending is dramatically cut.

The right wing has attempted to translate their ideas into law, further institutionalizing racial divisions and archaic sexist ideas about relationships between men and women. They have given new meaning to the notion that "might makes right," that our security rests in our ability to fight and win wars. It has achieved the power it presently enjoys because it has been well financed and well organized. At its core, its strength has been its ability to sustain campaigns that project certain specific notions about how people should lead their lives.

While the New Right seems to have gathered its present strength on single issue campaigns we would make a grave error to think that it is single-minded. Right wing ideologues, the same white men that now shape the policies and practices of the Reagan administration, have a coherent politic. Their anti-communism runs just as deeply as their racism. Their woman-hating runs just as deeply as their defense of capitalism. Their willingness to commit American troops to wars of intervention is just as strong as their hatred of gay people. Apple pie, motherhood and the American flag. It is an ideological whole with clear implications for the "correct" way to live. When people break away from the rules they too become the enemy, or at the very least sinners that have to be reformed and fit back into the mold.

There are lessons to be learned from the successes of the New Right, but it is important to remember that the New Right learned a great deal from the social movements of the sixties and seventies. The New Left of the sixties articulated the need for an inclusive politics that addressed the totality and complexity of the human experience. The New Right saw that the issues surfaced by the social movements of the last several decades were central in people's lives: the nature of race relations; the cavalier U.S. attitude toward the rest of the world; women's struggles against all forms of sexism including reproductive control and a criticism of compulsory heterosexuality. What the New Right has done so well is to play on people's confusions and fears— fears about change, confusions about how to alter the ways people relate to one another.

As the disarmament movement becomes stronger in this country, as I believe it will, we will run headlong into the organized right wing. When it is in power in government we will feel its attempts to repress us. When it has an impact on the mass media (as it certainly has today) we will see new images of militarism, racism and sexism. While it is understandable that the disarmament movement will first and foremost address the militarism of the New Right it is a mistake to think that we will be able to overcome its impact on foriegn and military policy if we do not address the other parts of right wing ideology and practice. It is a mistake to think the population will ultimately give its support to a left that fails to create an inclusive politic and an alternative approach to social and personal life. Again, the right, which learned crucial lessons from the left of the sixties, has its power partly because it has put forth a full program which ties several critical elements into a whole. We will have to do the same.

Given the tremendous energies that the right wing has put into campaigns around questions of sexual politics, we find ourselves again asking about how the disarmament movement relates to the concerns and struggles of the feminist movement. How do we integrate a feminist perspective into disarmament work *and* what relationship should the disarmament movement have to the work of the feminist movement? It is not merely a question of developing a politically richer disarmament movement. If the issues that women are struggling with today are vital to their survival, central to their equality and freedom, then at some point disarmament activists must look at them as they stand—as issues to be taken seriously on their own merit and not merely because they can be integrated into disarmament efforts.

I am not suggesting that it is the job of the disarmament movement to address equally all other legitimate and important social/political battles. There are still only twenty-four hours in every day and limits on the concrete work that any one person, any one organization, even any one movement can do. But to present this as all or nothing is not helpful. It is possible to identify specific issues or efforts in each struggle that we as disarmament activists might link with.

So far, the most controversial and difficult issue to come up in the effort to build links between the disarmament and women's movement has been that of reproductive rights. There is an attempt in this country, spear-headed by right wing ideologues and some religious institutions, to deny women the most basic of all human rights, the right to control one's own body. Our bodies are the physical manifestation, the concrete reality, of ourselves as human beings. Without our bodies we do not exist, and without control over our own physical being we reach less than our full human potential. In both the repression of female sexuality and the interference into our reproductive lives women are denied control over our bodies, and therefore our lives. Fundamental to women's equality and freedom must be the right to full reproductive self-determination and sexual autonomy. Without the option to decide if and when to have children, without the right of each woman to express her sexuality as she feels it, without these basic controls over our own bodies, women will never be free. Full reproductive rights must include the right for each woman to decide for herself the question of abortion.

There is a tremendous national debate on the issue of abortion (one used by the New Right for its own ends we might note). Countless arguments are presented on all "sides" of the issue. Indeed, abortion does raise medical, social, ethical and moral concerns. But it is precisely because it is such a complex issue that each woman must be able to make her own choices, free from economic or legal consequences. The feminist movement argues that we cannot outlaw a medical procedure because there are some who have religious or moral objections to it. The political struggle over abortion is critical to feminists, given the centrality of the human right to control our own bodies and the denial of that right to women. By playing on people's fears, confusions and honest concerns, the New Right has used the abortion issue as one of its stepping stones to political power. Of course, there are people who oppose abortion, or who would not choose one for themselves, who are not right-wingers, and there are right-wing people who oppose abortion in a non-opportunist way. But how seriously can we take the "pro-lifer" who is also pro-nuclear power, pro-nuclear weapons, pro-military intervention, anti-pollution control, anti-disarmament, etc.?

The disarmament movement, because it involves so many people, encompasses those who support the right to abortion and those who are opposed to it. We find within our ranks those who will not leave their basic feminist principles behind as they do disarmament work and others who are just as commited to outlawing abortion as they are to ending the arms race. This internal tension produces one of the most difficult problems within the disarmament movement.

I am certainly not neutral on this issue. As a feminist I am commited to full reproductive rights for all women. My political work before my present full-time involvement in the disarmament movement was in the struggle to secure women's reproductive self-control. It has not always been easy to work in coalition with people I know would outlaw abortion if they could. I also know that I will not leave this work, and do not want them to do so.

Let us accept the right of autonomous movements to define the issues that are central to them. Feminists state that reproductive rights and sexual freedom are basic to their politics. If the disarmament movement is to have a relationship to the women's movement it cannot ignore the struggle presently centered on the question of abortion. At the same time, to push the disarmament movement as a whole to take a position on this issue would surely tear it asunder, for there just does not exist a basis for agreement.

Where do we go with all this? While I do not have the long-term answers there are some things for the short run that are clear. To be a viable force for change, the disarmament movement will have to address the issue of its relationship to other social movements, and in so doing we will be called upon to take our stand on some pressing issues. As such a dynamic unfolds there are bound to be issues that call forth different responses, and are therefore seen as divisive. But it would be a mistake to stifle or limit discussion of such issues in the name of unity, for unity is not only a reflection of something we already agree upon. Unity also involves being willing to participate in a process where differences are aired, struggles are waged, and sometimes (for all sorts of reasons) minds are changed.

Whatever the limits are that now exist around the possibility that the disarmament movement might, with a common voice, take up the issue of reproductive rights, we must not silence the debate or cut off the discussion. Feminists cannot be asked to leave aside the issues that are basic to us in the name of unity. We have to be sensitive to how far an issue can be pushed, but we must not be asked to ignore our own concerns.

I personally hope that a day will come when the disarmament movement will be more outspoken on other issues, including those raised by the women's and gay liberation movements. Until that time many of us will feel slightly fragmented in our work, but we will not put the work aside. The relationship between the disarmament movement and other movements will eventually be sorted out because activists will continue to struggle in all those arenas at once.

*   *   *

For all of its strengths today, the disarmament movement has a tremendous amount of growing to do before the changes we work for can become reality. As we think about the tasks ahead there are several elements of movement-building that I hope will be kept in mind.

a) The ways we work today affect the changes we will see tomorrow. Change, be it reformist or revolutionary in character, is the outcome of complex interactions. The questions that we surface in our present work help set the terms for the political struggles before us. As our political efforts have been shaped by events that came before, so too does our work today become the foundation upon which the activists of tomorrow will function. It is self-defeating to believe that we can put off certain issues until some unknown later date. Of course, how we address those issues is determined by the circumstances we live in and the possibilities for struggle that exist. While we can and will change history, we cannot pretend that reality is anything more or less than it really is. The manner in which we approach that reality helps set the terms for our future efforts.

b) The character of our movement (the size of it, the breadth of participation, the tactics used, the political perspective articulated) stands in relation to the goals we work for. Dismantling nuclear weapons, ending the conventional arms race and wars of intervention, changing basic U.S. foreign and military policy, stopping the use of militarism to resolve disputes and conflicts between nations, confronting the many layers of violence in our daily lives—each of these goals requires different strengths. We might well argue that the present disarmament movement in this country is strong (one million people marching on June 12th, the thousands of new activists, even Congressional attempts to take up the call for a freeze). But if in fact we are attempting to deal with all of the issues mentioned above then we will have to be much stronger. We need the active participation of more people, of a greater diversity of people. We need an analysis and a strategy that ties these concerns together. We need a level of organizational coordination that does not exist today. And if we strive, as many say we should, to change the very structures which presently define our lives and the world we live in, then we will have to be all that much stronger. This is not said to be pessimistic about where we are today but rather to point out how much work there is still ahead of us.

c) Our movement must renew a commitment to local, grassroots organizing and activism. The goals of disarmament call for lasting changes. While some changes can clearly be made from the top (by government officials, corporate heads, military strategists), history teaches that the more lasting changes come when masses of people are involved in the process. Engaging large numbers of people means that we take our issues and our efforts to where those people are. The disarmament movement will not grow if it insists on people coming to it. We must go to where the people are—in their workplaces, communities, schools, etc.

d) For the grassroots activism to have national impact, for after all we are addressing national and international dynamics, there has got to be national coordination. This does not mean that some people decide on the work for everyone else, sending out the "line" on what should be done and how to do it. It does mean that we need mechanisms for sharing our local work, for looking at the overall picture, and for developing nationally coordinated efforts.

e) We cannot fall into the trap of setting priorities on people's struggles. The disarmament movement is especially vulnerable to this, in large degree because of the severity of the nuclear problem and the increasing dangers of nuclear holocaust. It just doesn't work to tell people that the issues in their daily experiences are not as important as the bomb. When we set up hierarchies of oppression, and when we say that other issues are somehow less deserving of our attention, then we cut ourselves off from people. Tell an unemployed worker, a battered wife, a political refugee, a welfare mother, the people who live at Love Canal or Three Mile Island, the black parents of Atlanta, families displaced by gentrification, gay men beaten, young men facing a draft, elderly with no income...tell all these people that their daily struggles to stay alive are less important and see what sort of response you get. We cannot build the disarmament movement on the notion that it, and it alone, is the most important issue on the agenda of the day.

f) Basic to the process of drawing out the connections that do exist between people is a respect for our diversity and the need for autonomy. Deeply entrenched sexism and racism, as well as class divisions, mean that people have very different realities. Add to that the varied ethnic, religious and cultural backgrounds of people, as well as regional differences given the size of this country, and we see that there is no way to identify one "typical American" experience or reality. In our autonomous formations we have the ability to explore our piece of the picture in greater depth. When we are strong in our autonomy we bring that particular reality to bear on an overall and coordinated process of change. So, as we do our disarmament work we must allow room for women, people of color, working people, any grouping of people that experiences a specific system of oppression to bring their insights into this work. By respecting autonomous formations we not only acknowledge our diversity, we also find what we have in common and thus build our unity. I believe it is a stronger, more powerful unity when people know they are respected for who they are and not asked merely to fit into yet another mold.

g) It is no less than all this that we have to keep in mind when we reach out to work with others. The form that perhaps best suits this is that of coalition. It is hard to work in coalition; no one group is in charge, differences are constantly being aired and we have to overcome decades, sometimes centuries, of divisions. But the alternatives (either working alone or asking everyone to submerge themselves into a new unit) just do not work. They don't work because they do not allow for actual experiential differences of people in this country. Once again, if we are not tied to people's realities then we will not be able to sustain their participation.

Having said all of this about the disarmament movement I think it is also important to say a word or two about the implications of this for the feminist movement. The feminist movement needs to develop a much more viable national presence. For us to function as the positive force inside the disarmament movement that I believe we can be requires a level of organizational cohesion that we now lack. Feminists need to take the concerns and insights of women more directly into disarmament work. We have to challenge the overwhelming male domination of the present disarmament movement, not because these are evil or bad men but rather because we do not want our structures to duplicate the power relations in society.

At the same time it is necessary that feminists continue to work in autonomous groups without men. In women-only organizations addressing disarmament issues women learn new things about the forces we are up against as well as about the nature of change. In fact, women's groups around the country have already begun exploring the relationship between what has been called the nuclear mentality and the role of patriarchy and sexism. Much of this work focuses on power relations, the use of force and violence in interpersonal dynamics as an extention of militarism (and vice-versa), and how the oppression of women is integrally tied to other forms of domination. A weakness in some of this work is a tendency to re-state traditional ideas of maternal instinct, again placing special emphasis on the role of biology. The idea that women are in some way "closer to the earth" seems to miss the depth of the analysis that feminism has to offer and again limits the very definition of woman. The effort to develop a coherent feminist analysis of militarism is still young. Even when we have disagreements with some of the particulars being articulated, the efforts of feminists to pursue these understandings is a vital process, and one that must be supported.

If we refuse to accept a hierarchy of oppressions/struggles then as feminists we have to take our perspective into various kinds of political work. And just as importantly, women must continue to be active in the struggles already surfaced by feminism. While the disarmament struggle is vital to our survival, the issues of sexual politics are also central to our lives and crucial to our liberation.

I believe that the people of the world will secure nuclear disarmament, that we can see an end to militarism, that the needs of people can come before the greed of profit, that it is possible to break down sexist and racist norms of behavior and live in a world where there is respect, trust and love, where people are allowed to reach their fullest human potential. In some ways it almost doesn't matter where you start from, the point is constantly to re-open the definition of the struggle and build on the links that already exist. In so doing we will gain the wisdom and gather the power not only to pull us away from the brink of nuclear annihilation but finally to insure that we never again face such a possibility.

4

RACISM: FUEL FOR THE WAR MACHINE
By Jack O'dell

Jack O'Dell is Director of International Affairs of Operation PUSH, (People United to Serve Humanity), a national human rights organization founded by Rev. Jesse Jackson and headquartered in Chicago.

Formerly Assistent Professor of Economic History at the Graduate School of Education of Antioch College in Washington D.C., O'Dell is a member of the International Economic History Association. His field of academic specialization is in the Comparative History of Colonialism.

A close associate of Dr. Martin Luther King Jr., in the movement to abolish segregation O'Dell was Director of Voter Registration, SCLC, (1961-1963). For nearly two decades he has served as Associate Editor of Freedomways *magazine—a quarterly journal of social sciences and the arts that has published many of his political essays.*

A former member of the Executive Committee of the "National Mobilization Committee to End the War in Vietnam," O'Dell was one of the National Organizers of the June Twelfth Disarmament Rally in New York last summer. He also serves on the Peace Education Division of the American Friends Service Committee.

In his capacity as International Affairs Director of PUSH, he has made several trips to Western Europe and the Middle East, and is active in the Anti-Apartheid Movement in support of liberation movements in Southern Africa.

When the June 12 Coalition faltered and threatened to disintegrate, one of the most explosive controversies centered on the relationship between the nuclear danger and the country's attitudes and practices toward its non-white populations. There were charges that important sections of the traditional peace movement were racist, and countercharges that militant blacks and their allies were trying to "take over" the coalition and use it for purposes that would prevent it from mounting the largest possible outpouring of sentiment against nuclear weapons and the threat of nuclear war. Jack O'Dell was one of the persons called in to play a healing role in the controversy. He didn't come in to develop a "magic formula" that would patch everything without coming to grips with the issues. He was invited to function on the staff and in the tense committee meetings as a person of proven insight and commitment for many years to both racial equality and coalition anti-war work.

With careful scholarship and without indulging in *ad hominem* attacks, O'Dell probes the interconnections between the country's "international relations" at home and its far-flung colonizing activities abroad. He examines the "great American chauvinism toward people [at home and abroad] of different ethnic and racial origins" and its connection to a foreign policy that has turned the United States into a military superpower with its finger on the nuclear button. This chapter destroys the illusion that foreign policy and domestic policy can be separated, or that the issue of racism can be either tokenized within or excluded from a movement that wants to succeed in ending the threat of nuclear war.

—D.D. & M.A.

What, then, are we to do, who desire peace and the civilization of all men? Hitherto the peace movement has confined itself chiefly to figures about the cost of war and platitudes on humanity. What do nations care about the cost of war, if by spending a few hundred millions in steel and gunpowder they can gain a thousand millions in diamonds and cocoa? How can love of humanity appeal as a motive to nations whose love of luxury is built on the inhuman exploitation of human beings, and who, especially in recent years, have been taught to regard these human beings as inhuman? I appealed to the last meeting of peace societies in St. Louis, saying, "Should you not discuss racial prejudice as a prime cause of war?" The secretary was sorry but was unwilling to introduce controversial matters!
—W.E.B. DuBois, "The African Roots of War," *The Atlantic Monthly*, 1915.

June 12th was a great day for peace; a great day in the history of our nation. For on that occasion, the peace sentiments of the people of our country affirmed themselves in a dramatic way. The June 12th march and rally was the largest demonstration in the history of the country. It was a by-product in many respects of years of work by traditional peace organizations who have held firm and carried the message that peace is a universal need.

It was an event which surpassed the most ambitious and extravagant hopes of the organizers; a powerful action. We can never go back to pre-June 12th days. It was also an act of internationalism, for it was in support of the UN Special Session on Disarmament. This particular special session was a result of an initiative of the Third World countries in the United Nations. These developing nations have repeatedly called attention to the fact that the nations of the world are spending hundreds of billions of dollars a year on nuclear and other weapons while on any day 200 million children in the world are out of school because they are too poor to attend. And so our movement on June 12th was responding to the concerns expressed by the nations of the Third World, of Africa and Asia and Latin America, for an end to the arms race. Quite appropriately, in the spirit of internationalism, thousands of people came from all around the world to join us. Yet June 12th was a landmark event produced by the people of the United States. It takes its place along with the march on Washington in 1963, the great demonstrations against the war in Vietnam in the late 1960's and early 1970's, the great demonstration in solidarity with the people of El Salvador and against intervention held in Washington in May 1981—as a milestone along the road of the people's struggle for human betterment.

Just as people came from around the world to join with us, the people of New York City played a pivotal role in hosting this great turnout. For an entire week there were activities in New York pointing to June 12th: a poetry reading at Carnegie Hall, a cultural fair up in Mt. Morris Park in Harlem, a performance of Beethovan's Ninth Symphony at St. Patrick's Cathedral, an international conference of the clergy, and an international conference of legal experts on the moral and legal aspects of the arms race. All this activity and more aroused the people of the nation and of New York to become a part of this great event.

The coalition of national organizations that gathered support for the June 12th rally and demonstration represents a new maturity on the part of the traditional peace movement. For the first time, its demand is to stop the arms race *and* direct the resources now being wasted on the military to those social programs serving urgent human needs. This is what we in the civil rights movement were saying at the time of our Poor People's campaign, in the middle of the Vietnam war, but the peace movement of that day lacked the maturity to understand that demand and never accepted it. A qualitatively different movement is emerging today, one that recognizes that peace and justice are indivisible and that the human needs of the people are a priority concern for those who seek peace and an end to the arms race. As a result, the traditional network of peace organizations is being transformed into a movement for peace which embraces many types of organizations.

The size of the demonstration was a message in itself. It was form and content made one. Eight hundred thousand people in New York and another 50,000 in San Francisco were saying in one voice: stop the arms race; cut the military budgets; redirect resources to meet human needs. The brief speeches by prominent individuals and representatives of organizations were an added significant dimension confirming support from the great cross-section of the national life of our country, and of the international life of the movement for peace and justice around the world.

Stop the arms race!
Take the toys from the boys!
Fund human needs—not the war machine!
Feed our cities, not the Pentagon!
No more Hiroshimas!
Jobs, not missiles!

The message rang clear from the posters and banners that were unfurled on that historic day in the summer of 1982.

People came from every state. Some travelled three or four days, by bus caravan or car caravan or train to be in New York to make witness to this mightiest expression of the people's will and determination to bring a lasting peace to the world in our time. We often hear that people are engaged in securing day-to-day survival in these days of economic crises, and therefore have no interest or time for such concerns as peace. But the movement to stop the arms race is a movement that has reached out to millions, convincing them that human survival is of transcendant importance, and that if it fails to achieve its objectives as a movement, the likelihood that another generation of Americans will be around to fight for jobs and affirmative action and health care, is indeed small. The people have become custodians of that message, as June 12th demonstrates beyond question.

On that day, through that event, our movement made a strong beginning towards changing the political agenda of this country. What is emerging is a movement that can effectively challenge the demagoguery that says "a strong America" is one based upon continuing to escalate the wasteful military budget, while taking food out of the mouths of school kids, cutting medical aid to the elderly, and crippling CETA job training programs for our unemployed youth.

The hundreds of organizers, in more than 500 cities and towns across the nation, who mobilized our country for this great event are midwives to the birth of a new movement, and all who participated are witness to the birth. To have participated was to leave the June 12th experience full of confidence that the people's will will prevail; no challenges are insurmountable; no obstacles cannot be moved; no pitfalls are inevitable; no arbitrary divisions will destroy that beginning unity that we have established. The creative energies of our people are being released in this awakening. We have joined the human community in a great effort to preserve life on this planet and all that we cherish in the democratic traditions and civilized achievements of our own nation. June 12th was our people's response to the worldwide movement for disarmament, and we have been inspired by the great mass demonstrations of the people of Europe, Japan, and elsewhere.

The anti-nuclear weapons movement in Europe which in this period rallies literally millions of people focused on the proposition that the new generation of Cruise and Pershing II missiles, which the leaders of NATO propose to introduce into Europe, is a serious threat to Europe's future and must be stopped. This movement challenges the established leadership in the various European countries and insists that they not become accomplices to those who glibly talk about and are preparing for so-called "limited nuclear war."

Our movement for peace and human needs is now consciously consolidating links with the international movements for disarmament. This lays the groundwork for recognition of the common interest that the people of the whole world have in ending the arms race and in common actions to follow. This enables the people of our country to break through the wall of

obscurantism and American provincialism that in the past has so
retarded our political development.

Demonstrations Against Nuclear Weapons
by the European and Japanese Peace Movements
(partial listing)

City	Oct.-Nov. 1981	Spring-Summer 1982
London	350,000 (Oct. 24)	250,000 (June 9)
Potsdam (GDR)	50,000	
Brussels	*200,000 (Oct. 25)	
Bonn	300,000 (Oct. 10)	350,000 (June 10)
Paris	30,000	350,000 (June 19)
Amsterdam	400,000 (Nov. 21)	
Bucharest		200,000
Vienna		70,000 (May 15)
Tokyo		(350,000)** (May 23)
Rome	250,000 (Oct. 25)	
Dublin		5,000 (June 12)
Dresden (GDR)		6,000 (February)

*2% of the entire population of Belgium
**32 million signatures on petitions were submitted by the
Japanese delegation to the U.N. Special Session. These petitions
advocated "total and complete disarmament."

Inspired by the qualitative growth in peace sentiment
throughout our country and encouraged by the prospects and

potential that the June 12th event has helped to crystalize, we are nevertheless mindful of the challenges that the objective situation holds. This birth of a new stage in the peace movement occurs at a time of general civilizational crisis in the country as a whole. People are losing their jobs, losing their homes, their health insurance, their family possessions.

We are living in the Great Depression of the 1980's, in which a large section of the working population is experiencing relative and absolute impoverishment. At this writing more than 12 million are unemployed and millions more can only find part-time work. Entire industries like steel, auto, lumber, and housing construction are in a long term slump and operating far below capacity. The fiscal crisis of the cities is spreading to ever larger units of our national life, affecting among other things a virtual collapse of the public school system. The number of farm bankruptcies is the highest since the 1930's, and the number of homeowners losing their homes is the highest since 1941. Small businesses are failing at an unprecedented rate. The social programs of government assistance to the poorer strata of the population are being systematically dismantled and abandoned, yet they represented only a minimum in fulfilling human needs, especially when compared with similar programs in other industrialized countries.

The spiritual and moral life of this society is deteriorating as long term unemployment makes its negative impact on family life and personal self-esteem. Medical illnesses associated with stress are in some areas reaching epidemic proportions. The very infrastructure of industrial and social development is decaying as bridges, roads, and dams stand in disrepair.

All of these trends have continued for more than a decade, but they have accelerated as a result of the Presidential elections of 1980. This process of social ruin is aggravated by military spending with its inflationary content and the waste of non-renewable resources so badly needed for the social reconstruction of our national life.

Therefore our efforts to reinforce the link between the arms race and redirect our national resources to meet human needs take on a special urgency: an urgency to work ever harder to mobilize people around an understanding of the link, and an urgency to guard against the insidious, divisive influences of racism. There are many examples of movements in the past that have floundered or have been derailed from their course by succumbing to this pathology.

Even in this time of crisis, we find human needs issues such as jobs, welfare, and slum housing perceived as "black issues" and projected as such by the media, even though most of the people they affect are white working people. We, Afro-American and Hispanic communities do, of course, suffer from these conditions in numbers disproportionate to our share of the population. Too often people view the issues that peace organizations raise as issues with which "blacks and Hispanics would not be concerned." This is put forward as a rationale by peace activists for not developing work in the black and Latin communities on issues of disarmament. Some leaders in the peace movement have also expressed feelings of apprehension that really involving the Afro-American and Latin communities in building the bridge between peace and human needs concerns would cause the traditional peace organizations to "lose control" or "be taken over" by these "militant" constituencies. While such attitudes expressed by white peace activists are not always motivated by racism, the organizational results are the same as if they were, because such attitudes coincide with and reinforce other experiences that are part of the real world of black Americans, Latinos, Native Americans, and the Asian population.

After all, this is a time in history when the Supreme Court has through the Bakke decision effectively diluted and in some cases reversed the affirmative action process in higher education and has through other decisions made it especially difficult for the victims of racism to secure justice in employment. This is a time when a conservative Senate has formally rejected busing as a remedy for those who have been denied equal access to quality education in the public schools. This is a time when the general policies of the Executive branch of government have created such havoc in the economy that the seniority system, originally designed to protect all workers, has now become a weapon against those who have always been the last hired and the first fired. This is a time when the majority of the population has met the lynching of a black youth in Mobile, Alabama, and Klan murders in Greensboro, North Carolina, or police killings of Mexican American youth in Houston, with general silence rather than with general outrage. Blacks and other direct victims of racism (white working people are indirect victims) see all this as an affront to their dignity and clearly understand that such official policies and unofficial attitudes are designed to keep them in a "disadvantaged" position in this society. This in turn engenders feelings of alienation, bitterness, and frustration because we have seen more than enough of this barbarism.

This fully takes into account that racism in America has undergone substantial modification during this century as a result of consistent struggle through the civil rights and other movements. Millions of white Americans now reject this ideology, both intellectually and emotionally—but they are still a small minority of the general population. What they represent is living proof that the social psychology of people can and does undergo change as a result of struggle and experience.

Racism is a major component of the historically-determined social psychology of the U.S. majority population. To understand this, let us look briefly at the institutional use of this mentality over the past several generations.

In U.S. national development, during the 19th century, racism became a pivotal component of the national belief system of this society. The idea of "white supremacy" and the implementation of its assumptions in concrete practice became one in the service of an economic system of exploitation for private gain. In this context, militarism and military aggression became a primary vehicle embodying the synthesis between racist theory and practice. The weaponry has evolved in its destruction from simple to complex, but the mentality remains essentially the same. For example, the idea of "bombing Vietnam into the Stone Age" and the idea that "the only good Indian is a dead Indian," as U.S. military policy undoubtedly belong to different centuries. Nevertheless, they represent one unbroken continuum in racist practice produced by this culture.

In 1830, some 55 years after the Revolution, the Indian Removal Act, passed by the Congress and implemented by the armed forces of the United States, removed the Choctaw, Creek, Chickasaw, and other Indian tribes from the eastern regions of the Carolinas and Georgia across the Mississippi and resettled them. This could be considered the beginning of U.S. colonialism, because the forceable removal of people from their national territory and the resettling of them at the will of the removers is of course one of the arrogances of colonialism.

The removal of the Indian population opened up the area of Alabama and Mississippi to the plantation system and African slave labor. The policy of annexing lands of Native Americans was, in fact, carried out under the Administration of President Andrew Jackson, himself a slaveholder in Tennessee. Jackson had gained much popularity earlier in the century as a general in the war against the Seminole Indians in Florida, which he lost. One of the major issues of this war was the rage of the slaveholders of Georgia because the Seminole often gave sanctuary to escaping Afro-American slaves.

After the removal of the Indians, the next act of U.S. colonialism was against the newly independent Mexican Republic. Mexico had generously permitted U.S. citizens to settle in that part of the Republic called Texas, on condition that they not bring any slaves. The revolution of 1821 had abolished slavery in Mexico. During the second Jackson Administration, the United States government encouraged these citizens to revolt against Mexican authority. In 1836 they did so, establishing the "Lone Star State." Nine years later, Texas was admitted to the United States as a slave state. Slavery had been reinstitutionalized in an area where it had once been abolished.

In the following year, 1846, the administration of President James K. Polk, a plantation slaveholder from North Carolina, launched a full-scale war for annexation of one-third of the Mexican Republic. The United States picked up the whole Southwest in this grand crusade, and while the Treaty of Guadelupe Hildalgo promised "full citizenship" in the United States to the conquered Mexican population in this area, this promise was as hypocritically made and as predictably broken as the many Indian treaties the United States signed.

In 1849, gold was discovered in the part of this newly annexed territory called California. The following year the California Territory was declared a state and admitted to the union. The westward gold rush was on. One of the first acts of the new State Legislature of California was to declare "null and void" all mining claims previously held by Mexicans. This policy of the state of California was religiously enforced by mobs of vigilantes who were protecting the right to ownership of the new colonialists.

One form of resistance to this tyranny and dispossession was the guerilla activity organized in the California mountains by Chicano revolutionary, Joaquin Murietta. We revere the memory of this man and of his deeds as we do those of Nat Turner, John Brown, Denmark Vesey, Chief Joseph, and other leaders of the many revolts against slavery and genocide.

The Mexican people in the Southwest became second-class citizens, and with this degradation came the subjugation of Spanish culture, which had flourished for 300 years. The racist stereotypes which had been systematically introduced nationally to prejudice people against Afro-Americans and thereby gain support for the institution of slavery were now applied to these Mexican-Americans. Through this colonial policy of conquest, the U.S. in its capitalist development inherited not only an area rich in mineral resources but also a highly developed cattle-breeding culture which had been transplanted from Spain in the 16th century. This crusade of plunder is treated in the history textbooks as a kind of idyllic pilgrimage called "the Westward expansion."

As is well known, one of the states carved out of this conquered territory and annexed is the state of New Mexico. An update of conditions since the dawn of the Atomic Age reveals that this area has been transformed into a militarily dependent region.

Activists in the peace movement in New Mexico call attention to the fact that Los Alamos, in the North, was the site for the research and development of the atomic bomb. The world's firt bomb was tested at Almogordo in the South. Then there are the Sandia Laboratories, which build nuclear weapons and the White Sands Missile Range where Pershing II's are tested. And Kirkland Air Force Base, Monzano Air Force Base and the storage of nuclear waste in the Carlsbad Caverns, etc.

Racism In American Intellectual Life and Institutions

The U.S. Republic soon faced a civil war brought on by the Southern slaveholders, who were prepared to break up the Republic in order to perpetuate slavery. In the midst of this challenge, the Lincoln Administration launched a second front—directed against the Cheyenne, Sioux, and other Plains Indians. This is undoubtedly the most infamous blot on the record of the Lincoln Administration, which was serving the interest of Northern finance capital by warring against Native Americans whom the United States had promised, by treaty, to leave alone. The conquest of this entire continent was now coming under the hegemony of the Eastern bank financiers, railroad magnates, and other sections of an emerging monopolistic class.

However, the Emancipation Proclamation in 1863 and the Thirteenth Amendment to the Constitution, which abolished slavery in 1865, were inspirational to the people of Puerto Rico and Cuba, which still remained under Spanish colonial rule. Puerto Rico had 40,000 slaves among a population of 650,000. The abolitionist movement in Puerto Rico organized the first political party founded on the island, the Liberal-Reformist Party. By historical coincidence, the unsuccessful uprising in Puerto Rico against the Spanish monarchy known as "El Grito Southern de Lares" occurred during the same year (1868) that the Pacific post-Civil War abolitionists in the United States were beginning the revolutionary Reconstruction efforts to abolish the remnants of the slave society.

In this same period the Chinese people began to migrate to the United States, the Boxer Rebellion having opened up China to the West. The building of the East-West Railroad and the

Southern Pacific was largely the result of Chinese labor—and the builders of the railroad were rewarded with the epithet "coolie." In 1868, the California Legislature passed an act that said "Chinese or Mongolians cannot be a witness in court in a case in which any white person is involved." Yet, in the previous year, 1867, Chinese had been murdered, largely by sheriffs in California who were enforcing the Mining Act. On October 25, 1871, the *Los Angeles Daily News* reported on the lynching of 14 Chinese in that city, part of a general campaign of intimidation of the Chinese community. Ironically enough, the victims lived in a ghetto called Negro Alley.

The year 1870, when the passage of the Fifteenth Amendment guaranteed the right to vote to all male citizens regardless of color, was also the year the Puerto Rico abolitionists, lead by the economist Joaquin Maria Sanroma, issued their famous manifesto. This was the beginning of the emancipation process in Puerto Rico, which extended over a period of about 10 years.

Meanwhile a protracted war for independence and the abolition of slavery was under way in Cuba under the leadership of the great Afro-Cuban patriot Antonio Maceo.

In 1876, the Hayes-Tilden Act began the betrayal of the Reconstruction effort, the consolidation of the political influence of the Ku Klux Klan, and the opening up of the South to terror and lynching. On the West coast an anti-Chinese movement was developing, and both the major political parties, Republican and Democratic, had anti-Chinese planks in their national platforms. Six years later, in 1882, the Congress passed a law prohibiting the immigration of Chinese for a period of 10 years. Actually, the law was renewed several times, so that this prohibition remained in force for a period of 25 years.

In 1883, the year the U.S. Supreme Court nullified the Civil Rights Act of 1875, racist mobs ran amuck in the Chinese quarters of Takoma, Washington, and San Francisco, burning them to the ground.

This entire process of developing a state system of racism in the United States during the nineteenth century was provided an intellectual shield by those spokesmen in cultural circles who advocated what was called the Teutonic Origins theory. This theory was, in essence, simple "white supremacy" given a fashionable dress of University endorsement. The Teutonic theorists argued that all Anglo-Saxon institutions of any worth had their historical roots in the Teutonic tribal institutions of ancient Germany and furthermore that "only the Teutonic races had been imbued with the ability to build stable governments."

In British intellectual circles, the leading advocates of the Teutonic Origins theory were Bishop William Stubbs and Edward A. Freeman, both historians at Oxford University. From England the theory spread to America towards the end of the 1870's. Its leading American spokesman was Henry Baxter Adams, one of the organizers of the graduate school at Johns Hopkins University. In 1884, Adams founded the American Historical Association. Freeman praised Adams' work in cultivating the Teutonic Origins theory and proceeded to modify his own views to say that Teutonic Origins theory "had three homes—England, Germany, and the United States."

Freeman came over to make a lecture tour in 1881 and is reported to have gotten into some difficulty when, in one of his lectures, he remarked: "The best remedy for whatever is amiss in America would be if every Irishman should kill a Negro and be hanged for it."[1] The date here is important, for it is a period of massive lynchings in the South; Afro-Americans were fleeing the South by the thousands in the face of Ku Klux Klan terror.

Professor Thomas F. Gosset, in his definitive and enlightening study of the history of racism in our country, tells us that "[t]he Teutonic Origins theory of government dominated the thinking of American historians during this period." In this context he mentions the leading theorists at "Harvard, Cornell, the University of Wisconsin and Columbia."[2] Most of these men had studied at German universities at some time in their careers. A case in point is John W. Burgess, who came from a slave-holding family in Tennessee (which had, however, supported the Union during the Civil War). Burgess studied at the Universities of Leipzig, Berlin, and Gottingen and returned to the United States to become the founder of Columbia's School of

Political Science, where he taught for 36 years. He sent dozens of his students to Germany and finally expressed the hope that his school was training the future leaders of the American nation.

During this period, the South became that region of the country where in defense of racial segregation the frontier traditions of mob rule and vigilante power were preserved as extensions of the police power of local government.

By the 1890's the counter-revolutionary forces in the United States had succeeded in bringing an end to the Reconstruction period. The racist institution of segregation was affirmed as national policy in the *Plessy v. Ferguson* decision of the Supreme Court. With the Plains Indians confined to reservations and blacks locked into a plantation system in the South as sharecroppers and tenants, the Manifest Destiny war machine was directed to overseas conquest. And so, from building an overland empire in the early part of the century, the United States now turned to extending itself overseas in the classic form of colonial rule.

The McKinley Administration in 1898 launched a war against Spain which was really directed at heading off the independence movements in Spain's remaining colonies— Puerto Rico, the Philippines, Cuba, Guam, and Hawaii. It was this historical intervention that resulted in Puerto Rico's becoming a colony of the United States. The Philippines suffered the same fate. Between 1899 and 1904, Guam, Puerto Rico, the Philippines, and Hawaii, all remnants of the Spanish empire, were annexed to the expanding United States empire. It was within this context that a Panama Canal Treaty was signed which gave the United States a zone of colonial domination in the newly established nation-state of Panama, which had just won its independence from Colombia.

The resistance to this classic pattern of colonialism expressed itself within our country in the formation of the Anti-Imperialist League. In this forum, a number of prominent Afro-American leaders spoke out actively against the colonialist aggression by the United States. Among them were Dr. W.E.B.

DuBois, the father of our modern freedom movement, and Bishop Henry McNeil Turner of the African Methodist Episcopal Church (AME).

Despite the resistance of some in this country, however, the *export of racism abroad* under American auspices was to become one of the major manifestations of the influence of racist ideology in the economic, cultural, and political institutional life and fabric of U.S. society.

The racist system of segregation and racial discrimination which was now pervasive throughout the United States was introduced into the Panama Canal Zone. Separate and unequal pay scales for Panamanian citizens and U.S. citizens in the Canal Zone, segregated housing, segregated public schools—the whole Jim Crow pattern was transplanted to Panama.

Even a separate judicial system was put into effect. A delegation from Operation PUSH visited Panama in 1977, in connection with efforts to secure U.S. Senate ratification of the new Panama Canal Treaties. We were informed that if a Panamanian citizen who had been tried in the U.S. court in the Canal Zone chose to appeal the verdict, the appeal went to the U.S. Circuit Court in Louisiana.

This comfortable little enclave of segregation established by the U.S. inside the sovereign territory of the Republic of Panama, a haven for civil servants from South Carolina and Georgia, in more recent decades became headquarters for the Southern Command. The latter is the U.S. military establishment's training center for police and military personnel from El Salvador, Guatemala, Nicaragua (under the Dictator Somoza) as well as counter-insurgency operations against socialist Cuba and other countries of the Caribbean area.

As a case in point, Puerto Rico furnishes another example. The colonial status of the Puerto Rican people, under U.S. domination throughout this century, has resulted in an intensification of a racial caste system in their society. This expresses itself particularly in the cultural sphere in trends that deny the African contribution to the Puerto Rican national culture. At the same time, one of Puerto Rico's islands, Viegas, and the waters around it which fisherman use for their livelihood, are currently used as areas of target practice for the U.S. Navy, a rather classic example of the organic unity between racism and militarism.

The great American war machine that had rolled across the Western plains was now, at the turn of the century, also directed towards colonial conquest in the Philippines. Its operation was an application of the Teutonic Origins theory. Its barbarities were forerunners of the atrocities the United States military would be committing in the Vietnam war 60 years later. Newspaper reporters of the day filed reports from the Philippines describing the use of dum-dum bullets against the Filipino freedom fighters, the torture of prisoners, and the mutilation of bodies by U.S. troops. Part of the conventional wisdom of the period held that many American civil servants who went out to the Philippines to work in the colonial government drew upon their experiences of "race relations" in the Deep South in forming attitudes about the Filipino people.

This situation mirrors the fact that U.S. foreign policy has been historically shaped in part by the prevailing "international relations" at home or has been carried out by people otherwise trained in the old traditions of great American chauvinism towards people of different ethnic and racial origins.

In the growth of the United States as a geopolitical unit, settlement was not a factor unto itself. Settlement went hand in hand with war, the annexation of territories, and plunder. The United States settled territories that it acquired in this manner in part with slaves plundered from the war on the African continent and in part with European immigrants—largely an impoverished population and often escaping from political repression.

With the war clouds gathering in Europe portending the massive destruction of World War I, the supply of immigrant labor which had flocked to the United States in the previous 30 years was drying up. During that period, some 14 million people had immigrated from Europe: Italians and Jews recruited for the sweat shops of the garment industry in New York; Poles and Czechs working the mines and steel mills of Pittsburgh; Finns and Scandinavians settling the farms of Minnesota and working the lumber camps of the Northwest; the Irish becoming the "groundhogs" digging out the subways of New York. World War I ended this as a pattern of exploitation by cutting off the supply of European immigrant labor. The captains of monopoly in our country dipped into the Southern plantation regions for a black labor supply to keep the war industry's production going in Pittsburgh, Chicago, and Detroit. They reached into the Rio Grande Southwest for their supply of agricultural labor to work such areas as the mechanized cotton fields of West Texas and the beet fields of Colorado.

The decade 1909-1919 saw the formation of the NAACP, with an agenda of fighting against lynchings and peonage in the South and rampant discrimination in the North. In 1919, a comparable movement, the League for the Protection of Latinos, emerged among the Mexican-American population. The League had an agenda of fighting against deportations and against the robbery of farm workers by such power centers as the Arizona Cotton Growers Association.

By the 1920's the old, formerly slave-worked Southern agriculture, with its sharecropping and other forms of impoverished tenant labor, was competing for the national market in cotton with the newer agricultural areas in the Southwest whose commercial farms had introduced the most advanced forms of mechanization and the widespread use of farm laborers who were transient and expendable.

"Master Race" Politics in the Atomic Age

During the course of World War II, the industrial power of the U.S. was greatly expanded while that of its industrial rivals in Europe was being decimated by the war. At war's end, U.S. military power had been dramatically demonstrated in the atomic devastation of Hiroshima and Nagasaki.[3] The economic royalists of America dreamed of long term economic supremacy in the world based upon a U.S. monopoly of atomic weapons. They entertained ambitions of taking over the old, fading colonial empires. The corporate elite of Western Europe were no longer able to hold onto these territories by direct rule because they had been relatively weakened by the devastation of the war. The more powerful U.S. empire builders hoped to reduce these Europeans to economic vassalage, or client states, through the Marshall Plan, while putting their colonial dominions under new management.

For those people of the countries under colonialism who aspired to be free and independent, U.S. policy makers put forward the "clean hands" interpretation of U.S. history: i.e., because the United States had been born through an anti-colonial revolution, it had clean hands and could be trusted to be supportive of the new revolutionary movements that were emerging in the Third World. As part of their interpretation, they explained institutional racism in the United States as mere "individual prejudice," a kind of family quarrel among Americans which was of no concern to the international community. With this economic, political, and propaganda offensive, the corporate elite held great hopes for dominion over at least the capitalist world economy.

The real possibility for that dream to materialize unscathed vanished within a few years. But this did not deter our empire builders, driven by the detemination to secure the maximum profits from overseas investments. They continued to pursue their fantasy about world supremacy—and the American tax-payer has been footing the bill for this fantasy ever since.

While world developments were confirming in many ways that the fantasy could never be realized, corporate America acquired an expensive habit. That habit is to get its profits guaranteed by the state through the manufacturing of expensive weapons under "defense" contracts, with their cost overruns, non-competitive bidding, and built-in graft. General Dynamics, Chrysler, McDonnell-Douglas, Lockheed, General Motors, Rockwell International, Texas Instruments, Livermore Laboratories, and a few dozen other giant corporations secured the "defense" of their corporate profit margins. The state is their servant. The expansion of U.S. corporate economic, and political influence abroad is still their purpose; building up a huge arsenal of nuclear and conventional weapons, and threatening to use them, is viewed as a means to that end.

U.S. diplomacy at the UN was consistent with the policy makers' larger geopolitical ambitions. It would be nice to believe that in its international relations, our country has remained consistent with the principles set forth in its own Declaration of Independence. Unfortunately, such is not the case.

Thirty years ago, in December 1952, when most countries of the Third World were still under colonial bondage. The U.N. General Assembly passed a resolution embodying the following principles:[4]

—The right to self-determination is a prerequisite to the full enjoyment of human rights.

—All means possible should be used to ensure self-determination for all peoples.

—Native peoples should take part in the government of their territories.

The U.S. delegation voted "No" on all three parts of the resolution. Again in 1957,[5] on a resolution affirming that independence should be given to Tanzania, Togo, and Burundi, the United States voted "No."

Of course no UN resolution gains independence for any country, but the UN sets a climate of world opinion favorable to such goals, and here we have an example of the United States voting against the idea that independence should be granted to colonized African countries.

Similarly, a resolution adopted by the UN in November 1961 resolved "to proclaim 1962 as the end to the era of colonialism." The U.S. delegation that voted against it was the delegation of the Kennedy Administration, appointed at a time when our movement here in the United States was gathering strength in its struggle against institutional racism and was pressuring the Administration to use its constitutional powers to abolish segregation.

A decade later, when the UN General Assembly passed a similar resolution,[6] the U.S. delegation—this time appointees of the Nixon Administration—again voted "No." Two years earlier the delegation had voted "No" on a resolution intended to focus world attention on the struggles of the people of Angola, Mozambique, and Guinea Bissau for independence from Portugese colonialism.[7]

The United States was the only country in the UN to support the Portugese colonialists.

The U.S. official tilt towards the racist apartheid regime in South Africa appeared quite early in the history of the UN. In 1946, the United States voted "No" on a resolution that the UN get a special report on the treatment of the Indians in South Africa. Thirty-two countries supported that resolution; the United States was among the fifteen that voted against it. Again in 1957, when the UN issued an "appeal to the Union of South Africa to revise its policy of apartheid," the United States voted "No," In 1969 the UN adopted an *International Covenant on the Elimination of all Forms of Racial Discrimination*. The United States remains one of the few countries in the world that has never ratified that covenant.[8]

Consistent with this pattern in foreign policy over more than three decades, in 1981 the U.S. delegation to the UN cast six consecutive vetoes against an African diplomat's becoming Secretary General of the UN, His Excellency Salim Ahmed Salim, the Foreign Minister of Tanzania and a past President of the UN General Assembly, was the choice of the overwhelming majority of the member states of the UN. His experience at the UN and general professional qualifications resulted in his candidacy being jointly put forward by the Organization of African Unity and the League of Arab States. Only the repeated U.S. vetoes in the Security Council prevented his election to the top post in the UN .

The Cold War of the mid-50's and massive U.S. purchases of South Africa uranium furnished the milieu in which official America's flourishing partnership with the racist apartheid regime began. That year South Africa purchased its first U.S. nuclear reactor. Later in the decade, with the cooperation of the West German nuclear industry, it laid the foundations for the events in the Kalahari Desert in 1979: the testing of a thermonuclear bomb. The most racist regime in the world today—a society in which the black majority population has no civil or human rights whatsoever—now has the capability of producing nuclear weapons. Its economic, political, diplomatic, and military relationship with the United States was indispensible to that accomplishment.

Such a development is obviously not the concern of only apartheid groups in our country. It deserves the attention of the entire peace movement. Aggressive, militaristic, racist South Africa, which uses its illegal occupation of Namibia as a base for frequent invasion into Angola, has created in Southern Africa the preconditions for a military confrontation that could lead to world war.

While Nelson Mandela, Walter Sisulu, and thousands of other courageous opponents of the regime among the South African people are languishing in jails or in forced exile and millions of blacks are disenfranchised, we must measure the success of our struggle against institutionalized racism here in the United States by the grim reality of continued official U.S. support for apartheid in South Africa. Foreign policy and domestic policy are inseparable.

On that point, the following quotation from a South African journal is appropriate:

> South Africa's credibility stood high in the United States, South Africa's top envoy, newly retired Mr. Donald Sole, told a luncheon of the Pretoria Press Club.
> He said the eyes of the U.S. were on South Africa to see what happened with new constitutional proposals.
> Mr. Sole said that South Africa's credibility in the U.S. had been at an all-time low during the Carter Administration—and that had been aggravated by the Biko affair. But now the country's credibility had been fully restored under the Reagan Administration and to an extent by links established with the American Secretary of State concerned with Africa, Dr. Chester Crocker.[9]

The apartheid regime does not hestitate to use this new-found "credibility" to its advantage. Taking their signals from American complicity in the recent Israeli invasion of Lebanon, they concluded that the time was ripe for another military sweep into the sovereign territory of Angola. They, too, are "only" going after "terrorists." In these military forays, which always resulted in the killing of untold numbers of people in refugee camps in Angola, the racist apartheid regime is really acting as a surrogate for the U.S. government since these actions are in full accord with the Reagan Administration's strategy of keeping the region destablized.

Sure enough, the *South African Digest* (August 20, 1982) reports the following:

> The Reagan Administration has understanding for the necessity of South Africa's most recent Angola operation. According to informed officials in Washington it is regarded as a new full-scale military campaign in southern Angola...
> The U.S. reportedly understands that South Africa cannot hold back at present just because delicate negotiations are in progress.

Such understanding is a well-kept secret from the American public although this administration has repeatedly told them that it is "returning government to the people."

Meanwhile, the armed might of the naval forces of the United States was roaming the high seas for several months (1981-1982) under orders from the President to intercept and turn back any boat carrying Haitian refugees seeking to enter our country. Though many Haitians are seeking political asylum, the government classifies them as economic refugees and under that status holds them in refugee camps until deported.[10]

In his essay from which we quoted earlier ("The African Roots of War"), W.E.B. DuBois analyzes the causes of World War I. Dr. DuBois identifies the Berlin Conference of 1884, when the great powers of Western Europe sought to carve up Africa among themselves, as the beginning of that world conflict. One hundred years later, these same European states, under the NATO military alliance, intend to introduce a new generation of American-made nuclear weapons into their arsenals. These Cruise and Pershing II first-strike weapons, undetectable by radar, will be stationed five minutes from Moscow. This means the world will from that day on be just five minutes from a nuclear war—a war in which the survival of the planet hangs in the balance.

In this regard, I am reminded of the conversation held at NATO headquarters in Brussels in November 1981. The American Friends Service Committee (AFSC) organized a delegation to meet with various leaders of the anti-nuclear weapons demonstrations in Western Europe. We visited Bonn and Cologne in the Federal Republic of Germany (West Germany); London; Amsterdam, and Brussels. We also met with Dr. Rolfe Hofsteder, head of the political department of NATO, who is assigned to that post from the FRG. Before leaving him, we summed up our discussion in order to make sure that we were bringing back to the United States an accurate account of what had transpired.

As we understood it, the NATO position was that an imbalance of forces exists between the Warsaw Pact and NATO in favor of the Eastern bloc and that the countries of the NATO bloc have neither the money nor the will to redress this imbalance through conventional means; and that therefore, NATO made the decision in December 1979 to introduce a new generation of nuclear weapons, deeming it better to risk nuclear war, even though it might destroy all civilization, than to leave the present imbalance intact.

Herr Dr. Hofsteder did not disagree with the substance of our summation, but he hastily interjected, "Yes, but you didn't say "deterrent." So that's the code word, the magic phrase, that supposedly makes everything alright. "Deterrent."

The world has witnessed a long history of episodes in which the "Western Mind" has conveniently stood reality on its head in order to provide the rationale for the purveyors of violence. Holding or trading in African slaves was "christianizing the natives." Hiroshima and Nagasaki were subjected to nuclear devastation in the name of "saving lives." The destruction of My Lai and other villages in Vietnam by napalm and defoliation methods was "saving them from Communism." The neutron bomb is endowed with a special value because it "preserves property"—and we must recognize that property is the most sacred item in the whole pantheon of values of the social system under which we live. The racist system of apartheid with its violation of human rights and the dispossession and relocation of black people in South Africa into economically sterile Bantustans, is called "Separate Development."[11]

The recent carnage in Lebanon and the mass murders in the Shatila and Sabra refugee camps in West Beirut have been rationalized as "stamping out terrorism," and building an arsenal of nuclear weapons that could destroy all human life on this planet is called "deterrent." The absurdity of the deterrence theory is evident in the fact that if it ever breaks down, the result could be a war that incinerates the planet.

From the depopulation and colonial amputation of the African continent to the depopulation of the whole planet: that's a devolution of human society that we must never allow the architects of "Master Race" politics to implement.

The Power to Be Organized

A century and a half ago, the people of the United States built a movement for the abolition of slavery which was ultimately victorious because slavery, and the economic class it directly benefited, had become destructive of the Union. In more recent times, we abolished segregation because this system of racist insult and deprivation violated the humanity of our citizens and became destructive to U.S. credibility in a changing world that rejected such institutionalized racism. Now we are challenged as a society to build a movement for the abolition of nuclear weapons because their continued existence threatens the survival of the United States and indeed the survival of life on this planet.

If the traditional peace organizations actively embrace the human needs dimensions of the struggle for peace, they have the opportunity to become the conscience of the nation—a center of moral authority and political power capable of reshaping in a progressive pattern the social outlook of the majority of the U.S. population. An America committed to changing through the freeze, reduction, and abolition of nuclear weapons will be a better America simply because it will be less dangerous to itself and the world. An America committed beyond just this objective, to reconstruct its economic and political life for full employment, health care, and quality education will not only be a better country because it is less dangerous; it will be more civilized, more humane, and more in step with world development. That's the preferred option. From embracing the goal of an end to the destructive arms race to establishing as a new national purpose the effective use of the national resources that are freed up through relief from the burden of the arms race: that's the transitional process we must seek.

Since ending the arms race, with all of its waste of human and financial resources, has now become a prerequisite for releasing the resources we need to meet human needs, activists in the traditional peace organizations have a concrete link to the activists in the human needs organizations. They reinforce one another's goals and objectives. The goals of the human needs movement will not be met short of drastic reduction in the military budget, and the goals of the disarmament movement will require the massive involvement of those constituencies involved in struggle for the various human needs issues. It is not only possible that we have this unity, it is imperative. Such unity serves mutual self-interest. The people of our country will improve the quality of life in direct proportion to the power they mobilize to prevent nuclear war and redirect the resources now going to the military to improve the material and cultural requirements of the whole population. That's a civilized course of action.

Nuclear weapons are a perversion of science and technology—our scientific intelligentsia certainly have more important work to do than simply figuring out how most efficiently to blow up the world. That's science enslaved to a false ethic.

For 37 years the United States has led the nations of the world in producing the arms race. Now we have the opportunity, combined with the moral obligation to the world and undergirded by our self-interest in securing a future for ourselves and our children, to lead the world in reducing the danger of nuclear war. Stopping the arms race and disengaging from continued possession of nuclear weapons—that's the *pivotal issue* in the human needs agenda of the 1980's. We *can* accomplish that agenda. But to do so we must direct our energies and talents to mobilize the national will, and we must not allow the charlatans of the political order and their counterparts, the pseudo-intellectuals in the media, to divert us into thinking it is unachievable.

I am not advocating unilateral disarmament by our country. Disarmament can best be achieved through bilateral negotiations with the Soviet Union, since there is approximate parity between the two countries, and through participation in international agreements such as those proposed by the UN Disarmament Commission. What I am suggesting is that our country take a unilateral initiative and set the pace for concrete steps towards the abolition of nuclear weapons. For more than 30 years, the United States set the pace for the arms race (atom bomb, hydrogen bomb, long-range bomber, middle-range bomber, atomic submarines, and so forth). Now let us be a pacesetter for the disarmament race so that the whole world will be convinced we are sincere about removing the threat of nuclear war from the human race.

The movement to stop the arms race in our country will organize people and move them by their fear of nuclear war, but that is not enough. We must provide people a cognitive framework within which to act, and out of which to draw a deeper understanding of the social causes of the arms race.

Racism has played a greater role in the development of the institutional framework of the United States as a society dominated by an oligarchy of corporate monopolies than it has in any other nation on earth except South Africa.

The emerging peace and human needs movement, as an alternative authority in organizing, educating, and interpreting events, is indispensible to the people of our country. It can provide the vision and confidence that would enable them to win victory over the masters of war and the ideology of racism-militarism. Some people want an America as is, with simply a freeze on further stockpiling of nuclear weapons. Some want an America as is, *minus* nuclear weapons. Both of these are looking in the right direction, but some of us must see further than this and champion the idea of an America without nuclear weapons as a constructive prerequisite to establishing a more civilized and humane social order.

In what has become a historically significant speech at Riverside Church in New York (April 4, 1967) Dr. Martin LutherKing, Jr. warned us that "A nation that year after year spends more on military defense than on programs of social uplift is approaching spiritual death." The human needs side or dimension of the social progress agenda has to be elevated as a desirable goal and given emphasis by the peace movement if that movement is to become a moral force that helps this society to avoid the "spiritual death" that Dr. King warned us about. It is conceivable that we could stop the arms race and if we did not insist on redirecting the resources to meet human needs we would still be approaching as a nation the moral suicide to which Dr. King called attention. The goal is for a society of peace with justice; this will represent a common effort to fulfill the principles set forth in the preamble to the Constitution: "...in order to form a more perfect union, establish justice, ensure domestic tranquility, provide for the common defense, and promote the general welfare for ourselves and our prosperity..."

In the course of the past ten years, a great cross-section of organizations and leadership in the black community have clearly decided that the foreign policy of the United States is as much our concern as domestic issues. We have decided not to let anyone "ghettoize" our concerns. Among the organizations to be commended are the Congressional Black Caucus in its outstanding legislative work, Trans Africa in lobbying, and the Coalition of Black Trade Unionists in pressuring the conservative AFL-CIO bureaucracy to take a positive position regarding the plight of the black majority workers in South Africa.

Several fact-finding missions to the Middle East by representatives of PUSH have associated that organization with the growing inquiry among the American public as to why U.S. policy in that area of the world is so one-sided. We, in PUSH, regard the "no-talk" policy toward the PLO as both ridiculous and insulting, and we insist that "terrorism" be measured by one yardstick.

The National Conference of Black Lawyers, in the finest tradition of the legal profession, has done much to make the public more aware of the UN Human Rights Charter. Together with many clergy of various denominations and with the SCLC, they have helped to create a climate of public debate around U.S. Middle East policy. Worthy of note also is the consistent internationalism of *Freedomways* magazine in its editorials and many articles, and the NAACP's formation of an International Affairs Department under the leadership of the distinquished Africanist, Dr. Broadus Butler.

Contributing greatly to the success of the June 12th demonstration were such New York-based groups as Asian-Americans for Disarmament, the Third World and Progressive Peoples Coalition, the National Black United Front, the Interdenominational Ministerial Association of Harlem, the Coalition of Hispanic Organizations for Disarmament and Survival and the Afro-American Executive Committee.

One should also take note of the growth and emergence of the Arab-American community as a new political force in the national life of our country. Some of their newly founded organizations are rapidly becoming experienced in the struggle against racism and militarism, and they represent an important reserve of strength for the coalition addressing the problems of peace and human needs. Racist stereotypes of Arabs, promoted by the U.S. media, the educational system, and by government institutions, is obviously not an accident. Taken in today's context, it is part of the psychological preparation designed to gain public acceptance of whatever adventures the Rapid Deployment Force might be ordered to undertake in the Middle East, allegedly to protect "our oil" in that region of the world.

We in PUSH have had the good fortune to share responsibilities on the battlefield with these and many other national and local organizations. Our common struggle in resistance to racism and deprivation, as well as our struggle for the full, unfettered development of our respective communities, has enabled us to share a common viewpoint on these fundamental issues of survival.

We believe America should join the world as a partner on the side of the oppressed and the disinherited rather than continue on its present course as an ally of every right-wing, repressive regime in the world. In relation to the Middle East, South Africa, and Latin America, we need a peace policy that serves our national interest rather than a war policy that serves special interests.

This commitment to human rights has deep roots in the Afro-American experience. We came here on a foreign policy issue; slavery was an integral part of U.S. foreign policy towards Africa. The greatest leaders of our people—among them Frederick Douglas, Dr. DuBois, Paul Robeson, Martin Luther King, Jr.—have always brought a world view to our freedom movement, and this was consistent with our struggle for a more civilized democracy in the U.S.

Speaking at an "International Conference on World Peace and Poverty" in Dublin, Reverend Jesse L. Jackson, the National President of PUSH expressed the connection between the arms race and human needs in the following:

> The human rights and the civil liberties of those struggling for more humane and just societies—in South Africa, Bolivia, the Philippines, Chile, Northern

Ireland, El Salvador or wherever in the world—must be protected and defended.... The deliberations at the conference have confirmed that the causes of poverty are rooted in economic injustices that have been institutionalized over centuries, while the arms race today aggravates and intensifies every aspect of the material and spiritual impoverishment of the human race.... Our economic justice movement (in the U.S.) is confronting government policy in which the whole public sector economy is being dismantled and the achievements of the last 40 years of social legislation are being either compromised or thrown out in the search for more tax dollars to pour into the nuclear weapons madness. A similar pattern is being carried out in England and to a lesser degree in other West-European countries....[12]

Organization is Decisive

The coalition of national and local organizations which united for the common purpose of producing the largest demonstration of our history on June 12th does not represent the formation of a new organization designed to replace in its work any of the existing organizations that made up the coalition. The unity it symbolized however, does represent the potential for being a new political influence crystallizing the public sentiment for peace and making possible thereby the expansion of the work of all organizations concerned with human survival and economic justice.

The coalition represents a larger constituency than any one or several of its organizations. If that unity is maintained, then it can speak more authoritatively to the issue of peace and human needs without usurping any of the prerogatives or programs of any *one* of the organizations which compose the coalition. To the contrary, the work of each organization is ultimately strengthened by the relationship it has to the larger configuration of organization and the collective impact on public opinion it can effect. It should be remembered that the June 12th coalition was built through struggle, a struggle to overcome mistrust, misperception, racist attitudes, and to arrive at a common appreciation among all the organizations of the challenge that organizing a massive demonstration represented. The most common feeling among us now is that whatever the difficulties, the event made it all worthwhile. Much has begun to change as a result of this experience, not only in the country at large but within the organizations that made up the coalition and among the activists themselves, who served as the co-organizers. Staying together, moving together, growing together, and winning victories together, that's the new challenge—to see June 12th as a very important beginning of a new period of human needs and peace activity, full of possibilities for altering the course of U.S. foreign policy and its domestic consequences.

We too must become "Great Communicators" and the millions of people in our country expect us to provide them with facts, insights and interpretation that they can act upon and give back to our movement their experiences.

If the traditional peace organizations assist the labor and civil rights groups in transforming the current depression of chronic joblessness into a movement for full employment, such activity would create a favorable context for explaining the role that military spending plays in aggravating the unemployment crisis and in creating inflation in the whole economy. We don't have any jobs for the jobless of our country. Mass movements are designed to be social change agents rather than social service agencies. What we do have is a sound interpretation of why so many millions of our citizens are without work and an explanation as to why neither government nor industry is making a serious effort to provide this essential human right.

As people understand the situation more clearly and it is increasingly the basis for mass action, the disarmament/human needs movement will gain a popular base of active supporters, not only in the ghettos and barrios across the country but in the working class communities of the Irish in South Boston and

Polish in Chicago and Cicero, Illinois. Building such a power-base among these constituencies is a critical part of the struggle against the pernicious ideology of race supremacy.

In a discussion last summer in Berlin, leaders of the Peace Committee of the German Democratic Republic made the point that there were many peace groups in Germany in 1932. Each was busy with its own agenda. The one thing they failed to do was come together in solid opposition to the war danger. In January 1933, Hitler was appointed Chancellor by Von Hindenberg, leader of the Social Democrats, and within a matter of months these peace groups were among the many organizations outlawed in the sweeping consolidation of power by the fascist regime. The opportunity for prevention had been lost, and the world paid the price in the devastation of World War II, and 50 million dead.

Our movement won't make that mistake. First of all, we won't make that mistake because we have the advantage of learning from the experiences of others. Secondly, we won't make that mistake because if we fail to prevent a nuclear war, humanity won't have another chance. Thirdly, we won't make that mistake because we have seen the fruits of unity in the June 12th demonstration—the largest on any issue in the history of our country. The wisest course of action for all of us is to build on that unity, that beginning, and expand and deepen the involvement of organizations that have roots at the community level, all across the country. This movement is still in the early stages of its growth.

The synthesis of peace and human needs issues makes for a more holistic analysis of the importance of peace and its necessity for the further progress of our society. In today's world the moral authority of a movement in the U.S. that is multiracial and multinational is far greater than if the movement were fragmented and narrow.

The power of organized, enlightened public opinion—that's the power to be mobilized if we are to redirect the current history of our country. That's the power of the people, affirmed, which can move our country off of this dangerous, literally dead-end detour road of national suicide represented by the arms race; the power that can put our society back upon the highway of national progress and social reconstruction.

The "experts" needed for this historical undertaking are not merely a small professional elite among the scientific community, even though their contribution can be enormous. Our experts include everyone who has experience organizing workers at a plant or mobilizing tenants in a public housing project. Everyone who knows how to communicate with the working people in the churches and fraternal lodges is an expert for our movement. Student leaders on the college campuses and in the high schools, people with organizational experience leading block clubs in the communities and consumer co-ops, all are experts for purposes of building our movement. An active commitment to the goals of this movement is the cornerstone of their expertise. When this is reinforced with systematic study of the issues (and study we must) the preparation is complete.

> There's a long road ahead of us. We may find it full of potholes, detour signs and every now and then danger points. Yet it's the road that leads to a more civilized society in our country.
> We have chosen mutually assured survival as the alternative to a policy of madness and mutually assured destruction.
> With determination and vision we will reach our goal.
> We *shall* overcome.

Notes

1. Reference to the Irish as an "inferior race" was quite common among the British political and intellectual elite; a racist attitude fostered by British colonialism

2. *Racism: The History of An Idea in America* by Thomas F. Gosset (Southern Methodist University Press).

3. The use of atomic weapons against the Japanese in August 1945 with its resulting 300,000 casualities and the further testing of such weapons on Bikini Atoll in June 1946 set up a standard pattern, repeatedly followed in the postwar era, of using the Asian and Pacific region and its people for all kinds of activities asssociated with the development of the U.S. nuclear weapons arsenal. This was an extension of the blatent act of racism by the U.S. government in rounding up Japanese American citizens on the West coast and putting them in American style concentration camps during the Second World War.

4. Resolution 637 VII, December 16, 1952.

5. Resolution 1064 XI, February 26, 1957.

6. Resolution 2787 **XXVI**, December 6, 1971.

7. Resolution 2507 **XXIV**, November 21, 1969.

8. *Objective: Justice*, A quarterly from the United Nations Office of Information. Vol. 8, NBR N4, Winter Issue 1976/ 1977. The United States' votes in the United Nations have been documented in a very significant article by Camille A. Bratton in *Freedomways*, Volume 17, Number 3, 1977.

9. *The Pretoria Citizen*, July 16, 1982. Donald Sole was formerly the South African Ambassador to the United States.

10. It is U.S. multinational corporations that benefit from the poverty of Haitian workers, many of whom are paid as little as $1.30 a day by such corporations' enterprises in Haiti.

11. Perhaps the most hopeful part of our discussion at NATO headquarters with Dr. Hofsteder was his frequent reference to his 16 year-old son, whom he repeatedly told us "does not agree with me". The young man has chosen to take an active part in the peace movement.

12. *The Irish Times*, October 5, 1982. This conference was chaired by Nobel Laureate and Lenin Peace Prize Winner Sean MacBride. It was held in observance of the 800th anniversary of the birth of St. Francis of Assisi.

5

AN ATOLL, A SUBMARINE AND THE U.S. ECONOMY

By Alex Cockburn &
James Ridgeway

Alexander Cockburn and James Ridgeway are staff writers for the Village Voice *and write a weekly column in that paper. Together they have contributed to the* New York Review *and other publications and have jointly edited* Political Ecology *and written* Smoke: Another Jimmy Carter Adventure. *Alexander Cockburn contributes another column, on the press, to the* Village Voice, *a monthly column to the* Wall Street Journal, *and has written* Idle Passion, Chess and the Dance of Death. *Irish by nationality, he lives in New York City. James Ridgeway has written* The Politics of Ecology, The Last Play, The Closed Corporation *and* Who Owns the Earth? *He lives in Washington D.C.*

One of the striking things about the disarmament movement is that there is relatively little attention paid to the interconnetions between problems of arms, war, and peace, and problems of economic structure. Of course the issue is not avoided entirely, but often disarmament activists are so focused on technical issues of arms policy and popular political possibilities that they overlook the equal importance of economic factors in determining the dimensions and texture of the arms race. Alex Cockburn and Jim Ridgeway contribute regularly to *The Village Voice*, perhaps the most established "alternative" weekly local newspaper in the country. Many of their articles have assessed, celebrated, or cajoled disarmament activists; often from the perspective of the importance of taking into account economic factors. We therefore thought they would be a good pair to ask for an article introducing the subject matter and accessibly and provocatively making the case for the importance of economic issues to the health and growth of disarmament activism. There contribution is an edited amalgam of some of their contributions to the *Voice* and adds another critical dimension to the overall case presented in *Beyond Survival*.

—M.A. & D.D.

About five hundred miles north of the equator and nearly twice the distance (as the missile flies) from California to Hawaii is the atoll of Kwajalein. Some 90 islands covering five and a half square miles enclose a 900 square-mile lagoon.

This lagoon lies at the heart of U.S. nuclear strategy: all the plans and scenarios for "massive response" or "counterforce" strikes against the Soviet Union rely on the testimony of Kwajalein lagoon, which is at the far end of the test range for land-based ICBMs launched from Vandenberg Air Force Base in California.

The islands scattered along the boomerang-shaped curve of Kwajalein lagoon have a similar historical significance. In the dreadful experience of their inhabitants—even though spared the horrors of some other Marshall Islanders—is etched a living history of the postwar nuclear age.

The islands were wrested from the Japanese by American troops in 1944, and subsequently employed as a testing site for A-bombs and later missiles. Beginning in the 1950s the military removed the native population from Kwajelein island, the largest and most populous of the island group. Inhabitants from Kawjalein and other tiny islets in the lagoon were made to live on Ebeye, where conditions soon became intolerable. There now are eight thousand people crammed into this hell hole of 65 acres. (Kwajalein island is 700 acres.) There is no grass, few trees. Roads are unpaved. There are no drains and the grey, muddy sand is covered with raw garbage and sewage. The drinking water must be imported weekly to a dock, and carried from there to homes and offices. Because of budget restrictions, there are no coffins to bury the dead. The shacks which serve as homes are so crowded that children sleep in shifts.

Three quarters of a million cans of beer per year play their part in anesthetizing the inhabitants—half of whom are under 14 years of age—from their misery. Visitors report seeing ten-year-olds too drunk to walk and 11-year-olds working as prostitutes for the U.S. personnel on Kwajalein.

Kwajalein by contrast is a pleasant place, with well manicured beaches, snack bars, a country club called the Kwaj

Lodge, another called the Yukway Yuk, and a PX known as Macy's East.

A few hundred people from Ebeye are permitted to come to work in low level jobs at the base or as domestics for American families. Even when they are educated in the U.S., Marshall Islanders who come back to Kwajalein atoll are not allowed to work at anything but low-level jobs; they are prohibited from living on Kwajalein island; they are searched whenever they enter or leave it; the food which they can buy cheaply in the commissary or snack bar on Kwajalein Island is confiscated when they leave; and when an American marries a Marshall Islander, the couple is not allowed to live on Kwajalein, but must go to Ebeye or elsewhere.

In sum, the situation is virtual apartheid.

The relationship between Kwajalein and Ebeye is well evoked by the following account of Dr. William Vitarelli, former trust territory liaison officer for Ebeye. During an epidemic of gastroenteritis, he testifies, "the Ebeye hospital ran out of intravenous fluids needed to sustain the lives of the Marshallese children, severely dehydrated from profuse vomiting and diarrhea. I took one Marshallese child who was very ill and put her on a skiff, and motored four miles to Kwajalein where the Americans live. We also needed to borrow some intravenous solution to take back to Ebeye."

"We were stopped at the beach by an American guard who would not let the child enter the island...She was Marshallese. The Marshallese nurse pleaded with the guard that the child was dying, and she could not receive appropriate therapy on Ebeye. The guard did not permit the child onto the island. She died on her way back to Ebeye...I went to the Kwajalein hospital. There I met with an American M.D. and asked for the intravenous fluid that we needed. He also refused my request. I then went to the medical warehouse in Kwajalein and stole several cases of intravenous fluid and took them back to Ebeye."

Since the days of the Titan II, the Vandenberg/Kwajalein test range has been the only such facility for the Air Force's land-based intercontinental ballistic missiles. Every few weeks or months, a missile will arc above the atmosphere on its east-west trajectory, and then plunge down into the lagoon. From the test results are constructed the data which are the currency of nuclear "deterrence" and "war-fighting" plans. Thus, when a nuclear strategist refers to the CEP (circular error probable) of a Minuteman III with MK 12A warhead as being .1 of a nautical mile, he is saying that half the warheads from that missile will fall within a radius of 200 yards, with an alleged 70 percent "probability" of "busting" a Soviet missile silo. These entirely hypothetical figures are all derived from the evidence of the test range and the lagoon.

What happens is this: the missile is fired and its course and the performance of its onboard instruments are monitored. The missiles then drop into Kwajalein lagoon after their 5,000-mile flight at varying distances—closely measured and held in deepest secrecy—from the target beacon. This process is regarded as ideal testing for a "real war" situation.

There are serious differences between the test and the real thing (no ICBM has ever been launched from an operational silo), which produce something colloquially known as the "bias factor."

The test results are built up after a series of corrections in trajectory and instrumentation, even though in real war, the first launch will be the only launch. The missiles speed over a track which is probably surveyed with more precision than any other equivalent portion of the globe. The surveying is useful, for a missile is affected (drastically, if silo-busting accuracy is desired) by the varying gravitational pulls of different portions of the earth's surface and by atmospheric variations such as jet streams and surface winds. Even under the carefully controlled and surveyed conditions of the Vandenberg/Kwajalein range, missiles have displayed unpredicted biases over years of testing, veering off course because of unexpected variations.

Yet all predictions of ICBM performance are based on the Kwajalein figures, and the Russians draw similar deductions from the performance of their missiles tested between Tyuratam and Kamchatka. In a real war situation, the missiles will be traveling over unsurveyed terrain, north instead of west. The biases will be, and must theoretically *always* be, unpredictable.

But a supposed accuracy is the motor of all modern debate about nuclear strategy. The MX and indeed Reagan's latest arms "reduction" proposals are similarly premised on accuracy: the notion that the Russians could launch 2,000 warheads which would land within 600 feet of their objective, all at the same time. The U.S. "response" or even "launch-on-warning" preemptive strikes are similarly based on such delusions of accuracy.

In 1974, Secretary of Defense James Schlesinger, the apostle of limited nuclear war-fighting, denounced such suppositions of accuracy, and the nuclear theology constructed on them. On April 30, 1982, he returned to testify before the Senate Foreign Relations Committee and once again stressed the all-important point. No newspaper saw fit to reprint his testimony. (We are grateful to the Federation of American Scientists for furnishing us with the passages quoted below.)

"Happily, no one has ever fought a nuclear war. Not only have ICBMs never been tested in flying operational trajectories against operational targets, they have not been tested flying north, and this may or may not introduce certain areas of bias into the estimates of accuracy. Nuclear weapons have never flown 6,500 miles through space, with the accompanying acceleration and deceleration, and, therefore, we have no real test data regarding failure rates. Consequently, neither the Soviet Union nor ourselves has appropriate test data to buttress the estimates regularly made about either nation's strategic forces. For leaders on either side who may be enticed into considering the utility of a major nuclear strike, I would hope there would always be somebody there under such hypothetical circumstances to remind them of these realities."

"For these reasons, perhaps the dominant element in measuring nuclear forces against each other is the unknown and immeasurable element of the possibility of major technical failure. It would tend to dominate any outcome. Given the spotty Soviet history in dealing with modern technologies, one would hypothesize that this must be a constant worry of the Soviet leaders—regardless of what others abroad may say about the supposed superiority of their forces."

In very careful language this indisputable hawk said that no one could have the slightest idea of what would happen to missiles in a real war situation, and that the Russians (any more than the U.S.) do not realistically have the capacity for first-strike silo-busting assault that has prompted the Reaganite scramble to close the "window of vulnerability" against their SS-18s.

*****

In the decade-long rekindling of the cold war, liberals and leftists have been overly prone to accept without question important propositions about the performance of nuclear armaments, perhaps on the assumption that there is no harm in over-rating (or accepting an exaggeration of) the lethal potential of such missiles and bombs.

Thus it was that the new cold warriors prevailed, almost unchallenged, in their claims about something first chastely described as the "perceived vulnerability" and then as the straightforward "vulnerability" of U.S. land-based missile silos. Pentagon claims of amazingly increased accuracy of Soviet missiles were accepted without demur. Turning to any handy weapon in the fight against the "Densepack" mode of basing the MX, liberals came forward with dramatic hypotheses: that a simultaneous ground-burst of two simultaneously arriving Soviet missiles would overcome the "Densepack's" presumed invulnerability to an entirely successful preemptive strike.

In December 1982 the administration sustained a serious reverse on its plans to deploy MX in the Densepack basing system, a reverse partly attributable to the political growth of the "freeze" movement after November 2 and partly attributable to publicly expressed reservations of the Joint Chiefs of Staff about Densepack. But only moments after this setback Richard Perle, a senior administration official in the Defense Department, was writing triumphantly—and correctly—in the *Washington Post* (December 13) that the arguments used by liberals against Densepack accepted many of the fundamental premises of the new cold warriors—"pinpoint accuracy" of Soviet missiles, consequent vulnerability of U.S. land-based forces, and so forth.

At first sight it may seem akin to obscene hairsplitting to challenge the view that a missile has a CEP of .1 or .9. In the minds of most people—with considerable justification and common sense—the warhead will explode and kill, regardless of whether it falls a few hundred yards or even feet nearer or further from its target. Yet even these decimal points should not be ceded to the cold warriors and nuclear theologians. To accept "pinpoint" accuracy is to accept silo "vulnerability." To accept "silo vulnerability" is to accept, in theory, the preposterous scenario of Soviet pre-emptive first strike followed by secondary blackmail of U.S. cities and consequent U.S. "surrender." To accept this is to accept, in some measure, the theoretical utility of an MX and a basing mode supposedly immune from surprise attack.

All claims about vulnerability disintegrate once critics return to first principles of physics and weapons' performance. The lesson, that hyperinflation of the performance of weapons should never be accepted, whatever the tactical temptations, holds true across the board. To accept the NATO thesis that supposed Soviet tank superiority in the central NATO theater demands a NATO nuclear "tripwire" against this imagined Soviet conventional superiority is to accept in some measure the logic which leads to the neutron bomb.

It is not good enough, therefore, to operate on the basis of an imagined symmetry of terror, as some advocates of a freeze do in an attempt to appear impartial. The movement should eschew apocalyptic rhetoric which—after a certain point—suffers diminishing returns in its mobilizing power, and deploy facts. Debates on the "throw-weight" of the Soviet SS-18 and its alleged menace to the West should not be abandoned to the cold war lobbyists, since once again an uncontested victory for the warmongers on "throw-weight" leads to less substantial intellectual opposition to MX or to supposed ICBM vulnerability.

Kwajalein also epitomises, in miniature, the price paid for the Cold War—in terms of suffering and deprivation—by Third World people, in this case the Marshallese. Their sufferings are not perhaps as profound as those in Latin America, Southwest

Asia and other areas subject to the crimes of international imperialism, often with complicity or prime guilt attributable to the U.S. But on a day-to-day basis the Marshallese are paying a horrible price. They are doing so—with almost no support in the U. S. The sit-ins on Kwajalein in late 1982 put the Marshallese on the very cutting edge of the disarmament movement. Yet their struggle evoked almost no echo on the mainland, not even on the MIT campus whence derive many of the technicians lording it on the Marshallese's former home.

*****

In the 37 years since the United States dropped the first atomic bomb on Hiroshima, the world nuclear arsenal has grown to some 50,000 nuclear weapons, mostly owned by the United States (about 30,000), the Soviet Union (about 15,000) as well as Great Britain, France, China, India, and Israel, with South Africa Pakistan, and Argentina well on the way to nuclear military status.

These nuclear weapons range in explosive potential from a nuclear artillery shell with a yield of less than one kiloton to a 20-megaton bomb. The Hiroshima A-bomb had a yield of 12.5 kilotons. Since one megaton equals 1,000 kilotons, one modern 20-megaton H-bomb can produce 1,600 Hiroshimas.

At the start of the nuclear age, the intended mode of delivery of these weapons was simple. They could either be carried by plane and dropped over a city, or be smuggled in parts across an opposing nation's frontier, reassembled, and set to explode. (This latter method, much feared by the U.S. in the 1940s, remains the most accurate and cheapest form of delivery.)

Methods of delivery have, of course, become vastly more sophisticated—though the accuracy of modern systems remains highly speculative. The U.S. has the choice of throwing a Minuteman III missile, with three warheads and a cumulative yield of 80 Hiroshimas, some 6,000 miles, or of firing a 203mm nuclear artillery shell some 20 miles, with a yield of one Hiroshima. The Soviet Union can hurl the mighty SS-18 missile 6,000 miles and produce the equivalent of 1,600 Hiroshimas with one 20-megaton warhead, or fire off a 180mm nuclear artillery shell with a yield of two Hiroshimas and a range of 25 miles. Nuclear munitions can be delivered by intercontinental ballistic missiles, from planes, from submarines, and, in the case of the United States, from low-flying cruise missiles to be delivered from planes, ships, or land.

If the point of nuclear weapons were simply to deter the enemy from attack on either NATO or Warsaw Pact territories, it would be enough for either side to possess no more than three five-megaton nuclear missiles each. It is rational to assume that the loss of Leningrad, Moscow, and Kiev would be intolerable to the Soviet Union, just as the loss of New York, Washington, D.C., and Los Angeles would be intolerable to the United States. Contrary to Pentagon claims, as we note above, three such missile silos would not be vulnerable to pre-emptive attack.

The questionable objective of mutual nuclear deterrence (that is, the threat of inflicting unacceptable damage on the other side) was thus achieved more than a generation ago, and the money and manpower which has been poured into nuclear research in the years since could have been devoted to more beneficial projects.

History discloses a very different objective. For one thing, U.S. strategists have never regarded nuclear warfare as "unthinkable." As Daniel Ellsberg points out in his excellent introduction to *Protest and Survive* (Monthly Review Press), those who engineered the first military use of nuclear devices on Japan, and their successors, have never abandoned the notion that a step over the nuclear threshold—or the threat to take such a step—is a "thinkable" expedient, and not "mutual assured destruction." And this attitude was not engendered with Casper Weinberger, or with Carter's famous PD59, or even with Schlesinger's equally publicized "counterforce strategy" of the early '70s. Nuclear warfighting with victory in view, rather than mutual assured destruction, has been U.S. nuclear strategy at least since the early '50s.

On no less than 12 occasions since Hiroshima and Nagasaki, on Ellsberg's computation, the U.S. has threatened to use nuclear weapons.[2]

Even in the early 1960s, when the Soviet Union had almost no ICBMs, and the U.S. had unquestioned nuclear superiority, the damage attendant on a nuclear "exchange" would have included U.S. civilian casualties in the millions. Yet, since the early '60s, we have seen relentless advance in nuclear refinement, initiated by the U.S. and subsequently matched by the Soviet Union. The latest developments include the cruise missile at one end of the spectrum, and the MX at the other—the latter commonly agreed to be a first-strike weapon which would restore the margin of *superiority* in the nuclear balance which has been the ongoing pre-occupation of the U.S. military-political high command of the post-war era.

With that matchless sense of timing which caused him to choose Hiroshima Day 1981 as the occasion to announce manufacture of the neutron bomb, Secretary of Defense Caspar Weinberger announced at the start of June 1982, just before the UN Special Session on Disarmament, a "clarification" of news stories about the Pentagon's plans to fight "protracted" nuclear war. "The United States' nuclear capabilities," Weinberger said, "must prevail, even under the condition of a prolonged war." This statement, by definition, is public notification that U.S. policy is to seek superiority, and that nuclear war can involve victory or defeat, rather than mutual annihilation.

Why the continued spiral? The causes of the revival of the cold war—spiraling of expenditures on nuclear and conventional arms, and escalation in bellicose rhetoric—are the subject of considerable argument.[3] There are those—most famously E.P. Thompson—who propose that "exterminism" has a momentum and internal, insane logic of its own. Others see more specific causes, preeminently an increasing sense of insecurity on the part of decisive political and military lobbies and interests in the U.S. from the early 1970s on: Nixonian detente did not produce a world balance overly favorable to the U.S. From Vietnam, through Mozambique, Angola, Ethiopia, Zimbabwe, Iran and Nicaragua—not forgetting OPEC—third world revolution recorded serious upsets for the U.S. in the seismic graph recording the fundamental conflict between capitalist and postcapitalist forces. (Monocular stress on the cold war conflict between the U.S. and the Soviet Union obscures the fact that casualties in the postwar period approaching the sum total of dead in the Second World War have come almost entirely from the Third World, where more than 140 wars have been waged.) Second, the Soviet Union has now arrived at a state of rough strategic nuclear parity with the United States. It could scarcely be said that Afghanistan, Poland, or Czechoslovakia have cooled cold war fires. Third, global recession, accelerated inflation and unemployment in the United States have engendered a reactive pugnacity which is understandable, but extremely dangerous.

The final reason, by far the most powerful in the sponsorship of the unceasing production and elaboration of nuclear and conventional armaments, is one that has been endlessly cited ever since it was first invoked by President Eisenhower in 1960, and which remains valid despite such repetition—namely the military-industrial complex, or the Iron Triangle: the nexus of defense contractor, Pentagon bureaucracy, and congressional promoters, to which should be added academic input from the military-intellectual research centers.

Here the incentive is straightforward: money and power are to be accumulated from the requisitioning and production of ever-more-elaborate weapons systems. Corporate balance sheets, and military-bureaucratic imperatives demand continued research, development, and investment in armaments. In answer to How Much Is Enough, their answer is Enough Is Never Enough.

Naturally, such continuing research and expense has to be justified, and this has been most simply done by disclosing a new "threat" posed by the enemy. There are inumerable examples. At a time when the Soviet Union had just *four* ICBMs, Kennedy declared the famous "missile gap," subsequently withdrawn in 1961. The installation of nuclear weapons in Europe by NATO was justified by reason of the supposedly overwhelming conventional forces possessed by the Warsaw Pact. Multiple independently targetable re-entry vehicles (MIRVs, which are clusters of warheads on ICBMs which drop away to separate targets as the vehicle or "bus" descends to enemy territory) were developed by the U.S. in response to the supposed Soviet anti-ballistic missile threat which did not in fact exist.

It is, in a sense, wrong to talk about an "arms race," for this implies a contest between two or more competitors. The U.S. arms buildup has proceeded in a fashion generally divorced from what the Russians have been producing. The introduction of MIRVs did not follow a new Russian "threat," though a particularly ludicrous one was invoked, but took place for reasons which had to do with then Defense Secretary Robert McNamara's ceiling of 1,000 Minutemen launchers. The addition of extra warheads while maintaining the decreed number of launchers was the U.S. Air Force's response. Similar patterns of defense investment can be found on the Soviet side—as Andrew Cockburn's work on the Soviet Defense establishment has made clear. So in the early 1980s, the U.S. military-industrial complex is once again seeking "threats" which are becoming patently more ludicrous: the supposed missile vulnerability to a Soviet first strike; the particularly outrageous allegation that "verification" of SALT II was a stumbling block to ratification. Now the next generation of nuclear technology—cruises, etc.—being introduced by the U.S. will make verification significantly more difficult than it was four years ago.

*****

Total world military spending rose in 1982 to over $650 billion, more than the entire income of 1,500 million people living in the 50 poorest countries. As a recent U.S. commission report puts it,[4] "The sums devoted to military research far exceed those for any other public research objective. Defense accounts for half of all publicly financed research in Britain and the U.S., and more than a third in France. In West Germany, by contrast, it accounts for only ten percent, and in Japan, two percent. Britain alone spends more public money on defense R&D than all OECD countries' publicly financed research or energy production, industrial growth and agriculture, and more than the entire public research expenditures of West Germany and Japan put together."

Third World military expenditure increased from a world share of 19 percent in 1971 to 25 percent in 1980. Third World arms imports have increased even more rapidly. As the Palme Commission pointed out, developing countries' arms imports are worth twice as much in absolute terms as the arms imports of all developed countries, and clearly represent one way the first world has offset the OPEC oil increases. Soviet arms exports also increased rapidly throughout the 1970s. "We are armor-plating the planet," as McNamara once remarked, and the world arms trade is adding significantly to the destitution and misery of the world's poor. Anyone looking at the political map of, say, Latin America and the complaisance of the arms-selling countries can see that this trade is likely to increase.

One rationale for U.S. military expenditure (aside from national security) is that it provides employment—an argument steadily advanced by the Democratic Party and the industrial unions. A 1968 U.S. government study showed that while defense employment accounted for 6.1 percent of all workers, it specifically accounted for 19 percent of all machinists, 22 percent of all electrical engineers, 38 percent of all physicists, 54 percent of all airplace mechanics, and 59 percent of all aeronautical engineers. With increasing emphasis on sophisticated "capital-intensive" weapons systems, these latter percentages are growing. The cream of the modern U.S. labor force is being scooped up and employed at high salaries in the development, manufacture, and deployment of weapons.

The "military Keynesian" argument is that defense-related employment provides jobs for those who would not otherwise have them, and research funds and capital expenditures which would not otherwise be made. It thus assumes that none of these engineers, machinists, etc., would find jobs in the civilian sector. But this is a matter of choice, not immutable fate. The most successful modern industrial nation—Japan—has chosen to allocate most of its human, technical, and capital resources in the civil sector. It has prospered and has the lowest unemployment figures in the advanced industrial world.

The United States is now spending more on military R&D than it did at the height of the Vietnam War. This investment will not alleviate unemployment and will contribute to inflation. And the U.S. is trying to export these problems to its trade competitors in Western Europe and Japan by forcing them to spend more on defense, lightening the "burden" of U.S. defense expenditures world-wide and diminishing the competitive trade threat.

So the "Keynesian" rationale for military expenditures holds no water. The only rationale for vast defense spending is national security, plus profits and employment for those already in the military-industrial sector.

A resolute disarmament movement must come to grips with the consequences of its demands for the national economy. About a quarter of the visible U.S. budget is now spent on defense, and this $220 billion figure is a very large understatement of the true state of affairs. The country is in a long term recession and its basic heavy industries—steel, autos, and aircraft—are tied to military procurement. In the years since 1946, when military Keynesianism was more or less proposed as national policy, critics have convincingly argued that the Keynesian effect of increased defense spending has eroded rapidly. As we have noted, the expenditure of money on high tech weaponry (while being a delightful bit of "Keynesianism" for those profiting from the subsidies) which removes scarce engineers from the civil sector and reduces productivity through DoD cost-plus contracts is different from building factories employing thousands to make army boots or bullets.

*****

Perhaps the best single example of the complexities involved in "conversion" is the story of the development of civilian nuclear power. It demonstrates the relationship between military and civilian sectors, shows how they are connected, what makes them separate, and provides a clue as to the underlying economics.

The story really begins beneath the waters of the North Atlantic during World War II. Although the German U-boats had ultimately failed in their objective of blocking American supplies of men and material to Europe, they had taken a terrible toll. Naval planners and strategists were keenly aware that if a true submarine were ever developed, it could change the shape of war forever. By 1945, the Germans seemed on the verge of bringing just such advanced submarines into production. Although the submarine already had a 40-year life behind it, it did not begin to approach the vessel envisaged by Jules Verne, in which Captain Nemo literally lived beneath the sea. The bastard contraption in use in the 1940s generally lived on the surface while stalking its prey, submerging only at the last moment to launch its torpedoes before attempting a dash to safety. Its electrical and diesel engines were short-lived and unreliable.

Immediately after the war the U.S. Navy, under the guidance of Admiral Chester Nimitz, began to survey its needs for the future. Nimitz had taken charge of the Navy in the Pacific in the month after Pearl Harbor and had built it into the most powerful battle fleet in history. He was a submariner and shared with Eisenhower himself the status of preeminent war hero. Nimitz and his planners soon saw one irresistible avenue of development.

Already, by the late '30s, the Navy had become aware of the potential of atomic power. In November 1939 the government, in response to scientific pressure (including that of Einstein), was grappling seriously with the same issue. Even at that time there was talk—in a memorandum by Dr. Ross Gunn, for example—of nuclear-powered vessels as well as bombs.

But during the war the Navy played only a small part in the Manhattan Project, which was controlled by the Army. In March 1946 the Navy's research laboratory issued a report arguing for construction of a nuclear submarine to be built in two years, based on advanced German hull designs. In that same month Monsanto Chemical Company proposed that the Navy, along with the other services, cooperate with private industry in building an experimental power reactor at Oak Ridge, in Tennessee.

Six Navy men traveled to Oak Ridge. At their head was the person who turned out to be the most influential figure in the development of U.S. nuclear power, both military and civilian, between that year and today.

Captain Hyman G. Rickover, at the time aged 46, had graduated from Annapolis in 1922 and had taken a masters degree in electrical engineering in 1929. He was qualified to command submarines, had worked as chief engineer on a battleship, and as commanding officer on a minesweeper. In 1939, he was assigned to the rapidly growing electrical section of the Navy's Bureau of Ships in Washington.

Rickover's genius showed in his mastery of naval bureaucracy, of wartime engineering requirements, and in knowing how to get what he wanted from the industrial sector. Whereas previously, for example, electrical equipment was based on designs dating to the 1920s, Rickover produced his own specifications—often based on British battle-damage reports and his own personal inspections—and forced the private contractors to build along those lines. He would personally select the contractor staffs. In doing so, Rickover built close working relationships with the major electrical contractors—most notably, General Electric and Westinghouse. He was one of the most single-minded, persistent, intelligent, and intractable personalities ever produced by the U.S. Navy.

Rickover and his team at Oak Ridge soon came to the conclusion that it was imperative for the Navy to build a nuclear-powered submarine. But Rickover became increasingly dismayed by postwar confusion and scientific meandering, which led him to believe that the reactor pile envisaged by Monsanto would never be built. Rickover was one of the first to understand clearly that for nuclear power to have military or civilian practicality it would have to be developed and controlled by engineers, not scientists.

As the Rickover team pushed forward, it suddenly found itself caught up in navel bureaucratic politics. Rickover himself was, of course, a relative nonentity in the Naval hierarchy. The prevailing sentiment among the brass was that the Navy should not get involved in a wild-goose chase toward a nuclear submarine, but should take what seemed to be a more secure road, and bank on the bomb. This trend was naturally keenly promoted by the ordinance officers, as opposed to Rickover's Bureau of Ships, which pushed propulsion.

It had always been Rickover's hope that the development of a nuclear submarine would be taken up by GE, which was not only a large corporation, but one equipped with a first-class laboratory. GE was interested, but there were problems. The company had agreed to run a plutonium-production plant for the government at Hanford in the state of Washington. The government had in turn agreed to provide GE with a nuclear-development laboratory in Schenectady. Soon enough, government bureaus and the Navy began to eye the giant electrical manufacturer nervously, fearing—in the case of the latter—that its new lab in Schenectady would prove a distraction from participation on a nuclear-vessel project. GE had decided to place the bulk of its effort in the development of a breeder reactor—a project many years from completion and which Rickover saw as being essentially off target, as indeed it was.

But Rickover continued to lobby for his point of view in Washington. He induced Nimitz to sign a letter to the Secretary of the Navy, endorsing the nuclear sub as a top priority. The secretary agreed. He fought hard to get the Atomic Energy Commission to cooperate in a reactor-research program, beyond its previous enthusiasms for the mere manufacture of bombs. His efforts paid off. The AEC, with Rickover ensconced in its command structure, opened a new section on reactor research and development. In the same year, Rickover induced Westinghouse to take seriously the possibilities of nuclear power.

He held classes for Westinghouse executives, set up a special division of the company, and plunged into the job of designing a nuclear submarine. He also persuaded MIT to set up a new department for training nuclear engineers, and his overall efforts in this direction provided much of the manpower for the nuclear industry over the next generation.

In 1953, the land-based reactor for the nuclear submarine Nautilus reached "criticality"—the first time in history that practical power had been obtained from the atom. A year earlier President Truman had officiated over the laying of the Nautilus' keel at Groton, Connecticut. In the course of his remarks, Truman said, "The peaceful significance of the Nautilus is even more breathtaking. When this ship has been built and operated, controllable atomic power will have been demonstrated on a substantial scale."

Thus it was Rickover, in the postwar years, with the help of Cold War sentiment, who shaped the organization of the nuclear industry and established its imperatives. Not that many other crucial figures weren't involved, but it was Rickover above all who understood the relationship of the state to corporations. In the end, it was Rickover who roged the essentials: a cadre of nuclear engineers, a system of contracting, nad a sense of direction amid bureaucratic anarchy.

The next turning point in the history of nuclear power in the U.S. came in April 1953, with Eisenhower's decision to terminate a Rickover project for a nuclear-powered aircraft carrier. At this point Rickover took the remnants of the carrier project and, with the blessing of the AEC, reshaped it into a program that culminated in the construction of the world's first full-scale nuclear electric generating plant. Under Rickover's overall control this reactor, designed by Westinghouse and built in conjunction with the Duquesne Light Company of Pittsburgh, was established at Shippingport, Pennsylvania. Ground was broken in 1954 and the reactor went on line in late 1957.

Rickover's victory at Shippingport stemmed from a broader political struggle, ultimately situated in the conflict between public and private power. It was less than two decades since the utility holding companies had been broken up and the Tennessee Valley Authority established in the 1930s. The Eisenhower administration was anxious to yield to private industry far greater latitude in the construction of the postwar U.S. economy. In 1951 the AEC had encouraged private utilities to take an interest in the long term prospects of nuclear power by making classified atomic data available to a group of companies. Industry responded favorably. Walter L. Cisler of the Detriot Edison Company, preeminent in the utility industry, stated that a group of companies under his leadership was prepared to undertake the construction of a power reactor.

Responding to this threat by private industry, the public-power advocates in the Interior Department and TVA hastened to form an alliance with the military adherants of a nuclear carrier. Their plan was to build a prototype multi-purpose reactor, which could run a carrier, produce plutonium for bombs, and generate electricity. Adroitly taking advantage of these conflicts, Rickover won support from the advocates of public power, especially the TVA. The TVA had been headed by David Lilienthal, who later became the first chairman of the AEC. Indeed, the role of the TVA had immense repercussions for the energy industry overall. In its early years, TVA had concerned itself largely with the construction of a web of hydroelectric projects, with the aim of modernizing the Tennessee Valley. As the cold war developed, TVA found itself having to rapidly expand its operations for very specific military reasons.

As a consequence of the arms race, larger and larger amounts of enriched uranium were needed for atomic bombs. The process by which uranium is enriched requires vast amounts of electricity. Much of that initial electricity was provided by TVA, which sent the power to the AEC enrichment plants in Kentucky. The hydroelectric facilities of TVA were not able to meet the demand of the enrichment plants during the 1950s and in order to step up generating capacity the Authority turned to coal. To this end TVA sponsored, through a series of unusual (at that time) long-term contracts with coal companies in Appalachia, the reorganization of the coal industry. The industry was mechanized, small operators were driven out, and the way was paved for the subsequent concentration of the coal industry, which finally fell under the control of the oil industry in the late 1960s.

The process then became circular. TVA created the electricity which enriched the uranium. These supplies of uranium, at first used to make bombs, later became the fuel for the nuclear power plants. Among the most important customers was TVA itself, which needed nuclear fuel to generate electricity in its reactors, which was used in part to create yet more fuel.

Thus the development of the civil nuclear industry in the U.S. stemmed not so much from rational assessment of the country's energy requirements—later touted as the lodestar of the nuclear option—as from military incentives.

While the nuclear industry itself—as we have indicated above—was first developed as a government-sponsored enterprise urging major corporations forward, it has come to depend in the most important respects on a network of petroleum and mining conglomerates.

Since the nuclear power plants operating in the U.S. today do not produce their own fuel (the aim of the "breeder" dreamed of by General Electric after the war), they must be supplied with constantly increasing amounts of uranium. Such a requirement has engendered a large industry, dominated by a handful of corporations.

The two biggest suppliers of uranium in the country are Gulf Oil and Kerr-McGee. Kerr-McGee alone is said to control 35.4 percent of all U.S. uranium reserves. Gulf follows with 19 percent. The control of these reserves again results from public policy decisions. Much of the uranium in the U.S. is found in public-domain territories, especially in the West. Government leasing policies, culminating in the 1960s, promoted this private domination of public assets. A 1974 Federal Trade Commission study showed that seven companies controlled 70 percent of the uranium business in the U.S. in 1971. At hearings held before Senator Edward Kennedy, Exxon officials said that oil company reserves of uranium amounted to 60 percent of total reserves. With the expansion of the nuclear industry, the search for uranium has gone well beyond the U.S. itself. Canada, South Africa, and Australia have become major suppliers. Here again, the resources are controlled by a small number of large companies.

Two firms in particular have played an important role in organizing the international uranium market. They are Rio Tinto Zinc, the British mining conglomerate much influenced by the Rothschild banking family, with extensive holdings in

Australia, Canada, and Southern Africa; and Anglo-American Corporation of South Africa, the huge mining concern run by the Oppenheimer family. Anglo-American produces uranium in South Africa as a by-product of gold mining. It also has a controlling interest in Engelhard Minerals, the U.S. company which is the largest producer of precious metals in the world. RTZ and Anglo-American are interlinked through their directors, and Anglo-American has maintained a financial interest in RTZ as well. In an apparent effort to maintain and increase, the price of uranium RTZ actually joined with the governments of Canada, France and South Africa in the formulation of a cartel in 1972.

The story of nuclear power demonstrates how the military successfully engaged two other important large industries—energy and mining—in its future development. As for the big engineering and construction companies, dependent on central power plant production along with military weaponry, nuclear power became absolutely crucial to their future survival. So, what had been narrowly conceived at the end of the Second World War as a military weapon, by 1980 had become a major industrial activity, on whose success depended the welfare of large industry.

Over time, the pronuclear policies of the government have been reinforced and invigorated by the academic institutions on which the government has depended for expertise and training since the origins of the Manhattan Project. These institutions, hovering between government and private sponsorship have manifest interest in maintaining the priority—nuclear—which brought them funding and eminence in the first place. The weapons scientists, and in particular the physicists at Los Alamos and Livermore remain a self-interested and determined group bitterly opposed to arms control. Originally there were two camps, those at Los Alamos siding with J. Robert Oppenheimer who wanted to go slow in developing the hydrogen bomb and those around Edward Teller and Ernest O. Lawrence who wanted to go full steam ahead and who in the process got a laboratory at Livermore.

Out of the friction between the two groups came what amounted to a heresy trial, over Oppenheimer's alleged disloyalty. The resultant enmity led to ferocious competition between the two laboratories as to who could make the better bomb and "superior" nuclear weapons.

The University of California has maintained a particularly profitable relationship with the Pentagon as the result of its bomb research. For example, Glenn Seaborg, former chairman of the AEC, had been chancellor at Berkeley and then propelled money back from the government to the university. John Foster, former director of research and engineering at the Pentagon, came from the University's radiation laboratory. These men set armament priorities for the whole research establishment. By the late 1960's, nearly half of all government expenditures to universities went to California, thanks to this cosy relationship.

But the prime example of the military/industrial/academic governmental nexus in this area must surely be Harold Brown, who came out of Livermore Lab, was director of research and engineering at the Pentagon in the early 1960s, became secretary of the air force (when he urged bombing of North Vietnam), then became head of Cal Tech, and subsequently President Carter's Secretary of Defense where he presided over PD59, the proposed mobile deployment of MX, the proposed manufacture of the neutron bomb (which he liked to boast that he designed) and the sabotaging of the SALT II Treaty, where Brown adroitly allowed Brzezinski to appear the main public hawk. Brown, a far more dangerous and effective operator, went relatively un-scathed in sustaining blame for the Carter administration's rapid conversion to the imperatives of the new cold war. Witnesses to his comportment and counsel in bureaucratic and decision-making sessions in the Carter administration attest that Brown was far more astute an artificer of cold war designs than the theatrical Brzezinski.

On the private side, favoring nuclear power, we find the uranium suppliers, which now include in this country the major oil companies—Kerr-McGee, Gulf, Conoco, Getty, and Exxon, along with the international mining companies (RTZ and Anglo-American). Most obviously dedicated to nuclear power are the manufacturers of the plants: General Electric (which now owns Utah International, which also mines uranium), Westinghouse, Babcock & Wilcox, and Combustion Engineering GE and Westinghouse are prime military contractors and participated in the earliest formation of the nuclear industry.

*****

Has the national security of the United States been increased by the vast investment in "defense"? The answer is clearly no. In 1960, the U.S. was threatened by precisely four Soviet ICBMs. Steady escalation of the arms race has now produced a situation in which the Soviet Union has attained a position generally conceded to be one of "rough parity" in strategic weaponry, in which its strategic forces have 8000 bombs and warheads, matched against 9400 for the U.S. strategic forces. A U.S. citizen can scarcely be described as "secure" when 147 serious false U.S. nuclear alerts—three of them nearly catastrophic—prompted by faulty systems, occurred between January 1979 and June 1980. On a less partial national level, the security of substantial portions of mankind has scarcely been enhanced by the deployment of 50,000 nuclear warheads, and the distinct threat on at least 12 occasions that nuclear weapons would actually be used.

Over the last year or so, the public has learned some important facts about the nuclear arms race. Among them, the idea that nuclear war is "fightable," or even "winnable," has been effectively discredited. Consider the results if nuclear weapons were to be used specifically against the opponent's military forces or missile installations (the so-called "counterforce" strategy, promulgated by the U.S. on various occasions over the last 25 years). The Palme Commission has drawn together some instructive examples.

In 1955, a military exercise code-named Sagebrush was held in Louisiana. It simulated the use of 275 nuclear weapons ranging between 2 and 40 kilotons. It was concluded that "the destruction was so great that no such thing as limited or purely tactical nuclear war was possible in such an area." In the same year, a second exercise, code-named Carte Blanche, was undertaken in Western Europe itself. In this case, the use of 335 nuclear weapons was simulated, 80 percent on German territory. In terms of immediate German casualties alone, excluding the victims of radiation disease and other secondary effects, it was estimated that between 1.5 million and 1.7 million people had died and 3.5 million more were wounded. As a result of this exercise, former West German Chancelor Helmut Schmidt stated that the use of tactical nuclear weapons "will not defend Europe but destroy it."

These are old studies. Experts recently assembled by the UN Secretary General constructed a scenario in which the two military alliances used a total of 1,700 nuclear weapons against each other's ground forces and nuclear arsenals in Europe. The weapons used in this "war" included one and five-kiloton artillery shells and 100-kiloton bombs dropped from aircraft. The test assumed no nuclear devices launched against cities. (There probably are in fact 10,000 intermediate-range and battlefield nuclear weapons deployed by NATO and the Warsaw Pact in Europe.)

The UN experts concluded that there would be a minimum of from five million to six million casualties from the immediate effects of the explosions, with military casualties estimated at about 400,000. For every one of the 200 larger weapons which went astray and hit a city, 250,000 fatalities should be added on.

How about nuclear wars "limited" to strategic targets in the U.S. and USSR? Estimates of fatalities resulting from an attack on U.S. strategic facilities range from 2 million to 22 million, with the low estimate assuming that the attack is restricted to missile fields, and that the civilian population has taken effective steps to shelter itself (a feat other studies have thought to be impossible). Equivalent U.S. studies of the effects of a strategic attack on the USSR show fatalities ranging from 3.7 million to 27.7 million.

This is not counting all subsequent disasters to the earth's environment, including puncturing of the ozone layer, disturbance of weather patterns, and hence famine, plagues, and so forth.

It should be added that no one actually knows what the effects of a nuclear attack would be. The entire edifice of so-called "scientific" data is absolutely speculative. No nuclear strategist really knows how "hardened" a silo has to be to resist the adjacent impact of a warhead. No scientist can tell with any precision the extent of damage of a nuclear device landing on a city. No missileer can tell how accurate his missile would be. The theology of nuclear weapons rests on two wartime nuclear deliveries and the 1,271 nuclear test explosions conducted between 1945 and 1980. No U.S. missile has ever been successfully test-launched from an operating silo.* Twenty years ago, for example, the U.S. air force denied the "fratricidal" effects of descending warheads—i.e., the proposition that the detonation of one warhead would throw the others off-course and thus disturb the calculations of the effects of a nuclear strike on a missile field. Today, the U.S. Air Force—in the interests of the Densepack System—accepts the notion of fratricide.

In sum, ideas of "protracted" nuclear war—most recently advanced by Defense Secretary Weinberger—are dismissed by all objective observers as deranged.

From 1974 to the present day, the nuclear arms race gained impetus (with a sudden late-70s surge in defense spending) under the rationale that the United States had fallen behind the Soviet Union in the capacity of its military forces.

The fact is that innumerable studies and statements, ranging from such sources as Carter's secretary of defense Harold Brown to Reagan's ex-Secretary of State Alexander Haig accept "rough equivalence." Haig said on June 5, 1981, that "I would put in the central strategic nuclear area the fact that we are

---

*[Editor's Note] In an article arguing for production of a "more efficient" missile, Gregg Easterbrook, a staff writer for the *Atlantic* writes: "The Air Force has never successfully launched a Minuteman from an operational silo. Four attempts to do so ended in failure; during three, the missiles didn't even clear their pads. Thereafter the Air Force cancelled testing from operational silos, on the grounds that crippled Minutemen might crash into populated areas around their missiles bases...The Vandenberg tests...are more like moon shots than realistic drills: The missiles are combed over by white-coated technicians before launches scheduled months, not minutes, in advance. Even under these laboratory conditions, one of nine Minutemen launched last year failed." (*New York Times,* Op. Ed., February 18, 1983).

still in an area of rough equivalence." "Bean-counting" is a slippery art, brought to perfection by propagandists for increased military spending. It is the game of estimating forces on the basis of partial numbers. Thus proponents of the "overwhelming Soviet threat" will point to Soviet superiority in tanks, but omit NATO superiority in anti-tank weapons. They will stress the Soviet advantage in missile submarines, but omit the fact that they carry far fewer warheads. They will point to the superior "throw weight" of some Soviet nuclear missiles, but omit the fact that most Soviet ICBMs are still liquid-fueled, and hence some 20 years behind U.S. technology. ("Throw weight" is the sum of the weight of warheads and the "bus" that carries them on the first stage of their flight. Russian rockets have less miniaturization, are larger and cruder, hence have more throw weight. Liquid fuel is less stable than solid, produces more corrosion, and presents more complexities in storage and launch—particularly on submarines. The U.S. Navy would not accept liquid-fueled ICBMs, unlike the Soviet submarines.)

They will point to the alleged boom in Soviet defense expenditure without disclosing that such figures are often arrived at by applying U.S. defense costs to the Soviet Union or that the Soviet Union has a smaller economy, but is committed to the maintenance of "parity" with the U.S. Thus, if there is a cost-overrun on the C5A transport, the Soviet defense budget goes up. Having a smaller economy, the Soviets do devote a higher percentage of GNP to defense. Nevertheless, Soviet defense spending has remained constant in recent years. NATO currently outspends the Warsaw Pact.

Manpower "bean-counting" is similarly deceptive. Very often, Soviet civil engineering units are included in the overall Soviet military total, and some Western forces, such as the French army, are excluded from the NATO total. Considerations such as training quality, morale, internal problems (are Polish troops likely to fight hard for the Warsaw Pact?) are excluded. Unlike the U.S., the Soviet Union has no permanent bases outside the Warsaw Pact.

The sum conclusion is that the West's more advanced economies and techno-industrial base continues to produce forces and equipment not inferior to, and almost certainly superior to, the Soviet or Warsaw Pact equivalents (and this includes the Chinese threat to the Soviet Union).

We have a situation in which arms expenditures on both sides are increasing, and the dangers of nuclear war are increasing with them. The next generation of nuclear systems, ever more narrowly geared to "launch on warning," will produce a greater likelihood of accidental nuclear conflict, unstoppable after the first detonation. Nuclear technology continues to proliferate. In this situation, the disarmament and freeze movements have grown rapidly, first in Western Europe and now in the United States.

A "freeze" can mean a number of things. It can mean the freezing in place of the present nuclear arsenal. It can mean a ban on further testing of nuclear devices and the means by which they are carried to the target. This latter and more desirable objective would best be accomplished by signing and ratification of a Comprehensive Test Ban. A test ban on weapons and in-flight systems would halt the forward development of the arms race. The last effort to negotiate it, slowed down by the right wing in the United States, occurred in 1978. This should be an elementary demand of any "freeze" or disarmament move-ment. Even the partial test ban of 1963 at least led to a diminution of the high death rate attendant on atmospheric testing. A Comprehensive Test Ban is viewed with horror by the military-industrial complex, since an untested system is far less likely to get through the procurement process, let alone deployment.

The next step after a test ban would be actual reduction in the nuclear arsenals by both sides. The latest Reagan proposals are specious gestures in this direction, since they permit deployment of the MX—conceded to be, in potential, a first-strike weapon—and of cruise missiles. Real reduction would be accompanied by continually expanding nuclear-free zones—in both hemispheres and most particularly in Europe.

It is just conceivable, though highly unlikely, that the mounting pressure of peace movements in Europe and in the U.S. will force a treaty leading to actual freezing and even reduction of nuclear arsenals. It should be remembered that all the SALT talks and other talks of the past generation have never removed one warhead already deployed, unless it was obsolete and ready to be replaced by a more sophisticated successor.

When the abolitionists of the nineteenth century assailed the evil of slavery, they did not speak of a "phased reduction" of slaves on plantations throughout the South, or bow to the argument that the outlawing of slavery in the United States would give its economic opponents disastrous economic advantage. They said slavery was evil, and should be abolished.

There is a parallel in the nuclear situation today. As we said at the outset, the questionable goal of "nuclear deterrence" could be adequately maintained if the United States and the Soviet Union (and indeed any other country) had but three nuclear missiles in its arsenal. At the moment, official U.S. policy will not even permit a guarantee of "no first use." The freeze movement now extends from citizens who would stop at that demand, through those who would like to see a "freeze in place," preceded, in Reagan's case, by an arms escalation designed to intimidate the Russians into negotiations, through a mutual arms reduction.

But the time has come for this movement to contain at least a sector which goes beyond the rhetoric of "phased mutual reduction" and such appeals, to serious advocacy of nuclear arms reduction by the United States, regardless of what the other side may or may not be doing. It should be stressed that such a program, which allows for the U.S. to retain the ability to slaughter 12 million Russians (just to take Moscow and Leningrad) is not a unilateral declaration of surrender. It is a refusal of the exterminist mindset which assumes that politicians and generals can rationally assume the deaths of ten or twenty percent of their citizenry to be "tolerable."

If the U.S. nuclear arsenal was reduced by a factor of 95 percent, this nation would still have the capacity to destroy the Soviet Union, not to mention much of the rest of the world. There is no need to "trust the Russians" in order to urge reduction of the United States' arsenal. To deny this is to plunge down the rhetorical escalator on which Weinberger and his colleagues now stand.

To remain mired in exterminist logic is not only immoral but stupid, since such logic and such rhetoric will slow or even destroy the momentum of the peace movement and debauch its vigor. To reverse the momentum of arms spending in the United States requires, in the end, a new social and political order— perhaps one alien to many mustering to the freeze movement today. A broad movement must, self-evidently, remain broad, but the demands of "consensus" should not extinguish political debate or seemingly uncomfortable propositions.

The problem with the "freeze movement" is that it is, at one and the same time, less and more than it seems. On the one hand it says simply that nuclear war is bad and that right-thinking Americans are against it to the degree—*pari passu*—that right-thinking Russians are against it. On the other hand, logical sequences lead from an initial freeze "posture" to much more radical conclusions confronted in this collection—from less comfortable propositions about the allocation of responsibility for escalation of the cold war and the arms spiral; to propositions about the national security state and balance of terror in the Third World; to the real challenges posed to the system by calls for disarmament or slow-downs in the arms race more substantial than SALT proposals so far.

The contradictions in the freeze movement were plain for all to see on June 12, when hundreds of thousands gathered in Central Park in New York to call for a freeze, even as a nuclear power, Israel, invaded Lebanon and provided a real-time enactment of the kind of geopolitical crisis which could lead to nuclear war. Most proponents of the nuclear freeze simply refused to admit the relevance of the invasion of Lebanon, or even its existence, and attacked efforts to raise the issue within the freeze/disarmament context as "divisive", "irrelevant" or even "anti-Semitic".

This double standard in the discussion of nuclear peril is on permanent political display. In the congressional vanguard of freeze advocates is Senator Edward Kennedy, who is also one of the most vocal supporters of Israel. Three weeks after the vast rally on June 12, Democratic Party members gathered for a mid-term convention in Philadelphia and there hammered out an exceptionally woolly pro-freeze resolution. At the same time they passed, *without one dissenting voice,* a resolution actually commending Israel for its invasion of Lebanon, this at a time when the Israeli forces were bombing and shelling hospitals in Beirut. A freeze movement this unable and unwilling to face reality does not oppose but confirms the priorities it pretends to challenge. A "respectable" freeze movement will be constantly zealous to protect its virtue and to insist on its political purity. Each spasm of red-baiting from Reagan and his associates is thus quelled by outraged assertions that the insinuations are without foundation. To assert that an insinuation is without foundation is to accept the legitimacy of making the insinuation in the first place. In making its defense, the freeze movement concedes the legitimacy of the attack, and draws its skirts ever more tightly around its ankles to avoid contagion from possibly "suspect" groups—such as those organizing against U.S. intervention in Central America. A movement thus narrowly conceived will be vulnerable to the simplest maneuver by the war party: a supposed concession in arms negotiations, the demolition of one weapons system. Those doubting how rapidly a "respectable" disarmament movement can be demobilized should recall the early '60s and the partial test-ban signed by Kennedy and Khrushchev in 1963 which had about the same effect on the arms race as the ban on tv cigarette advertising and the surgeon general's warning had on the vitality of the tobacco industry.

Consider the debate which informed and changed the environmental movement in the years since it "took off" in 1970. At that point it concerned itself with the superficials of a cleansed environment: billboards, broken bottles beside the road, and the froth of detergent in local streams and rivers. Soon however, the movement had to start grappling with the basics of energy infrastructure, fundamental to the nation's economy. Even though the environmental movement was and is made up of middle-of-the-road and essentially conservative people (its political champions have always been moderate Republicans) there was no flinching in coming to grips with the basic economic issues and debating them: when to go forward with oil and gas, coal and synthetic fuels or nuclear power. Out of this debate came the proposals of those such as Amory Lovins and

Dennis Hayes for the "soft path" energy future which projects an entirely fresh economic base for an American energy system.

Contrast this achievement with the freeze movement's inability thus far to look squarely at the logic of its demands, at the consequences of any assault on the economic and political underpinnings of the military industrial complex. As Raymond Williams once remarked, "To refuse nuclear weapons, you have to refuse much more than nuclear weapons. The freeze movement has to become as radical as reality itself."

6
LABOR & DISARMAMENT
THE MEETING
OF SOCIAL MOVEMENTS

By Paula Rayman

Paula Rayman teaches sociology at Brandeis University, Waltham, Massachusetts with special focus on urban studies, industrial and labor organization, and social movements. Among her publications are Nonviolent Action and Social Change, *Irvington Press, 1980 (coeditor Severyn Bruyn);* The Kibbutz Community and Nation-Building, *Princeton University Press, 1982; and* Out of Work, *Simon and Schuster, forthcoming (co-author Barry Bluestone). She has been on the National Boards of the War Resisters League and SANE. As a founding member of the Bay State Conversion Project, she has done writing and speaking on the militarized economy. She is presently involved with research on the private and social costs of unemployment in the United States.*

As the economy is an important factor in determining the character of the arms race, the labor movement will necessarily be a key actor in disarmament efforts. Labor is an organized, well financed, progressive force in U.S. politics whose power is undeniable but whose allegiance to non-union causes has often been limited. Can the disarmament movement and labor movement relate to each other's priorities and to the linkages between economic and peace concerns?

Paula Rayman examines the possibilities for communication between the disarmament and labor movement by assessing some of their past relations and current interconnections. She reviews the life and work of A.J. Muste who was both a peace and labor activist and, drawing lessons from his experience, concludes that cooperation between the movements is necessary, possible, and potentially mutually beneficial. She proposes as one main avenue for joint activity struggles for economic conversion—the transfer of machinery, skills, labor power and resources from military to human needs production—and reviews some contemporary efforts in this direction.

Recently in the *New York Times* two articles appeared on the same day which have important bearing on the issue of the need for relations between the labor and disarmament movements. The first concentrated on the federal government's raising the national debt level largely to accommodate the increasing military defense budget. From the end of World War II until 1980 one trillion dollars had been earmarked for defense spending. The Reagan administration has outlined a program that will commit $1.5 trillion in just the next five years. This translates to an amazing statistic: we will be spending $34 million every hour for the next five years for military purposes.

The second article announced new unemployment figures indicating that one out of every five workers had experienced job loss during the previous year, at a rate not equalled since the Great Depression. Figures did not include those so discouraged from seeking new work that they were no longer counted in official records. The article continued that over 31.8 million individuals were living in the United States below the official poverty level, that home foreclosures were nearing a 400,000 annual rate and that there has been a 45 percent increase in business failures.

Looking at the national budget can not only contribute to an analysis of the consequences of a militarized economy but also provide a perspective on the prevailing norms and values of our society. It would seem that such an examination, to which the two newspaper articles provide an orientation, would result in the clear recognition that there is indeed much common ground for labor and disarmament activity. Already, during the June 12th demonstration there was ample evidence that at least some of labor had joined forces with the disarmament effort. Banners proclaimed the presence of industrial trade unions representing the auto workers (UAW), the machinists (IAM), the steel-workers, and the electrical workers as well as unions representing the public service sector of the economy (AFSCME and SEIU). While the official AFL-CIO position on the demonstration was at best non-committal, labor leaders such as Victor Gottbaum, William Winpisinger, and Douglas Fraser went public with their support.

However, moments of unity between the disarmament and labor movements have been sporadic, often reflecting a kind of "boom and bust" cycle. Though both movements appear linked in their common calls for social justice and human rights, historical events have often evoked differing and even opposing responses. If the question before us is, "will the tentative joining of forces demonstrated on June 12th mark a new, emerging era of mutual activity?" consideration must be given to the roots of the boom and bust history. When before in U.S. history have the efforts of the two movements been intertwined? What has been the basis for continuing eruptions of suspicion and even distrust between the movements, or at least large segments of the movements? Does the present moment in history offer and perhaps demand possibilities for firmer cooperation? What kinds of joint activity are either already in progress or exist on progressive planning agendas?

History of Internal and External Struggle

The development and struggles of the United States labor and disarmament movements have occurred within a changing global capitalist economy, an emerging cold war politics and a dangerously escalating arms race. By beginning the review of the two movements during the World War I period our examination starts at a time when U.S. economic and political supremacy was on the rise but not fully achieved, when assembly lines and Taylorism were new methods affecting the workplace, and when "conventional war" was the only type fought. From the First World War through the present years the United States' role in the world has undergone significant transformation, in many ways making the tasks confronting labor and nonviolent activists more difficult than ever. As monopoly capital took hold and state bureaucracies enlarged, power became increasingly centralized and the mechanisms of social control more routinized, and, in the nuclear age, more deadly.

The labor and nonviolence movements each have faced their own internal forces of change, factionalism and re-grouping. Trade unions have not been unified in their arguments against business interests, nor in assessing "correct" methods for labor resistance. Between the Wars the labor movement umbrella covered such diverse union organizations as Gompers' American Federation of Labor, the Industrial Workers of the World, and the Congress of Industrial Organizations. With the rise of the Cold War many of labor's most progressive and socialist leaders and rank and file members were purged or re-molded into neo-conservative American patriots. The Vietnam War again caused a rupturing within the labor movement. Today persons such as William Winpisinger of the IAM remain quite apart from the reigning labor order of Lane Kirkland. This divergence is important to note since the causes of dissension within the labor movement have also been keys to elements of unity with the disarmament movement.

As for the disarmament movement, it too has housed sharp differences within its borders. Religious pacifists, many of whom had been deeply involved with the Abolitionist and early women's suffrage movement largely rejected A.J. Muste's notion that "In a world built on violence, one must first be a revolutionary before one can be a pacifist." The split, reflecting arguments regarding the relationship of pacifism to radical social change efforts, arose again during the emergence of CO's in World War II, the issue of women's and gay liberation and over support for the NLF during the Vietnam War. What constituted nonviolent action also was a sore point of debate— for instance whether, as the Berrigan brothers maintained, nonviolence could be utilized to attack property, in their case smashing the nosecones of weaponry with a hammer and pouring blood on them.

However, there have been many moments during this century that have united the majority of those in the two movements. The points of common struggle have reflected a joint commitment to a transforming vision of U.S. society. The vision has included notions of participatory democracy, workers' control of the workplace, egalitarian distribution of goods and services, and peaceful resolution of conflict. How labor and the disarmament movements together struggled towards this vision can perhaps best be briefly demonstrated through a short biographic accounting of the activities of Abraham Johannas Muste (A.J. Muste). His life provides an explication of the

circumstances uniting the movements as well as why such unity
has been hard to maintain.

A.J. Muste: A Labor Pacifist

A.J. Muste was a radical activist who utilized his profound
analysis of global social, political and economic problems to
guide his leadership roles in both the labor and pacifist
movements.[1] Graduating from the United Theological Seminary
in 1913 at the age of 28 he contended that Christian ideals
necessarily had revolutionary implications. He spent the remaining 54 years of his life organizing to transform humanitarian
ideals into political reality.

As a Presbyterian minister for a white middle-class congre-
gation in Newton, Massachusetts, Muste joined with other local
pacifist religious leaders to form The Comradeship. This
religious community was bound to nonviolence and a very
Gandhian notion of the search for truth. In 1919, as the labor
situation among textile workers in Lawrence, Massachusetts was
reaching the point of general strike, The Comradeship decided to
offer its services to the workers. Muste wrote:

> We had also a feeling that nonviolence had to prove
> itself in actual struggle; otherwise it was mere abstrac-
> tion or illusion....Here a struggle was developing in our
> own backyard. Did our nonviolence have any relevance
> to the impending conflict?

The 30,000 Lawrence millworkers were mostly immigrants, and
the AFL, representing only skilled craftsmen and opposing
industrial unionism, refused to support their demands. Cut off
from the larger labor movement, workers asked The Comradeship for aid, resulting in A.J. Muste's becoming the executive
secretary of the strike committee. He was successful in maintaining nonviolent discipline among the workers, stating,

> ...to permit ourselves to be provoked into violence
> would mean defeating ourselves; that our real power
> was in our solidarity and our capacity to endure
> suffering rather than give up the right to organize;
> that no one could weave woolens with machine guns.

After fifty weeks of striking, the management gave in to the workers' demand for a 48 hour week at 54 hours' pay.

Following World War I, as labor struggles grew to organize against a resisting company/government bloc, Muste became director of the Brookwood Labor College in Katonah, New York. Brookwood became a haven for pacifists concerned with workers' education and labor leadership training, from which many future CIO leaders emerged. Perhaps no other single place in American history has stood so clearly for the common ground linking the two movements.

After serving as chair of the pacifist Fellowship of Reconciliation, Muste began taking a new path that led to the formation of the Conference for Progressive Labor Action (CPLA). The CPLA became the radical labor alternative to the Communist Party USA which was then following a strict pro-Stalin line. Muste had temporarily given up on pacifism and supported the utilization of violence in the cause of labor struggles if the situation arose. Even during this period, though, Muste was instrumental in re-introducing the use of the non-violent direct action "sit-in" as a labor method of organizing. The use of the sit-in, which women garment workers had successfully employed in the early 1900s, was a key ingredient in the strikes organized throughout the 1930s, especially in the Goodyear Tire, Akron, Ohio plant and the Fisher Body plant in Flint, Michigan. In the Flint struggle, The Women's Emergency Brigade, constituted by the wives, sisters and women friends of the workers, barred police from entering the plant by using a non-violent tactic of linking arms and blocking the main gate.

Renouncing an orthodox left approach to social change after a visit with Trotsky in 1936, Muste's return to the pacifist fold was marked by a new type of pacifist formulation. He increasingly called for a non-violence of mass direct action and committed to revolutionary prescriptions of socialist economy and nonviolent civil defense methods.

After World War II, he was almost alone as a non-communist in keeping contacts with those being purged by McCarthyism and in his leadership role with FOR helped to inititate the emerging non-violent civil rights movement. As the

Vietnam War era came onto the scene. Muste pushed for a left position which tied together the rights of workers, the rights of minorities, and the need to end foreign intervention and move toward disarmament. Muste's life was thus a rich example of the ways in which the philosophy and methods of nonviolence were made relevant to the U.S. labor movement.

It becomes evident from a biographic sketch of A.J. Muste that the marriage of the movements very much rested upon the extent to which members of each movement saw themselves in opposition to the established order and were willing to work actively towards an alternative vision of society. While the June 12th demonstration has indicated that the basis for the marriage still exists and can be renewed, there are critical elements within each movement which present significant obstacles.

Limits of Labor Struggle

Those seriously concerned with progressive social change movements have assumed that the working class would be an important part of that struggle. The questions usually have centered on whether the working class would play the vanguard role or an associate role, and upon the issue of who in fact constituted the working class. Consensus has nevertheless evolved that labor participation is essential for a successful left movement. Thus, trade unions, if not at the heart of the battle, are key organizations.

As George Ross has discussed in his thoughtful article, "What Is Progressive About Unions?" labor progress can be measured according to two distinct functions.[2] The first concerns the degree to which trade unions have protected workers against the claims of capitalism. The second concerns the degree to which the unions inspire class unity and concrete visions for an alternative social order. Going beyond protective functions usually occurs only when unions have cemented a close affiliation with a national political party so that political and economic agendas are coordinated.

Within the United States, unlike most advanced industrial nations in Europe, there is no labor party, no socialist party forging a strong working relationship between labor representatives and party professionals. U.S. unions have for the most part been "business unions," labor organizations concerned only with protectionism on job related issues for their membership. Sticking to wage and job condition issues, U.S. unions, with a few notable exceptions, have avoided a push for working class solidarity. A particularism limiting the fight for rights and gains to its membership has resulted in the typical U.S. union not only being divorced from "the workers of the world" but also separated from the struggles of other workers in the United States. For instance, we have already seen how the AFL refused to support the struggle of the Lawrence workers. More recent examples include the Teamsters effort to break the back of the farm worker strike, and most unions' refusal to offer strong support for the PATCO strikers.

By and large the particularism of business unionism in the United States has been shaped by the failure of the unions to see themselves in opposition to the capitalist order. The marriage of trade unions to the management demands of capitalist firms has prevented progress in bringing notions of democracy into the workplace. However the current crisis of the U.S. economy which is having a deep effect on the health of unions, particularly in the primary blue-collar industries, is forcing U.S. trade unions to confront their former attitudes and positions. It has been all too clear that a stance of protectionism is inadequate in an age of capital mobility and transnational corporation structures. As the "capital mobility option" has allowed corporations to move from the old industrial cities to the sunbelt, from the United States to overseas, cheaper labor locations, it has greatly reduced the power of unions to meet the basic labor need of job security. Cities are battling against cities, states against states, regions against regions to entice new industry with all sorts of tax incentives and relaxations of regulation. Unions are not only losing their memberships, they are being forced to compete for whatever jobs are left, pitting new workers against older workers, blacks against whites, women against men. In a study just completed on unemployment in the aircraft industry, for example, one out of four of the unionized males sampled blamed affirmative action for job loss.[3]

Only 20% of the U.S. labor force is organized and even this percentage is under the barrage of rising unemployment. What options remain for the trade union movement in the United States? Will a new direction emerge necessarily linking peace issues with issues of the economy? Before entering into a response let us first examine the forces within the peace movement which have caused difficulty in forging common ground.

Limits of the Peace Movement

Before World War II there were important occasions when pacifists and those committed to the use of nonviolence to solve conflict joined the struggles of labor. Early on, Abolitionists worked with the Knights of Labor, and later the life of Muste demonstrated points of convergence. However, with the rise of the cold war distance between the movements seemed to grow. Some of the explanation has to do with the acceptance on the part of U.S. trade union leaders of the cold war ideology, and in the case of those such as George Meany, the tendency to become leading Cold Warriors. The threat of communism became more central than the threat of capitalist control of the workplace. Labor leaders often became the voices behind the call for more defense spending as a belief was instilled that militarism was good for job creation.

Another aspect of the explanation for the distancing of the peace and labor movements, though, has to do with the constituency of much of the U.S. nonviolent movement and the limits of its response to economic issues. Particularly since the 1950s, the central organizations of the nonviolent movement, such as the American Friends Service Committee, War Resisters League, SANE, Women's International League for Peace and Freedom, and Fellowship of Reconciliation, have had a membership that has been largely the white middle class. The need for nonviolence and the pressing for disarmament, including calls for test-ban treaties and nuclear freeze, have rested on ethical concerns and moral judgments. But the language and organizing tactics of the peace movement often demonstrated a great ignorance of the daily life struggles of the working class and the poor. While expecting manual laborers and welfare recipients to see the urgency of the nuclear issue, for example, "peaceniks" seemed blind to the urgency of inner-city decay and occupational health and safety issues in workplaces. It was not uncommon during the anti-Vietnam War actions for young college age students, fresh from the suburbs, filled with passionate critiques of the War to label workers in the defense plants as "pigs," "war-monsters" and "baby-killers." In turn, some workers responded by wearing hard hats and taunting the students with shouts of "pinkos" and "go to Russia." In back of all the name calling and labeling was the undeniable fact that for the most part the post-World War II peace movement had failed to creatively address modern economic issues. Confronting the privilege and ethos of middle class background was not often or easily accomplished. There were important breakthroughs. Some were sparked by those in the civil-rights movement such as Martin Luther King who increasingly before his death linked economic issues to those of civil rights.[4] Cesaer Chavez, from his leadership position in the United Farm Workers union, opened the eyes of many in the nonviolent movement to the plight of the migrant laborers.[5] Yet, the peace-movement organizations still did not make much headway in directly responding to how issues of national security were inherently tied to issues of a militarized economy and thus economic realities. Almost nowhere in the programs and literature of the nonviolent movement are there discussions and debates on issues important to labor such as job security, pension plans, costs of retirement, comparable worth or job re-training. It is as if there were two ships passing in the night, each with its own passengers and baggage, each tooting the horn for its own destination. Of course both the ships are traveling in the same sea and there exists the promise or at least the possibility for fuller cooperation.

Toward Joint Efforts

Both ships, to carry the metaphor a bit further, are traveling on a stormy sea, with waves of nuclear disaster and economic decline fast approaching. Within this environment of serious concerns, there have been a number of ventures, here in the United States and abroad, that have brought the peace and labor movements into bonds of joint effort. These efforts are still largely geo-politically defined by national boundaries, but more and more there seems to be recognition that peace issues and labor issues are in fact international issues. Morever there are healthy signs that labor leaders and peace movement leaders, and the rank and file of both movements, are listening with greater interest to each other so neither will drown.

The most promising and widespread of the joint efforts is centered on the concept of economic conversion—the transfer of machinery, skills, labor power and resources from military production to production of civilian needs. Organizing efforts towards economic conversion, led by both labor and peace activists, is taking place both in Europe and in the United States. From the nonviolent movement side, they reflect a strategy of speaking about jobs with peace, instead of war is good for jobs. From the labor side, it empowers workers to have greater responsibility over what they are producing as well as the conditions of production. It has provided the means for those in the nonviolent movement to listen to workers about conditions of employment and for those in labor to hear how military spending sparks inflation, job loss and economic skidding.

The mobilization for economic conversion is not new in U.S. history. This country has already experienced massive economic conversion after both World Wars. During World War I, military production was primarily of ordinary peacetime goods produced in regular peacetime facilities and conversion of the facilities back to the civilian economy was simple. By World War II, over one half of the military production was special purpose equipment, but still at the end of the war most facilities were able to convert back to civilian production with no special problems. However, today 90% of the material needs of the military consist of specialized equipment produced in specially designed facilities. Obstacles to conversion, therefore, are considerably greater today than in the past.

The challenge to implement alternative use planning—to come up with specific blueprints on how to convert a particular plant—has involved the energies of shop-floor workers with peace-movement organizers, community officials, business representatives and technical consultants. Often the initiative for alternative use planning has come from workers facing permanent layoffs from their worksite. One of the best known of such cases involved workers at the Lucas Aerospace company.[6]

Between 1970 and 1974, 5000 workers at Great Britain's largest private military contractor, Lucas, lost their jobs. As a result the planning was begun by unionists that resulted in the Alternative Corporate Plan being presented to management for negotiations in 1976. Although the Lucas workers have not won implementation of their comprehensive plan they have seen some of their ideas realized and have almost completely prevented layoffs for five years. As a result of the initiatives of the Lucas workers and the Centre of Alternative Industrial and Technological Systems (CAITS, organized by the Lucas workers with NE London Polytechnic), other shop-stewards committees have prepared their own alternative plans for major British industries like Vickers and Rolls Royce. In addition to producing plans, alternative products have been built including a novel heat pump, an energy efficient low pollution diesel/electric power pack, and a road/rail vehicle. These plans were based on suggestions and answers to questionnaires distributed to rank-and-file workers who came up with 150 socially useful products which could be produced with existing equipment and skills.

Within the United States nearly a dozen economic conversion projects exist, usually focused on local or regional military-industrial facilities. At various stages of organizational development and sophistication, each conversion project has chosen its own tactics to further educate the public regarding conversion and to enlist the support of labor, business and community activists. The Mid-Penninsula Conversion Project has been concerned with the Silicon Valley, heart of the electronics industry in California's Santa Clara region. For educational and organizing outreach they publish the *Plowshares Press* and have also issued a detailed study of how electronics firms dependent on military work, could be converted to produce solar-energy products. Having built a broad coalition in support of conversion including firm technicians, labor union representatives, plant managers and community leaders, the Mid Penninsula Project has held public hearings relating unemployment, energy conservation and industrial growth to military spending. Staff members from the project have testified at California State hearings on economic development, traveled to Europe to learn more from similar efforts abroad and are active in linking issues such as the nuclear freeze campaign on one hand and workplace democracy on the other hand to the overall strategy for conversion.

The St. Louis Economic Conversion Project has completed a vast amount of research on defense contracting in the St. Louis area. They have detailed the contrast between dollars for military contracts and dollars for the region's auto and transportation industry. Along with research activity, SLECP has mounted a direct-action campaign at McDonnel Douglas stockholder meetings to pass resolutions calling for the organization of an economic-conversion committee made up of labor, management and community representatives. It also publishes a newsletter which has documented the loss of local area union jobs and the growth of sub-contracting military contracts.

The Austin, Texas Conversion Project, affiliated with the local branch of the American Friends Service Committee, publishes *Common Ground.* Their research has looked at the rapidly growing dependency of the state on military contracts. A new related group in Amarillo, Texas, sparked by the organizing efforts of the Catholic Bishop, has instituted a trust fund for workers no longer chosing to continue jobs in the local military industrial plant.

The Bay State Conversion Project of Boston, Massachusetts for the past five years has researched and published, *The Case for Economic Conversion: Massachusetts.* The booklet has served both as an educational tool for those initiating discussion on conversion and for those wishing to translate conversion concepts into activism in their own communities. The BSCP has worked closely with related groups in the region including the Jobs With Peace campaign, the Allanthus Group attempting to disarm Draper Lab (a military-contracting firm doing research and development in nuclear and non-nuclear weapons), and Worcester County Peace Network which holds weekly nonviolent vigils in front of the gates of the military contracting firm, GTE. During the past year the BSCP has begun to work closely with two local trade unions, the IUE based at the largest military-contract firm in Massachusetts, General Electric in Lynn, and the International Maritime Workers Union of the General Dynamics' Quincy Shipyard. Leaders in both local unions had recognized that although military spending was on the rise during the Reagan administration, job security for their workers has been steadily diminishing. The Quincy Shipyard has been especially hard hit by layoffs, with over 5,000 workers receiving pink slips during the past five years. The company also has attempted to weaken seniority protection for older workers. The response of a group of laid-off Quincy workers is worth looking at more closely.

Work -in-Progress: The South Shore Conversion Committee
     The issues facing the workers in the Quincy shipyard reflect the central economic concerns in our country today: declining industries, widespread unemployment, the collapse of metropolitan communities and the power of multinational corporate investment decisions. The South Shore Conversion Committee was initiated by a small group of laid-off shipyard workers in 1982 as a grass-roots effort to push for an alternative production plan at Quincy that would ensure job security, social responsibility to the community and the creation of socially useful products. Realizing their efforts involved political as well as economic considerations the workers expanded their meetings to include local church leaders, community social-service personnel, small business proprietors, and government representatives.
     The task the Committee has set for itself is formidable. As the nation's number one defense contractor, General Dynamics builds the F-16 jet fighter, the Trident nuclear submarine, tanks for the army, the Cruise missile and defense electronics. The company has shown little interest in local community economic problems or in capital investment in product alternatives for

shipyards. The ship-building industry globally has been declining, with ship orders in 1981 only one quarter of annual orders eight years earlier. In 1982 no major U.S. shipyard received a commercial shipbuilding contract. The nature of Navy defense contracting keeps those shipyards still open "like a hungry pack of wolves chasing a few rabbits," as put by a Navy officer.

The Quincy Shipyard has been the mainstay of the region's economy for over 50 years. During World War II employment peaked at 30,000, during the 1970's it was held to 7,000 and in the early 1980's fell to under 2,000. This boom and bust cycle, endemic to military defense industries, has taken its toll on workers, their families and communities. The workers have traditionally clung to the hope of new defense contracts coming to Quincy at the expense of other equally needy yards in other locations. General Dynamics short-lived diversification program into LNG ships proved to be a major miscalculation: while predicting 200 new ships would be contracted, only 10 were built before the market evaporated

The South Shore Conversion Committee has stated that there needs to be a national approach to the ship-building problem. For conversion activity to be successful local efforts must be tied to larger educational and organizing activity. Towards this end, the Committee hopes to sponsor a national conference for ship-building unions to address the industry's decline and call for alternatives. In terms of alternative use planning, the Committee has suggested that the union complete an inventory of the capabilities of the yard and the workers' skills. Suggesting that other steel fabrication or transportation products could be produced at the yard the Committee has begun to research offshore Thermal Energy Conversion-ships that use the change in water temperature to create electricity. This would not only create a viable alternative product for the yard, but aid in the nation's energy self-sufficiency. The Committee is also pressing for greater federal and state government action to aid a conversion program. At present there are few incentives for companies to invest in the research and development and risk-taking that conversion production would entail.

The promise of the work of the South Shore Conversion Committee will very much depend on the enlargement of its circle of support. On one front national unions are moving ahead on the conversion issue. The IAM recently commissioned a report entitled, "The Costs and Consequences of Reagan's Military Buildup." In the foreword President William Winpisinger of the IAM wrote the following:

> The IAM joined in comissioning this study for two reasons. First, as a trade union whose membership includes a large number of workers engaged in military production and maintenance of our national security forces, we have a duty and obligation to provide those members with objective information, which will enable them to think about and act upon the war-peace issues, free from employer intimidation and fear of job loss. Secondly, we owe it to all of our members—their families, their communities and, indeed, the nation at large—to provide the means for rational and informed discussion on the impact and consequences of the staggering costs of the arms race. It is they and ordinary working people everywhere, who are bearing the oppressive burdens and sacrifices exacted by mega-military budgets.

Much of the motivation on the part of the IAM and other unions to begin seriously taking a look at the costs of military spending comes from the worsening job security situation for their membership. For example, in 1970 IAM had 24,000 members at McDonnell Douglas, St. Louis. By 1982 membership had fallen to 11,000 although prime contract awards to McDonnell Douglas jumped from $1.4 billion in 1975 to nearly $2.8 billion in 1978 and has been growing at a similar rate since that time.

Whether the conversion efforts prove to be a new reform within the present political economy or a more radical element of systemic change is yet to be seen. However, economic conversion appears to be an issue whose time has come and speaks directly to concerns of both the labor and nonviolent movements.

Final Note
It is clear that we have only begun to explore the dimensions of the problems and possibilities facing the labor and peace movements today. Necessarily international in their reach, we have been focusing on domestic historical and current evidence. To be sure, there is a great deal to be learned from labor struggles and nonviolent movement activity in other industrialized countries and from Third World examples. Strategies for greater economic democracy, visions of a more just society are being discussed, attempted, disbanded and renewed elsewhere. Just as in the United States, the working out of these strategies often demonstrates factionalization among progressive movements. Within European countries, for example, labor parties and trade unions frequently are not on the same side of the barricades as anti-nuclear and environmental supporters. These struggles are instructive to what may be points of unity or discord here.

In hard times, a history of internal conflict and mutual distrust among social movements is difficult to overcome. At the same moment, the reality of painful recession and the rise of the New Right suggest there will be more nonviolent activists at Solidarity Days, and more trade-unionists at demonstrations such as June 12th. Recognition of mutual interests will greatly affect the future of both movements, separately and collectively.

Notes
1. Nat Hentoff (ed.), *The Essays of A.J. Muste* (Simon and Schuster: N.Y., 1967).
2. George Ross, "What Is Progressive About Unions," *Politics and Society*, 10, 1981, pp. 609-643.
3. Paula Rayman and Barry Bluestone, *Out of Work: The Consequences of Unemployment in Hartford's Aircraft Industry* (National Institute for Mental Health, Research Grant No. 5-RO1-MH33251-02, 1982).
4. Robert Cooney and Helen Michalowski (eds.), *The Power of the People* (Peace Press Inc.: Culver City, Ca. 1977).
5. Susan Abrams, "The United Farm Workers Union," in Severyn Bruyn and Paula Rayman (eds.), *Nonviolent Action and Social Change* (Irvington Press, 1979) pp. 102-127.
6. Mike Cooley, *Architect or Bee?* (South End Press: Boston, 1981).

6

MANY PATHS TO WAR
RIGHT, CENTER & LEFT
By Holly Sklar

Holly Sklar is Director of the Institute for New Communications (INC) in New York City. INC is producing a Popular Pamphlet Series and Public Policy Pamphlet Series with South End Press, and sponsoring a Speakers/Workshop Bureau on a wide range of economic, political and social issues. Holly is editor of Trilateralism: The Trilateral Commission and Elite Planning for World Management *and coauthor of the poster guide "Who's Who in the Reagan Administration." She has codesigned workshops to demystify global corporate strategies and speaks frequently on elite planning and U.S. Foreign and domestic policy.*

One of the more difficult and often underplayed problems facing any movement for social change is understanding the actual thinking and strategy of those whom they are opposing. The disarmament movement has done an excellent job of discovering and communicating the character and horror of nuclear war and a reasonable job of discerning many of the material relationships associated with the arms race and the use of weaponry throughout the world. It has been less effective in understanding exactly how various armament and disarmament options are viewed by members of "our" governing political elite.

Holly Sklar's contribution is a survey of the nuclear policy attitudes of various leaders and sectors of leaders in position to influence decision-making directly. What are the real parameters of their choices, the real aims of their policies, the real costs and gains—in their eyes—of their competing perspectives? In particular, what are the potential impact, breadth, and limits of Reagan's MX plans, the Kennedy-Hatfield Freeze resolution, and, for that matter, the No First Use proposal put forward by Robert MacNamara, et. al.?

To improve our chances of creating a powerful movement we need to take advantage of confusions and weaknesses within the "power elite," to benefit from their own hesitant efforts at disarmament proposals, to avoid cooptation, and to understand the likely ways our own movement's efforts will percolate into the elite's thinking and acting—not by changing their minds but by raising pressures that they cannot ignore. Holly Sklar provides critical information and insights on these matters.

—M.A. & D.D.

Secretary of Defense Caspar W. Weinberger said today that the Reagan Administration had formulated a plan to wage a protracted nuclear war to avert what he called a "hair trigger situation."...

Mr. Weinberger also assailed those critics of the Administration's policy who have protested against provisions that call for the United States to "prevail" in nuclear war by ending the conflict on terms favorable to the United States and with some nuclear weapons intact....

Mr. Weinberger reiterated his view that nuclear war was not winnable. But he added that "we certainly are not planning to be defeated."

...Asked whether a prolonged, calibrated nuclear war was possible, Mr. Weinberger said, "I just don't have any idea; I don't know that anybody has any idea."

New York Times, August 10, 1982

Interviewer: *Do you honestly think, in the final analysis, as a human being, a Christian, a father, that you could actually recommend to the President to push the button and kill millions of people?*

Zbigniew Brzezinski: *I don't know whether I would. Certainly I think I would and I certainly think I would without too much hesitation if I thought that someone else was launching a nuclear attack on me. Because if I didn't have the conviction that I have the determination and will to do it, I think I would enhance the probability of war, by eliminating the deterrent effect.*

Interviewer: *Even though that might make the chance of the regeneration of human society that much more difficult, even impossible?*

Brzezinski: *Well, first of all, that really is baloney. And I do emphasize the importance of the deterrent effect...As far as human society and all that is concerned, it sounds great in a rally. The fact of the matter is — and I don't want this to be understood as justifying the use of nuclear weapons, because we don't want to use them and we're not going to use them first in an attack — the fact of the matter is that if we used all our nuclear weapons and the Russians used all their nuclear weapons, about 10 per cent of humanity would be killed.*

Now this is a disaster beyond the range of human comprehension. It's a disaster which is not morally justifiable in whatever fashion. But descriptively and analytically, it's not the end of humanity.

Washington Post, October 1977

Windows of Insanity

In the last Democratic Administration we had a national security adviser who assumed that "if we used all our nuclear weapons and the Russians used all of their nuclear weapons, about 10 per cent of humanity would be killed." That takes care of the Soviet Union and the United States. How about other NATO and Warsaw Pact nations? Off-target missiles? How about global radioactive fallout? Destruction of the ozone layer? In *The Fate of the Earth*, Jonathan Schell writes, using data available to Brzezinski in 1977 and before: "In judging the global effects of a holocaust, therefore, the primary question is not how many people would be irradiated, burned, or crushed to death by the immediate effects of the bombs but how well the ecosphere, regarded as a single living entity, on which all forms of life depend for their continued existence, would hold up."[1]

In the current Republican Administration we have a Secretary of Defense who doesn't "have any idea" and who doesn't "know that anybody has any idea" as to "whether a prolonged, calibrated nuclear war was possible." But he is planning to spend over 1.6 trillion dollars on a five year plan to fight that war and any other war on and in the ground, sea, air, and space. All simultaneously, of course. This "global war" doctrine employs three basic strategies: *vertical escalation* from conventional to nuclear weaponry; *horizontal escalation* by retaliating or "setting fires" anywhere around the world the United States perceives an advantage (e.g. Cuba or Vietnam); and *decapitation*—destroying the Soviet military and political power structure.[2] The doctrine calls for a 600 ship navy to "control the sea lanes" around the world in war or peacetime. And it calls for a vast expansion of military operations in space and "civil defense" on the ground. The *Harvard Lampoon's* Fall 1982 *Newsweek Parody* wins the T.K. Jones Nuclear Fleece Prize with this portrait of Weinberger wisdom:

> According to Pentagon calculations, in the event of a nuclear war Soviet citizens would only be killed 21 times over, while their American counterparts risk being annihilated 45 to 50 times over. 'We must close this large and unacceptable gap in the overkill ratio,' declared Caspar Weinberger at a recent press conference.

The military budget for space is to increase at a rate of 10 per cent above inflation while the overkill, *oops* overall military budget rises at annual rates of 7 to 9 percent. As the Air Force Space Command's deputy commander puts it: "Space is not a mission, it is a place. It is a theatre of operations. It is now time that we treat it as a theatre of operations." One role for the space theatre is to house reconnaisance satellites which will "scan the Soviet Union after an initial nuclear exchange, spotting military forces that are being reassembled, thus providing vital information for 'waging protracted nuclear war.'"[3] Defense analyst Thomas Powers' point is well taken as he concludes a recent article with this remark:

> Strategic planners hesitate to say what the world would look like after a nuclear war. There are too many variables. But they agree—for planning purposes, at any rate—that both sides would 'recover,' and that the most probable result of a general nuclear war would be a race to prepare for a second general nuclear war. As a

practical matter, then, a general nuclear war would not end the threat of nuclear war. That threat, in fact, would be one of the very few things the pre-war and post-war worlds would have in common.[4]

The current five year Defense Guidance Plan is not so much an expression of Weinberger's wildest fantasies as it is a more brazen follow-up to Jimmy Carter's Presidential Directive (PD) 59 of July 1980. PD 59 officially revised U.S. nuclear strategy to plan to fight a so-called "prolonged but limited" nuclear war. With "silo-killing" counterforce weapons, such as the Minuteman-3, M-X, Trident-2, and Cruise missiles, fighting a nuclear war need not mean mutual assured destruction (MAD). For many among this country's "best and brightest," the possibility of a "disarming first strike" made nuclear war both thinkable and winnable.

In his article, Powers analyzes the evolution of PD 59 (and earlier nuclear war doctrine). He describes a 1977 meeting which was chaired by then National Security Adviser Brzezinski to consider the "Military Strategy and Force Posture Review," (Annex C) of Presidential Review Memorandum (PRM) 10. PRM 10, says Powers, was a potential instrument for arms control since it "assumed that we had more than we needed for 'deterrence.'" Annex C outlined four strategic options with different criteria of destruction for deterring war. According to Powers, Brzezinski interrupted a briefing on these matters to ask "Where are the criteria for killing Russians?" The briefer was surprised because "It is a kind of unwritten rule among strategic planners that one does not target 'population per se.'" But he explained that "If you attack Soviet economic and industrial targets, you're bound to kill a lot of people"; Annex C estimated that a major nuclear war would kill some 113 million Soviet citizens. According to Powers, Brzezinski responded, "No, no, I mean *Russian* Russians." Powers goes on to explain:

> Brzezinski had something severely practical in mind. It was Russians who ran the Soviet Union, Russians who

were the enemy. If you wanted to deter war you had to deter Russians. If deterrence failed, it was Russians you had to kill. Killing Russians *qua* Russians would speed the breakup of the Russian empire...It could be done the same way the Russians might target white neighborhoods in a segregated American city, and for much the same reason—because whites are afraid of blacks, just as Great Russians fear submergence in a sea of Asians. Thousands of warheads are available for such tasks. They *can* be selectively targeted in such a way...

Powers concludes the section by stating, "With one question, Brzezinski summed up the reasons for the demise of Annex C of PRM 10. It didn't address the right question—how to fight the war."[5] Confident in their new technologies with their "surgical precision," the NUTS—to use Paul Joseph's abbreviation for nuclear-use theorists—were overtaking the MADs.[6]

This article will analyze how rightwing, centrist, and liberal elite opinion-and-policy-makers address the questions of how to fight the Russians and how to preserve perceived U.S. interests in the Third World. And it discusses centrist and liberal strategies for arms control such as the Kennedy-Hatfield Freeze Resolution. One can't dismiss nuclear war as morally unthinkable while rationalizing intervention in the Third World in terms of perceived costs and benefits (economic, political, strategic). One can't reduce the risk of nuclear war on the one hand by building up the conventional war machine on the other. But too many "arms control" advocates do just that. If the peace movement is to succeed it must understand the contradictory stances of elite disarmament allies in the dominant political spectrum and address the question of nuclear armament and disarmament in a larger foreign policy context. This article is a contribution in that direction.

Freeze! And We'll Shoot?

By the time this book appears, the disarmament movement will have won a round of local electoral victories on the nuclear freeze front. The constituency comprising the nuclear freeze campaign is a diverse one. Establishmentarians who have endorsed the freeze include former Secretary of Defense Clark Clifford, former CIA Director William Colby, former Deputy Secretary of State Warren Christopher, former Special Envoy to the Middle East Sol Linowitz, former Vietnam Peace Negotiator Henry Cabot Lodge, former Deputy Secretary of Energy John Sawhill, and former Director of the Arms Control and Disarmament Agency Gerard Smith.

Kennedy and Hatfield call the freeze (the real thing—not the Jackson-Warner version) "a first but essential step back from the nuclear precipice" and "a firebreak, encircling and containing a weapons race threatening to break out of control."[7] We should all applaud the freeze as a much needed first step. And it may well become a firebreak around the development and deployment of first-strike weapons. But whether it provides an enduring firebreak for the overall superpower arms race and for war-making around the globe depends upon the vitality of that part of the nuclear disarmament movement which is anti-militarist and anti-interventionist. As Michael Klare argues in a recent issue of *The Nation*, "A Nuclear Freeze Isn't Enough."

It isn't enough, in part, because of a kind of linkage which is often side-stepped: the "little war-big war link." While the freeze campaign is tryng to put a firebreak around the nuclear arms race, the designers of military weaponry are working to eliminate the firebreak between the use of conventional and nuclear weapons. As Klare observes:

> Just as the designers of conventional weapons are being encouraged to think big and create weapons of greater destructiveness, the designers of nuclear weapons are being encouraged to think small in order to create 'mini-nukes'—bombs with the same kill radius as large conventional bombs. The object is to develop conventional arms and nuclear arms that are interchangeable on the battlefield.[8]

Three well-publicized "brushfire wars" have been fought during the lifespan of the freeze campaign. The Iran-Iraq war is still raging. The Falklands/Malvinas war offered a demonstration of the new generation of "smart" missiles like the Exocet, made famous with the sinking of the British destroyer Sheffield. Luckily for Thatcher, the potential of these "great equalizers" (the words of retired Admiral Gene La Rocque) in the Anglo-Argentine war was limited by Argentina's short supply.[9]

The still-smouldering Israeli invasion of Lebanon showcased the capabilities of electronic warfare and modern conventional weaponry. Israel demolished Syrian Soviet-built SAMs (surface to air missiles) and shot down numerous MIG fighters with virtual impunity. "Cluster bombs of the type used in Lebanon," writes Klare, "scatter 'bomblets' that kill or maim all exposed people over an area ranging in size from a football field to seventy-five square city blocks." And, says Klare, "A bomb of that type with the kill radius of a small nuclear weapon is now being developed for NATO forces as a result of the mounting opposition in Europe to the deployment of nuclear weapons."[10]

Furthermore, the arms race cannot just be frozen at the superpower level. Israel is the world's seventh largest arms exporter, a supplier of arms to Argentina, and a major supplier to South Africa. South Africa is the largest arms producer in the Southern Hemisphere, though it exports less than Argentina and Brazil. Israel and South Africa have nuclear weapons capability; Argentina and Brazil are on the threshold between "peaceful" nuclear power and weapons development.[11] In December, 1981, Israel's Defense Minister Ariel Sharon made a 10-day visit to South African forces in illegally-occupied Namibia. While it receives little attention in the U.S. media, South Africa has repeatedly invaded Angola and occupies an increasing area in southern Angola in its campaign to destroy SWAPO (the Namibian liberation force) and support UNITA, the Angolan counterrevolutionary force led by Jonas Savimbi.[12]

"Little wars" between the allies of the superpowers can lead to direct superpower intervention and global nuclear conflagration. Indeed, "little wars" can go nuclear without direct super-power intervention. "You can help prevent nuclear war"—to use the Kennedy-Hatfield phrase—by helping to prevent war, period. I can't help but think of Smoky the Bear saying "You can prevent forest fires." But wars are not caused by the accidental or careless cigaret smokers and campfire builders. War is more like arson for profit.

"Let Him Who Desires Peace Prepare for War"

The Roman maxim quoted above could have come from Ronald Reagan's November speech announcing plans to deploy the MX missile—the one Reagan calls (are you listening Orwell?) "Peacekeeper." War has been called "the extension of politics by other means." If we are to achieve peace, we must understand the political and economic causes of war, and build a movement which addresses the root political and economic issues. What are some of these issues? Well, I could say the issues of markets, resources, and labor and then review familiar radical arguments about militarism and intervention. But I prefer to hear it direct from the horse's mouth wherever possible. And for this I turn to *BusinessWeek* (or *Forbes* or *Fortune* or *Foreign Affairs* or *Business International...*).

In 1979 *BusinessWeek* did a special issue on "The Decline of U.S. Power: The New Debate Over Guns and Butter." It featured a weeping Statue of Liberty on the cover. A weeping multinational corporate executive would have been more appropriate. In the words of the Middle East chief of a major U.S. bank:

> It was easy in the pre-Vietnam days to look at an area
> of the map and say, 'that's ours' and feel pretty good
> about investing there. That's no longer the case, as Iran
> has made so terribly clear. American investment
> overseas is going to happen at a reduced rate until we
> can redefine our world.

"That somber prediction," says *BusinessWeek*, "expresses what the leaders of many U.S. multinational corporations think in their darker moments as they confront a far more dangerous world than the one that cradled their globe-girdling growth from the 1950s to the early 1970s."[13]

A fuller quote from *Business Week* offers a corporate sketch of the decline of U.S. power:

> Historical parallels can be overdrawn. But in historical terms, the U.S. emerged from World War II as an imperial power and has had to live with the problems of empire ever since. For great powers 'to survive— and perhaps even to flourish,' in the words of former Secretary of State Dean Acheson, their leaders must understand the connections between the military, political, and economic aspects of power. Only once since World War II, with the establishment of the Marshall Plan in 1948, did the U.S. fully grasp these connections...
>
> **1956-1965:** *When empires cannot produce a commodity vital to their survival within their borders, they become vulnerable to decline unless they secure their sources of supply by effective military or political means.* For the Roman empire it was grain from the then-fertile fields of Egypt and North Africa. For the U.S., beginning with the mid-50s, it has been the relatively cheap oil from the Middle East.
>
> John Foster Dulles saw the Suez crisis of 1956 as an anachronistic exercise in 19th century colonialism. It may have been, since France was the country that had built the Suez Canal and Britain was the country that used it as an imperial lifeline. But by provoking Egypt into nationalizing the canal with the withdrawal of U.S. financing of the Aswan Dam in July and then forcing its allies [France, Britain, and Israel] to withdraw from the canal when they attacked it in November, the U.S. failed to recognize the magnitude of the oil threat to the economic health of the West.

The Suez miscalculation gave the Russians an opening into the Middle East.

Another failure for the U.S. in dealing with its principal allies was unwillingness to insist that its European and Japanese partners share the economic burden of military security. Thus began the erosion of the dollar...

Cuba was to show another of the recurring problems of maintaining the American "empire"—an inability to contain and channel the process of radical economic and social change in the Third World...

1965-1970: Having taken on too large a share of the costs of collective security, *the U.S. discovered in Vietnam another of the ancient problems of empire: the high cost of resources of defending its perimeters.* With the Gulf of Tonkin resolution in 1965, the Senate almost blindly followed President Lyndon B. Johnson in committing an unsuspecting U.S. public to a land war in Asia. The costs of this war for a society that was beginning to commit more and more resources to meeting the ambitious social goals began to produce the economic strains—inflation and a weakened dollar—that have haunted the U.S. for nearly 15 years.

1971-1979: The failure to protect oil supplies that began with Suez, combined with the economic and political strains caused by Vietnam, produced a long series of reversals for the U.S. in the 1970s, including the failure to deal with a Soviet-backed Cuban intervention in both Angola and the Horn of Africa...The decade began with the collapse of the Bretton Woods monetary agreement after the dollar was cut loose from gold on Aug. 15, 1971. That year also produced the first U.S. trade deficit of the 20th century, which fed protectionist sentiments in the U.S., including a domestic political assault on U.S. multinational corporations...

The most serious blow of the decade, though, was the loss of control over oil supplies represented by OPEC's successful power grab in 1973. The quadrupling of the price of oil plunged the world economy into the first global crisis since the 1930s. And unless the U.S. can find the military, political, and economic equivalent of a Marshall Plan to deal with the new problems raised by the fall of the Shah of Iran, the greatest period of economic growth the world has ever seen may come to an end.[14] (italics added)

Whew! And that's before the Soviet intervention in Afghanistan in late 1979 gave Washington an official excuse to reassert U.S. power in the Middle East, activate draft registration, and legitimize the Rapid Deployment Force. And that's before the overthrow of Somoza made U.S. elites more nervous about looking at Central America on the map and saying "that's ours." And it's not till later on in the lengthy article that *Business Week* gets around to discussing the United States' loss of clear strategic superiority over the Soviet Union. The imbalance which had prevailed throughout most of the post-World War II period emboldened U.S. presidents to make numerous threats of nuclear use or shows of nuclear force (Berlin Blockade, June 1948; Korea, 1950 and 1953; Dienbienphu, Indochina, 1954; "Lebanon Crisis," 1958; Quemoy islands off mainland China, 1958; Berlin crisis, 1961; Cuban missile crisis, 1962; Vietnam, 1968-72) and repeated covert and conventional interventions (e.g. Iran, 1953; Guatemala, 1954; Lebanon, 1958; the Congo, now Zaire, 1960; Cuba, 1961; Brazil, 1964; Dominican Republic and Indonesia, 1965; and Chile, 1973.)73.)[15]

The Carter Doctrine clarified the Middle East's place in the U.S. empire. In January 1980, during his last State of the Union address, President Carter declared:

An attempt by any outside force to gain control of the Persian Gulf region will be regarded as an assault on the vital interests of the United States of America, and such an assault will be repelled by any means necessary, including military force.

And that includes nuclear force!

The Carter Doctrine was publicly announced after the Afghanistan intervention rather than years before, when it was actually initiated, because the public was expected to swallow the rather ludicrous proposition that Afghanistan was a Soviet stepping stone to the Persian Gulf oil fields, and hence the "new" U.S. policy was justifiably countering an expansionist Soviet thrust.[16] President Reagan has also reissued the Monroe Doctrine (which originally told the Europeans to keep out of the "Americas") in the name of the Soviet threat to vital U.S. interests. In testimony before the Senate Subcommittee on Hemispheric Affairs (February 1, 1982), Assistant Secretary State for Inter-American Affairs Thomas Enders warned:

> There is no mistaking that the decisive battle for Central America is underway in El Salvador. If after Nicaragua, El Salvador is captured by a violent minority [alias Soviet-Cuban backed terrorists], who in Central America would not live in fear? How long would it be before major strategic United States interests—the Panama Canal, sea lanes, oil supplies— were at risk?

Disarray in the "Politically Relevant Spectrum"

Ruling elites today are debating the issues raised by *Business Week* and more: What is to be done to best secure markets, resources, and labor power and revitalize the international capitalist system; contain and channel radical economic and social change in the Third World—and at home, where a "crisis of democracy" persists; balance the political and economic costs of defending the empire; manage relations with the allies—Western Europe and Japan; and deal with China and the Soviet Union.[17] We often hear that the goal of U.S. policy is to

preserve freedom. To corporate executives freedom's just another word for profit. The president of Business International,
Orville Freeman (!), describes what "freedom" meant in the
postwar period in the film "Controlling Interest": "freedom to
invest, freedom to trade, freedom to have economic intercourse."
A 1981 article in *Foreign Policy* provides a good introduction for
us to demystify foreign and military policy debates in the post-
detente era:

> Few in the politically relevant spectrum these days
> would challenge the notion that the Soviet Union is a
> menace. Yet there is still disagreement about the
> nature of the beast and how to tame it.[18]

Today's "politically relevant spectrum"—on foreign and
domestic policy—is skewed heavily to the Right. As Ronald
Reagan has said, "Sometimes our right hand doesn't know what
our far right hand is doing." Far Right figures such as Senator
Jesse Helms and Heritage Foundation bankroller-Kitchen Cabinet member Joseph Coors flank such Reaganauts as National
Security Adviser William Clark and Neoconservative Committee on the Present Dangerites such as U.N. Ambassador
Jeane Kirkpatrick and ex-Arms Control and Disarmament Agency
Director Eugene Rostow. Secretary of State George Shultz (like
General "I'm In Control" Haig before him), Vice President Bush,
and foreign policy guru Henry Kissinger hold the much lauded
center ground, remarkably appearing as "moderates" and "pragmatic conservatives" in the glare of the right-wing ideologues.
Cap The Butter Knife Weinberger is your basic megamilitarist,
but he distances himself from the ideology-firsters with his
Bechtel-bred Saudi sensitivity. There are no liberals in the
Reagan Administration; Interior Secretary James Watt explains
there are two kinds of people in the United States: Americans
and liberals. Inside the Democratic Party liberals have regrouped
under the more conservative banner of Neoliberalism. The Left
(old and new) is excluded from the nationally-broadcast "politically relevant spectrum."

Three different forms of containment/intervention have emerged as competing guides for U.S. policy toward the Soviet Union and international relations generally: "containment of communism" or unlimited containment; "moderate containment" or limited containment; and "containment without confrontation" or liberal containment. All agree that the U.S. must "draw the line." They don't agree on where, when, and how.

Unlimited Containment

Unlimited containment is, of course, a contradiction in terms. A more accurate characterization would be unlimited intervention. Right-wing ideologues say draw the line everywhere, and redraw it in Angola, Nicaragua, and the Soviet bloc itself. For these ultra-hawks the detente era of Kissinger's non-ideological *realpolitik* was a time when, to use the words of *Commentary* editor Norman Podhoretz, "the chairman of Pepsi Cola and other luminaries of American business with more strategically important goods to sell were rushing to Moscow laden with the 'rope' that Lenin famously predicted the capitalists would provide for their own execution at the hands of Soviet hangmen."[19]

These right-wingers really do see the Soviet Union as a demonic, expansionist goliath bent on global domination by any means necessary, including nuclear war. For them peaceful coexistence is unthinkable. The United States can and must have nuclear superiority over the Soviet Union to prevent nuclear blackmail and prevail in an actual nuclear war. Economic warfare and covert action should be the bottom line of Cold War confrontation. The goal? Roll back the Iron Curtain. Anything less is spineless capitulation. A year and a half ago Podhoretz chastized "certain Europeans and their American counterparts" for their "hypocritical plans for the neutralization of Afghanistan and plaintive prophecies to the effect that a Soviet invasion of Poland would be the worst thing that could happen to the Poles," saying:

How do these people know? Might not a Soviet invasion be the worst thing that could happen to the Soviets? Might they not encounter a degree of resistance from the Poles they did not meet with in Hungary or Czechoslovakia? And might this not trigger other uprisings against Soviet rule?[20]

A year later, in an article titled "The Neoconservative Anguish Over Reagan's Foreign Policy," Podhoretz reiterated George Will's observation that the Reagan Administration "loves commerce more than it loathes Communism." Shortly after the Polish regime declared martial law, the U.S. government paid the interest due on the Polish debt. Walter Laqueur (of the Georgetown University Center for Strategic and International Studies) speaks for most Neoconservatives, says Podhoretz, when he observes "that even Lenin...could never have imagined that we would rush to give them the money to buy the rope."[21]

The ideology-firsters would never sell out the loyal anti-communists on Taiwan for a billion potential Coca-Cola drinkers and anti-Soviet footsoldiers on the Chinese mainland. And if the namby-pamby Europeans won't go along with Born-Again America, that "shining city on a hill," then the U.S. will go-it-alone.

When it comes to the Third World, the traditional foreign policy establishment has its geostrategics. But right-wingers prefer Egostrategics. It's very simple. You're either for or against us. If you're for us, you're the "moderate autocrat" of a "moderately repressive regime"—like the dearly departed Somoza of Nicaragua and Shah of Iran. If you're against us, however, you're "totalitarian"—like the Sandinistas of Nicaragua and the MPLA of Angola. If you're for us, you're a "freedom fighter"—like UNITA leader Jonas Savimbi. But if you're against us, you're a Soviet-Cuban backed international "terrorist"—like the Salvadoran and Guatemalan revolutionaries.

Jeane Kirkpatrick is a whiz at the kind of disinformation and double-speak which characterizes Egostrategics. "Traditional autocrats," says Kirkpatrick, "tolerate social inequities, brutality, and poverty while revolutionary autocrats create them."

> Because the miseries of traditional life are familiar, they are bearable to ordinary people, who growing up in the society, learn to cope, as children born to untouchables in India acquire the skills necessary for survival in the miserable roles they are destined to fill.[22]

"Ordinary" Third World people don't make revolutions. Change isn't inevitable. Kirkpatrick scoffs at such notions: "So what if the 'deep historical forces' at work in such diverse places as Iran, the Horn of Africa, Southeast Asia, Central America, and the United Nations look a lot like Russians or Cubans?"[23] When religious workers challenge the notion that poverty, brutality, and inequality are predestined in the natural order ("the poor shall always be with us") and preach the messages of liberation theology ("the poor shall inherit the earth") Kirkpatrick is outraged: "As for the Catholic left," she taunts, "its interest in revolution on this earth has waxed as its concern with salvation in heaven has waned."[2] The Maryknoll sisters and layworker who were raped and murdered in El Salvador got what they deserved. And when the ordinary people—the campesinos—rise up against dictatorship, economic peonage, hunger, disease, illiteracy, torture, death squads, and countless crimes against humanity, Kirkpatrick and company blame it on Soviet subversion and sanction repression by any means necessary. Hear Kirkpatrick's own words in a paper prepared for the American Enterprise Institute in December 1980 and titled "The Hobbes Problem: Order, Authority and Legitimacy in Central America." As Alexander Cockburn said when he excerpted the paper for his *Village Voice* column (March 30, 1982), "for unabashed racism, and, to be frank about it, undiluted fascism, the following extracts almost defy belief."

> General Maximiliano Hernandez Martinez, who governed El Salvador from 1931 to 1944, was minister of

war...when there occurred widespread uprisings said to be the work of Communist agitators. General Hernandez Martinez then staged a coup and ruthlessly suppressed the disorders—wiping out all those who participated, hunting down their leaders. It is sometimes said that 30,000 persons lost their lives in this process. To many Salvadorans the violence of this repression seems less important than that of the fact of restored order and the thirteen years of civil peace that ensued.

The leader of that rebellion was Jose Faribundo Marti, the name assumed by today's revolutionary front in El Salvador. Hernandez Martinez's name endures also, as Kirkpatrick points out:

> The traditional death squads that pursue revolutionary activities and leaders in contemporary El Salvador call themselves Hernandez Martinez brigades, seeking thereby to place themselves in El Salvador's political tradition and communicate their purposes.

Hernandez Martinez, says Kirkpatrick, is a hero, a person who makes "a special contribution to highly valued goods." In the order of things described above the lives of passive ordinary people count little, the lives of ordinary people in pursuit of liberation count even less.

Since the 1950s, the Right has sprouted a lot of new institutions: the Heritage Foundation, the Committee on the Present Danger, *Conservative Digest*, the National Conservative Political Action Committee, and even electronic churches. But their ideas have stood still, or regressed. New Right direct mail tycoon Richard Viguerie formed his political views in admiration of the "two Macs," General Douglas MacArthur and Senator Joseph McCarthy.[25]

Limited or Relatively Moderate Containment

Proponents of limited containment reject—in the words of Trilateral Commission architect Zbigniew Brzezinski—"nostalgia" for the Pax Americana of the fifties. And they reject the "escapism" of the post-Vietnam seventies.[26] They look back on detente as overly optimistic. But they reject the idea of regaining meaningful nuclear superiority over the Soviet Union as dangerous, unattainable, and destructive to the Western alliance. In short, they reluctantly recognize limits on U.S. power.

Limited containment is the basic posture of two 1981 reports associated with the Council on Foreign Relations (CFR): *The Soviet Challenge: A Policy Framework for the 1980s*, by the CFR's Commission on U.S.-Soviet Relations, and *Western Security: What Has Changed? What Should Be Done?*, jointly prepared by the directors of the CFR, the British Royal Institute of International Affairs, the French Institute of International Relations, and the German Society for Foreign Affairs' research institute. It is also the explicit thesis of a 1980 *Foreign Affairs* article by Robert Tucker, a conservative member of the CFR Commission on U.S.-Soviet Relations, and professor of political science at Johns Hopkins University.

The CFR commission reflected a mix of views from the "politically relevant spectrum," from Stanley Hoffman of Harvard University on the relatively liberal end to Paul Nitze, then head of policy studies for the Committee on the Present Danger and now chief U.S. negotiator for European arms control in the Reagan Administration, of the more rightest persuasion.* While commissioners didn't agree on everything, such as what to do about SALT II, they did achieve a measure of consensus on major recommendations.

---

*Other members on the CFR commission: Henry A. Grumwald, editor-in-chief, Time Inc.; W. Michael Blumenthal, chairman, Burroughs Corporation and Secretary of the Treasury under Carter; William S. Cohen, Senator from Maine; Milicent Fenwick, Congresswoman from New Jersey; William G. Hyland, senior fellow, Georgetown University Center for Strategic and International Studies and former Deputy National Security Adviser; Joseph Kraft, nationally syndicated columnist; Walter Laqueur, Center for Strategic and International Studies; Harry C. McPherson Jr., partner, Lipfert, Bernhard & McPherson; Walt W. Rostow, professor of economics and history, University of Texas at Austen (and

To meet military commitments in Europe, Asia, the Persian Gulf, and elsewhere around the world, the U.S. "must have more, not merely restocked and upgraded, forces, including more men under arms." Substantial military spending increases should be undertaken at (politically and economically) sustainable rates, reaching a level of perhaps six percent of the U.S. gross national product. West European and Japanese allies should share the political and economic burden of a sustained military effort which may "involve a role for the West Germans outside Europe and for the Japanese outside the Japanese homeland." The Rapid Deployment Force must "be assured of a consolidated and enlarged network of facilities in various countries, permitting rapid and efficient moves to danger points."

The commission urges improving the quality and readiness of the armed forces and comments on the apparent failure of the all-volunteer force: "In the short run the Commission recognizes that we can only hope to attract and retain qualified people by providing better pay and benefits. In the longer run the problem may only be solved by instituting some form of compulsory military service."

In the strategic nuclear area, commissioners underscore "the need to preserve an effective, suvivable triad of forces" (land, air, and sea). They divide on the question of developing a "first strike" "silo killing" ICBM force such as the MX. A minority believes "that such a capability would be destabilizing, pushing the Soviets into hair-trigger 'launch-on-warning' tactics." But there is no reported dissent on the recommendation that the U.S. go forward with plans to deploy the modernized theatre nuclear forces which NATO decided upon in December 1979. These plans for Cruise and Pershing-2 missiles should not be delayed pending (highly unlikely) progress in arms control negotiations, but adjusted later if warranted. Commissioners add: "Realistically, the United States must face the possibility

Eugene Rostow's brother); Robert Scalapino, Director Institute of East Asian Studies, University of California at Berkeley; and Helmut Sonnenfeldt, guest scholar, The Brookings Institution and former counselor, Department of State.

that the apparent European political consensus in favor of the 1979 deployment decisions might fall apart for lack of sufficient public support in key countries. This would constitute a serious setback to the cohesion and effectiveness of NATO. And it would be seen by the Soviets as a victory."

On arms control, the commission has this to say: it "believes that in the recent past arms control has been the centerpiece of U.S. policy toward the Soviet Union, and that this was wrong." While commissioners do not call for superiority, they do assert that "Arms control cannot be expected to correct deficiencies in the military balance that have arisen over the last decade." At the same time, they attempt to distance themselves from the more rightist position, for example, by defining linkage more flexibly: "There is, in fact, a double link to the larger political context of U.S.-Soviet relations: For, as arms control efforts cannot flourish in periods of high tension, so neither can they be expected to bear the whole responsibility for improving relations." Moreover, "Where the Soviet Union has significant security goals at stake—for example, in Afghanistan or Poland—the disruption of arms control negotiations is unlikely to affect its decisions." And the commission is realistic about the fact that the U.S. public and the allies demand significant arms control efforts. More specifically, the commission argues that future arms control negotiations "may help to reduce the risks of advances in anti-submarine and anti-satellite warfare, for unconstrained developments in these areas are likely to have seriously destabilizing effects."

On current treaties and negotiations, commissioners see possible renegotiation of the antiballistic missile pact "to permit hard-point defense," in the course of a restructuring of U.S. land-based nuclear forces. On the SALT II agreement, commissioners divide into three basic option groups: revising and extending the SALT II agreement into a mutually acceptable SALT III treaty; replacing SALT II with a more modest agreement; or ratifying a minimally-amended treaty as a step toward negotiating further limitations under SALT III. Treaties and negotiations which are deadlocked or no longer pertinent should be shelved. "For example, there is no point in pursuing naval limitations in the Indian Ocean (where the United States is required for the indefinite future to maintain major forces to meet regional contingencies)." The commission also argues that it is not realistic to "expect to negotiate limits on conventional arms transfers while broader understandings about restraint in regional conflicts are missing." It calls for continuation of the Mutual and Balanced Force Reduction talks in Vienna as a useful forum for contact between NATO and Warsaw Pact countries. But it calls for suspension of the Comprehensive Test Ban negotiations, "at least until the United States can review its nuclear needs." Finally, the commission believes that efforts to limit the spread of nuclear weapons under the Non-Proliferation Treaty have been encouraging, and continued U.S.-Soviet cooperation in this area is recommended.[27] The Commission, it seems, prefers to take two steps back for every step forward.

Of the commission members, two are listed in the Kennedy-Hatfield book as supporters of their freeze resolution: Millicent Fenwick and Stanley Hoffman.

The CFR commission addresses policy toward the Third World in a section titled "Conflict in Third Areas" which assumes that trouble in so-called third areas "constitutes the most frequent and most likely source of confrontation" between the U.S. and USSR. Commissioners call for flexible policies, recognizing that "much of the turmoil is, at least in the first instance, indigenous and unrelated to Soviet actions." But the Soviets still get the blame for fanning the flames and serve as the ever-ready enemy for propaganda purposes. The U.S. population is not likely to approve of intervention in the Third World to defend the freedom of multinational corporations.

"As a world power," says the commission, "the United States no doubt has some degree of interest almost anywhere." But the U.S. "cannot and should not involve itself—at least militarily—wherever adverse trends appear." What's lacking are established priorities for U.S. "involvement" (read "intervention"). The Persian Gulf has the highest priority, but the commission is divided on whether to stop short of stationing combat troops permanently in the area (relying on a regional infrastructure for the Rapid Deployment Force, de facto security relationships with friendly states, naval forces in the Indian Ocean, etc.). There is no attempt to rank other "third areas" of U.S. interest in Africa, Southeast Asia, and the Western hemisphere. Rather there is a general call for the U.S. to "again be ready and able to use military force in unstable or threatened regions," as a last resort, of course. Using verbal subterfuge, covert action is included with political, economic, and diplomatic activity in the non-force category. The commission doesn't adhere to the "for or against us" criteria of the right: "We should not be reluctant to support local political forces ready to keep Soviet influence to a minimum, even when they are not vocally anti-Communist or pro-United States."[28]

While the CFR commission begs the question of defining priorities for selective intervention in the Third World, outside the Persian Gulf, Robert Tucker addresses it head on in his article, "The Purposes of American Power."

Limited Containment: Take II

Tucker's guide for limited or moderate containment is the ability to distinguish between "need" and "want." To illustrate, Tucker contrasts the case of the Persian Gulf with Central America.

The West "needs" Persian Gulf oil, says Tucker, and thus has a vital interest in countering any external Soviet moves in the area and safeguarding the *internal order* of pro-west regimes. That is, given a "need," it is perfectly okay for Washington to ignore the rights and desires of indigenous movements *within* countries and to impose its own aims instead. A very frank statement of imperial logic, indeed. Thus, ground troops should be stationed permanently in the region. Central America, on the other hand, is only a case of "want." Resources, not political or human rights is the stuff of Tucker's cost-benefit principles. Thus, Tucker argues that Central America has no vital resources which make it a legitimate security concern worth the risk of intervention. The U.S. "wants" Central America because of Central America's historic role in the U.S. sphere of influence—a sphere in which the U.S. by Tucker's frank admission "regularly played a determining role in making and unmaking governments." But, says Tucker:

> We have now passed the period of overthrowing an Arbenz in Guatemala [1954], when disposing of governments to which we took offense was a quite easy undertaking.[29]

Military superiority or no, the U.S. should keep hands off. The way to prevent post-Somoza Nicaragua and other radical regimes from following "in the footsteps of Cuba with intolerably close relations with the Soviet Union is to offer economic aid as an inducement." This, says Tucker, may be properly seen as a "euphemism for blackmail."[30] And, indeed, this was the policy of the Carter Administration when the Sandinistas came to power.

Yet, even from a purely imperialistic perspective a major problem with Tucker's cost-benefit containment is that his criteria of vital interest are themselves problematic. For there is no consensus as to what constitutes "need." For example, if oil is the vital resource which gives the U.S. a license based on "need" to intervene in the Middle East, then what about oil and potential oil in Mexico, Guatemala, and the Caribbean? Where some dismiss Southern Africa as strategically unimportant, others point to its uranium, gold, cobalt, and so forth and call it "the Persian Gulf of minerals."

We should also note, lest anyone think that Tucker's rule is "to each country according to their need"—and abundant U.S. grain is the rightful preserve of all countries who need it—that there are different rules for "great powers" and "small powers." As Tucker tells us, "the great object of American foreign policy ought to be the restoration of a more normal political world, a world in which those states possessing the elements of great power once again play the role their power entitles them to play."[31] Might does indeed make right in Tucker's world.

In a later article, "Trading Poland for the Gulf," Tucker argues that "the claim that Moscow has neither the right nor the need to intervene in Poland constitutes a denial of the Soviet Union's interest in Eastern Europe." Such a denial flies in the face of post-war "great power" reality. "The crises in Poland and the Persian Gulf," asserts Tucker, "invite comparison not only because in both instances the vital interests of a superpower are at stake but also because in both instances force may have to be employed to preserve these interests against movements that enjoy undoubted legitimacy." The United States may have to employ force against "movements that enjoy undoubted legitimacy?" Tucker freely speaks the conventionally unspeakable:

> American interests may be imperiled by contingencies other than an 'outside force' intent on gaining control of the Persian Gulf. As recent events have shown, it is plausible to assume that the more likely threat to Western interests in the Gulf will come from inside the region rather than outside...At any time, the United States may find itself confronted by a threat that follows from an action expressing the effective will of a people, an action otherwise recognized as within the domestic jurisdiction of the state.[32]

Tucker is a world-order power broker, not an ideologue. In contrast, Norman Podhoretz says that an "anti-communist strategy of containment" which aims for the "breakup of the Soviet empire" has "terrible risks," but they are risks worth taking.[33] Tucker says no, "In both Poland and the Persian Gulf, the issue today is above all one of order, not of justice." While the "postwar order, which is at hazard in the twin crises, has not been ideal" it compares favorably with the orders of the past and "We cannot know the consequences of bringing it down."[34] The right claims God on its side in its nuclearized crusade to vanquish the antiCapitalist. But Tucker dispenses with moral masquerades completely. The issue, he says—lest we believe the propaganda of the politicians—is "one of order, not of justice."

Relatively Liberal Containment

Advocates of liberal containment are the "doves" in today's foreign policy establishment spectrum. They want containment with minimal confrontation in U.S.-Soviet relations and maximum accommodation in U.S.-Third World relations. The liberal approach is to use reform to stave off or co-opt revolution and preserve Western dominance over the international economic system (in its subtler, neocolonial form). In the words of a Trilateral Commission report, *Towards a Renovated International System*, "A minimum of social justice and reform will be necessary for stability in the long run." Stability for the freedom of multinational economic intercourse, that is.

Two publications in particular stand as liberal counterparts to the works discussed above. The first is a 1980 *Foreign Policy* article by Robert Legvold, director of the CFR's Soviet Project, titled "Containment Without Confrontation." The other is a 1981 report by a panel on U.S.-Soviet Relations sponsored by the United Nations Association of the U.S.A. First, the Legvold thesis.

Legvold argues that "An effective Soviet policy must proceed on two tracks:"

> one of firmness, military strength (but not by seeking military superiority), and a will to act (requiring a public readied for the possibility); the other of cooperation, the extended hand, and a renewed interest in dealing with problems jointly rather than in turning problems against each other.[35]

More specifically, the latter track emphasizes arms control as central to national security policy and calls for cooperation in economic policy and a "serious attempt to open the one area of detente that never got started, namely, crisis management." The military track calls for "a reinstated draft, real progress on NATO's long-term defense program, an effective Rapid Deployment Force, and, as lesser priorities, a solution to the vulnerability of land-based intercontinental ballistic missiles and a response to new Soviet theatre nuclear weapons," and the strengthening of U.S. military power in the Persian Gulf region.

Legvold's "containment without confrontation" position is hardly nonconfrontationalist. Like most strategists in the "politically relevant spectrum," he supports military assistance to the Afghan resistance to "draw the line" against such interventions in the future. Legvold doesn't offer criteria for intervention in the Third World. But he poses a series of rhetorical questions (based on particular assumptions a set of which, as with other direct quotes of this sort, I refrain from systematically refuting in the limited space of this article) which continue to be debated in elite circles today:

> ...what realistic limits are Americans shooting for? The United States will seek to deter further Afghanistans, obviously—that is, no more military invasions to make or save 'revolutions.' Presumably as well, any further joint Soviet-Cuban expeditions to force the outcome in fluid settings such as Angola are unacceptable. But will Americans oppose support for so-called freedom fighters such as the Patriotic Front in preindependent Zimbabwe; or intriguing with groups such as the Sandinistas in Nicaragua? Will U.S. policy oppose Soviet intervention even where, in effect, international norms are being upheld, as in the Horn of Africa?[36]

The United Nations Association of the U.S.A. (UNA-USA) Panel makes more extensive and specific recommendations than Legvold's article. The report, *US-Soviet Relations: A Strategy for the '80s,* represents "a broad consensus of the diverse perspectives of the Panel members."[37] The Panel was headed by William Scranton, former UN Ambassador and Governor of Pennsylvania and a member of the CFR and Trilateral Commission executive committee, and included representatives from business, academia, media, and former government and military officials. (The Chair of the UNA-USA National Council is former Secretary of State Cyrus Vance; UNA-USA chair is former Attorney General Elliot Richardson.[38])

The UNA-USA report argues that in strengthening U.S. military power "choices must be selective, because America's financial, manpower, and production resources are limited." The "readiness" of conventional armed forces to carry out missions around the world is singled out as the most "important and pervasive weakness" in the U.S. military posture. The familiar key is rapid deployment: "In the 1980s—a decade likely to be characterized by sudden and unpredictable events affecting US interests in distant parts of the world—US forces should be flexible and mobile." In classical liberal containment language, the report adds: "This does not mean that the U.S. should necessarily adopt a more interventionist foreign and military policy." It should just be ready to intervene where "necessary."

The panel calls on the Reagan Administration to "reassess the personnel policies of the US armed services" and to "analyze alternative forms of mandatory national service," noting that the reinstitution of a peace-time draft "would have the advantages of cost-savings and better-educated recruits, but would raise grave political problems."

According to the report, the U.S. faces three basic sets of security problems:

> (1) to deter nuclear and nonnuclear attacks or coercion through credible threats against the U.S. and its allies in Western Europe and the Western Pacific;
> (2) to offer sufficient assistance to friendly states elsewhere to assure their defense against aggression or coercion; and,
> (3) to secure access to essential resources overseas, especially to Persian Gulf oil, and to protect the sea lanes as conduits for commercial and naval traffic.

The panel bases its recommendations on an assumption which is controversial even among panel members: "While deterring a nuclear attack against the United States and its closest allies is essential for national survival, it is at the same time the least likely contingency to confront the U.S. and the one for which its forces are best prepared."[39]

Nonetheless, the report urges the U.S. to continue strengthening NATO forces, "including the development and deployment of cruise missiles and Pershing II missiles, while pursuing balanced agreements to limit conventional and nuclear forces in the European theatre." It agrees Western Europe and Japan should spend more on the military, and it gives Japan some extra attention. "Japan," says the report, "with a gross national product close to that of the Soviet Union, has the potential to play a pivotal role in shaping the future of Asia." Since "it would be unproductive to attempt to pressure the Japanese into assuming a military posture for which their public is not prepared"—not to mention other Asian nations—the U.S. should encourage Japan to use its "economic strength to bolster Western security interests in other ways—by giving greater economic aid to Turkey and Pakistan for example." The report might have added South Korea, since it goes on to state that country's importance to U.S. security. Interestingly enough, the panel calls on the U.S. to "encourage South Korean leaders to pay greater respect to basic human rights so that the society can resume its earlier path toward a more democratic form of government."[40] It doesn't mention the autocratic leaders of Pakistan and Turkey.

In a section on "Soviet-American Rivalry in Third Areas," the UNA-USA panel warns that "dynamic indigenous forces for change, such as Islamic nationalism in the Near East, decolonization in Africa, and political radicalization in Central America, continue to develop largely beyond Soviet and American control....A dangerous disjunction is thus developing between the great powers' growing interests and rivalry in the Third World and their decreasing ability to control events in these areas." The panel assigns the U.S. some of the responsibility for this growing rivalry in "third areas." The U.S. should increase foreign economic assistance and adopt more flexible and pragmatic political policies "to lessen the opportunities for Soviet involvement." The U.S. should also be "raising the costs to the Soviet Union of intervening." A successful policy toward the Third World "depends upon identifying where real U.S. and Western interests are involved and when American involvement is likely to yield positive results."

This requires distinguishing between leftist regimes whose behavior is inimical to Western interests and those with parallel interests; between Soviet-aided but indigenously controlled movements and Soviet-dominated forces lacking genuine roots in the local society; and, finally, between pro-Western regimes whose stable and responsive governments make them potentially reliable partners and those whose days are numbered because they are out of touch with the needs of their own people.

Unfortunately, no examples are given. Is this criteria applicable in Central America, which, according to the panel, has along with parts of Africa and the Persian Gulf "gained immense strategic importance" due to "abundant oil and natural gas resources"?[41] The rights and desires of indigenous peoples are always balanced against the economic and strategic claims of the United States, on the one hand, and the costs of intervention versus reform on the other.

When it comes to arms control the UNA-USA panel takes a generally positive and pragmatic view:

The economic burden of the continuing arms race is becoming prohibitive for both countries. As both now stand on the threshold of a new generation of even more destructive weapons, the responsibility for pursuing consultations aimed at preventing a direct Soviet-American military confrontation becomes impelling.[42]

The panel argues that since the SALT II Treaty will not be ratified by the present U.S. government, talks should be undertaken to modify it in a mutually acceptable manner. "In the long term," says the report, "SALT discussions could focus on more effective qualitative limitations as well as on deeper quantitative reductions." The panel urges continuing negotiations on limiting antisatellite weapons, and on limiting theatre nuclear forces and pursuing mutual and balanced force reduction in Europe. It further urges renewed efforts to discourage nuclear proliferation, ratification by the U.S. of the Threshold Test Ban Treaty and the Treaty on Underground Nuclear Explosives for Peaceful Purposes, continuing negotiations on a Comprehensive Test Ban, and U.S. participation in multilateral efforts to limit chemical weapons, radiological weapons, and "especially injurious conventional weapons," and in arms control discussions at the United Nations.[43]

One Step Forward, Two Steps Back?

Since the writing of the reports discussed above, the Reagan Administration has undertaken the START talks. A significant number of non-rightwingers in the "politically relevant spectrum" have shifted somewhat to the left on strategic issues, prompted by genuine fear of first strike bellicosity, the economic disaster of an insatiable military budget, and last but not least, political expediency. Four establishmentarians have called on the U.S. to embrace a policy of no first use of nuclear weapons (McGeorge Bundy, former Ford Foundation President and National Security Adviser; George Kennan, former Ambassador to the Soviet Union and Yugoslavia; Robert McNamara, former President of the World Bank and Secretary of Defense; and Gerard Smith, chief negotiator of SALT I and North American Chair of the Trilateral Commission).[44] According to one observer, the majority response to no-first-use within the establishment, "official and otherwise, has been unambiguously negative," and the NATO foreign ministers officially re-endorsed the first-use strategy option in May 1982.[45]

The most far-reaching initiative with backing in the politically-elected establishment is, of course, the Kennedy-Hatfield Freeze Resolution. Since the writing of the UNA-USA report discussed above, with its generally pro-arms control stance, a grass-roots disarmament movement has injected a strong measure of popular urgency into the arms control debate. The freeze is rooted in that well-deserved sense of urgency. In mid-1979, former nuclear weapons engineer Robert Aldridge warned: "Time is short. All of these first-strike programs will be in or near production by 1982 or 1983....So the next three years are crucial—either we halt this momentum toward genocide or nuclear cremation will strike again."[46]

We must work to turn back the momentum toward a first-strike, and we must work to turn back the march toward "limited nuclear war" in Europe and the Third World. But we will not succeed by supporting "instead" a conventional arms buildup and globe-trotting rapid deployment forces.

When Kennedy and Hatfield discuss the secondary goals of a freeze, they contend:

> A freeze will also help to strengthen our economy and other areas of our national defense, both of which have heavily suffered from neglect and from the cost of this nuclear buildup. The $90 billion that a freeze alone could save in the next five years could be spent on conventional defenses and domestic priorities.[47]

In fact, as Michael Klare points out in the discussion of nuclear-conventional linkage addressed earlier, some 85 percent of Reagan's "defense" buildup involves conventional and inter-ventionary forces.[48] Conventional weapons are part of the problem—not the solution. Kennedy and Hatfield would tame the fires of militarism with one hand, and feed them with the other.

Within the "politically relevant spectrum" there is consensus on two things: one, the "readiness" of conventional forces must be improved, and two, the Persian Gulf region is of vital strategic importance. Ted Kennedy (the more liberal of the duo) does not dissent from this consensus. In a recent op. ed. piece in the *New York Times*, Kennedy argues that "Soviet control of Iran would be the most serious strategic defeat for the West since World War II."[49] In the interest of finishing this essay I have to forego a discussion of the assumptions underlying Kennedy's Cold War view of events and concentrate on the implications of his policy recommendations.[50] Kennedy argues that the Soviet Union is likely to achieve domination through political rather than military means and "American military precautions are a last resort to be possibly invoked if diplomacy fails; they are no substitute for the political, economic and social ties that constitute the best guarantee of Gulf stability." In 1980, Jimmy Carter announced that U.S. interests in the Gulf would be defended by force if necessary. Kennedy agrees. Carter did not preclude nuclear force. Does Kennedy?

Kennedy describes the basic elements of "a coherent overall strategy for the entire Middle East" this way: "that means opposition to the extremism of the Libyan leader Muammar el-Qaddafi and Palestine Liberation Organization terrorism, rebuilding Lebanon physically and politically, and making progress on the Palestinian issue in accord with the mandate and vision of Camp David. It also means working to end the Iran-Iraq war and coming to grips with the external and internal issues plaguing the Gulf." Let's leave aside the question of PLO participation in resolving the 'Palestinian problem" and the meaning of "rebuilding Lebanon physically and politically" (along with the other issues such as Israel's role as an arms supplier to Iran) and take up Camp David's conventional corollary.

Writing in March 1982, before the Israeli invasion of Lebanon, Klare observed that as part of the Camp David Treaty package, the U.S. "would supply Egypt and Israel with an additional $4.5 billion worth of sophisticated arms and military services, over and above the $1.5 billion annual military subsidy already promised those countries....These and other recent arms transactions, have boosted U.S. weapons exports to record levels, and helped fuel an increasingly precarious arms race in the Middle East. And, unless some unforseen developments contribute to a reduction of tensions in the area, it is only all too likely that Carter's and Reagan's 'peace offerings' will sooner or later be unsheathed for war."[51] And, indeed, they were. In the wake of Israel's military victory, Syria and the other Arab states will rush to narrow the vast technological gap exposed by the fighting in Lebanon even as they pursue a peace plan Washington can accept.

A viable disarmament policy must deal with both ends of the conventional/nuclear war spectrum. And it must deal with both ends of the nuclear fuel cycle. That means nuclear energy as well as nuclear weapons and it means the role of multinational corporations in all stages of the nuclear fuel cycle from the mining of uranium on Indian lands in the United States or in Namibia, to the export of reprocessing technology, to the dumping of nuclear waste in the fishing grounds of Pacific islanders. Bechtel Corporation offers a case in point.

Much has been heard about the Bechtel-White House connection and the Bechtel-Middle East connection. Secretary of State Shultz is former president of the Bechtel Group, Secretary of Defense Weinberger is former vice-president and general counsel, Special Middle East Envoy Philip Habib is currently consultant with Bechtel along with former CIA Director and Ambassador to Iran Richard Helms. Less well known is the fact that Deputy Secretary of Energy W. Kenneth Davis is Bechtel's former vice-president for nuclear development (before that Davis was the Atomic Energy Commission's director of reactor development). With Davis back inside the government, Bechtel is pushing the administration—successfully—to loosen nuclear nonproliferation restrictions on plutonium reprocessing and nuclear sales abroad.[52]

On the first day of George Shultz's confirmation hearings, his Bechtel ties were raised in a critical light by some members of the Senate Foreign Relations Committee, mainly in suspicious regard to Shultz's attitude toward Israel and the Arab nations. But the next day, according to the *New York Times,* Senator Paul Tsongas "declared without anyone's dissenting that 'the Bechtel issue is a nonissue'." Tsongas is a front-running neoliberal and an endorser of the nuclear freeze. At the hearings Tsongas endorsed Bechtel, saying "he had a father-in-law and brother-in-law who worked for Bechtel and he had decided that it was 'a remarkable company,' without any particular political orientation and 'for a major company that is a plus.'" (Funny thing—the Bechtel Foundation has given money to such right-wing groups as the Heritage Foundation and anti-environmentalist Pacific Legal Foundation; perhaps its grants to the Trilateral Commission, American Enterprise Institute and Georgetown University Center for Strategic and International Studies give it the neutrality Tsongas applauds.)[53]

Guns, Butter, and Business

In 1979, *Business Week* asserted:

If the decline in U.S. power is to be arrested, the trend toward spending a smaller share of the federal budget on defense must be reversed, and economic policy must change in a way that encourages investment at the expense of consumption.[54]

The guns and butter debate is back on the table, this time with less butter and more guns.

A 5-year, 1.6 trillion dollar military budget—before cost overruns—is more than as big as it sounds. It's been calculated to equal "a year's worth of all the goods and services—the combined Gross National Products—of Latin America, Australia, Africa, Southeast Asia, and India, plus all the oil produced in the Middle East."[55] Pentagon officals see higher target budgets of up to 1.9 trillion dollars. While that may be good for military contractors and the military arms of major corporations, it's not seen as good for the corporate economy generally.

Reagan's magic show was supposed to cut taxes, hike military spending, balance the budget, and stimulate the economy. The real world didn't behave. Business investors are soaking up cash from the banks to conduct their merger wars; unemployment, business bankruptcies, and farm foreclosures are at post-war highs; the federal deficit is soaring; and Wall Street is jumping up and down in the largest leaps since 1929. Having gotten much of the wage roll-backs, social welfare cuts, deregulation, and tax breaks they wanted, corporate influentials (from the Business Council to the National Association of Manufacturers) are now taking aim at Social Security (and other middle class "entitlement" programs) as well as the military budget.

In a recent special report on "Guns Vs. Butter," *Business-Week* argues that "The crisis is so severe that it is no longer the old problem of giving up one for the other, but of giving up a lot of both." *Business Week* goes on to assert that "a consensus is emerging among elected officials, business leaders, and other influential citizens [not to mention ordinary people] that the enormous increases the Reagan Administration is asking for—almost doubling the budget over the next five years—can be cut back substantially without weakening the nation's defense." Not too substantially, of course. Among *Business Week's* recommendations: put a cap on spending increases (after inflation) of perhaps 5%; cancel the MX and forgo any antiballistic missile system which would accompany it; cancel the Navy's two Nimitz class aircraft carriers; drop the Air Force's F-18 and maybe the B-1 bomber also; consider dropping the Army's M-1 tank. More controversial is the suggestion to consider abandoning the land-air-water strategic Triad and relying on air/space and water-based missiles. *Business Week* would bet our money on an even higher-tech military revolving around "smart missiles" with "one-shot, one-kill" capability; relatively invulnerable Trident subs, stealth technology to make weapons invisible to radar, and space lasers.[56]

The *Business Week* approach isn't safer—just ostensibly more cost effective. Indeed, each technological leap brings new dangers. Take the Stealth bomber for example:

> 'There is no one today who has the slightest idea of how to win a war without radar,' declares Stansfield Turner, a retired four-star admiral and former Central Intelligence Agency Director. But 'with Stealth technologies, radar may not be useful anymore.' It could 'mean a revolution in warfare.'[57]

The world can't afford another "revolution in warfare" from which there may be no return. The country can't afford the current military budget, much less real growth in spending of five percent.

Studies have shown that military spending is certainly not good for the economic health of the rest of us; boosts in military spending lead to a net jobs loss, not a jobs gain as we often hear.[58] There is one big exception, of course. Military spending is good for jobs in the military. The unemployment draft has joined the poverty draft to make the local armed forces recruiting station a thriving enterprise. "The recession," says the *New York Times*, "has all but made the armed services a major American job program.''[59] Numbers are up, quality is up, and the worries of the all-volunteer (sic) army are down. President Reagan's Military Manpower Task Force recently reported there would be no need for a draft in the foreseeable future because enough qualified enlistees were signing on. One recruiter explains that among his more qualified volunteers are "young men who had dropped out of college because their money had run out.''[60] Social welfare cutbacks are good for the military in more ways than one.

Conclusion

The Pentagon would give us jobs with war. There is a growing campaign for Jobs with Peace. In the 1982 election Jobs with Peace referenda—calling for an increase in spending on social services paid for by a reduction in unnecessary military spending—passed in all 50-plus cities and towns where they were on the ballot with an average yes-vote of 66 percent (from Baltimore, to Pittsburgh, to San Jose).

U.S. soldiers might well be fighting another war—this one in El Salvador—if not for strong public opposition. Popular protest has kept U.S. intervention in Central America on a leash, but the leash is getting longer with dangerous increments of military aid, advisers, and covert operations. The Pentagon may never take the politically explosive and militarily costly step of sending U.S. ground forces to the region. Still a regional war is being ignited. We must redouble our anti-intervention efforts.

What if the Iranian Revolution were happening today? Would the movement against U.S. intervention be strong enough, or would the Cold Warriors prevail? The nuclear tripwires of the Middle East must be short-circuited. And southern Africa cannot be seen as the "Persian Gulf of minerals." The U.S. public must demand a reappraisal of Washington's "needs" as well as its "wants." People around the world are demanding self-determination, an so should the people of the United States. Without a just international order there will be no peace—and no survival.

Work for a nuclear freeze, nuclear and conventional disarmament, and a non-interventionist foreign policy must go hand in hand with the pursuit of justice and equality at home.

Democracy means rule by the common people and practice of the principle of equality of rights, opportunity, and treatment. In the United States today inequality, racism, sexism, and anti-unionism have all gained renewed respectability along with militarism. Blaming the victim has become a favorite pastime of the privileged. People of color and women are blamed for their disproportionate levels of poverty, unemployment, and under-employment. Workers are blamed for plant shutdowns and runaway shops. Average citizens are blamed for not spending the country out of recession and for not luring business to invest with greater and greater tax breaks and giveaways.

Enough is enough. Today in the United States, the richest country in the world which exploits and consumes most of the world's resources, one out of seven people are poor—most are women and children. Unemployment is nearing 11 percent for all workers, and not predicted to go much lower for years to come. For people of color—from the ghettos of the cities, to the reservation/*bantustans* of Native Americans to the last of the struggling small farmers—this is a depression. This is obscene.

In a forthcoming pamphlet on "Poverty in the American Dream," a Black mother of two tells how her job as a Vista organizer of food and nutrition programs was eliminated by the Reagan Administration and how she has struggled to make ends meet:

> I couldn't take it anymore. My welfare check and food stamps were cut and I had to choose between paying the rent or buying food and school clothes for my growing boys... I went down and enlisted in the army. It's my last chance to try and support my family.[61]

That is the poverty draft in action. The system at work there is obscene.

In the days ahead there will be much tactical manuevering as longtime disarmament activists and newer advocates of capping defense spending attempt to achieve legislative victories. It must be remembered that the goals of each are different. It must be remembered that the strength of the peace movement cannot be measured in increments of "respectability" doled out at the level of elite opinion, but in the vitality of grassroots activism which forces political elites to pay heed.

The introduction to *Southern Exposure's* "Waging Peace" issue provides an appropriate concluding perspective:

> The policies of our current government have one end product in common: death. Its military policies— including direct intervention, military aid to repressive governments, sales of armaments by the government and corporations—kill people directly. The domestic policies kill people by taking away food, housing, health, jobs,...the means of life....With "Waging Peace" we intend to help build links between the committed members of the traditional peace groups and people from this much wider range of constituencies, including people from civil rights, women's, religious, neighborhood and workers' organizations. Through a self-conscious process of cooperation, the advocates of international peace can build the organizations and thinking that can defeat those who are taking our communities and our nation down the path to the last war.[62]

Notes

1. Jonathan Schell, *The Fate of the Earth* (Knopf: New York, 1982), p. 21.
2. *Washington Post*, 17 July 1981; *New York Times* 30 May 1982.
3. *New York Times*, 17 October 1982, first of three articles on the space buildup by Richard Halloran.
4. Thomas Powers, "Choosing a Strategy for World War III," *Atlantic Monthly*, November 1982, p. 110.
5. *Ibid.*, pp. 86, 91.
6. Paul Joseph, "From MAD to NUTS: The Growing Danger of Nuclear War," *Socialist Review* No. 61 (Jan.-Feb. 1982).
7. Senator Edward M. Kennedy and Senator Mark O. Hatfield, *Freeze! How You Can Help Prevent Nuclear War* (Bantam: N.Y., 1982), pp. 132, 142.
8. Michael Klare, "A Nuclear Freeze Isn't Enough," *The Nation*, 25 Sept. 1982, p. 264.
9. La Rocque appeared on CBS Special Report on the Falklands/Malvinas, "Winner and Losers," 15 June 1982. Also see Alexander Cockburn and James Ridgeway, "The Lessons of HMS Sheffield," *Village Voice*, 18 May 1982.
10. Klare, op. cit. Also see "Killer Electronic Weaponry," *Business Week*, 20 Sept. 1982, pp. 74-84.
11. For an analysis of ties between South Africa, Argentina, and other Southern Cone Regimes, their relations with the United States, and the implications of the Falklands/Malvinas war, see Paul Horowitz and Holly Sklar, "South Atlantic Triangle," *NACLA Report on the Americas* XVI: 3 (May-June 1982). Also see Nicholas Burnett, "The Israel-South Africa Connection," *The Nation*, 20 May 1978; and *New York Times*, 13 March 1981 and 13 December 1981.
12. On Sharon's Namibia visit see *New York Times*, 14 December 1981. For continuing coverage of South African occupation of an intervention in Namibia and Angola, see *Southern Africa* magazine, *Africa News* weekly, and reports by the American Committee on Africa (N.Y.), Washington Office on Africa and TransAfrica (Wash. D.C.).
13. "The Decline of U.S. Power," *Business Week*, 12 March 1979, p. 74.
14. *Ibid.* p. 40-41.
15. List of nuclear threats compiled by Daniel Ellsberg in E.P. Thompson and Dan Smith, eds., *Protest and Survive* (Monthly Review Press: N.Y., 1981), p. v-vi.
16. See Michael Klare, *Beyond the "Vietnam Syndrome": U.S. Interventionism in the 1980s* (Institute for Policy Studies: Wash D.C., 1981). Also see Sidney Lens, *The Day Before Doomsday: An Anatomy of the Nuclear Arms Race* (Beacon Press: Boston, 1977), pp. 23-24.

17. The phrase "crisis of democracy" comes from the most famous of Trilateral Commission reports, *The Crisis of Democracy: Report on the Governability of Democracies to the Trilateral Commission* by Michael Crozier, Samuel Huntington, and Jojo Watanuki (NYU: N.Y., 1975). For an analysis of this report and trilateralist strategies for the '70s and '80s, see Holly Sklar, ed., *Trilateralism: The Trilateral Commission and Elite Planning for World Management* (South End Press: Boston, 1980).

18. Dimitri K. Simes, "Disciplining Soviet Power," *Foreign Policy*, Summer 1981, p. 33.

19. Norman Podhoretz, "The Future Danger," *Commentary* April 1981, p. 32.

20. *Ibid.* p. 45.

21. Norman Podhoretz, "The Neo-Conservative Anguish Over Reagan's Foreign Policy," *New York Times Magazine*, 2 May 1982, p. 88.

22. Jeane Kirkpatrick, "Dictatorships and Double Standards," *Commentary*, November 1979, p. 44.

23. *Ibid.* p. 40.

24. Jeane Kirkpatrick, "U.S. Security and Latin America," *Commentary*, Jan. 1981, p. 34.

25. Alan Crawford, *Thunder on the Right: The "New Right" and the Politics of Resentment* (Pantheon: N.Y., 1980), p. 43; *New York Times* 2 October 1981 and 6 January 1982.

26. Zbigniew Brzezinski, "Looking Back—and Forward," *Trialogue* No. 25 (Winter 1980-81), p. 17; "What's Wrong With Reagan's Foreign Policy" *New York Times Magazine*, 6 December 1981; "A Conversation with Zbigniew Brzezinski," *Bill Moyers Journal, WNET/Thirteen*, N.Y., 14 November 1980.

27. *The Commission on U.S. Soviet Relations, The Soviet Challenge: A Policy Framework for the 1980s* (Council on Foreign Relations: N.Y., 1981), pp. 11-17.

28. *Ibid.* pp. 18-22, on "conflict in third areas."

29. Robert Tucker, "The Purposes of American Power," *Foreign Affairs* 59:2 (Winter 1980-81), p. 271.

30. *Ibid.* p. 272.

31. *Ibid.* p. 273.

32. Robert Tucker, "Trading Poland for the Gulf," *Harpers*, April 1981, p. 17.

33. Podhoretz, "The Future Danger," op. cit. p. 47.

34. Tucker, "Trading Poland for the Gulf," op. cit. p. 18.

35. Robert Legvold, "Containment Without Confrontation," *Foreign Policy*, Fall 1980, p. 93.

36. *Ibid.* p. 89.

37. United Nations Association—USA National Policy Panel on US-Soviet Relations, *US-Soviet Relations: A Strategy for the '80s* (United Nations Association of the United States: N.Y., 1981), p. 2.

38. Vance served on the Independent Commission on Disarmamanet and Security Issues, *Common Security: A Blueprint for Survival* (Simon & Schuster: N.Y., 1982). Commissioners came from the Soviet Union and Third World countries as well as the West.

39. See *US-Soviet Relations*, pp. 45-48 for quotes.

40. *Ibid.* pp. 36-39, on NATO and Japan.

41. *Ibid.* pp. 32-33, on "third areas."

42. *Ibid.* p. 1.

43. *Ibid.* pp. 52-55.

44. McGeorge Bundy, George F. Kennan, Robert S. McNamara, Gerard Smith, "Nuclear Weapons and the Atlantic Alliance," *Foreign Affairs*, Spring 1982.

45. Jonathan Dean, "Beyond First Use," *Foreign Policy*, Fall 1982, p. 37. Also see Karl Kaiser, Georg Leber, Alois Mertes, Franz-Josef Schulze, "Nuclear Weapons and the Preservation of Peace: A German Response to an American Proposal for Renouncing the First Use of Nuclear Weapons," and General David Jones, Earl Ravenal, et. al., "The Debate Over No First Use," *Foreign Affairs*, Summer 1982.

46. Robert C. Aldridge, *First Strike*, (South End Press: Boston, 1983).

47. Kennedy and Hatfield, *Freeze!*, p. 133.

48. Klare, "A Nuclear Freeze Isn't Enough," p. 266.

49. Edward M. Kennedy, "Seeking More Stability in the Persian Gulf," *New York Times*, op. ed., 15 September 1982.

50. Fred Halliday critiques the Cold War view behind U.S. policy in Afghanistan, the Middle East, and the Horn of Africa, and analyzes Soviet policy in the region in *Soviet Policy in the Arc of Crisis* (Institute for Policy Studies: Washington D.C., 1981). Also see Klare, *Beyond the Vietnam Syndrome*, op. cit., and Alan Wolfe, *The Rise and Fall of the Soviet Threat* (Institute for Policy Studies: Wash D.C., 1981).

51. Michael Klare, "The Global Arms Trade," *New Catholic World*, March/April 1982.

52. William Greider, "The Boys From Bechtel: Will Ronald Reagan Reverse U.S. Policy on Nuclear Nonproliferation?" *Rolling Stone*, 2 September 1982.

53. *New York Times*, 15 July 1982. For more on Bechtel, see Mark Dowie, "The Bechtel File," *Mother Jones*, September/October 1978; "Bechtel: A Reclusive Giant," "Bechtel and Its Link to Reagan," and "Bechtel Orchestrates Building of New Saudi City," in *New York Times*, respectively,

8 July 1982, 5 December 1980, and 13 February 1978. Also see Senate Foreign Relations Committee, hearings on the nomination of Geroge Shultz as Secretary of State, July 1982

54. "The Decline of U.S. Power," *Business Week*, p. 37.

55. "Defense, Dissent and the Dollar," *Bill Moyers Journal*, transcript, WNET/Thirteen, New York, 8 May 1981, p. 1.

56. "Guns Vs. Butter," *Business Week*, 29 November 1982, pp. 68-76, 120.

57. *Ibid.*, p. 73.

58. See, for example, Marion Anderson, "Neither Jobs Nor Security: Women's Unemployment and the Pentagon Budget" and "The Empty Pork Barrel: Unemployment and the Pentagon Budget," 1982 edition, from Employment Research Associates, Lansing, Michigan.

59. *New York Times*, 13 October 1982.

60. *Ibid.* 19 October 1982.

61. Barbara Ehrenreich and Karin Stallard, *Poverty in the American Dream—Women and Children First*, forthcoming Spring 1983 from the Institute for New Communications and South End Press.

62. Marc Miller, Introduction to "Waging Peace," *Southern Exposure*, November/December 1982, p. 2.

7

WHAT DIRECTIONS
FOR THE
DISARMAMENT MOVEMENT?
INTERVENTIONISM
AND NUCLEAR WAR
By Noam Chomsky

*Noam Chomsky is a long time peace activist, a writer
and a professor of linguistics at M.I.T. in Cambridge,
Massachusetts. He was a tireless contributor to the
anti-Vietnam War movement, and has remained
active in the effort to preserve the history of the period
in the face of "mainstream" attempts to obscure the
truth by a "rewritten history." He regularly speaks and
writes concerning contemporary problems of U.S.
foreign policy, international affairs, and human rights
and is currently completing a book dealing with
Israeli/U.S/Palestinian relations. Chomsky has written many other articles and books about international
relations including, most recently,* Toward A New
Cold War *(Pantheon: N.Y., 1982) and the two volume
study* The Political Economy of Human Rights *with
Edward Herman (South End Press: Boston, 1979).*

Within the disarmament movement a central focus of debate has revolved for some time around the issue of interventionism. How much emphasis should disarmament activists place on opposition to U.S. intervention in El Salvador and throughout Latin America? Should they address the Israeli invasion of Lebanon? South African incursions into Namibia? U.S. complicity in Honduran attacks on the Nicaraguan Sandinistas? Or are these focuses distractions from the more ultimate danger—nuclear war? Should disarmament activists seek reductions of conventional weapons or solely of nuclear weaponry?

As we write this brief introduction, The Union of Concerned Scientists is circulating a movie, "No First Use," that argues in favor of expanding conventional armaments in order to minimize the risk of getting forced by military defeat into starting a nuclear war. Other disarmament activists argue that to expand any part of the military establishment is to increase the likelihood of so-called small wars, especially in the Third World. This they see as immoral in its own right, contradictory to a concern for peace, and counterproductive to the effort to diminish the likelihood of nuclear incineration.

Noam Chomsky's contribution is a succinct and compelling argument that disarmament activism will be ineffectual without an anti-interventionist emphasis.

—M.A. & D.D.

The recent growth of concern over the danger of nuclear war has been dramatic and impressive. It is also eminently realistic. Any rational person who considers the scale and character of contemporary military power, the current vast expansion of military arsenals of the superpowers, and the proliferation of armaments throughout the world, would surely have to conclude that the likelihood of a global catastrophe is not small.

One might argue, in fact, that it is a miracle that the catastrophe has not yet occurred. From November 1946 to October 1973, there were 19 incidents in which U.S. strategic nuclear forces were involved (we do not have the record since, nor the record for the USSR and other powers).[1] That means, to put it plainly, that every U.S. President regarded the use of nuclear weapons as a live policy option, a point that Daniel Ellsberg has emphasized. The examples are instructive. Here are a few:

1. In February 1947, long-range bombers assigned to the Strategic Air Command (SAC) were flown to Uruguay in a show of force at the time of the inauguration of the president of Uruguay.

2. In May 1954, SAC bombers were flown to Nicaragua as part of the background planning for the successful CIA coup in Guatemala in June.

3. In 1958, U.S. strategic nuclear forces were involved in the U.S. intervention in Lebanon. According to the report of one participant, the use of nuclear weapons was threatened if the Lebanese army attempted to resist. Rockets with nuclear warheads were available had fighting developed.[2]

4. In 1962, according to memoirs of participants, the "best and brightest" estimated the probability of nuclear war at one-third to one-half at the peak of the Cuban missile crisis, but were unwilling at that point to accept a settlement that would have resolved the crisis peaceably, with complete withdrawal of Russian missiles from Cuba. The barrier to this settlement in the view of Administration planners was that it entailed simultaneous withdrawal of U.S. missiles from Turkey—obsolete

missiles, for which a withdrawal order had already been issued (but not implemented) before the crisis erupted since they were being replaced by Polaris submarines. One analyst of the crisis aptly remarks:

> Never before had there been such a high probability that so many lives would end suddenly. Had war come, it could have meant the death of 100 million Americans, more than 100 million Russians, as well as millions of Europeans. Beside it, the natural calamities and in-humanities of earlier history would have faded into insignificance. Given the odds on disaster—which President Kennedy estimated as "between one out of three and even"—our escape seems awesome. This event symbolizes a central, if only partially "thinkable," fact about our existence.[3]

This surely must be one of the low points of human history. It is a fact of some significance that it is generally regarded here as a glorious moment, "one of the finest examples of diplomatic prudence, and perhaps the finest hour of John F. Kennedy's Presidency,"[4] to cite one of many examples.

Blechman and Kaplan conclude from this record that "In short, the United States has used nuclear threats sparingly"— only 19 times in the period surveyed—noting also that there were "215 incidents in which the United States employed its armed forces for political purposes between 1946 and 1975." They also observe that "Like Army ground troops deployed overseas, strategic nuclear forces serve vital political objectives on a continuous basis, perhaps thus obviating the need for discrete and explicit utilization," a cool and no doubt accurate evaluation.

We can learn a good deal by studying these 19 cases—and they are not the only ones when the use of nuclear weapons was seriously considered and possibly threatened.[5] Other powers have also issued nuclear threats, e.g., the USSR at the time of the Israeli-French-British invasion of Egypt in 1956, and apparently Israel in the early stages of the October 1973 war, when Egypt and Syria attacked the Israeli occupying army in the Sinai and

Golan Heights.[6] Furthermore, there have been numerous occasions when radar misidentifications, computer failures, or programming errors have produced false alarms of Soviet nuclear attack and only human intervention aborted the programmed reaction.[7] It is only reasonable to assume that the same (or worse) is true for the Soviet Union, and that the future will be even more hazardous than the past in these respects, as the time span for human intervention is reduced. Those who speak of the likelihood of nuclear war are hardly alarmists. To reduce this likelihood is imperative. The question is: What directions should such efforts take? How should energies be distributed if they are to be maximally effective in averting this catastrophe?

The primary question that should concern us is this: How is a nuclear war likely to break out? We may realistically assume that any military conflict between the superpowers (and others, in the not-too-distant future) will quickly become a nuclear conflict, and an unlimited one. While there are elaborate scenarios assuming the contrary, they can hardly be taken very seriously. The central questions, then, reduce to these: What are the likely sources of superpower conflict and what can be done to reduce the likelihood of such conflict?

Some years ago it was perhaps realistic to suppose that Europe was "the tinderbox," but such a judgment hardly appears accurate today.[8] If war does break out in Europe, it will probably be in reaction to conflicts arising elsewhere. Brutal repression will no doubt continue under Soviet rule, but it is extremely unlikely that it will lead to Western intervention; the day is long past when the U.S. was actively supporting guerrilla armies established by Hitler in the Carpathian mountains or attempting to carry out coups in Albania, as part of its "rollback strategy,"[9] though it may be that the Reagan Administration harbors dangerous fantasies on this score.[10] It is also hardly likely that the USSR would intervene within Western domains, even at or near its borders, any more than it has in the past: e.g., when the U.S. was engaged in destroying the former anti-Nazi resistance in Greece in the late 1940s, or backing the restoration of fascism in Greece in 1967, or supporting a ruthless military dictatorship in Turkey since 1980.[11] Nor is it likely that either superpower will launch a military attack in Europe, or that either will attack the other directly.[12] Judgments must necessarily be speculative, but prospects such as these appear to be highly remote contingencies. The attention they receive, in my opinion, reflects certain mythical elements in Cold War ideology to which I will return.

But war may very well break out elsewhere, engaging the superpowers. Possible examples, by no means remote eventualities, are all too numerous. Consider a few of the many cases, from recent and current history:

1. Secretary of the Navy John Lehman recently observed that a U.S. attempt to impose a blockade on Cuba and Nicaragua might lead to a U.S.-Soviet naval war. The navy "cannot conceive that a naval conflict which engaged Soviet forces could be localized," he stated; "It is instantaneously a global war." He added that he envisioned a conventional rather than nuclear war, but this is hardly credible.[13] These possibilities are not far removed. Since the summer of 1981, the U.S. has been conducting major war games and large-scale maneuvers in the Caribbean area, obviously aimed at Grenada, Cuba and Nicaragua. And only a strong public reaction in the U.S. prevented moves towards blockade and perhaps direct U.S. military intervention in El Salvador in the early months of the Reagan Administration, in my view.[14]

2. Turning to another part of the world, consider the 1979 Chinese invasion of Vietnam, surely with at least tacit U.S. backing. This might well have elicited a Russian response and U.S. countermoves, bringing the superpowers into conflict. A recurrence is not out of the question, with Vietnamese troops in Cambodia and the U.S. and China supporting Pol Pot as part of the policy of "bleeding Vietnam."[15]

3. Moving west, the U.S. is now committed to arming the military dictatorship of General Zia in Pakistan, allegedly to protect Pakistan from Soviet expansionism. It is difficult to imagine that the USSR would invade Pakistan, and if it were insane enough to do so, the arms being sent would hardly be a credible deterrent. The arms will very likely be used, however: for internal repression, as in the mid-1970s when U.S. equipment supplied by the Shah was used by the Pakistani army in attacking

the Baluch, who now appear somewhat ambivalent, not surprisingly, about the Soviet presence in Afghanistan. Interviewing the "triumvirate" of Baluch leaders, Selig Harrison found that each was thinking of the possibility of seeking Soviet support in response to U.S.-backed government repression: "If the Americans pump weapons into the Punjabis, obviously we have to stretch our hand to another superpower," one stated.[16] Further repression might well lead to a call for Soviet assistance, triggering renewed cries of a Soviet "march to the Gulf" and a U.S. reaction, leading to a superpower conflict. Arms to Pakistan also fuel the Indo-Pakistan arms race, with nuclear weapons on the horizon. It is also likely that the heavily-armed Pakistani military dictatorship will come to serve as part of the elaborate base structure for the U.S. Rapid Deployment Force, designed for intervention in the Middle East.[17] Meanwhile, Pakistani troops protect the Saudi monarchy against possible domestic insurgency.

4. The Iraqi invasion of Iran and the recent reversal of fortunes in Iran's favor have created a situation of great instability, in some ways reminiscent of Afghanistan in early 1978 before the Russians won that particular skirmish in the Great Game, but with much higher stakes and far greater dangers. The superpowers are no doubt maneuvering to pick up the pieces, and others are also hovering in the background, in particular, Israel, which sees it in its interest to break up Iraq into separate states and to press for a post-Khomeini military coup in Iran that will restore the Irano-Israeli alliance of earlier years.[18] U.S. support for the Turkish military dictatorship is motivated in part by plans to use Eastern Turkey as an intelligence center and a base for projection of American power in this region.[19] The USSR is presumably making similar preparations along its own southern border. Again, the possibility of a superpower conflict is not negligible.

5. It had been clear, certainly since mid-1981, that "Sooner or later, Israel will probably find a pretext for another invasion of Lebanon [following the 1978 invasion and the heavy bombardment in subsequent years] in an effort to administer the

coup de grace to the PLO and to disperse the [Palestinian] refugees once again."[20] Through early 1982, Israel appears to have attempted to provoke some PLO action that could serve as a pretext for the planned invasion, but without success.[21] When pretexts were not forthcoming, they were manufactured. In April, Israel bombed Lebanon with heavy civilian casualties after an Israeli soldier was killed by a mine—in southern Lebanon! The Israeli claim that this constituted a PLO "provocation" was, remarkably, accepted as plausible fairly generally in the U.S. The *Washington Post*, for example, responded editorially to the Israeli bombing of Lebanon as follows:

> So this is not the moment for sermons to Israel. It is a moment for respect for Israel's anguish—and for mourning the latest victims of Israeli-Palestinian hostility.[22]

The wording is typical: it is *Israel's* anguish that we must respect when Israel murders more Arabs,[23] victims not of Israeli bombing but of the more abstract "Israeli-Palestinian hostilities"; and the nature of the "provocation" merits no comment. Emboldened by this rather typical U.S. reaction, Israel responded to the attempt to assassinate Israeli Ambassador Shlomo Argov in London, apparently carried out by an Arab group that had been engaged in a running battle with the PLO for years, with additional heavy bombing in which many civilians were killed. The retaliatory PLO shelling of northern Israel then served as the long-awaited pretext for the outright invasion. The border had been quiet since the July 1981 cease-fire apart from Israeli actions, and the events leading to that cease-fire had also been provoked by Israeli military actions, breaking an earlier period of calm, a recurrent pattern.[24] Israel alleged that the June 1982 invasion was an exercise in "self-defense." In the *Jerusalem Post*, for example, Elmer Winter wrote that "Israel's decision to push the PLO back from the Israeli-Lebanon border came after 11 months of escalating terrorist attacks against its northern towns and villages, and only after overwhelming evidence that the UN forces, which were supposed to maintain the cease-fire and prevent such incursions, were unable to do so," an exercise of "its 'inherent right to self-defense' under Article 51 of the UN Charter."[25] While the U.S. press and government did not offer these transparent falsehoods in justification for the invasion, nevertheless the Israeli claim to be acting in "self-defense" was widely repeated by government spokesmen and in press commentary, and was accepted as a legitimate justification for the long-planned invasion.[26] The only real issues that arouse concern are the level of civilian casualties and the threat to American (or Israeli) interests, not the Israeli aggression itself.

Israel's attack quickly brought it into conflict with Soviet-backed Syria, raising a serious and imminent threat of super-power conflict. A senior Soviet official "expressed concern the Mideast fighting may provoke a full-scale confrontation between Israel and Syria, triggering greater Soviet involvement," and it has been alleged that "the Russians had threatened to intervene military, if the fighting did not stop," evoking U.S. attempts to limit the Israeli attack.[27] Both U.S. and Soviet fleets were present in force in the Eastern Mediterranean.[28] Once again, the world approached the brink of a final catastrophe. The latest of the strategic nuclear alerts listed in the Blechman-Kaplan survey cited above was at the end of the October 1973 Arab-Israeli war, under circumstances which might well have recurred in the course of the Lebanon invasion.

The Middle East, for obvious reasons, is the most likely candidate as the trigger that will set off a nuclear war.[29] General Thomas Kelley of the NATO southern command (AFSOUTH) observed plausibly that "If we have a WWIII, it will probably start here in the Mediterranean when a local conflict burns out of control."[30] The largest recipients of U.S. military aid for Fiscal Year 1983 are, in order: Israel, Egypt, Turkey, Spain, Pakistan, Greece.[31] A prime concern, in each case, is to strengthen U.S. dominance in the Middle East. In addition, the U.S. is selling vast quantities of arms to Saudi Arabia and, as already noted, is developing a base structure ringing the Gulf region for U.S. intervention forces. While the official justification is the threat of Soviet aggression, a more reasonable interpretation is that the perceived threats are indigenous to the region, including the threat of local uprising against the regimes of the oil-producing states that are, for the most part, closely allied to the U.S. and see themselves as dependent on U.S. power to defend them against radical Arab nationalism.[32] General Kelley's speculation is realistic, if we understand "Mediterranean" to mean "Eastern Mediterranean extending to the Gulf."

There are other examples of situations in which local conflicts or outside intervention may come to engage the superpowers, leading to global nuclear conflict. The rational conclusion from a survey of possible cases of this sort is straightforward: if we are concerned to avert nuclear war, our primary concern should be to lessen tensions and conflicts at the points where war engaging the superpowers is likely to erupt. The size of nuclear arsenals is a real but secondary consideration, though technological advances may pose an extreme hazard for reasons discussed below.

Even if nuclear arsenals were vastly reduced, a nuclear interchange would be a devastating catastrophe; in fact, even if they were reduced to zero, the capacity to produce nuclear weapons would not be lost and they would soon be available, and would be used, in the event of superpower conflict. Furthermore, the relation between the size of nuclear arsenals and the likelihood of the use of nuclear weapons is not an entirely simple one. Recall that on the one occasion when nuclear weapons were used to massacre civilians, there were exactly two available—and if two more had been available, in the hands of the Japanese enemy, it is quite likely that there would have been no atom bombing, for fear of retaliation.[33] Nuclear deterrence probably does work, to some extent at least, a fact that cannot be lightly dismissed. Consider, for example, the U.S. terrorist war against Cuba for the past 20 years.[34] It is possible that the U.S. was inhibited from escalating a large-scale program of state terrorism to direct invasion by fear of widened, perhaps nuclear conflict, and similar concerns may have inhibited each of the superpowers on other occasions as well.[35] Suppose that reduction of the deterrent capacity would tend to increase the aggressiveness of one or the other of the superpowers, not an unlikely consequence.

Then it would increase the likelihood of superpower conflict, and with it, the likelihood of nuclear war. It is not obvious that the prospects for peace and survival are enhanced by efforts to eliminate or reduce nuclear arsenals if these efforts are not an integral part of a more general program to constrain state violence.

Once again, a central concern of the disarmament movement should be to lessen tensions and conflicts at the points where war is likely to erupt. If we are willing to face this issue, we will find that there is often a great deal that we can do, since not infrequently U.S. policy has been instrumental in maintaining and enflaming such tensions and conflicts. This is of course not invariably the case, nor is the U.S. alone in this regard, but nevertheless it has been true often enough.

A case in point is the last and most threatening of the examples just discussed, the Israeli invasion of Lebanon. The U.S. stood alone (with Israel) against the rest of the world in blocking international efforts to bring the aggression to a halt, as is required under the UN Charter; such action might also have averted the significant danger of superpower conflict and nuclear war.[36] In earlier years as well, the U.S. had frequently blocked attempts to achieve a peaceful settlement that would have recognized the national rights of both Israel and the Palestinians. For example, in January 1976 the U.S. vetoed a Security Council resolution calling for a two-state settlement with recognized borders and guarantees for territorial integrity and security. In this case, the resolution was backed by the "confrontation states" (Syria, Jordan, Egypt) and by the PLO and the USSR, and opposed by Israel (under the Labor government, with a reputedly "dovish" cabinet), which announced that it would have no dealings with any Palestinians on any political issue and would enter into no negotiations with the PLO even if it recognized Israel and renounced terrorism.[37] These and many similar facts do not prevent American commentators from insistently claiming that only the Arab refusal to accept the existence of Israel blocks the possibility of a peaceful settlement. On an earlier occasion, Israel (with U.S. backing) rejected Sadat's

February 1971 proposal for a peace treaty on the pre-June 1976 borders that made no mention of Palestinian rights, allegedly the issue that now blocks the so-called "peace process." Sadat's offer was more favorable to Israel than his proposals on his trip to Jerusalem in November 1977, but was flatly rejected.[38]

Sadat's 1971 peace offer, like the 1976 Security Council resolution and much else, has been effaced from the approved historical record, since it is incompatible with the required image of well-intentioned U.S. and Israeli policy and of "the Arab mentality." In Israel and Egypt, Sadat's 1971 offer is described as his "famous" attempt to establish a genuine peace with Israel.[39] In the U.S., this "famous" attempt has been dropped down the memory hole. According to the official story, Sadat was a typical Arab fanatic who went to war intent on destroying Israel in 1973, and then, under the benign influence of Washington, learned the error of his ways and became the first Arab leader to seek peace with his dramatic trip to Jerusalem. In actual history, Sadat attempted to achieve peace with Israel immediately after becoming President of Egypt in 1970, and when his attempts to do so (and, incidentally, to convert Egypt to an American client state) were rebuffed, he warned repeatedly that he would have no alternative to war. The surprising Arab successes in the 1973 war finally awakened Kissinger to some of the realities of the Middle East, leading to his diplomatic efforts to exclude Egypt from the conflict while permitting Israel to move towards gradual integration of the occupied territories apart from the Sinai, and ultimately to the Camp David agreements under Carter, which extended this process, a fact that was predictable and predicted at the time and is now evident in retrospect.

The official story is presented, for example, in a lengthy two-page encomium to Sadat by Eric Pace, Middle East specialist of the *N.Y. Times*, after Sadat's assassination.[40] There is no mention here of the real history, as briefly sketched above; indeed, in the *N.Y. Times* version the well-documented facts are explicitly denied. Thus, referring to Sadat's trip to Jerusalem in 1977, Pace writes:

> Reversing Egypt's longstanding policy, he proclaimed
> his willingness to accept Israel's existence as a sovereign
> state. Then, where so many Middle East negotiators
> had failed, he succeeded, along with Presidents Carter
> and Reagan and Prime Minister Menachem Begin of
> Israel, in keeping the improbable rapprochement alive.

An elegant example of what has sometimes been called "historical
engineering,"[41] that is, redesigning the facts of history in the
interests of established power and ideology, a crime of which we
justly accuse our enemies.

The full historical record is complex and involves numerous
interactions and much mutual terror, in which Israeli initiatives
played a more prominent role than is acknowledged in mainstream commentary and analysis here.[42] It is also highly unlikely
that the actual history will obtain much of a hearing in the U.S. as
long as state policy is committed to Israel as a "strategic asset."
But it is nonetheless beyond question that the U.S. refusal to join
the international consensus on a two-state settlement—a consensus explicitly rejected by both major political groupings in
Israel while accepted in varying degrees and form by most of the
Arab states and the PLO—has been a significant factor in
maintaining and often enhancing tension and the risk of war.[43]

This is only one example, though a particularly important
one, of how U.S. policies have contributed and still contribute to
the risk of war—putting aside the not insignificant question of
their import for the people directly involved, year after year.
Simple logic leads to the conclusion that these issues should be a
major focus—I think, *the* major focus, for reasons already
explained—for the disarmament movement.

In this connection, we should note that the distinction
between nuclear and conventional weapons is too crude. In the
latter category, there is an important difference between, say,
anti-tank weapons designed for deterrence in Europe, and attack
carriers or the Rapid Deployment Force (which has nuclear
capability as well). Intervention capacity constitutes a large
component of the U.S. military budget,[44] though it is often
disguised in the official rhetoric of "deterrence." It may increase

the danger of nuclear war even more than a new generation of nuclear monsters. More crucial still are policies that the U.S. has pursued that contribute to tensions that may lead to war, engaging the superpowers. The U.S. is, of course, not alone in this respect, but it cannot be stressed too often that it is U.S. policies that American citizens can hope to influence directly, a consideration that is of obvious significance in a democratic society where the public can exert some influence on foreign policy. This is a category of questions that deserve much more attention than they have received in the general policy debate and specifically, within the disarmament movement itself.

When I say that the question of the size of nuclear arsenals is a secondary factor, I do not mean to suggest that it is unimportant; and the character of these arsenals is a matter of still greater concern. President Reagan's sabre-rattling evoked mass popular movements of protest, which in turn impelled his administration to at least a rhetorical commitment to curbing the arms race. In his most recent proposals for START negotiations (Eureka Illinois, May 9, 1982), the crucial phrase was that "many years of concentrated effort" will be required to implement his proposals[45]—perhaps 10 to 15 years, to judge by accompanying comment from administration figures. During these "many years," weapons development will continue, including the MX missile program, which, as Air Force Chief of Staff Lewis Allen has stated, will have "a counterforce first-strike capability,"[46] and Pershing II missiles which will have a five to six minute flight time to Moscow if deployed, as planned, in West Germany. These developments may impel the U.S. and the USSR to adopt a "launch on warning" strategy, which means that tensions that fall well short of actual military conflict may lead to nuclear war.[47] Thus, proposals for a nuclear freeze, ratification of SALT II, and reduction of the world's nuclear arsenals, are obviously very significant.

The disarmament movement—specifically, those elements in it that have been the focus of media attention—has concentrated on demonstrating the awesome consequences of nuclear war and on various plans to halt or reverse the arms race. One might feel that the first of these endeavors is an insult to the intelligence, but perhaps those who judge otherwise are correct. If so, then the task of reiterating the obvious is an important one. The second line of action is also important. But the most significant issues for those concerned with reduction of the likelihood of nuclear war may well lie elsewhere.

There has been much discussion within the disarmament movement as to whether to concentrate programs and organizing objectives solely on controlling the nuclear arms race or whether to include also an "anti-intervention plank." The argument against extending the scope of activities to include interventionism, which has often prevailed, is based on two assumptions: first, that the consequences of nuclear war would be so horrendous that other issues pale by comparison; and second, that a "single issue" focus will draw broader support.

The second point is arguable. At least with regard to elite groups, the argument probably holds true. It is difficult, for example, to imagine that the movement would retain its remarkably favorable media image[48]—quite unusual for popular movements of protest—if it were to concentrate on the broad range of issues that fall under the rubric of "intervention," including such examples as those mentioned earlier. With such a shift of direction, even with no change in style, to the ideological organs the movement would no longer be "sober" and "responsible" but would become "violent," "extremist," and "emotional." In general, a favorable media image is restricted to those who do not challenge power and privilege in any serious way. It is important to avoid being seduced by unaccustomed favorable attention in the mainstream ideological institutions, and to think clearly about what this means, and about the appropriate distribution of effort if the movement is to be effective in realizing its goals. Furthermore, though this tactical judgment may indeed be accurate with regard to elite groups, I suspect that it is wrong with regard to the population at large. Activists in the disarmament movement should ask themselves whether they are not, in fact, holding back the popular forces that they see themselves as mobilizing. To cite one suggestive example, the

Boston Jobs with Peace group succeeded in placing on the November 1981 ballot a resolution urging that "the City Council call upon the U.S. Congress to make more federal funds available, for local jobs and programs—in quality education, public transportation, energy-efficient housing, improved health care, and other essential services—by reducing the amount of our tax dollars spent on nuclear weapons *and programs of foreign military intervention*" (my emphasis). The resolution carried every ward in Boston, winning 72% of the vote citywide. It received the backing of the Justice and Peace Commission of the Catholic Archdiocese in Boston, as well as support from labor and ethnic groups. This was the result of a relatively small organizing effort, but it evidently touched a sensitive nerve, and though the anti-intervention issue was not the central focus of the campaign, it was quite clearly and explicitly included.[49]

But it is the first argument that is most seriously flawed. Let us accept the assumption that prevention of nuclear war should dominate all other concerns—an assumption that might not be regarded as obviously correct by a substantial part of the human race, e.g., the tens of millions who die of starvation every year. It then follows, as discussed earlier, that a prime concern should be the class of issues that fall broadly within the rubric of "anti-intervention," and more generally, foreign policy initiatives concerning the Third World, where a nuclear war is most likely to break out. Consideration of other related questions seems to me to reinforce this conclusion.

Before turning to these questions let me emphasize that I am restricting attention here to the U.S. disarmament movement. The movement in Europe should be considered in a rather different framework. It forms part of the long-term process in which Europe is slowly extricating itself from the bipolar world system established as a result of World War II, which has been eroding in the past years, to the discomfiture of the superpowers.

It is worth noting that the European movement has received a fair amount of harsh criticism in the U.S. media, perhaps reflecting an appreciation of the fact that it does pose a serious challenge to American power. At times, this criticism has taken on a remarkable tone. It is interesting, for example, to compare Butterfield's admiring (though narrowly restricted) account of the American anti-nuclear movement with an article in the same journal by John Vinocur, chief of the *N.Y. Times* bureau in Bonn, on the anti-nuclear movement in West Germany.[50] West Germany is affected by a serious "malaise" in his view: "something has shaken loose" in the country, as reflected by the fact that "more young people favor an attempt at achieving neutrality than favor continuing a military alliance with the United States." "Public feelings of angst and loss of control have led to increased pacifism," and for a significant part of the population, "a furious embrace of the illusions—or, at least, the serious miscalculations—of the last 10 years," in particular, the belief in the possibilities and importance of detente. There is "a crisis of national identity—a reality crisis, really—because it expresses fear and anger about the nation's being locked into the facts: its loss of unity and of total independence as a result of World War II." These irrational currents have recreated the "traditional notion of a German middle way between the West, often denounced as mercantile and impure, and Eastern Europe, seen as more romantic and less corrupt." With the collapse of detente, "there is hurt pride, frustration, anger and a more intense nationalism. With them come great emotion and a weakened hold over the rational— both very unhappy filaments in the Germans' past." One indication of this "weakened hold over the rational" is the belief that the U.S., as well as the USSR, poses dangers to world peace, an illusion that affects "the so-called peace movement." Throughout, Vinocur describes this so-called peace movement as a symptom of a general disease, a "problem" that the West Germans must somehow overcome in a country whose "agonies are deep," and irrational.

In this "malaise," Vinocur perceives signs of a revival of the Hitler era. As his evidence, he cites a press report

> that people opposed to the Frankfurt Airport Author-
> ity's building a new runway through a wooded area
> think the plan is a NATO-United States plot. The

mood is captured in a remarkable admonition—the vocabulary could have come out of a Hitler-era time capsule—tacked to a tree in the controversial woods: "Tremble before this tree. It was holy to your forefathers. Doing anything against the tree is a sign of an inferior people and base individual morality.[51]

But all is not lost. Chancellor Helmut Schmidt "still represents pragmatism and a pro-Western orientation in the country," and according to a confidant, feels "that the country's mood, sour and angst-ridden, comes in part from an insufficient exercise of authority on all levels," an impression that Vinocur appears to share. Note that this concern over "an insufficient exercise of authority on all levels" does not evoke memories of the Hitler era, in contrast with a concern to save trees from destruction.

Once again, it is interesting to compare the generally favorable media treatment of the American disarmament movement, in the *N.Y. Times Magazine* and elsewhere, with Vinocur's lament over the irrational concern for peace and detente and equally irrational belief that both superpowers, not just the Russians, exhibit threatening behavior. His reaction can perhaps be understood as a manifestation of a fear that "the so-called peace movement" in Europe constitutes part of a long-term development towards a more independent role in world affairs for a European community of nations that might, if recent trends persist, become a really serious rival to the United States, with an economy on the scale of our own, a high level of education and technology, independent access to resources and raw materials, and interests that do not necessarily coincide with those of dominant groups in the U.S.

Mary Kaldor is, I think, quite right when she argues that a motivating force in the European peace movement is "the sense within the movement of political emancipation," a sense that is international in scope and is "related to a growing awareness of European identity": "For the peace movement, the idea of a

Europe free of military blocs and free from the artificial division of the continent—seen to have been imposed by the super-powers—is at least as important as the demand for denucleari-zation." The significance of such proposals as "no-first-use," she argues plausibly, is that if it is "seen as a way of *de-emphasizing* the role of nuclear weapons in NATO and hence loosening the relationship between the United States and Western Europe, this might help to initiate a very different kind of reciprocal process, one that could eventually lead to the detachment of both halves of Europe from the superpowers."[52] This aspect of the "no-first-use" policy, she notes, was completely ignored (not very surprisingly) by the "four eminent members of the American establishment—Robert McNamara, George Kennan, McGeorge Bundy and Gerard Smith" in their "widely publicized proposal for a 'no-first-use' nuclear strategy for NATO" in the Spring 1982 issue of *Foreign Affairs*, just as they overlooked "the political nature of the demand for a nuclear-free Europe," namely, the "sense of emancipation" it reflects.[53] A variety of important questions arise in this connection that are surely related to those that specifically concern the American disarma-ment movement, and to the shape of the future world more generally.

As this discussion indicates, it is misleading to isolate concerns over the size and character of nuclear arsenals from a much broader nexus of issues. It is also important to bear in mind that strategic nuclear forces and "conventional forces" tend to grow in parallel, and for good reasons. The real function of the strategic weapons systems can sometimes be discerned in pronouncements of planners, for example, in the January 1980 statement to Congress by President Carter's Secretary of Defense on the proposed military budget. "The programmed rates of growth," he argued, "are needed for two basic reasons." One is "the sustained expansion in the Soviet defense effort," and the other is "the growth in international turbulence, illustrated by recent developments in the Caribbean, Southeast Asia, Korea,

Afghanistan, and Iran." The U.S. thus faces "simultaneous demands." "Our strategic nuclear capabilities," he said, "provide the foundation on which our security rests... With them, our other forces become meaningful instruments of military and political power."[54]

This is the heart of the matter. In fact, for each superpower, strategic nuclear capacities provide a protective cover for programs of state violence that it undertakes or supports in its own domains, which for us, have included much of the Third World. When B-52s drop bombs in the Egyptian desert in Operation Bright Star in the fall of 1981, it is not the USSR that is under threat, but the people of the Middle East and Africa. When the U.S. carries out naval maneuvers in the Caribbean, the target is not the USSR, but Grenada and Cuba, Nicaragua and El Salvador. And as already noted, the primary function of the Rapid Deployment Force, despite rhetoric to the contrary, is not to prevent Russian aggression but to control and repress indigenous forces in the Gulf region that might threaten U.S. dominance.

Similarly, it is not very likely that tactical nuclear weapons will be used against the Soviet Union, but they may well be used against opponents too weak to strike back. General Nathan Twining, Chairman of the Joint Chiefs of Staff from 1957-60, argued that "These weapons, if employed once or twice on the right targets, at the right time, would, in my judgment, stop *current* aggression, and stop *future* subversion and limited wars before they start."[55] He gave examples of the "world-wide subversion" that he had in mind: the Congo, Cuba and Vietnam. And there is little doubt that by "aggression," he meant to refer to the kind of "aggression" that was carried out by South Vietnamese peasants against the U.S. and its clients. Tactical nuclear weapons, then, can be used in a pre-emptive strike to prevent "subversion" before it becomes too firmly implanted, one of the "lessons of Vietnam," already well-learned when Twining wrote in 1966. Similar observations hold quite generally of the doctrine of "limited war," hardly a plausible strategy in the face of an enemy that can respond in kind, but available for use against those who cannot strike back. When we attack South Vietnam, as we did 20 years ago under the Kennedy Administration, then all of Indochina a few years later, it was limited war for us but a total war for the victims, a fact that it is all too easy for us to ignore and to forget.

The parallel growth of nuclear armaments and an intervention capacity is clear from recent history. The Kennedy Administration set off the current phase of the arms race by a huge strategic weapons program, justifying this build-up on the basis of a fabricated "missile gap." At the same time, it inaugurated the "era of counterinsurgency," an era of subversion and outright aggression that brought death and misery to many millions of people throughout the world.

The consequences in Southeast Asia are familiar, but it should not be forgotten that this program was much broader in scope. The impact was particularly striking in Latin America. In 1958, President Eisenhower's Secretary of Defense, Neil McElroy, had informed Congress that military aid to Latin America "is primarily for the purpose of the maintenance of internal security and also a very modest preparation for defense against any incursion from offshore."[56] This modification of the official rationale was opposed in the Senate, but after the Cuban revolution,

> The concept of hemispheric defense was abandoned in favor of internal security, which quickly became the single goal of military aid to Latin America. By 1962, for example, the Department of Defense announced that "in recognition of the fact that the principal threat faced in Latin America is Communist subversion and indirect attack, the primary emphasis of the military assistance program was changed from hemispheric defense to internal security in FY1962...The danger of internal subversion has not diminished;...rather, it has

increased significantly. This threat is not peculiar to one or two or even a few of the Latin American countries. It exists in every country."[57]

The results were awesome, as much of Latin America was turned into a torture chamber as a result, in large part, of U.S. policy initiatives.[58]

The meaning of the "era of counterinsurgency" for Latin America is vividly described by Charles Maechling, who led counterinsurgency and internal-defense planning for Presidents Kennedy and Johnson while in the State Department from 1961-66. Discussing the current state terrorism in Central America, he writes:

These atrocities are not just a tragic by-product of civil war. Nor are they accidental. Not understood by the American public, and concealed by the Reagan Administration, is that the Latin American military—Salvadoran, Guatemalan or Argentine—routinely employs terror to exterminate guerrillas and insurgency movements. Devised by the Nazis for occupied Europe, perfected by Argentina and now passed from hand to hand by Latin military staffs, the strategy involves torture and murder of anyone suspected of association with "subversives." Guilt or innocence is immaterial; the object is to exterminate the opposition and, by cowing sympathizers into submission, deprive the guerrillas of support...In their endless quest for "stability" south of the border, U.S. Administrations repeatedly turn a blind eye to the rapacity and cruelty of the Latin American military. Not until 1961, however, was there direct complicity (as opposed to occasional direct interventions) by the U.S. government in aiding domestic repression in Latin America. In that year, under pressure from the Pentagon, the Latin American military role was changed from "hemispheric defense" to "internal security"; U.S. assistance programs were retooled to strengthen the hold of the local military forces over their own people...Under guise of "civic-action" programs, Latin American officers have been encouraged to meddle in government and civilian affairs. There has been little screening to weed out the drug racketeers and war criminals, and no indoctrina-tion in civilized standards of warfare. Senior officers indistinguishable from the war criminals hanged at Nuremberg after World War II have passed through the Inter-American Defense College in Washington. Neither in training programs nor thereafter does the Pentagon insist on compliance with the Geneva Conventions regarding humane treatment of prisoners and noncombatants. Equipment is given without strings.

For the United States, which led the crusade against Nazi evil, to support the methods of Heinrich Him-mler's extermination squads is an outrage.[59]

The Reagan Administration programs are remarkably similar to those instituted by the Kennedy liberals, including another vast expansion of the strategic weapons system and an accompanying intensification of counterrevolutionary violence and support for internal repression. Reagan's programs continue and sharply escalate those developed in the latter stages of the Carter Administration, which by late 1978 had announced its plan to expand the military budget at the cost of social welfare programs, exploiting the subsequent Iranian hostage crisis and Soviet invasion of Afghanistan to put these plans into opera-tion,[60] a familiar pattern. As in the Kennedy period, there is a clear link between the vast expansion of the strategic weapons system and the parallel intensification of subversion and counterinsurgency. Strategic weapons guarantee that there will be no impediment to intervention—the preferred term is "peace-keeping"[61]—and, if necessary, the establishment of programs of state terrorism and violence to enforce the desired social order. Meanwhile, at the ideological level, since intervention is typically masked as "defense" against the superpower enemy, it is often necessary to build up the image of a fierce and threatening adversary who must be "deterred," when an era of counterinsurgency is inaugurated. It is not surprising, then, that the Kennedy programs of global subversion and aggression were accompanied by a "missile gap" and a strategic arms build-up to counter it, and that the record is being replayed today. This has been the repeated pattern since 1947, when Dean Acheson and others learned that opinion could be mobilized in support of an activist foreign policy, and in particular for a murderous counterinsurgency campaign in Greece, by conjuring up a Russian threat to take over the world,[62] by "scar[ing] Hell out of the country," in Senator Vandenberg's phrase. I will return to this important matter, and to other and more subtle ideological connections between strategic weapons programs and what Edward Herman has appropriately called "the *real* terror network."[63]

There are two other crucial issues that must be addressed if we hope to avert nuclear catastrophe: the domestic factors that drive the Pentagon system, and the dynamics of the Cold War. Unless these questions are squarely faced, efforts to control and reverse the arms race are unlikely to attain their ends.

As for domestic factors, U.S. planners have repeatedly turned to military Keynesianism as a device of economic management. In effect the Pentagon system has come to serve as the state sector of the economy, offering a guaranteed market for high technology production, subsidizing industrial research, and in general, functioning as a system of industrial policy planning. In principle, other mechanisms are available to achieve these ends, but reliance on military production offers many temptations and once the system is established, it is not easy to dismantle it and to construct an alternative. In a society such as ours in which business interests dominate ideology and political life, state intervention must be designed in such a way that it does not diminish or threaten the prerogatives of the masters of the private economy. The natural policy choice for state-induced production, then, is the production of waste rather than for the competitive market. Furthermore, in an advanced industrial society this must be high technology waste, preferably, rapidly obsolescing if state intervention is to be a persistent factor in stimulating economic growth. Military production admirably meets these conditions. There are also political questions that must be faced: taxpayers must be persuaded to foot the bill, as they will do if they feel that their lives and society are threatened by an implacable enemy bent on their destruction. And finally, it is preferable for such state-induced production to serve at least some utilitarian purpose—for example, providing both the direct means and the general framework for intervention and subversion along the lines just indicated along with arms sales to client regimes (by now a non-trivial contribution to "economic health"),[64] and creating a climate of submissiveness and obedience among the population.

Again, it is difficult to imagine an alternative to the Pentagon system that so readily satisfies all of these conditions. And, of course, once established, the system has its own dynamics, as important segments of industry and labor develop a stake in its maintenance. The system also poses many hazards, but, as Edward Herman points out, "the gains from an aggressive militarism are in the short-run, the threat of mutual incineration is more remote."[65]

The advantages of military-based state intervention in the economy were perceived within the business community at an early stage of the Cold War. A 1949 *Business Week* analysis of the merits of the Pentagon system noted that military spending was rising and would probably continue to do so, but it was concerned that there might be a downward shift in this trend.[66] Specifically, it noted that "There's some evidence that Stalin's 'peace offensive' is serious," so that "Businessmen need to weigh the possible results":

> True, Stalin's 'peace feelers' have been brushed aside. Until the North Atlantic pact is safely signed and ratified, Washington is convinced it would be foolhardy

to entertain the idea that the Russians might be serious. But for the businessman, right now, it isn't Washington's feelings that matter; it's Stalin's. And there is some evidence that Stalin actually is eager to get off the hook of the cold war.

The article then investigates the impact of "the prospect of ever-rising military spending," in particular, its function "as a ceiling on the ambitious social-welfare projects that the Truman Administration has its heart set on." In contrast, "a constant or declining military budget" would provide the President with "more financial elbow room for his welfare programs, public works, and resource development projects," while increasing the threat of deflation and diminishing the threat of inflation.

The article then turns to Stalin's moves, suggesting that they may indeed be serious, and asks "What problems would it raise or ease for the U.S. businessman" if this proves to be the case. The conclusion is that these problems should not be too serious: "the transition [to a peacetime economy] would be easy, almost painless." So far so good, but there remain serious problems. Foremost among them is the one just noted: "the Truman Administration would get its chance to go ahead with civilian spending programs that the big military budget has kept under wraps," including "elaborate plans for development of natural resources, expansion of public works, broadening of social welfare programs." These would be "Truman's answer to a fundamental problem that would emerge as soon as military spending slacked off—the problem of making the business boom go on indefinitely under its own steam."

Why should business oppose these measures, preferring military spending to social spending and thus hoping that Stalin's "peace offensive" either will prove illusory or can be "brushed aside," as in the current foreign policy planning in Washington? The answer is simple:

But there's a tremendous social and economic difference between welfare pump-priming and military pump-priming. It makes the government's role in the economy—its importance to business—greater than ever. Military spending doesn't really alter the structure of the economy. It goes through the regular channels. As far as a businessman is concerned, a munitions order from the government is much like an order from a private customer. But the kind of welfare and public works spending that Truman plans does alter the economy. It makes new channels of its own. It creates new institutions. It redistributes income. It shifts demand from one industry to another. It changes the whole economic pattern.

Though the transition to a peacetime economy could be easily managed, the impact on the society would be significant, weakening the dominant role of business interests and permitting other forces to develop. As income is redistributed, new popular elements enter into the formation of policy, and new social and economic institutions arise. Since this outcome is intolerable, the state must confine its intervention in the economy to inducing military production; that is the clear message. State intervention in the economy is fine, indeed necessary, but only if it contributes to existing private power and privilege.

There has always been a kind of love-hate relation between business interests and the capitalist state. On the one hand, business wants a powerful state to regulate disorderly markets, provide services and subsidies to business, enhance and protect access to foreign markets and resources, and so on. On the other hand, business does not want a powerful competitor, in particular, one that might respond to different interests, popular interests, and conduct policies with a redistributive effect, with regard to income or power. It has never been an easy problem to solve.[67]

The message expressed in the *Business Week* analysis, and elsewhere, was well-understood in planning circles. By early 1950, the National Security Council had produced NSC 68, which called for a vast increase in military spending to combat the alleged Russian threat of world conquest, while conceding that the West retained overwhelming military and economic dominance. It also called for "a large measure of sacrifice and discipline" among the American people—sacrifice as social welfare programs are curbed, and discipline in order to overcome "the excesses of a permanently open mind" and "dissent among us," which may become a "vulnerability" of our society.[68] The Korean war provided an appropriate pretext for adopting this program, which was approved by Truman on September 30, 1950 "as a statement of policy to be followed over the next four or five years."[69] Note again the familiar pattern of 1947, 1950, 1960, and again today, along wth numerous incidents along the way: militaristic or aggressive policies are designed to serve perceived needs, then implemented when some international event makes it possible to conjure up a Russian scare (or, for a time, a Chinese scare), whatever the available facts may be.

As a number of commentators have noted, "there is a striking similarity between America's defense-related and aerospace programs, and other nations' industrial policies that are expressly designed to accelerate the development of emerging industries," in particular, Japan's Ministry of International Trade and Industry (MITI).[70] Reich notes that the Pentagon now funds some 30% of U.S. research and development. The percentage of government funding for these purposes is higher in the U.S. than in Japan, where the government "is expressly committed to promoting Japan's emerging industries." The American computer industry relied heavily on government support in the 1950s ("In 1954, the government was the only major purchaser of computers; by 1962, the government market still represented almost one-half of total computer sales"). The government continues to provide a substantial market for aircraft, radio and communications equipment, engineering and scientific instruments, and other indusries. MITI and the Pentagon are now "squaring off," Reich notes, in development of integrated circuits, robotics, fiber optic communications, lasers, computer software, "and a host of other technologies."

There are, however, important differences between the Pentagon-based industrial policy system and such competitors as MITI:

Apart from the Pentagon's broad concern for the economic health of U.S. defense contractors and NASA's recent flirtation with commercial applications for its space shuttle, the Department of Defense and NASA have no interest in the successful marketing of new products. Indeed, defense and aerospace programs actually may have jeopardized the international competitiveness of American manufacturers. By contrast, the efforts of our trading partners, particularly Japan, have been focused directly on world competition for commercial markets.

Furthermore, MITI fosters competition in marketing, while the Pentagon system discourages competitive bidding and is unconcerned with economic efficiency. Most important, "MITI sees to it that new technologies are diffused rapidly into the economy, and incorporated into countless commercial products," while such concerns are foreign to the Pentagon system of industrial policy planning, and in fact, "rather than encourage American commercial development, defense spending on emerging high technologies may therefore have the opposite effect over the long term, diverting U.S. scientists and engineers away from commercial applications."[71]

In short, the Japanese system of state industrial policy planning is oriented towards the commercial market, while the otherwise rather similar U.S. military-based system is concerned primarily with military applications. It is "perhaps significant," Chalmers Johnson notes, "that aviation, space vehicles, and atomic energy are all sectors in which the United States is preeminent, just as Japan is preeminent in steel production, ship-building, consumer electronics, rail transportation, synthetic fibers, watches, and cameras."[72] It is hardly very surprising that U.S. industry is finding it increasingly difficult to compete with Japan, despite its enormous advantages of scale, access to resources, domestic market, and penetration of the international economy. It should also be noted that the current flurry of concern over the alleged fact that the Pentagon is designing military equipment so complex that it may be unusable is somewhat misplaced, once the broader role of the Pentagon system of industrial policy planning is brought into consideration.

In this context, it is not surprising that the Reagan Administration, like its predecessors in the 1970s, has sought to impel Europe and Japan to increased military expenditures: they must damage their economies too if we are to remain competitive in world trade. This effort has largely failed. Similarly, Reagan's efforts to rekindle Cold War enthusiasms,[73] the natural concomitant of a massive arms program, has also failed to evoke a positive response either domestically or abroad, and in fact has contributed to considerable conflict within the Atlantic alliance, particularly, with the attempts to block the gas pipeline from the USSR to Western Europe—which, incidentally, would have the effect of contributing to European independence from largely U.S.-controlled Middle East petroleum. These facts have significant consequences.

Before considering them, let us return briefly to the similarities noted above between Reagan's programs and those of the Kennedy liberals 20 years earlier. Specifically, both Administrations came into office with the promise and intent of overcoming the perceived lethargy of the recent past and "getting the country moving again" by expanding what amounts to the state sector of the economy—namely, the guaranteed market for high technology waste production—along with a much enhanced program of global aggressiveness. The comparison, which in fact goes further than this (compare Reagan's "supply side economics" with the major domestic achievement of the Kennedy Administration, a regressive tax cut to spur business investment), tells us something about the real spectrum of politics in the United States.

But there are also striking differences. The Kennedy Administration evoked much enthusiasm and admiration among the liberal intelligentsia, but there is no Camelot today. In part, this difference reflects the fact that Reagan dismisses the intelligentsia with contempt, while Kennedy offered them a place in the sun, a chance to rub shoulders with those in power and even to share in its exercise. But more important, Kennedy's programs largely succeeded, while Reagan's uniformly fail. The difference reflects the decline in American global hegemony over the past 20 years, a decline that has also affected the superpower enemy despite much rhetoric to the contrary.[74] The Kennedy Administration was concerned over the viability of the Japanese economy.[75] This is hardly the concern of American planners today. At a time of U.S. dominance over the global economy, military Keynesianism could be adopted as an industrial policy program without undue concern for our rivals in the world economy, but that is no longer true.

There are other problems too that the Kennedy planners did not have to face. The population can no longer be easily mobilized for militarism and aggression. When Kennedy attacked South Vietnam in 1962—the year when the U.S. air force began its direct participation in the bombing of the South Vietnamese countryside—there was no public outcry. When Reagan attempted to mobilize public opinion in support of direct military intervention in El Salvador, he succeeded only in organizing a large-scale popular movement of protest and was forced to limit himself to an extension and escalation of Carter's efforts: support for the forces conducting a major massacre of peasants and dissidents, instead of a crusade against an outpost of the global enemy. Kennedy's brinkmanship and nuclear adventurism aroused much admiration, as noted earlier, while Reagan's rhetoric—which so far falls far short of Kennedy's actions—has, in contrast, provided a major impetus for an international disarmament movement. Case by case, the same comparison holds.

High-level Pentagon planners may believe that "The U.S. is going back to becoming the world's policeman,"[76] but their joy in this prospect is overly optimistic. It is doubtful that the U.S can return to those wonderful days when intervention, subversion and direct aggression could be freely undertaken with much success throughout a large part of the world while the intelligentsia lauded our noble commitment to Wilsonian principles of freedom and self-determination and the inspiring humanitarianism that distinguishes the U.S. from all other powers in history. With the failure of the effort to impel our rivals/allies to undertake major rearmament programs, the inability to whip up war fever, and the negative effects of the enormous expenditures for armaments on the American economy, the Reagan program of "reindustrializing America" by the familiar devices of military Keynesianism will no doubt have to change course. "A Wall Street Journal/Gallup survey of top corporate executives last week showed 83 percent favoring a reduction in defense spending in order to reduce the federal deficit."[77] A significant change after a year of failure in the programs of an administration that was heavily backed by big business. It is likely that there will be significant conflict within business circles over the coming years between those who hope to retain the traditional Pentagon-based system of industrial policy planning and others who believe that it will no longer serve in a period of decline of American hegemony, when industrial rivals can no longer be controlled or dismissed and the domestic population is not so malleable as heretofore, so that new methods of state intervention in the economy will have to be devised.

How do these tendencies relate to the disarmament movement? In several ways. First, it should be recognized that the participation of elite groups in the campaign to control the strategic weapons build-up, and the unusual spectacle of a popular movement receiving relatively favorable treatment in the media, reflect the fact that powerful elements in American society are now opposed to increased reliance on the traditional devices of military-based state economic planning. In brief, they regard the disarmament movement as potentially "their troops" in a forthcoming political struggle—as long as the movement does not go too far or take a dangerous path, of course. Second, we may expect increasing support for the kind of arms control agreement that will permit unending technological advances while limiting the number of weapons. The American comparative advantage, after all, lies in high technology, not in actual production; and the concentration of state resources on subsidies to high technology industry should continue to benefit emerging industries in those areas where advantages should accrue to American business enterprises (though with the problematic features already noted). One may also expect renewed efforts to induce Europe and Japan to expand their conventional forces, at considerable expense to them and without posing a major threat to U.S. dominance. At the same time, U.S. military production will have to be geared increasingly to ensuring an adequate intervention capacity in a world in which the U.S. cannot rely on surrogate powers to perform its work, as the collapse of the Nixon-Kissinger doctrine indicated. This is only a piece of a complicated story, but once again, one that must be considered seriously by the disarmament movement if it hopes to further its quite different goals.

This leads finally to what may well be the main question: the dynamics of the Cold War. Much intellectual energy has been devoted to the study of the origins of the Cold War, particularly since the mid-1960s, when the orthodox doctrine that the U.S. role was purely defensive and reactive was challenged by so-called "revisionist" critics. Their work could not be readily dismissed as the popular movements of the period insistently demanded a reopening of this and many other questions, causing much dismay among establishment figures. Henry Kissinger lamented that as "American self-doubt" became "contagious" in the 1960s, "European intellectuals began to argue that the Cold War was caused by American as well as by Soviet policies," while "a vocal and at times violent minority"[78] in the United States challenged "the hitherto almost unanimous conviction that the Cold War had been caused by Soviet intransigence alone."[79] The orthodox position collapsed with remarkable swiftness when it was exposed to critical scrutiny. By now, major theses of the "revisionist critique" have been incorporated in some fashion within mainstream scholarship. Apart from some holdouts such as Kissinger, few would now be scandalized to read that "the Cold War cannot be understood simply as an American response to a Soviet challenge, but rather as the insidious interaction of mutual suspicions, blame for which must be shared by all."[80] In fact, the observation is common now among mainstream historians, e.g., John Lewis Gaddis, who concludes that "The Cold War grew out of a complicated interaction of external and internal developments inside both the United States and the Soviet Union."[81]

The reaction to the revisionist critique, however, deserves some notice, from Arthur Schlesinger's early statement (later amended) that it is time to "blow the whistle" on this heresy to Walter Laqueur's recent claim that "The inability to accept the permissible limits of rewriting history was the undoing of the Cold War revisionists"; in his analogy, "It is one thing to admire Stalin, it is another to depict him as a great humanist whose sole aspiration was to cooperate with the West in a spirit of goodwill, peace and mutual benefit."[82] Gross distortions of the revisionist critique are common: e.g., Herbert Feis, who writes that Alperovitz "apparently thinks [that the Soviet government] was merely the hapless object of our vicious diplomacy" (see above), or Adam Yarmolinsky, who perhaps unknowingly reiterates major conclusions of revisionist historians, then writing that "This is not to argue, as the historical revisionists of the New Left have done, that the menace of Soviet and Communist power in the postwar world was largely invented in Washington."[83] Even Gaddis, who is much more careful, misstates when he writes that "Historians, revisionist and nonrevisionist, now generally agree on the limited nature of Stalin's objectives"; it would be more accurate to say that nonrevisionist historians have now come to accept this standard revisionist point. Gaddis also offers a wholly irrational criticism of the revisionists, claiming that they place themselves "in the odd position of employing a single-cause [essentially, economic determinist] explanation of human behavior, yet criticizing the subjects they deal with [American policy-makers] for not liberating themselves from the mechanistic framework which they, as historians, have imposed." But to identify (not "impose") social and economic factors that play a crucial role in policy formation is not to conclude that these are laws of nature that leave no choice of action. In fact, it is misleading even to refer to the "revisionist critique," etc., since the historians assigned that title have differed substantially among themselves on major issues.

But while there has been much useful study of the origins of the Cold War, less attention has been devoted to the question of why it persists. In particular, why do the superpowers amass these growing arsenals of destruction? Each has an answer, and it is the same answer. Each superpower describes its armaments as "defensive." Each is concerned only to deter its violent opponent, whose aim is to take over the world. There is an element of truth in each of these competing stories, but basically they are myths. If we hope to do more than protest impending destruction, and to protect the actual as well as the potential victims, then we must come to understand the reality that lies behind the elaborate mythology of the Cold War and the reasons for its persistence. With not too much effort, and a little attention to recent history, we can extricate the real nature of the Cold War from ideological obfuscations. The basic and crucial fact is that the Cold War system has proven highly functional for the superpowers, which is why it persists, despite the likelihood of mutual annihilation if the system breaks down by accident, as sooner or later it very likely will. The Cold War has provided a framework within which each of the superpowers can use force and violence to control its own domains, appealing to the threat of the superpower enemy to mobilize its own population and recalcitrant allies. As H.L. Mencken once observed, "The whole aim of practical politics is to keep the populace alarmed (and hence clamorous to be led to safety) by menacing it with an endless series of hobgoblins, all of them imaginary," a lesson that leaders of both superpowers, and many others, understand quite well. A survey of the historical record brings out this fact with brutal clarity.

Consider, for example, the U.S.-organized invasion of Guatemala in 1954, which destroyed a brief and hopeful experiment with political democracy and social reform, turning the country into a literal hell on earth, with periodic infusions of U.S military assistance (particularly under the liberal Democratic Administrations of the 1960s) to ensure that the gangsters in power will be able to maintain their bloody rule. It would have been difficult—in fact, ludicrous—for the U.S. government to claim that the United States was threatened with destruction when a moderate government, with policies resembling those of the New Deal, instituted desperately needed reforms and attempted to expropriate unused lands of the United Fruit Company to turn them over to miserable peasants, offering as compensation exactly what United Fruit had claimed the lands were worth in a standard tax fraud, an offer that aroused much indignation in the U.S.[84] Matters appeared quite different when the U.S. government claimed that Guatemala was the outpost of international Communism, an advance base for a superpower aiming at global conquest, armed with nuclear weapons, with an ample record of brutality and atrocities. With the cooperation of the press and scholarship, this ridiculous tale was told, and believed, justifying U.S. intervention to save the Free World from destruction by an enemy of Hitlerian proportions. Blechman and Kaplan find it "fascinating that the 1954 decision by the Arbenz government in Guatemala to accept military aid from the Soviet bloc [following ample evidence of U.S. intention to sponsor an invasion and extensive Guatemalan efforts, rejected by Eisenhower, to arbitrate disputes and avoid a confrontation] was sufficient to occasion a major response from the United States, which included the temporary deployment of strategic bombers to Nicaragua—meant, it would appear, as a signal of American commitment—and the movement of an aircraft carrier task force, a reinforced marine amphibious battalion and air-wing, land-based patrol aircraft squadrons, and several related actions"[85]—including the illegal interception of ships at sea, bombing by U.S. pilots, a major psywar campaign, etc.

When the USSR invaded Hungary two years later, it resorted to essentially the same rhetoric, with the obvious changes of names. The Soviet leaders did not even have the originality to change the record; the Khrushchev doctrine was merely a transposition of the doctrine devised to justify the destruction of Guatemalan democracy.

Similarly, the Johnson Doctrine constructed to justify the U.S. invasion of the Dominican Republic in alleged defense against global Communism was reiterated in virtually the same terms in the Brezhnev Doctrine issued to justify the Soviet invasion of Czechoslovakia.[86] Both were "defensive interventions," undertaken to ward off the threat of the superpower enemy, which was seeking to establish an advance base for its nefarious designs.[87] I do not know whether current Soviet propaganda refers to these interventions as "peace-keeping missions" (see note 61).

The rhetoric accompanying current U.S. support for massacre in El Salvador and the Soviet invasion of Afghanistan, the U.S. support for a martial law regime in Turkey and the Soviet support for a similar regime in Poland, is essentially the same. In fact, the same has been true throughout the history of the Cold War, since the Truman Doctrine was used to disguise the first major U.S. counterinsurgency effort, in Greece, at a time when Stalin was attempting to call off the Greek guerrillas, recognizing that Greece, at the periphery of the Middle East, was "American turf."

Conventional doctrine has it that the superpower conflict is the central axis of postwar history. Thus the standard periodization is in terms of "containment," "detente" (which allegedly failed because of Russian intransigence), and a return to some form of containment. The rhetoric is defensive, as is typical of the propaganda of every state, and focuses on the bipolar superpower conflict. There is surely some truth to this picture; the conflict between the U.S. and the USSR certainly exists. But the picture is a highly self-serving one, for the reasons already indicated, and should not obscure more fundamental elements of the Cold War system: crucially, its utility as a device to disguise the aggression and subversion carried out by the superpowers to maintain control over their respective domains, and to justify the often harsh means undertaken to these ends. And we should bear in mind that the U.S. has often taken the lead in this macabre dance.

We should also recall that the victors in World War II generally had a conception of how the postwar world should be organized that differed from the vision of leading forces in the countries they were liberating from the Axis yoke. In the domains conquered by the Red Army, the point is obvious enough, and too familiar to require discussion. It is less often observed, within our own ideological institutions, that the U.S. also engaged in a systematic attempt to impose its own form of global order, often in alliance with fascist collaborators and in opposition to the forces that had fought against the fascist powers. Consider a few examples.

In North Africa in 1942, the U.S. placed in power Admiral Darlan, a leading Nazi collaborator who was the author of the Vichy regime's anti-Semitic laws. Stephen Ambrose comments:

> The result was that in its first major foreign-policy venture in World War II, the United States gave its support to a man who stood for everything Roosevelt and Churchill has spoken out against in the Atlantic Charter. As much as Goering or Goebbels, Darlan was the antithesis of the principles the Allies said they were struggling to establish.[88]

As the American army drove the Nazis out of Italy, it restored the rule of fascist collaborators while dispersing the Italian resistance, which had fought courageously against up to six German divisions, after it had liberated much of Northern Italy.[89]

In Greece, the British army took over after the Nazis had withdrawn, imposing the rule of royalist elements and Nazi collaborators and suppressing the anti-Nazi resistance. When the brutality and corruption of this regime evoked further resistance that Britain was unable to control in its post-war decline, the U.S. stepped into the breach under the Truman Doctrine and conducted a murderous war of counterinsurgency in support of such figures as King Paul and Queen Frederika (former leaders of the Greek fascist youth), crushing labor unions and the former anti-Nazi resistance based among the peasantry and working classes and led by Greek Communists.[90]

In Indochina, the British army prepared the way for the return of French imperialism, soon to be supported by the U.S. in its attempt to reconquer its former colonies and to suppress the Viet Minh led by Ho Chi Minh, who had cooperated with the American OSS in the anti-fascist war and was recognized by the U.S. to be the only credible nationalist figure in Indochina.[91] Subsequently the U.S. took over the anti-nationalist struggle itself, with consequences that are well-known, though it is predictable that a more acceptable history will soon succeed in replacing the actual historical record.

In neighboring Thailand, by the late 1940s the U.S. found itself supporting the military regime of Phibun Songkhram, a former ally of fascist Japan. By 1954, Pridi Phanomyong, who was the leader of the Free Thai movement that had fought with the U.S. against Japanese fascism and had attempted to develop a liberal democratic regime, found himself in Communist China, a consequence sometimes described as "ironic" in American scholarship—as indeed it may seem, if viewed in isolation in the customary fashion.[92]

In the Philippines, the peasant forces that had fought against the Japanese were suppressed by the U.S. and the regime (including many Japanese collaborators) the U.S. had imposed.[93]

In the former colonies the story was often similar, though specific motivations varied. Meanwhile in Europe, the western victors of the anti-fascist war, with the early collaboration of Stalin, succeeded in controlling leading elements of the anti-Nazi resistance, while the U.S. moved to abort steps towards a form of "national capitalism" (let alone socialism) that might have led to independence from the American-controlled global order.[94]

In general, the United States was committed to the establishment of what wartime planners called a "Grand Area," a region including at a minimum the Western hemisphere, the former British empire and the Far East, which would be subordinated to the needs of the American economy.[95] By 1961, as noted earlier, the U.S. changed the mission of the Latin American military, which it substantially influenced or controlled, to "internal security," leading to a "plague of repression" (in the words of the Linowitz Commission) that had no parallel in the bloody history of the continent, as terror-and-torture states spread throughout the region with a notable domino effect, generally supported by the United States.[96] Meanwhile "aid" to Latin America "has tended to flow disproportionately to Latin American governments which torture their citizens," "to the hemisphere's relatively egregious violators of fundamental human rights," quite uncorrelated with need, including military aid intended for internal repression.[97] The CIA was soon directed to covert operations, including "the support of terrorism around the world," in the words of the document that launched these operations,[98] but primarily subversion, some of the main targets being democratic governments that appeared to be drifting out of U.S. control. In the Middle East, the U.S. largely displaced Britain and France and has since attempted with much success to maintain in power what are called "moderate" (meaning pro-U.S.) regimes, relying on Israel (and for a time, Iran under the Shah) to serve as a barrier to radical Arab nationalism,[99] and under the Eisenhower Doctrine, intervening with military force in Lebanon to achieve this end. The same has been true in parts of Africa, though here the U.S. has largely tended to rely on other powers, particularly France, whose forces help "keep West Africa safe for French, American, and other foreign oilmen," in the approving words of *Business Week*.[100]

This is the barest sketch of a pattern that is highly systematic. We have no hesitation in attributing the systematic behavior of the USSR in the regions it conquered to the structure of power within the Soviet Union, to the desire of the ruling military-bureaucratic elite to impose and extend their rule. Similarly, we do not find it difficult to explain the commitment of this ruling group to military production rather than satisfying human needs in terms of their desire to extend their domestic power and imperial control.[101]

To impose the same rational standards on oneself, however, appears to be a difficult if not impossible task even though the pattern of U.S. behavior is obvious, there is a fair amount of direct documentation concerning planning at the highest levels that makes the pattern clear enough, and the mechanisms by which those who largely own and manage the economy use the instrument of state power to pursue their interests are also quite transparent.[102] Nevertheless, the topic is under a virtual taboo in American scholarship,[103] and those who attempt to apply a single rational standard to both the U.S. and other powers are frequently accused of "extremism," "dangerous radicalism," or, remarkably, of a lack of "evenhandedness" and of invoking "a double moral standard."

Typically, U.S. behavior is described as disinterested, reactive, defensive, governed by high idealism ("excessive moralism," some critics charge), committed to freedom and democracy. "Unlike the Soviet Union, the U.S. does not want to convert anyone to a specific political, social, or economic system," two well-known commentators proclaim, offering this pronouncement as a Truth that requires no factual support, on a par with the revealed truths of other organized religions, and therefore not affected by actual U.S. behavior in Latin America, Southeast Asia, and elsewhere.[104] As Hans Morgenthau once explained, we should not "confound the abuse of reality with reality itself," where "the abuse of reality" is the actual historical record with its many deviations for the "transcendent purpose" of the United States, and "reality itself" is the unachieved "national purpose" as revealed by "the evidence of history as our minds reflect it"[105]—at least, those minds that are properly trained and disciplined.

Some go still further. In the lead article of the Spring 1982 issue of the *Political Science Quarterly*, Harvard professor Samuel Huntington assures us that

> When it had an effect, however, the overall effect of American power on other societies was to further liberty, pluralism, and democracy. The conflict between American power and American principles virtually disappears when it is applied to the American impact on other societies.[106]

Judging by Latin America or the Philippines, then, we must conclude that "American principles" are to foster mass murder, high technology torture, child slavery, starvation and other such noble ideals. [107] Huntington explains further that "The interventions by United States Marines in Haiti, Nicaragua, the Dominican Republic, and elsewhere in these years often bore striking resemblances to the interventions by federal marshals in the conduct of elections in the American South in the 1960s: registering voters, protecting against electoral violence, ensuring a free vote and an honest count," nothing more. Even Chile proves the case: if "the United States had been as active in the popular election of 1970 as it had been in that of 1964, the destruction of Chilean democracy in 1973 [by some unknown and mysterious force] might have been avoided"—to translate into real world terms: the U.S. would not have been required to commit itself to overthrow Chilean democracy and to support the subsequent slaughter and oppression, if only it had intervened with sufficient effectiveness to guarantee the "right outcome" in the democratic election of 1970. As for the Congressional Human Rights program of the 1970s,[108] it is a reflection of the decline of American power:

> When American power was clearly predominant, such
> legislative provisions and caveats were superfluous: no
> Harkin amendment was necessary to convey the
> message of the superiority of liberty. The message was
> there for all to see in the troop deployments, carrier
> task forces, foreign-aid missions, and intelligence
> operatives.

One can only stand in awe in the face of this amazing record of virtue, unique in history.

We can learn a good deal about our own society and its intellectual life by considering such examples as these—and while this last may appear to be an extreme case, a review of American scholarship shows that it is not too far beyond the norm[109]—and noting that they are regarded as reputable scholarship, in contrast to "extremist" views that would not be permitted expression in such journals. We might ask, for example, how we would react to an account of Soviet behavior of a similar level of veracity (and audacity) in a Communist Party journal. It is a useful exercise.

In the post World War II period, these American enterprises in defense of freedom were typically justified by the rhetoric of the Cold War. What is crucially important about Cold War propaganda is that it works, or has worked until quite recently. We do not, of course, have public opinion polls and the like for the Soviet Union, but from the reports of travellers and journalists it appears that the bulk of the population, including the intelligentsia, accepted the incredible thesis that the invasion of Afghanistan was a benevolent act undertaken in defense of the oppressed people of Afghanistan from brutal terrorist gangs supported by Western imperialism (a thesis which, as in the case of most state propaganda, rests upon a particle of truth). The West, of course, rejects this absurd idea with derision, noting correctly that "an invader is an invader unless invited in by a government with some claim to legitimacy."[110]

The justified contempt for the vile propaganda of a totalitarian state might be expressed in somewhat less self-righteous tones if we were willing to take an honest look at some achievements of our own. Twenty years have passed since the U.S. attacked South Vietnam, and seventeen years since the outright invasion of South Vietnam by an American Expeditionary Force, yet one will search in vain in American mainstream journalism or scholarship for recognition of the simple fact that in this case too "an invader is an invader unless invited in by a government with some claim to legitimacy"; the South Vietnamese client regimes imposed by U.S. force were recognized by U.S. planners to be artificial implants, and were regularly overthrown when they appeared to be making dangerous gestures towards a peaceful settlement, while the indigenous opposition was estimated at about one-half the population, well above what George Washington could have claimed. Nevertheless, such words as "aggression" or "invasion" are unpronounceable when the U.S. attacks and brutalizes South Vietnam and then all of Indochina. Rather, this is a noble defense of freedom against terrorist gangs serving as agents of Soviet (or Chinese) imperialism.[111] Here we have a record of long-term subservience to state propaganda that any dictator would envy.

It is sometimes argued that it is wrong to describe American planners as duplicitous when they invoke Cold War imagery to justify subversion or aggression, since they really believe what they say in justification of their actions. Thus, in an important study of the 1954 Guatemalan intervention, Richard Immerman objects to the view that it was the domestic programs of the Guatemalan government that impelled the U.S. to action (specifically, as other analysts put it, that "The takeover of United Fruit land was probably the decisive factor pushing the Americans into action"[112]). Immerman takes note of the negative U.S. reaction to the reform program in Guatemala and the close connections of United Fruit and the Executive Branch of the U.S. government, and observes that

> the reform did damage [the United Fruit Company's] interests and thus came under the contemporary definition of a Communist program. Linked with other similar evidence [relating to New Deal-style reforms], the agrarian reform convicted the revolutionary government.

Why, then, is it incorrect to describe these reform measures as the causal agent that led to U.S. intervention? The reason is that "In the cold war ethos, it was a simple step to interpret the enactment of a long-overdue agrarian reform, official opposition to Yankee-supported Latin American dictators, labor legislation, or other nationalistic policies that failed to coincide with those of the United States as proof of Communist intrigue."[112] The documentary record, he concludes, shows that U.S. planners really believed that Guatemala had already "succumbed to Communist infiltration," in the words of the President's brother, Milton Eisenhower.[114] Thus under the "cold war ethos," it was natural for Spruille Braden ("an ardent crusader for United Fruit") to state that:

we may be compelled to intervene...I should like to underscore that because Communism is so blatantly an international and not an internal affair, its suppression, even by force, in an American country, by one or more of the other republics, would not constitute an intervention in the internal affairs of the former.[115]

What we call, *mutatis mutandis*, the Khrushchev-Brezhnev Doctrine.

Immerman's review of the documentary record is persuasive, and he is no doubt correct in concluding that top American planners and corporate representatives closely linked to the government (or running it) really believed that Guatemala's moderate reforms constituted proof of "the penetration of Central America by a frankly Russian-dominated Communist group,"[116] justifying U.S. intervention in defense of freedom. Similarly, Asia scholar John King Fairbank is at least half-right in stating that "Our role in defending the South [Vietnam] after 1965 was...aimed at forestalling a southward expansion of Chinese communism."[117] But the point made by Immerman, Fairbank, and many others, is considerably too narrow. A comparable investigation of the record of other powers— including the USSR and even Hitler Germany—would no doubt reveal that their leadership too comes to believe the propaganda they produce in an effort to justify brutal and murderous acts undertaken in the interests of dominant domestic forces. It is a rare individual who, in personal or public life, consciously believes that what he does is genuinely evil. Rather, one easily comes to believe what it is comfortable to believe. The rational conclusion, which we draw with no hesitation in the case of official enemies or precursors in imperial aggression, is that the true interests are disguised in propaganda, perhaps even disguised to those who propound it, a fact of interest, perhaps, for the study of the psychology of leaders and the population they attempt to manipulate, but of little relevance to the study of state policy. It is only in studying the record of our own state that such elementary rationality is proscribed, and quite effectively suppressed—incidentally, quite a typical stance of elite intellectuals with regard to one or another Holy State.

There is, however, a related point that is of some significance for the study of state policy. A system of rationalizations and propaganda, once constructed and internalized, may come to be a factor influencing or determining policy decisions as ideology overwhelms interests. The same may be true of other irrational factors, such as those that entered into decision-making at the time of the Cuban missile crisis, to cite only one example (see also note 111). A close analysis of policy will generally unearth a structure of rational calculation based on perceived interests at its core, but in the complex world of decision-making and policy-planning many other elements may also intervene, sometimes significantly, including the system of self-serving beliefs that is regularly constructed to disguise —to others, and to oneself— what is really happening in the world.

Returning to the superpower conflict, while it surely has been a major factor in world affairs, it is simplistic and misleading to ignore its functional utility in providing a deceptive cover for subversion and aggression. The costs of the Cold War have been great, primarily of course for the direct victims, but also for the superpowers themselves. There are, in the first place, the material costs of a militarized society. And in addition, there are the moral costs. Very few people are gangsters by nature. Few people, for example, would steal a morsel of bread from a starving child if they happened to be hungry and knew that the child could not resist; such behavior, on the individual level, would be regarded as pathological. It is therefore necessary to conceal the fact that we engage in it on a vast scale, for example, when we impose and maintain regimes in Latin America that encourage the production of crops and beef for export to the United States while much of the population starves.[118]

Hence the need for organs of propaganda—the media, the schools, the universities and academic scholarship, with disgracefully too few exceptions. We must be protected from suffering the moral costs of our actions. It is not nice to think about the reality of Guatemala, where tens of thousands of children die of starvation every year while agricultural land is converted to export crops, where 80% of the agricultural population lives under conditions of semi-slavery while peasants, teachers, union leaders, priests, centrist political figures and others are gunned down by death squads directed from the Presidential Palace—conditions that result directly from repeated U.S. intervention over many years and direct U.S. military and economic support, or more recently, military support from Israel, in effect, indirectly from the U.S.[119] Or to think about the fact that in Brazil, people advertise their eyes and kidneys for sale in a desperate effort to survive, or sell their blood for export to the point where some die because they have "almost no blood," doctors report.[120] This is but one consequence of an "economic miracle" much praised in the United States after a U.S.-backed military coup in 1964 instituted a regime of torture and oppression in what Ambassador Lincoln Gordon described as "the single most decisive victory for freedom in the mid-twentieth century"[121]—something that he no doubt believed, just as Brezhnev no doubt believes that the USSR is selflessly defending the people of Afghanistan from U.S.-backed terrorism.

In these and innumerable other cases, it is much nicer to believe that we are defending someone from the Russians (or Chinese). The Cold War system has enabled us to maintain this pretense, as it has for our tacit partner in global oppression. It has enabled us to avert our eyes from many terrible scenes throughout the world, and also to contribute to perpetuating them. For us, the Cold War has been a war against much of the Third World, to a significant extent, while for the USSR, it has been a war against their subject populations. This is the real meaning of the Cold War, and we should not forget it, when we turn our attention to the fact that this system of massacre, torture and oppression may, in the end, engulf us as well.

What, then, are the proper directions for the disarmament movement? It should, certainly, be concerned with controlling and reversing the strategic arms race. It should also be concerned with the proliferation of nuclear weapons, and with the vast arms sales of the major (and some minor) powers, which are placing enormous means of destruction in the hands of states that will use them for internal repression or aggression; and with the fact, which Michael Klare has emphasized, that so-called "conventional arms" are reaching a point of destructiveness not far below that of nuclear weapons, so that "small" or "limited" wars will be extremely costly in human lives while "the so-called 'firebreak' between conventional war and nuclear war is vanishing," as conventional weapons become more destructive and low-yield nuclear weapons are devised, with the consequence that steps up the escalation ladder to full-scale thermonuclear conflict become ever more likely.[122] But there are other issues that cannot be dissociated from this complex and that are in many respects even more crucial: the domestic factors that drive the arms race, the dynamics of the Cold War and its impact on many millions of people, the extraordinary dangers (and horrors) of superpower intervention, the policies that contribute to maintaining or enflaming conflicts and tensions throughout the world, which, apart from the cost to the victims, are the most likely cause of a potential final holocaust.

The drift towards mutual annihilation has a seemingly inexorable quality. The factors and powers involved appear to be out of control, beyond our ability to influence or constrain them. We can only hope that this perception is false. One effect of the development of nuclear weapons has been to induce a feeling of powerlessness on the part of much of the population, and at the same time, to reinforce the doctrine that the state must be free to conduct its affairs without popular involvement or even scrutiny, given the awesome forces that it and its enemy commands. Recall the concern expressed in NSC-68 in 1950 that our society would be "vulnerable" if dissent were to be too freely tolerated. During that period, the Communist threat to our survival was successfully manipulated to impose conformism and passivity. So-called "McCarthyism" was an extreme variant, one that was quickly eliminated when it passed beyond helpless victims and extended to such powerful institutions as the U.S. Army. But the attempt to reduce the population to apathy and obedience went far beyond such excrescences.

The return to a more free and open society in the 1960s, with steps towards meaningful popular participation in the political process and challenges to reigning ideology, evoked much concern on the part of state authorities and the "secular priesthood" as well. The state undertook major programs of domestic terrorism and repression (see note 78), while elite circles shuddered at the collapse of authority during "the time of troubles." These fears were codified in the first major study of the Trilateral Commission, which warned of a "crisis of democracy" now that those glorious days had passed when "Truman had been able to govern the country with the cooperation of a relatively small number of Wall Street lawyers and bankers."[123] It called for a return to a more becoming state of apathy, so that democracy, in the preferred sense, could survive.

A particular concern has been what has been labelled "the Vietnam syndrome," that is, the insight into the real world that began to develop among substantial parts of the population as ideological constraints eroded, and the accompanying feelings of sympathy and concern for suffering people, many of them victims of our policies, a development that is quite intolerable to the approved moral code. It was widely believed that this dread ailment had been overcome in the quiescent '70s, a hope that was quickly shattered by the response to Reagan's attempt to rekindle the aggressive enthusiasms of the New Frontier. It is, in fact, remarkable that the '70s have so commonly been described as a period when popular movements were tamed. In fact, as many people know from their own experience, this allegedly quiescent period was one of wide-ranging activism; it was precisely in this period that the feminist movement became a major force, with a far-reaching impact on social life, along with the environmental movement and much else, often on a local level. The growth of the disarmament and solidarity movements in response to the "Resurgent America" programs of the later Carter and Reagan Administrations should come as no real surprise.

The disarmament movement, which forms part of a much broader complex, faces tasks of prime importance. Extending and deepening the much-feared "crisis of democracy" and "Vietnam syndrome" lie at their very core, and may, perhaps, offer some hopeful prospects in a period when prophecies of doom have an unfortunate ring of plausibility.

1. Barry M. Blechman and Stephen S. Kaplan, *et al.*, *Force without War: U.S. Armed Forces as a Political Instrument* (Brookings Institution: Washington, 1978).

2. Wilbur C. Eveland, *Ropes of Sand* (Norton: New York, 1980). According to Eveland, who was present as a mediator under CIA auspices, U.S. troops landed with atomic-armed rockets. In Blechman and Kaplan, *op. cit.*, William Quandt states that the troops had "nuclear-capable howitzers" but did not bring ashore nuclear weapons, though "the use of nuclear weapons was considered." Chairman of the Joint Chiefs of Staff Nathan F. Twining writes that State Department "back peddling" prevented the actual deployment of nuclear weapons, which remained off-shore, so that, had fighting developed, "the absence of these primary weapons from the battlefield, in the hour of need, could have been most serious" (*Neither Liberty Nor Safety*, Holt, Rinehart and Winston: New York, 1966, p. 65). Quandt notes Eisenhower's evaluation that there was a risk of "general war with the Soviet Union," an opinion shared by some of his advisers, who felt that "we should face the risk now as well as any time" (Loy Henderson).

3. Graham T. Allison, *Essence of Decision* (Little, Brown and Co.: Boston, 1971), p. 1.

4. *Ibid.*, p. 39. These statements are cited by Ron Hirschbein in his discussion of "atomic cultism" in his *Nuclear Theologians*, forthcoming.

5. For a review and an acute analysis of many examples, see Daniel Ellsberg, "Call to Mutiny," in Edward P. Thompson and Dan Smith, eds., *Protest and Survive* (Monthly Review Press: New York, 1981).

6. See my *Towards a New Cold War* (henceforth, *TNCW*) (Pantheon: New York, 1982), pp. 321, 458.

7. Roger Molander, "How I Learned to Start Worrying about Nukes," *Manchester Guardian Weekly*, April 4, 1982.

8. The contrary view is expressed by Jeremy Stone, Director of the Federation of American Scientists, who states that "Europe is still the tinderbox," David Shribman, *N.Y. Times*, June 24, 1982. Shribman reports "one common scenario": an uprising in Eastern Europe supported by West German sympathizers, then NATO forces. This seems far-fetched. There have been repeated uprisings in Eastern Europe with no hint of such a development, which seems less likely today than some years ago.

9. Thomas Powers, *The Man Who Kept the Secrets* (Knopf: New York, 1979). See *TNCW*, pp. 21f., for discussion in the context of the early postwar "rollback strategy" enunciated in NSC-68 (April 1950). On attempted coups in the Balkans, see Martin O'Shea, *N.Y. Times*, June 20, 1982. Blumenthal writes that the U.S. was "dropping agents into the Balkans by parachute in the early 1950's to foment revolts," and that among people influential in Washington were former Nazi collaborators who are held responsible for major massacres under the Nazis.

10. A new five-year Reagan Administration defense plan is reminiscent of the thinking of NSC-68, according to the account by Richard Halloran N.Y. Times, May 30, 1982. The policy aim emphasized in NSC-68 was "to hasten the decay of the Soviet system" from within. The new plan "asserts that the United States and its allies should, in effect, declare economic and technical war on the Soviet Union" (Halloran). It urges that the U.S. should "open up new areas of major military competition and obsolesce previous Soviet investment." Space should be exploited for U.S. military needs; intervention capacity should be rapidly expanded and special operations improved. The plan discusses "protracted" nuclear war (meaning anything beyond a single exchange of nuclear weapons). In such a war, "to exploit political, economic and military weaknesses within the Warsaw Pact and to disrupt enemy rear operations, special-operations forces will conduct operations in Eastern Europe and in the northern and southern NATO regions," with particular attention to eroding support within the Soviet system. With regard to intervention, "the strategy for Southwest Asia, including the Persian Gulf, directs American forces to be ready to force their way in, if necessary, and not to wait for an invitation from a friendly government" (Halloran).

The feasibility of these plans for "protracted nuclear war" is questioned by David C. Jones, retiring Chairman of the Joint Chiefs (Richard Halloran, N.Y. Times, June 19, 1982), on the grounds that the U.S. no longer has the nuclear superiority of earlier years that permitted it to send large forces overseas, as in Korea and Vietnam. Secretary of Defense Caspar Weinberger denied that the Reagan Administration was planning to fight a protracted nuclear war, though it was "preparing to prevail if the Soviet Union started such a conflict," Halloran, N.Y. Times, June 21, 1982.

11. For discussion of the U.S. response to martial law in Poland and Turkey, see Edward S. Herman, The Real Terror Network (South End Press: Boston, 1982), pp. 11, 144, 208f.

12. Shribman (op. cit.) cites Pentagon officials who "speak of the possibility that the Soviet Union might launch a sudden, unprovoked attack if they were to conclude that one planned in great stealth might disarm the United States of its retaliatory force." I think that such rhetoric, which is common, should be regarded as propaganda for a military build-up inspired by other motives, which is not to say that it may not be believed. See below for further comment.

13. David Woods, L.A. Times—Boston Globe, March 17, 1982.

14. See TNCW, pp. 35ff., for discussion of the interaction of government planning, popular reaction and media response during the early months of the Reagan Administration.

15. See "Bleeding Vietnam White," cover story, Far Eastern Economic Review, December 25, 1981. See TNCW for a number of examples. It

should be noted that although the reasons advanced vary, this is a typical U.S. response to radical nationalist movements that seek to extricate some country from the Western-dominated global system. With remarkable consistency, U.S. policy in the post-World War II period has been constructed to drive such societies into the Russian orbit, a consequence then exploited to justify further U.S. harassment, terrorism and intervention. When behavior is systematic, it would seem reasonable to search for a unifying cause, a task that does not seem difficult in this case.

16. Selig S. Harrison, *In Afghanistan's Shadow* (Carnegie Endowment for International Peace: New York, 1981), p. 51. For further discussion of why the Baluch "could easily become the focal point of superpower conflict," see Harrison, "Baluch independence," *The Nation*, November 14, 1981. For more on this topic, see *TNCW*, pp. 196f.

17. See Leila Meo, ed., *U.S. Strategy in the Gulf* (Association of Arab-American University Graduates, Belmont Mass., 1981), particularly the chapters by Michael Klare. See also Klare, *Beyond the "Vietnam Syndrome"* (Institute for Policy Studies: Washington, D.C., 1981).

18. See my articles in the *Guardian* (London), July 12, 1982; *Middle East International* (London), July 16, 1982; *Inquiry*, August 1982; *Merip Reports*, September 1982; END papers, Spokesman Pamphlet No. 81 (Bertrand Russell House: Nottingham, U.K., 1982).

19. See Claudia Wright, *New Statesman*, May 14, 1982; also *Counterspy*, February 1982.

20. *TNCW*, p. 297.

21. See Robin Wright, "Israeli 'provocations' in southern Lebanon fail to goad PLO—so far," *Christian Science Monitor*, March 18, 1982.

22. Editorial, *Washington Post*, April 22, 1982.

23. The *Post* cites in particular Israel's problems in "suppressing" the "Palestinian nationalist movement" in the West Bank and Gaza, and its "great pain" in evacuating settlers from the Sinai. As for the latter, the U.S. press has had little to say about the great pain of many thousands of Arabs violently expelled from these areas, their communities bulldozed, to prepare the ground for an influx of Israeli settlers a few years earlier; or about the fact that many of them remain a short distance away in the desert, "obliged to perform menial and seasonal agricultural chores for the Israelis at a daily wage of less than $2," Clive Robson, *Middle East International*, January 29, 1982; parts reprinted in *Palestine/Israel Bulletin*, P.O. Box 53, Waverly, Mass., 02179, February 1982. Nor did the *Post* or other journals take note of the fact, widely reported by Israeli journalists, that the "national trauma" of the Sinai evacuation was largely staged, with cooperation between the settlers and the army, for a domestic and American audience. See Amnon Kapeliuk, "Conjuring up a trauma," *New Statesmen*, May 7, 1982; for extensive discussion in the Israeli press of what Ha'aretz (April 27, 1982) called "Operational National Trauma '82'," See *Israleft News Service*, No. 205-6, May 20, 1982 (P.O. Box 9013, Jerusalem, Israel).

24. See *TNCW*, pp. 296f., 321, for some examples.

25. Elmer Winter, "The task facing American Jews," *Jerusalem Post*, June 18, 1982.

26. A spokesman for the conference of Presidents of American Jewish Organizations stated that "we had been well prepared for the invasion by General Sharon, who briefed the organization a little time ago." Michael Hamlyn, *London Times*, June 16, 1982. The invasion had been predicted for months in the Israeli press, often with sharp criticism.

27. Ned Temko, *Christian Science Monitor*, June 23, 1982; Claudia Wright, *New Statesman*, June 18, 1982.

28. UPI, *Boston Globe*, June 23, 1982.

29. See "Armaggedon is well-located" and other essays in *TNCW*.

30. Cited by Michael Klare, *Mother Jones*, April 1982.

31. Sheila Ryan, *Merip Reports*, May 1982. The next four include Tunisia and the Sudan.

32. In the past, Israeli power has also been perceived in this way, at least by U.S. intelligence, perhaps by Saudi ruling circles as well. See *TNCW*, chapter 11. That the primary threat is indigenous is recognized by many advocates of U.S. intervention, e.g., Robert W. Tucker, who advocates the use of U.S. military force if we are "faced by threats that, if permitted to go unmet, could result in sacrificing interests on which the nation's economic well-being and the integrity of its basic institutions depends," specifically, access to resources ("The Purposes of American Power," *Foreign Affairs*, Winter 1980/81). For discussion of this still more extreme proposals for military intervention that Tucker advances, see *TNCW*, chapter 8. See also note 10, above.

33. Since the U.S., rather than some hated enemy, was the perpetrator of these acts, they have not generally been regarded as blameworthy here, and in fact have often been justified on spurious grounds. Others have taken a different view. For example, in his dissenting judgment at the Tokyo Tribunal, Indian Justice Radhabinod Pal stated that the decision to use the bomb was "the only near approach to the directives...of the Nazi leaders" in the Pacific war. See my *American Power and the New Mandarins* (Pantheon: New York, 1969) for extensive quotes and references.

34. For discussion, see *TNCW*, pp. 48f., Herman, *op. cit.*, pp. 64f., and references cited.

35. Recall the comments of General David Jones, cited in note 10 above.

36. On June 26, 1982, the U.S. voted against all other Security Council members, vetoing a resolution calling for a limited withdrawal of Israeli forces from Beirut coupled with the withdrawal of PLO armed forces to "existing camps" outside Beirut, on the grounds that this plan "was a transparent attempt to preserve the P.L.O. as a viable political force" (Bernard D. Nossiter, *N.Y. Times*, June 27, 1982). A few hours later, the U.S. and Israel alone voted against a General Assembly resolution (adopted with two negative votes and no abstentions) calling for Israeli withdrawal from Lebanon and cessation by all parties of "all military

activities within Lebanon and across the Lebanese-Israel borders" (UPI, *Boston Globe*, June 27, 1982). Excerpts from the texts appear in the *Times*, June 27. Earlier, the U.S. had vetoed a Security Council resolution condemning Israel for ignoring the earlier demand for withdrawal of Israeli troops (*Boston Globe*, June 9, 1982).

The front page of the *N.Y. Times* on June 27 displays a remarkable conjunction of three adjacent stories: one, on the U.S. veto; a second on the vast destruction caused by the preceding day's "fierce Israeli strikes" and previous attacks; and a third on the national conference of the Democratic Party, which "adopted a statement highly sympathetic to Israel's recent attacks in Lebanon, qualifying it only with an expression of regret over 'all loss of life on both sides in Lebanon'." In contrast, the foreign ministers of the European Community adopted a resolution "vigorously condemning the new Israeli invasion of Lebanon" as "a flagrant violation of international law and the most elementary humanitarian principles," which "presents an imminent danger of leading to a generalized conflict" (*Le Monde*, June 11, 1982).

37. See *TNCW*, pp. 267f., 325, 461. General Haim Herzog, who was then Israel's ambassador to the UN, describes the January 1976 plan as "prepared by the PLO," and as "more moderate" than the Saudi Arabian plan proposed in 1981 (the Fahd plan). He cites also the PLO condemnation of the U.S. veto. ("Nothing new from Fahd," *Jerusalem Post*, November 13, 1981). David Krivine of the *Jerusalem Post* points out quite accurately that the reason for Israeli (hence also U.S.) refusal to deal with the PLO is "not because they are nasty people"; rather, "The obstacle is the subject on the agenda," which "can only be the creation of a Palestinian state on the West Bank, and that we can't agree to" since Israel will "have to retain part of it." Letter, *Economist*, July 10, 1982. The point has long been well-understood outside of the U.S.

38. See *TNCW*, pp. 324-5, 460-1.

39. "...Sadat was the first Arab leader who, a year after coming to power, declared his willingness to make peace with Israel in his famous reply [February 1971] to Dr. Jarring's memorandum" (editorial, *Ha'aretz*, October 8, 1971); four days after Sadat's "initiative, later known by his own name, for solving the Middle East problem," Gunnar Jarring presented his "famous report of 8 February 1971...to which Egypt gave a positive reply," Ghali Shoukri, *Egypt: Portrait of a President* (London: Zed Press, 1981), pp. 50-51.

Commenting further in *Ha'aretz* (November 13, 1981; *Israleft News Service*, No. 195, November 17, 1981), Amos Elon writes of the "panic and unease among our political leadership" regularly caused by Arab peace proposals; "The most extreme instance, though not the only one, was in early 1971, when Sadat threw Israel off balance with his announcement, for the first time, that he was willing to enter into a peace agreement with Israel, and to respect its independence and sovereignty in 'secure and recognized borders'." Elon describes the harshly negative reaction of the

Israeli government and the silence of most of the press. The occasion for his article was the similar reaction to the Saudi peace plan, just announced. There have been numerous other examples.

40. Eric Pace, "Anwar el-Sadat, the Daring Arab Pioneer of Peace with Israel," *N.Y. Times*, October 7, 1981.

41. Frederic L. Paxson, one of a group of American historians who offered their services to the state for this purpose during World War I; cf. *TNCW*, p. 70.

42. See *TNCW* for documentation and references.

43. On these matters, see *TNCW*, chapters 6, 9, 11, 12; Joe Stork, "Israel as a strategic asset," *Merip Reports*, May 1982; Meo, *op. cit.*; Seth P. Tillman, *The United States in the Middle East* (Bloomington, IN: Indiana University Press, 1982); and many other sources.

44. For some estimates, see the report of the Berkeley Study Group in *Science for the People*, May/June 1982. Intervention capacity is currently being considerably extended; see Richard Halloran, *N.Y. Times*, July 19, 1982, on special operations, one component of it.

45. *N.Y. Times*, May 10, 1982.

46. R. Jeffrey Smith, "Pentagon Moves Toward First-Strike Capability," *Science*, May 7, 1982.

47. *Ibid.* The Soviet defense minister, Marshal Dmitri Ustinov, "issued a veiled warning that the Soviet Union may adopt a 'launch on warning' defense posture—or an almost instant retaliatory strike largely decided by machines—in response to President Reagan's arms buildup," in particular, the proximity of Pershing missiles; Dusko Doder, *Washington Post - Boston Globe*, July 13, 1982.

48. See, for example, Fox Butterfield, "Anatomy of the Nuclear Protest," *N.Y. Times Magazine*, July 11, 1982.

49. See *The Boston Peace Budget* and other literature of Jobs with Peace, 10 West St., Boston, MA 02111. In his article on the nuclear protest (see note 48), Fox Butterfield, who is chief of the *Times* bureau in Boston, observes that "An important facet of the peace movement has been the degree to which Boston and Cambridge have been its breeding ground." There is no mention of Jobs with Peace or other similar programs.

50. John Vinocur, "The German malaise," *N.Y. Times Magazine*, November 16, 1981. One should, however, place Vinocur's discussion of the German peace movement in the context of his more general reporting from Germany. When the *N.Y. Times* sent him from Bonn to Paris, the West German journal *Die Zeit* bid him farewell with an editorial (August 6, 1982) describing him as a correspondent "who couldn't stand our country" and "missed no opportunity to comment in detail on the unfavorable and to represent the Germans to his country in that light." Cited by Alexander Cockburn, *Village Voice*, October 5, 1982.

51. The following day the *Times* ran a dispatch from Bonn reporting that demonstrators oppose the runway extension "on the grounds that it will destroy extensive forests and that it will serve to increase the military

potential of the airport, which is used by United States Air Force units assigned to the North Atlantic Treaty Organization," a fact that Vinocur neglected to mention in describing the irrational delusions of "the so-called peace movement." Special to the *N.Y. Times*, November 16, 1981.
52. The European peace movement has aroused an echo in East Germany, a fact of some interest. See Elizabeth Pond, "East Berlin's peace rally for writers takes a shot at *both* superpowers," *Christian Science Monitor*, December 16, 1981; John Tagliabue, "4,000 East Germans Dispute Official Defense Policy," *N.Y. Times*, February 15, 1982; also July 6, 1982.
53. Mary Kaldor, *The Nation*, June 26, 1982. McNamara, Bundy and Smith were subsequently awarded the $50,000 Albert Einstein International Peace Prize (*Boston Globe*, October 8, 1982). One wonders what Einstein's reaction reaction might have been to this choice.
54. *Report of Secretary of Defense Harold Brown to the Congress on the FY 1981 Budget, FY 1982 Authorization Request and FY 1981-1985 Defense Programs*, U.S. Government Printing Office, Washington, DC, January 29, 1980. See note 10, above.
55. *Op. cit.*, pp. 244-245. Emphasis in original.
56. Cited in Lars Schoultz, *Human Rights and United States Policy toward Latin America* (Princeton: Princeton University Press, 1981), p. 218.
57. *Ibid.*, p. 219.
58. For discussion, see Chomsky and Edward S. Herman, *Washington Connection and Third World Fascism World Fascism* (Boston: South End Press, 1979); Penny Lernoux, *Cry of the People* (Garden City: Doubleday, 1980); Herman, *op. cit.*; and the references of note 96, below, among others.
59. Charles Maechling, Jr., "The Murderous Mind of the Latin Military," *L.A. Times*, March 18, 1982. On the role of U.S. military assistance programs, see Miles D. Wolpin, *Military Aid and Counterrevolution in the Third World* (Lexington: Lexington Books, 1972).
60. See Klare, *Beyond the "Vietnam Syndrome"; TNCW*, pp. 189f.
61. See Peter Kihss: in the Dominican Republic, "Civil war broke out in April 1965, and President Johnson sent 23,000 troops to seek peace"; Jacob K. Javits: in Lebanon, the U.S. sent marines in 1958 "to avoid the very chaotic and religious war that has torn Lebanon apart," with Israel in a supporting role, and "Now Israel can again serve in this peace-producing role." *N.Y. Times*, July 5, 1982. Examples are legion.
62. For discussion, see *TNCW*, pp. 195ff.
63. *Op. cit.*
64. "The United States will sell a record $30 billion in arms overseas this year, far surpassing the Soviets and topping the $17 billion sold by the Ford administration in 1975" (*Christian Science Monitor*, April 21, 1982), citing a study by the Center for Defense Information); see *Defense Monitor*, April 1982.

65. Edward S. Herman, "Military Spending: The Last Externality," paper presented at the Conference on Social Scientists and Nuclear War, CUNY, June 4, 1982, a discussion of the dynamics of the military system.

66. "From Cold War to Cold Peace?", *Business Week*, February 12, 1949.

67. On this topic, see Gabriel Kolko, *Main Currents in Modern American History* (New York: Harper & Row, 1976).

68. See *TNCW*, pp. 22f.

69. Gregg Herken, *The Winning Weapon* (New York: Knopf, 1980).

70. Robert B. Reich, "Making Industrial Policy," *Foreign Affairs*, Spring 1982.

71. *Ibid.* These topics have been investigated for many years by Seymour Melman. See, e.g., his *Pentagon Capitalism* (New York: McGraw-Hill, 1970).

72. Chalmers Johnson, *MITI and the Japanese Miracle* (Stanford: Stanford University Press, 1982), p. 312.

73. On the sources of this effort in Reagan's domestic programs of alms for the wealthy, see *TNCW*, pp. 17f.

74. See the analysis of Soviet power by the Center for Defense Information (*Defense Monitor*, January 1980), concluding that it peaked in the late 1950s, declining since in capacity to coerce and influence.

75. See Fred Bergsten, "Crisis in U.S. Trade Policy," *Foreign Affairs*, July 1971, on Kennedy's concern for developing new markets for Japan.

76. *Business Week*, April 26, 1982.

77. Brad Knickerbocker, "Defense spending no longer off limits to budget-cutters," *Christian Science Monitor*, April 21, 1982.

78. There was some violence on the fringes of the movements of the 1960s, a good part of it caused by government provocateurs, though it did not begin to compare with the violence employed by the state in its efforts to disrupt the civil rights movement, the peace movement, the ethnic movements, and others. See my introduction to N. Blackstock, ed., *COINTELPRO* (New York: Vintage, 1976); Morton H. Halperin *et al.*, *The Lawless State* (New York: Penguin, 1976); Robert J. Goldstein, *Political Repression in Modern America* (New York: Schenkman, 1978); Lennox S. Hinds, *Illusions of Justice* (Iowa City: School of Social Work, University of Iowa, 1978); Christy Macy and Susan Kaplan, eds., *Documents* (New York: Penguin, 1980).

79. Henry Kissinger, *The White House Years* (Boston: Little, Brown & Co., 1979), pp. 57, 65.

80. Gar Alperovitz, *Cold War Essays* (Garden City: Doubleday & Co., 1970), p. 31.

81. John Lewis Gaddis, *The United States and the Origins of the Cold War* (New York: Columbia University Press, 1972), p. 316.

82. Arthur M. Schlesinger, letter, *New York Review of Books*, October

20, 1966; Walter Laqueur, "Visions and Revisions," *Times Literary Supplement*, March 5, 1982.

83. Herbert Feis, cited in Alperovitz, *op. cit.*, p. 135; Adam Yarmolinsky, "The military establishment," *Foreign Policy*, Winter 1970-71. On "the general failure of orthodox historians to engage the revisionist argument," see Christopher Lasch's introduction to Alperovitz, *op. cit.*

84. See Blanche Wiesen Cook, *The Declassified Eisenhower* (Garden City: Doubleday & Co., 1981); Stephen Kinzer and Stephen Schlesinger, *Bitter Fruit* (Garden City: Doubleday & Co., 1981); Richard H. Immerman, *The CIA in Guatemala* (Austin: University of Texas Press, 1982).

85. *Op. cit.*, p. 51.

86. See Thomas M. Franck and Edward Weisband, *Word Politics* (Oxford: New York, 1971), for comparison of the rhetoric employed in these cases.

87. "The overriding U.S. concern during the Dominican revolution," Jerome Slater points out, was "to avert at all costs a second Cuba" (Blechman and Kaplan, *op. cit.*, p. 307). On the bitter consequences of this effort to "seek peace," see Chomsky and Herman, *op. cit.*, chapter 4, section 4; Lernoux, *op. cit.*; Lisa Wheaton, "'Democratization' in the Dominican Republic," in Holly Sklar, ed., *Trilateralism* (Boston: South End Press, 1980); *TNCW*, pp. 381-82.

88. Stephen E. Ambrose, *Rise to Globalism* (Baltimore: Penguin, 1971).

89. See Gabriel Kolko, *The Politics of War* (New York: Random House, 1968); for a participant account, see Basil Davidson, *Scenes from the anti-Nazi War* (New York: Monthly Review Press, 1980).

90. See Lawrence S. Wittner, *American Intervention in Greece* (New York: Columbia University Press, 1982).

91. See Archimedes L.A. Patti, *Why Viet Nam?* (Berkeley: University of California Press, 1980). In September 1948, the State Department was concerned over "the unpleasant fact that Communist Ho Chi Minh is the strongest and perhaps the ablest figure in Indochina and that any suggested solution that excludes him is an expedient of uncertain outcome." For citation and discussion, see my *For Reasons of State* (New York: Pantheon, 1973), p. 32. This and much similar evidence has not prevented leading American Asia scholars from claiming that "the reason for our failure" in Vietnam (that is the harshest term that can be used) was that we did not recognize that the Viet Minh was a nationalist force. See *TNCW*, pp. 80, 400-401, for some examples.

92. See Frank C. Darling, *Thailand and the United States* (Washington, D.C.: Public Affairs Press, 1965).

93. See Stephen Rosskamm Shalom, *The United States and the Philippines* (Philadelphia: ISHI, 1981). On Thailand and the Philippines, see Chomsky and Herman, *op. cit.*, chapter 4, and sources cited there.

94. See Kolko, *Politics of War*; Joyce and Gabriel Kolko, *The Limits of Power* (New York: Harper & Row, 1972); Fred L. Block, *The Origins of*

International Economic Disorder (Berkeley: University of California Press, 1977). For further discussion, see chapter 1 of my *At War with Asia* (New York: Pantheon, 1970), and sources cited there.

95. See Lawrence H. Shoup and William Minter, *Imperial Brain Trust* (New York: Monthly Review Press, 1977).

96. See Richard Fagen, *Foreign Affairs* (Winter 1979), cited in *TNCW*, p. 206. See Wolpin, *op. cit.*; Jan Knippers Black, *United States Penetration of Brazil* (Philadelphia: University of Pennsylvania Press, 1977); Chomsky and Herman, *op. cit.*; Lernoux, *op. cit.*; Herman, *op. cit.*

97. Lars Schoultz, "U.S. Foreign Policy and Human Rights Violations in Latin America," *Comparative Politics*, January 1981. For a study with similar conclusions, see Chomsky and Herman, *op. cit.*., pp. 42-46, and Herman, *op. cit.*, pp. 128f.

98. Cited by Morton H. Halperin, *Militarism and Freedom* (Riverside Church Disarmament Program, July 26, 1981), p. 3. On some curious examples of apparent military-CIA involvement in terrorist training, see Philip Taubman, "The Secret World of a Green Beret," *N.Y. Times Magazine*, July 4, 1982.

99. See *TNCW*, particularly chapters 2, 11, 13.

100. *Business Week*, August 10, 1981.

101. At the same time, one should not discount the fact that the U.S. has regularly had the initiative in the nuclear arms race. See Roy A. Medvedev and Zhores A. Medvedev, "Nuclear Samizdat," *The Nation*, January 16, 1982. Up to very recent years, the point is not seriously disputed, and with regard to technological superiority, the conclusion remains clear. For recent discussion, see *SIPRI Brochure 1982*, Stockholm International Peace Research Institute, 1982.

102. To mention only the most obvious fact, the executive branch of the government has largely been staffed in top decision-making positions by representatives of major corporations or law firms that cater to their interests; see Gabriel Kolko, *The Roots of American Foreign Policy* (Boston: Beacon Press, 1969); Richard J. Barnet, *Roots of War* (Boston: Atheneum, 1972). This is only the most direct of the means by which business interests influence foreign policy. Nevertheless, the issues are more complex, and there are often second-order conflicts between the short-term needs of various sectors of the private economy and the long-term interests represented by the state, which has less parochial concerns; see *TCNW* for several examples. See Steven D. Krasner, *Defending the National Interest* (Princeton: Princeton University Press, 1978), for an illuminating discussion of this issue from a somewhat different point of view.

103. For an indication of the force of this taboo, see *TNCW*, pp. 103f.

104. Walter Laqueur and Charles Krauthammer, *The New Republic*, March 31, 1982.

105. Hans J. Morgenthau, *The Purpose of American Politics* (New York: Vintage, 1964).

106. Samuel P. Huntington, "American ideals versus American institutions," *Political Science Quarterly*, Spring 1982.

107. Huntington takes little note of such marginal features of human existence, limiting himself to the issue of what he calls "free elections," as in Greece, after the class enemy was suppressed by the U.S.-organized counterinsurgency campaign, a standard prerequisite for "genuinely free elections." On the actual role of the U.S. in "promot[ing] free elections in Greece" (Huntington), see Wittner, *op. cit.* Elsewhere, Huntington alludes to the fact that areas under U.S. control have their flaws, but the reason is the decline of American influence. Thus the U.S. "held few effective levers with which to affect the course of Philippine politics" when President Marcos instituted his martial law regime in 1972. In the real world, the U.S. held very effective levers, and used them effectively to support this brutal regime, which had the signal virtue of staving off a potential nationalist threat to U.S. investors. On the facts, see Shalom, *op. cit.*; Chomsky and Herman, *op. cit.*, among many other sources. The *Far Eastern Economic Review* correspondent in the Philippines, Sheilah Ocampo, observes that "analysts contend that Marcos is secure so long as he maintains the twin props of his rule—military support and foreign investment—particularly from the US" (October 17, 1980).

108. As Lars Schoultz notes, "Over the open and intense opposition of the Nixon, Ford, and Carter administrations, since 1973 Congress has added human rights clauses to virtually all U.S. foreign assistance legislation" ("U.S. Foreign Policy and Human Rights Violations in Latin America"). See his book cited in note 56 for more details.

109. See *TNCW* and earlier work of mine for numerous examples.

110. "Don't forget Afghanistan," *Economist*, October 25, 1980.

111. As late as 1969, Henry Kissinger regarded China as "the more aggressive of the Communist powers" (*op. cit.*, p. 173), without, however, citing specific examples of its worldwide aggression. But China lost this role when it became a U.S. ally. One indication of the inability of American planners and analysts to conceive of the possibility that the Vietnamese might have their own ideas is given by the quite remarkable fact that the Pentagon Papers historians, surveying a documentary record of 20 years, were able to discover only one intelligence document (a staff paper of 1961) that even raised the possibility that Hanoi might have nationalist goals, instead of serving as an agent of the Kremlin or "Peiping." For discussion, see *For Reasons of State*, p. 51.

112. Kinzer and Schlesinger, *op. cit.*, p. 106.

113. Immerman, *op. cit.*, p. 183.

114. *Ibid.*, p. 133.

115. *Ibid.*, p. 127.

116. *Ibid.*, p. 128, a paper by Adolf Berle on behalf of a study group of the Council on Foreign Relations, advising the State Department's representative, John Cabot.

117. See *TNCW*, p. 401, for references and discussion. Note that Fairbank does not doubt that we were "defending the South," though he regards this as an error, resulting from "an excess of righteousness and disinterested benevolence," as explained his Presidential address to the American Historical Society in December 1968; *ibid.*

118. "In Latin America, per person production of subsistence crops *decreased* by 10% between 1964 and 1974 [that is, after the direct involvement of the U.S. in promoting military rule and internal repression; see above] while in the same period per person production of export crops increased by 27%" (Richard Franke, "Why Hunger?: an Anthropologist's View," paper presented at the Victor Johnson Symposium on World Hunger, Amherst College, Amherst, MA, December 3, 1981. For background, see the regular publications of the North American Congress on Latin America (NACLA), e.g., Roger Burbach and Patricia Flynn, *Agribusiness in the Americas* (New York: Monthly Review Press, 1980). pp. 104-105.

119. See *TNCW*, pp. 290f.; Israel Shahak, *Israel's Global Role: Weapons for Repression* (Belmont, MA: Association of Arab-American University Graduates, 1982); "The New Latin American Arms Market," *Washington Report on the Hemisphere* (Council on Hemispheric Affairs), June 29, 1982, noting in particular Israel's central role in Guatemala.

120. Kenneth Freed, "A Brazilian Tragedy: Desperation: Selling Your Eye, Kidney," *L.A. Times*, September 10, 1981.

121. Cited by Black, *op. cit.*

122. Michael Klare, *Bulletin of the Atomic Scientists*, June/July 1982; *Des Moines Register*, April 16, 1982; "The inescapable links: Interventionism and nuclear war," unpublished, June 1982.

123. Samuel P. Huntington, in M.J. Crozier, S.P. Huntington and J. Watanuki, *The Crisis of Democracy* (New York: New York University Press, 1975). See Sklar, *op. cit.*, for background and discussion. Also *TNCW*, pp. 68f.

8

WHAT ABOUT
THE SOVIET THREAT?
By David Dellinger

Ronald Reagan seems to think that the disarmament movement has its headquarters in Moscow, that disarmament activists are dupes of the Kremlin, and that the leaders of the movement—presumably those who organize (or publish?) widely on the matter—are communist agents.

It might be good dinner-time banter to hypothesize whether Reagan actually believes this phobia, or instead promulgates it solely for the fear-mongering effect it might have in the media and across the country. With him it is sometimes hard to distinguish dangerous ignorance from venal manipulation, unlike many other leaders from whom we have come to expect only the latter form of disinformation.

Be that as it may, the question of the Soviet Union's foreign policy, of people's fears of Soviet imperialism, and of how these should be addressed by a sensitive disarmament movement are of first-rank importance. The problem of dealing forthrightly with the ills of Soviet policy and the character of the Soviet state without falling into the trap of "anti-communism," is a serious one. With red-baiting on the rise from media and political elites, and with the existence of real fears about the Soviet Union among the populace at large, the disarmament movement faces a difficult juggling problem. How do we evolve a logic and practice that is honest, communicates clearly, *and* addresses people where they are at? It is these matters which Dave's second contribution, "What About The Soviet Threat?" addresses.

—M.A.

There can be no doubt that large numbers of Americans and West Europeans are undergoing profound attitude changes toward nuclear weapons, or that these changes are causing other changes in our consciousness, with implications that none of us fully understand as yet. We are in the early stages of powerful movements that aim to force our governments to abandon their reliance on the politics of nuclear brinkmanship, and that show signs of being determined to take whatever steps prove necessary to accomplish this. But our calls for disarmament frighten a lot of people. What about Eastern Europe and the Soviet Union, they say. Unless the people there have the same sense of urgency, and freedom to protest and change the policies of their governments, what good are our efforts? If we succeed in getting the United States to reduce its nuclear arsenals (let alone abolish them), will we not be adding to the danger by assuring Soviet leaders that they can launch their bombs and missiles against us without fear of reprisal?

It is important for American advocates of disarmament to recognize the logic and power of this belief. So far as appearances are concerned, our critics may be right. There are compelling answers to their fears, some of which I will mention shortly, and we should make them. But they do not consist of arguing that the Soviet government is blameless in the present emergency. For all its rivalry with our governments (and their rivalry with it), it is closer in its thinking and politics to them than to the new modes of thought that are responding to the cosmic crisis and energizing the anti-nuclear movement.

In terms of both conventional politics and our own explorations of alternative ways of thinking and acting, there is no reason to trust the government of a country that invaded Afghanistan in 1980 (and is acting there today much as the United States acted for more than a decade in Vietnam). Or that invaded Czechoslovakia in 1968 (three years after the United States invaded the Dominican Republic and five years before it overthrew the democratically elected government in Chile). How can we trust, or ask others to trust, a country that sent its troops into Hungary in 1956 to suppress popular uprisings and install a regime that would be more capable of rendering the people powerless while it placed the interests of the Soviet Union ahead of their interests? (This happened two years after the United States overthrew the democratically elected government of Guatemala and installed a pro-American military regime, with terrifying results that persist to this day; three years after the C.I.A. staged a coup in Iran to prevent nationalization of its oil resources by replacing the reformist Mossadegh with the brutal Shah Pahlevi).

It's not absurd to be wary of a country that maintains rigid control of its East European satellites, through puppet governments, economic manipulations and the use of armed force when necessary (in other words, by roughly the same methods that the United States maintains "friendly authoritarian" regimes in its client states in Central America and other areas of the world that it considers crucial to its "vital [i.e. corporate] interests" or supposed military security).

Americans may know a lot more about Soviet attempts to bolster an oppressive regime in Poland than about U.S. efforts behind the scenes to destabilize it; and almost nothing about U.S. actions to preserve a right-wing dictatorship in Turkey, its NATO ally on the Soviet border, against the stirrings of its people. But that's no reason for those of us who believe in justice and peace everywhere to overcompensate by arguing that Soviet actions are justified, or scoffing at those who are frightened by them.

Finally, it's not hard to understand why people are ready to believe the worst of a ruling Party that, after sixty five years in office, still won't allow freedom of speech, press or assembly and arrests anyone who tries to organize an independent peace movement. In this area, the situation is not nearly so bad in the United States—and not worse, as it is in the case of the many U.S. interventions in countries close to the Soviet Union. Our civil liberties traditions and current practices are clearly superior, at least for most white people. But there are more serious limitations on our own freedoms than most Americans realize, and the disarmament movement will have to contend with them as it proceeds to organize the types of action that will be necessary to eliminate the nuclear danger. When it begins to organize a general strike, and other actions similar to the ones our government is so enthusiastic about in Poland, the response will not be gentle.

Confronting Fear and Hostility

I offer this (partial) list of Soviet and U.S. crimes for two reasons. The first is that for reasons we should understand many Americans are sincerely worried that the Soviet leaders might decide to get rid of their superpower rival tomorrow, if they thought they could do so without having their own country wiped out in the process. This fear, in turn, makes them afraid of the disarmament movement. I am not suggesting that this should lead us to moderate our program; certainly not by agreeing that the United States should continue its senseless production of arms until after the Soviet Union has agreed to stop. The situation is far too desperate for that.

Every new weapon the United States produces constitutes a new threat *to us,* whether the Soviet Union is foolish enough to try to keep pace or not. But as we expand and intensify our resistance, we had better learn to face suspicion and hostility without losing touch with the understanding that has given us enough hope to become active in the first place. That is the insight that fear and antagonism can be overcome with honest information, nonviolent actions and the type of sister- and brother-love that comes from consciousness that we are all members of the same threatened family.

The following words by Edwin Markham may not constitute great poetry, but they make for sound politics, particularly in the nuclear age.

> He drew a circle that shut me out—
> Heretic, rebel, a thing to flout.
> But love and I had the wit to win:
> We drew a circle that took him in.

Our country must adopt that approach in its dealings with other countries if the world is to survive. If we want it to do so, we should be equally creative in our relationships with those within the country who oppose and challenge us. Specifically, we should refuse to accept the role of "enemies," even when we are treated as such. Here again the "personal" and the "political," the "local" and the "global" are one. So should be the means we employ to achieve the ends we seek. As A.J. Muste used to say, "There is no way to peace; peace is the way."

It is a mistake to think that a politics based on "love" implies an excess of sentimentality at the expense of common sense, hard-headed analysis and militant action. Martin Luther King, Jr. often said that the only politics that will get us out of the mess we are in is a politics dominated by love for all our fellows. But more often than not he quickly added that we don't have to *like* everyone—or allow them to abuse us.

A realistic politics based on the sacredness of all person-hood, including our own, rejects and resists *institutions and actions* that oppress ourselves or other people. It restrains us from abusing those who abuse us. It is a logical extension of the secular revolutionary insight that draws a distinction between oppressive institutions and the people who are victimized by them. To mean anything, this has to apply to people who are victimized psychologically or spiritually, or driven by economic necessity, to act as agents of the oppressive institutions. A similar distinction is made in many religious traditions between the "sin" and the "sinner." The importance of both distinctions for a movement devoted to justice and peace rather than to retaliation and "seizing power" is not lessened by the failure of Marxist Leninists (by definition), many "Christians" and other leftists and religionists to live up to them.

Beginning in late 1968 and early 1969, the anti-Vietnam war movement was seriously weakened by instances of "trash-ing," screaming epithets (such as "pig" or "fascist") against those who opposed us, or deriding as class enemies or personal cowards people who had begun to turn against the war but differed from us in their methods of opposing it or prescriptions for ending it. As if breaking store windows, smashing public phone booths or (in a few rare cases) exploding a bomb in the washroom of a corporate office building would encourage people to think more clearly about the war or turn against the government or corporation instead of against a movement that did such things. As if those who had begun to change their politics but weren't changing as fast or as far as we wanted would join us more quickly and with a healthy attitude if we forced our own ideological loyalty oaths on them or used unhealthy forms of pressure to conscript them for actions they were not ready for. No wonder that during those years many people turned against the war and against the anti-war movement, depriving themselves and us of needed cross-fertilization and strength.

In the nonviolent atmosphere of today's mass demonstrations and civil disobedience actions, these examples may seem extreme. But now is the time to extend and deepen that spirit for the testing times that are inevitable. In doing so, it will help to remember that *many of our opponents are motivated by the same overriding sense of the danger of nuclear annihilation that we are, but draw opposite conclusions as to the best way to prevent it.* One of the most dangerous groupings of powerful people in favor of nuclear brinkmanship and U.S. domination of the entire world knew what it was doing when it cleverly called itself Committee on the Present Danger. For us to overlook this reality in the thoughts and feelings of millions of ordinary people—our neighbors and potential allies—and become self-righteous about our superior virtue, as evidenced by our concern for humanity and their supposed lack of it, will be politically self-defeating, even without a return to the acts of physical violence that crept into sections of the movement in the late Sixties.

Self-righteousness violates the growing awareness of human unity that characterizes our movement at its best and that I have been so bold as to call the beginnings of a psychic breakthrough. I call it that not because there have not always been a lot of people who have had a similar awareness (and most everyone for brief moments), but because I think that the universality and extremity of our plight have made it more real to more people in more countries at the same time than ever before. Our peril is leading more people to treat this awareness as pragmatic reality, something rapidly becoming more realistic than the so-called practical politics that treats our hostile divisions as inevitable and ineradicable. More people are coming to understand that no matter how great our differences may seem, in their essence all peoples of the world are one and must find ways of acting as such or the species will perish. To paraphrase a 19th century English writer, a truly aware person is one who realizes that the things that seem to separate us from our fellows are as nothing compared to the things that unite us with all humanity.[1]

No Double Standard

My second reason for listing a few of the actions by governments on each side of the Cold War that produce fear in the populations of the other side is to call attention to another error that can undermine the integrity of the disarmament movement and isolate it from the bulk of those we want and need to reach out to. It is to speak as if either side were solely responsible for the present impasse. We need constantly to challenge the double standard of those who one-sidedly condemn and fear the Soviet power elite more than they fear and condemn our own military-industrial complex. That is an urgent task, particularly in view of the efforts of ambitious politicians who are wedded to the U.S. power elite to jump on the nuclear freeze bandwagon—and the politically unrealistic belief of many peace advocates that the support of a Kennedy, Bundy or MacNamara is more important than developing a people's movement that understands the realities of U.S. imperialism. But we cannot carry out this task honestly or successfully if we fall into a similar double standard on the other side. Even at the most superficial level, to argue that Soviet participation in the arms race (whether to catch up, stay even, or get ahead), and its many acts of repression at home and abroad, are justified by our arms buildup and their defense needs is to accept the very arguments about how a country has to respond to external threat that we refuse to accept when they are put forward by our own militarists.

It is one thing for us to publicize and protest the many U.S. actions that lead the Soviet people to fear our government and are used by their government to justify the actions that cause our people to fear it (and back and forth to infinity, or however close to infinity the nuclear holocaust will take us). Clearly our primary responsibility as Americans is to put an end to such actions by our own government and society, not only to lessen the dangers of nuclear war but also for the sake of the immediate victims at home and abroad. But it is another thing to claim that Soviet actions do not add to the dynamic of the arms race, or are any less harmful to *their* victims at home and abroad.

Being realistic about the many crimes of the Soviet Union does not prevent us from pointing out that historically the United States has been the initiator and driving force behind the Cold War and the nuclear arms race. The U.S. military-industrial elite literally scared the wits out of the American people by raising the threat of Soviet power and dominance at a time when the Soviet Union was lying devastated from World War II, with twenty million war dead and its economy in shambles. It did this not out of honest fear of Soviet attack but in the service of its own power drives, its hatred of any attempt anywhere (even today in little Grenada) to build a non-capitalist society, and its eagerness to use the government-subsidized arms industry as a high-profit method of priming the economic pump. Earlier it dropped the bombs on Hiroshima and Nagasaki after Japan was defeated militarily and suing for peace. It did so not to save American lives but to demonstrate the awesome power of the weapon that was supposed to establish U.S. domination of the post-war world (the so-called American Century).[2] (On the Soviet side, Stalin also refused to respond to Japanese peace overtures, anxious that the war in the Pacific not end until he had moved a substantial body of troops into the Orient to strengthen the Soviet postwar position.)

Eight short months after Hiroshima and Nagasaki, the United States threatened to drop a nuclear bomb on the Soviet Union if it did not remove its troops from the unsettled areas of Northern Iran that border on the Soviet Union. The Soviet Union complied, but it is not hard to surmise that this humiliation strengthened the hand of those in its power elite who argued they needed their own nuclear bombs to "deter" such threats in the future. (To be realistic, this is how "deterrence" works. It spurs the opposing side to build up its destructive capabilities until no one is safe, not the countries temporarily and insecurely deterring each other, and least of all smaller, less powerful countries.) Many times since, the United States has "used" its nuclear weapons against the Soviet Union and other countries in a similar fashion. It has used them to extend its power and ability to rob Third World countries of their resources, much as a hold-up man "uses" a gun to rob his victims, whether he actually fires it or not.[3] The aim of the present military buildup is not to gain parity with the Soviet Union. America's strategic inferiority today is as fictitious as it was in 1960 when John F. Kennedy rode his claims of a disastrous missile gap into the presidency. It is an attempt to regain the overwhelming genocidal superiority that will permit the U.S. to throw its weight around without fear that the Soviet Union will be able to stand up to it.

Given facts such as these, it is not surprising that some well-meaning members of the disarmament movement tend to make excuses for the Soviet Union. But to jump from knowledge of U.S guilt to a position that holds the Soviet Union blameless, is to ignore a whole set of other facts. There is room for legitimate difference of opinion concerning the relative degrees of U.S. and Soviet complicity. But by now this debate has become as irrelevant to world safety as the meaningless debates over which country has the ability to wipe out the most millions of people and "emerge as number one, not number two" after a nuclear holocaust. Even those who are inclined to take the many Soviet disarmament proposals at face value while wisely distrusting those of the United States, must acknowledge that at the very least the Soviet Union has failed to respond to U.S. military imperialism with sufficient imagination to prevent its arrival with the United States in a no-win situation. Like the United States it relies on nuclear blackmail for a precarious survival that seems doomed not to last unless both countries reverse course. By now, Soviet bombs are as apt to go off by accident as ours; be launched by some fearful or "insane" members of their power elite as ours; or provide the excuse for a similarly catastrophic decision by their counterparts here. For us to state these facts simply and straightforwardly, in our domestic campaigns and in international conferences sponsored or attended by the Soviet Peace Committee is an indispensable prerequisite for achieving a healthy climate for the work that has to be done in both countries and between the peace-loving people of both.[4]

Mirror, Mirror on the Wall

As long ago as the mid-fifties, Vinoba Bhave, an Indian disciple of Gandhi, said,

> Russia says America has dangerous ideas so she has to increase her armaments. America says exactly the same thing about Russia.... The image in the mirror is your own image; the sword in its hand is your sword. And when we grasp our sword in fear of what we see, the image in the mirror does the same. What we see in front of us is nothing but a reflection of ourselves. If India [or the United States or the Soviet Union— D.D.] could find the courage to reduce her army to a minimum it would demonstrate to the world her moral strength. But we are cowards, and cowards have no imagination.

We may all be cowards, in one respect or another, though usually I try to avoid that pejorative concept. But if we are, the time has come when even cowards must use their imagination and moral strength to break the pattern of violence and counterviolence that threatens to destroy the world. To achieve the spiritual and political strength necessary for a whole country to break out of this pattern requires a totally realistic assessment of the forces at work on both sides of the conflict. It would not be realistic for us to appeal to the Soviet Union to disarm because the C.I.A., Pentagon and U.S.-based multinational corporations have clean hands and the best interests of the Soviet people in mind. It is no more realistic to tote up the peace offers made by the Soviet Union, talk about the defensive aspects of its arms build-ups and foreign interventions and urge our country to disarm because of the peace-loving nature of the Soviet government.

Some people fear that to be frank about the country against which the U.S. militarists say we must arm (to the point of widespread poverty and imminent suicide) will make it more difficult to persuade the American public of the wisdom of disarming. But in the long run, nothing can make that task more difficult than refusing to level with the American people. Trying to sweep unpleasant facts under a rug of silence will not prevent the media and government from blaring them forth in distorted headlines and newscasts, out of context, and with far more frightening implications and conclusions than people would fall for if they had access to honest facts and analysis from a movement they have learned to trust.

It is not hard to show that the real competition between the United States and the Soviet Union is not over preparations by either country to invade, occupy, and administer the daily affairs of the other. It is competition for control of the resources, labor, and markets of Third World countries. From the point of view of the danger of nuclear war, it makes little difference whether the profits sought are largely private (with some "trickle-down" effects), as in the case of the United States, or mostly "national" (but unequally shared), as with the Soviet Union. If a few right-wing fanatics in either country harbor illusions about occupying their super-power rival, nuclear arms are not the way to prevent them. Possession of a "defensive" nuclear strike force capable of inflicting massive "assured destruction" may act as a deterrent for a while. But it also leads step by step to the psychology, politics and hair-trigger, accident-prone technology that by now have made nuclear war virtually inevitable without a reversal of course.

The natural pride, patriotism, and grass-roots resistance of the people would provide the most practical method of turning an attempted invasion into a disaster for anyone foolish enough to attempt it. Already the Soviet Union has more than it can handle trying to pacify Eastern Europe, Afghanistan, and Eritria, let alone its problems on its border with China. The United States, for all its financial and military power, has its hands full in tiny El Salvador, Nicaragua, South Korea, the Philippines, etc., not to forget its recent inability to occupy and pacify Vietnam. The only insane way either superpower could think of successfully occupying the other would be by destroying its populations in a first-strike nuclear attack. But that wouldn't work either, because radiation would make the country unoccupiable—and probably their own country as well.

Dealing With Anti-Communist Hysteria

Other people caught up in an outdated, end-justifies-the-means distortion of "progressive" politics, fear that to speak honestly about Soviet guilts is to encourage the one-sided anticommunist hysteria that is promoted by the government and media. But here again, there is no cure more effective than the truth. This means publicizing the real facts when the United States invents scurrilous tales of Soviet domination of an indigenous liberation movement as a cover for its own attempts to dominate the country in question. And it means exposing the lies and evasions of our government about peace proposals of the Soviet Union that could provide the basis for a positive response by an American government that wanted multinational arms reductions. But it also means being frank about Soviet actions that violate not only the enlightened socialist or communist ethics of the past but also the new political ethics that are developing along lines that were once considered utopian but have become the only practical way to respond to today's peril.

To argue that this is anti-communist or will encourage blind anti-communism in others is as false as to argue that to take a public stand in opposition to the terrible crimes of Israel against the Palestinian (and other) people is anti-semitic or will encourage anti-semitism. Ironically, some of those who place their hopes, if not in the Soviet Union as it is today then at least in a more enlightened non-authoritarian form of communism, understand that it is not anti-semitic to speak the truth about Israel but think it is anti-communist to speak truthfully in public about the Soviet Union. This is a by-product of the traditional, ultimately self-defeating tendency of so-called political realists to choose a "lesser-evil" side and tailor their arguments (and ultimately their thinking) to its benefit.

To state the matter bluntly, the kind of movement that will become capable of doing what is necessary for survival of the species cannot afford to repeat the mistake made by a lot of well-meaning progressive people in the thirties and forties. They dismissed the Stalinist blood purges and death camps as capitalist propaganda, even after the evidence had become overwhelming. Others, in their confusion, tried to side-step unpleasant facts in a manner caricatured in a macabre joke of the time: "Q: What about the slave labor camps? A: What about lynchings in the South?" This during a period, when, under Stalinism, more people were imprisoned, tortured and killed than in Germany under the Nazis.

Sometimes, tragically, it is not a case of *either/or* but of *both/and*. When we protest the crimes of one country and evade or make excuses for those of the other, on the theory that the United States is "democratic" or that the Soviet Union is "socialist," we encourage the narrow partisanship in ourselves and our opponents that keeps us divided and makes it more likely that the crimes of both will continue.

In the thirties, those who clung to the Soviet Union in this blind partisan way paid a heavy price, first in their loss of public trust and influence, later *in their own disillusionment and loss of hope*. Not enough attention has been given to the fact that the vicious red-baiting of Senator Joseph McCarthy was able to wreak more damage than otherwise would have been politically possible because of the internal disarray of those sections of the progressive movement who had made this heart-breaking mistake.

Today the Soviet Union is free of Stalin and the most massive and monstrous crimes of his regime, but it has not changed its basic characteristics or policies, including its internal authoritarianism. So militarized is its economy that it can provide arms to Third World peoples struggling to gain their freedom (and to governments within its orbit that are struggling to suppress freedom) but cannot provide food, civilian goods, or a model of freedom.

Meanwhile, the imperialistic drives of the Pentagon, the U.S.-based transnational corporations, and the government that serves their interests, under both parties, have become more blatant and far-flung. The changes that take place when liberal Democrats replace not so liberal or compassionate Republicans (or Democrats) are merely cosmetic. *Plus ca change, Plus c'est la meme chose.* (The more things change, the more they remain the same.) More and more people around the world and even inside the United States are becoming aware that these drives are ruining them economically and are leading step-by-step to a nuclear holocaust.

The disarmament movement will suffer grievous losses in external influence, internal morale and staying power, if it does not face up to *both* of these realities. It cannot afford to be misled by the peaceful rhetoric of either government. It dare not be fooled by the occassional positive steps one or the other takes in the course of the twists and turns through which it tries to keep the public in tow while pursuing its dangerous policies.

In particular, the American disarmament movement needs the active contributions of two groups that are not fully active in today's white-middle-class-dominated anti-war movement. One consists of Third World populations inside the United States. They are prime victims of the system at home, and many of them are acutely aware of what the U.S. corporations and government are doing in Africa, Central America, the Middle East, the Philipines, etc. They can help guard against the movement's tendency to over-estimate the "peace-loving," "democratic," nature of the United States. Their participation and leadership are necessary to the movement's integrity and vision.

The second is comprised of ethnic groups of immigrants from Soviet dominated countries, who know too much to believe that the case for disarmament rests on the peaceful nature of the Soviet Union. Sometimes this important section of the population is dismissed from consideration because of the reactionary, pro-U.S. lengths to which some of their members take their anti-Soviet bitterness, and the uses to which the C.I.A. has put it.

But it makes absolutely no sense to dismiss them all as ex-members of the nobility or fascists, 65 years after the Russian Revolution and nearly forty years after the creation of the Soviet bloc in Eastern Europe. Second and third generation immigrants from these countries tend to be more realistic about American realities than their parents. Their first-hand experience is to suffer grievously from unemployment, runaway shops and other indignities imposed on them by a profit-dominated, anti-worker economy. They can help forge necessary links between the labor and anti-war movements, if we don't alienate them with well-meaning but inaccurate defenses of Soviet injustices.

People-to-People Rebellions

Our current peril flows from the unfortunate similarities between the governments of the United States and the Soviet Union, whatever differences there may be in economic and political systems and the methods by which a tiny elite in each country maintains undemocratic and unsocialistic control. Our hope lies in the similarities between the people of these two countries, whatever our differences in language, culture and politics. The bulk of the people of both countries are eager for survival through peace. So are the people of Europe. The nuclear threat and other unpleasantnesses in their everyday experiences are stimulating the populations in both East and West Europe to make efforts to break out of Cold War blocs that subordinate their interests to those of the superpower "protector."

Our job is to communicate with the people of these countries, not so much through summit conferences of political leaders we cannot trust, or arms control negotiations between governments not committed to disarmament, but through people-to-people contacts. The surest, most powerful way for Americans to communicate is by continuing and expanding the mass protests and nonviolent resistance actions that demand a transfer of research, labor and funds (governmental, corporate, and academic) from military to civilian projects and an end to direct and indirect military interventions abroad.

Despite a media blackout in Soviet countries and dimout here, a number of visitors, smuggled documents and a few news stories indicate a growing perception within the Soviet bloc that the threat of nuclear annihilation requires people to take actions they did not consider reasonable or necessary a short time ago. These actions are not prudent for anyone thinking in terms of individualistic advancement, or in some cases even survival. But news of the mass rallies and other more militant actions in the West has strengthened the determination of similarly alarmed people in those countries to launch their own forms of protest. When asked recently about such activities, Pastor Rainer Eppelman of East Berlin testified that "Our peace work depends...on the anti-nuclear armament groups in the West."[5]

Eppleman launched a protest petition, called the Berlin Appeal, in late January, 1982. It calls for a nuclear-free zone from the Urals to the Atlantic and removal of NATO and Soviet "occupation forces" from West and East Germany. It raises for consideration bans on war toys, military parades and civil defense drills, and opposes military training in the schools. After a couple of months, *Der Spiegel* (a West German publication) reported that more than two thousand East Germans had signed the appeal, despite severe penalties for signing it. After visiting East Germany in the summer, Adam Hochschild of *Mother Jones* magazine reported that the number of signers "by now...is far greater."[6]

Eppleman's decision to launch the Berlin Appeal and the positive response it received were undoubtedly influenced by the circulation in West Germany of the Krefeld Appeal. The West German petition did not go as far as the East German one. It demanded a public referendum on the deployment of American Cruise and Pershing 2 missiles. Although it was signed by two million West Germans, the government "asserted that the constitution did not allow for public referendums on such military matters."[7]

As yet most of the protests in Soviet countries are not as extensive as here, and the forms tend to be more muted and certainly less massive. This is a natural consequence of the fact that the forms of repression are traditionally less muted and more massive than they usually are here. I say "usually," because, as almost every black or other Third World person in this country knows, and as the most determined protestors of the Sixties discovered regardless of their race, this country is capable of the most extreme forms of repression. Here they take place when the power elite perceives what the Supreme Court calls a "clear and present danger." The danger they perceive is not the one the disarmament movement sees today and usually does not threaten anyone's legitimate human rights. Customarily it is a "danger" to the undemocratic privileges and power of a tiny minority.

The Message from Poland

The obvious exception to the lack of massive, country-wide protests within the Soviet Bloc is Poland. At first glance, and with an assist from our media and politicians, the Polish resistance may appear to be an argument *against* our disarmament efforts rather than in their favor: "See how bad the Soviet Union is! That's why we have to have military superiority." I believe the opposite; namely, that even after we take into account the naively pro-American sentiments of some sections of the Polish movement, their actions make our actions more relevant and important.

One reason for drawing the wrong conclusion from the Polish actions is that their anti-nuclear opposition is somewhat overshadowed by their attention to more immediately pressing grievances rooted in poverty and repressive domination by a foreign power. On the surface and without more information than our media provide, it can be argued that their concerns are not our concerns and they are not like our disarmament movement at all. This seems especially true if one accepts the myth that our movement is a single-issue movement made up of people without other pressing demands. But for those who do not view the nuclear issue as an isolated problem, it is not necessary for it to predominate in Poland in order to see parallels between their movement and ours. This is especially clear if one saw the plethora of signs at the June 12th protest proclaiming a symbiotic relationship between a military mentality and a host of other social malignancies that interact as both cause and effect.

Polish economic problems, like ours, have been intensified by the diversion of productive energies and resources to the arms industry, and both Solidarity and KOR make this clear. Some of the accompanying anti-military demands have been aimed primarily at the Soviet Union, their supposed protector and direct tormentor. But this is not so different from what has been happening in the United States. As our economy has worsened, demands to cut the *U.S.* arms budget, *even in the absence of a bi-lateral freeze*, have become more insistent. To their credit, some of the previously most rigid advocates of a single-minded concentration on the horrors of nuclear weapons and the need for a bi-lateral agreement now make this demand.

It is perfectly logical for the worst sufferers in both countries, and those who empathize with them, to stress the need for immediate relief from the *results* of a militarized economy, as experienced in an intensification of already existing injustices. As I write (at the close of 1982), demands of this type are as fervent and widespread in the United States as demands for an end to the nuclear threat itself. There is a flood of activities focussing on unemployment, threats to social security, utility rates, mortgage sales of family farms, gentrification of the inner cities, police and other crimes against blacks, civil liberties abuses in the name of "national security," etc. But this does not mean that anxiety about nuclear extinction has disappeared or ceased to act as a powerful energizing force.

Just as there is a handful of American protestors (without significant influence) who tend to romanticize the "peace-loving, socialist" Soviet Union, so in Poland there are opponents of the regime who romanticize the "peace-loving, democratic" nature of the United States. In both cases, the enemy of their enemy is thought to be their friend. For historical reasons connected with Soviet totalitarianism and Polish poverty, American civil liberties and affluence, and the still persistent (but rapidly disappearing) myth of U.S. devotion to human rights, the number who take this position is far greater in Poland than in the United States. But again this should not obscure the underlying similarities between the goals and basic drives of the

Polish and American movements—for a better life, for a greater say in the decisions that affect their lives, for survival through peace.

Concerning the goal of survival, there is, of course, more information about the Polish movement than our media readily provide. Few Americans realize that Solidarity calls for the *abolition of all nuclear weapons*. Hard pressed as they are, they consider this demand a part of their program and close enough to the hearts of the Polish people to put it forward as one of several organizing themes for their demonstrations. The underground *Solidarity Information Bulletin*, No. 10, May 29, 1982, calling people to a protest on June 13, stipulated

> We demand the destruction of nuclear arsenals! Begin US-USSR Talks Now! (*Catholic Worker*, December 1982)

The American media, with their assumptions of what constitutes "news" and their preoccupation with the *differences* between the Soviet Union and the United States rather than the similarities, may play down these correlations between the Polish and American movements, but we should not overlook them.

For my part, I wonder if the Polish example does not encourage us to expand the similarities by making an even stronger identification between our opposition to the attitudes and institutions that have produced the nuclear threat and our support for the needs and demands of *those sections of the American population whose lot, for whatever reason, is not substantially better than that of the Polish people.*

I also wonder if their example does not support the view that the primary responsibility and natural inclination of people on both sides of the Cold War is to press for unilateral initiatives in their own country, as a first step toward creating the international climate for multinational disarmament. Well intentioned disarmament leaders whose personal lot is more comfortable sometimes underestimate how natural it is for people suffering from the burdens as well as insecurities of a nuclearized economy to do this. Spokespersons for the power elite, who have their own selfish reasons for arguing that the United States cannot disarm until the Soviet Union does, may have some success in counteracting this natural tendency. But those of us who understand the urgency of beginning the process without delay should not unwittingly encourage this fallacy by constantly "reassuring" people that we are proposing only simultaneous bi-lateral disarmament and are not in favor of unilateral *beginnings* that go beyond mere talk. Whatever the (dubious) merits for using this as an initial organizing tactic, it has now become counterproductive, providing the Reagan administration with a ready-made basis for obfuscation and stalling.

However, consideration of these two questions should not divert us from realizing the one inescapable message from Poland. *Polish events demolish the arguments frequently heard in this country that our disarmament movement is unrealistically (and unfairly) taking advantage of freedoms that exist here but whose denial in Soviet dominated countries makes impossible the rise of significant resistance movements.* To cap their error, most of the people who make this argument extol the Polish resistance and decry even more moderate programs and actions here. If one considers that the Polish people are resisting their colonization by the Soviet power elite and the American people are in an early stage of challenging our colonization by U.S. based multinational corporations, one sees the basic parallelism between the two movements, whatever the differences in form. One also understands why those who speak for our colonizers take the positions they do. In effect, they take the same attitude toward our efforts to intervene in the political process that the Soviet leaders take toward the Polish efforts, and for basically the same reasons.

Superpower Policies

An interesting and useful case can also be made that the attitudes of the two superpowers toward resistance movements in the homeland of the other and in its major, historically acknowledged, satellite areas of Europe are similar, though they are different than the attitude attributed to the Soviet Union by rightist critics and to the United States by many leftists.

There are indications that both Soviet and U.S. policy is to encourage and assist dissident movements in the belly of the other beast but not so much that they get out of hand by becoming too successful. The United States benefits from having Polish resisters (and Soviet dissenters) harass and embarrass the Soviet Union but does not want the people in either country to overthrow their rulers and gain their freedom. Without Soviet tyranny how could the United States justify its frantic, highly lucrative arms buildups and world-wide sales to "threatened" countries, its interventions and bases all over the world, its mammoth expenditures and obscene activities in behalf of corporate interests and American power by the C.I.A. and other "intelligence" agencies, its extensive recourse to "classification" and secrecy that undermines the public's right to know, its violations of the right to privacy and other civil liberties?

As the cliche goes, if the Soviet Union did not exist, the United States would have to invent it. Since it does exist, why allow its offensive and frightening character to disappear and thereby destroy its usefulness? This realpolitik, together with an overriding capitalist desire to keep milking Poland and eventually get a full return on their investments, helps explain the decision by U.S. banks, (supported by governmental suspension of the laws governing such transactions) not to foreclose on Poland's loans, despite that country's flagrant defaults on both interest and principal payments.

As if this were not enough, freedom anywhere is contagious. This realization and the fear it aroused was the misstated essence of the much maligned domino theory that led the United States to continue its aggression in Vietnam long after it became economically and politically unprofitable in short-run terms. The ridiculousness of that theory is not in the accurate understanding that underlies it, but in the topsy-turvy manner in which it is applied. If one accepted U.S. claims to have been fighting for freedom in Indochina, and to be doing so now in El Salvador, Guatemala, Africa, etc. in order to prevent the falling domino effect one would have to believe that the establishment of tyranny anywhere inspires other people to rise up and insist on being tyrannized too. Of course, in contrast, the obvious reality that the United States is fighting in support of tyranny makes it easy to understand the "domino effect" of successful opposition movements.

A similar understanding of the dangers of allowing freedom to exist anywhere explains why the United States, despite its pretensions to the contrary, consistently acts on the principle that if it cannot dominate and control a Third World country it would prefer to see it become a Soviet satellite rather than an independent non-aligned state. In particular it fears and acts to prevent the emergence of independent non-totalitarian socialist (or other humane, post-capitalist) societies which might serve as powerful models not only for other Third World countries, but for the citizens of industrialized Western and Eastern bloc nations as well. The United States not only argues that Cuba, Vietnam and now Nicaragua are controlled by the Soviet Union *but does its best to turn the claim into a reality*, despite strong indigenous sentiments in all these countries and the efforts of all three to avoid that fate. All three have tried to enter into friendly relations with the United States in order to exist as fully independent entities that can relate to both superpowers (and the rest of the world) without becoming dependent on any foreign power. But the United States rejects all overtures and imposes embargoes on everything from manufactured goods, agricultural instruments and raw materials to food, medicine, disaster relief and foreign loans. It tries to force its allies to do the same. If anyone doubts that the reason for this is the one I have ascribed, consider that the United States does not pursue a similar policy toward the Soviet "monster." Instead, it harasses the Soviet Union from time to time, and underlies its role as dangerous aggressor (as in Afghanistan) by boycotting the Olympics and placing a temporary embargo on wheat sales, etc., but that is all. If the motive for boycotting Cuba, Nicaragua, and other Third World countries seeking an independent road is punitive, or ethical and somehow aimed to hurt "communism," why aren't the same policies applied to the Soviet Union itself?

Indirect support for this analysis also comes from understanding Soviet policy in Vietnam for fifteen years as well as current U.S. policy in respect to Afghanistan. In both cases the objective has been to keep their rival bogged down in a quagmire while avoiding a confrontation. I am not talking only about an all-out military confrontation but anything that would seriously upset detente. U.S. rhetoric aside, detente is practiced by both sides, with each having a somewhat different view as to how far it should extend. Hence, the Soviet·Union's red-carpet reception for Nixon in Moscow in 1972, in the midst of an escalation in Vietnam that killed Soviet seamen in the port of Haiphong. Hence U.S. covert aid to the "rebels" in Afghanistan but lack of interest in serious international pressures that would destabilize relations with the Soviet Union. (The relations are not seriously destabilized by the arms build-up since the reasons for this have more to do with domestic economic and political considerations and competition in the Third World than with any intention of attacking the Soviet homeland, and the Soviet rulers know this.)

I am not suggesting that these policies are publicly articulated, or even agreed to by all contending sections of the American or Soviet establishment. In both countries there undoubtedly are eager-beaver adventurers who argue for crushing the evil enemy. If so, either power has gone to their heads or they are genuine "true believers" who put ideology and ethnocentric devotion to what they think of as American freedom or Russian socialism ahead of "practical" considerations. Or they may be Pentagon boys in love with their toys and anxious to try them out. But U.S. administrations tied to the corporate establishment prefer to avoid such silliness. And of course the opposition of all Soviet administrations to such suicidal adventurism has been obvious for years to anyone who pays more attention to their words and deeds than to U.S. propaganda efforts to justify its own armaments and interventions.

Fear of the destabilizing internal effects of external freedom (particularly in its satellite areas) and a concern for Great Russian power interests led the Soviet Union to crush efforts to establish "socialism with a human face" in Czechoslovakia in 1968 and Hungary in 1956, and to oppose politically liberalizing trends elsewhere. For similar reasons it wiped out a whole generation of anti-Nazi resistance leaders after World War II. *The Soviet Union pursues these policies despite the fact that the establishment of a humane and democratic socialism would encourage the rise of anti-capitalist movements in the United States and in its subject and allied countries by giving hope to people suffering under the status quo by providing alternative models.* And it would encourage them to support a Soviet Union that related positively to such developments. Similar considerations have dominated the Soviet bureaucracy's treatment of Communist Parties all over the world, even though its high-handed methods have caused severe strains and periodic mass defections, as happened in France, Italy, England and the United States after the invasions of Hungary and Czechoslovakia. It would be unrealistic to imagine that other loyalties would dominate its efforts to influence Western disarmament movements. And they don't.

Communist Influence

Working as best it can through the World Peace Council and local Communist Parties, the Soviet Union welcomes and encourages the U.S. and West European disarmament and anti-intervention movements because of their ability to embarrass and discredit the United States and serve as restraints on U.S. interventionism and adventurism, both of which can get out of hand and send Soviets as well as Americans up in radioactive smoke. But most members of these organizations scrupulously avoid public anti-capitalist propaganda and discourage anti-capitalist trends in the disarmament movement. They try to soften anti-Soviet attitudes and naturally avoid discussions of Afghanistan, trying desperately to change the subject if it comes up. Despite their obviously sincere devotion to the cause of peace and the welfare of America's numerous minority groups and powerless majority, their politics are far closer to those of their elitist Soviet model than to the spirit and practice of most American groups in the 1980s. They press for summit meetings and agreements between members of the U.S. and Soviet power elites and they try to rally support for liberal, safely pro-capitalist politicians such as Edward Kennedy. Earlier the Communist Party worked to get the American peace movement to support Henry Wallace, Adlai Stevenson, Lyndon Johnson (after he had faked the Gulf of Tonkin affair and bombed North Vietnam), Hubert H. Humphrey (a virulent anti-Communist who had proposed outlawing the U.S. Communist Party) George McGovern and Jimmy Carter. For years it opposed calls for withdrawals of U.S. troops from Vietnam, putting forward instead slogans favoring negotiations between the Vietnamese and U.S. governments and making discrete references in high-level anti-war circles to the fact that Vietnam could not hope to win and should accept a divided country.

Sometimes I wonder if the Right Wing in this country know how pathetically conservative, irrelevant to a dynamic anti-war movement, and discredited the American Communist Party and any organization it succeeds in influencing are. My guess is that the more "populist" Red-baiters are the simplistic ideologues I have already referred to, and that the more sophisticated screamers are just playing the game, knowing the advantages to the American power elite of frightening the public with an imaginary Red Menace.

It is, of course, an insult to the intelligence of the millions in this country who have marched, rallied or supported anti-nuclear and Jobs with Peace referenda to suggest, as Ronald Reagan has done, that they are not capable of listening to both sides of the nuclear weapons debate and making up their own minds as to the reality of the danger and the need to take action. Given the flood of high-level propaganda, disinformation and dire warnings based on secret "intelligence sources," all aimed at establishing the need for a nuclear build-up, it is fatuous to claim that the contrary decision of millions results from the more clever manipulations of a handful of pro-Soviet ideologues or agents. Ironically, the words and deeds of the last two administrations dramatized the real danger and convinced infinitely more people of the need for disarmament than could possibly have been accomplished by any attempted manipulations by equally duplicitous Soviet forces as opposed to the welfare of the American people as Reagan is.

The Dresden Five Thousand

The lessons of Poland aside, five or maybe six thousand East Germans gathered in Dresden on February 13 1982 to protest the nuclear weapons and foreign policies of both the Warsaw Pact and NATO countries. The remarkable fact about this protest was not only that it took place in a country ruled by the most rigid and subservient of the Soviet satellite governments and with a more prosperous economy than Poland and some of the other countries. Equally significant, it occurred on the anniversary of the night in 1945 on which British and American airforces firebombed Dresden, an unarmed, officially designated hospital city, burning more people alive than were killed in the atomic bombings of Hiroshima and Nagasaki combined. (Who says that after 37 more years of high-technology weapons development the freeze/abolition of genocidal armaments should be limited to nuclear weapons?) Yet it condemned equally Western arms and Soviet military "defenses" against the countries that had perpetrated this atrocity.

As Hochschild tells the story:

> The authorities, used to organizing and controlling any kind of public demonstration, panicked. Protestant officials offered to invite the young people into Dresden's *Kreuzkirche*.... The government quickly agreed, 'The state felt the church could do its job of containing this thing,' says Pleitgen [a West German TV reporter who covered the event].... The pews were full; people were standing; they were in the aisles; the galleries were full. Nobody knew what would happen.

While speeches and discussions were still going on:

> at 10:15 p.m.—the exact moment when the allied bombing had begun...—much of the audience, about 2,000 according to Pleitgen, rose, filed out and walked to the ruins of *Frauenkirche*, another church half a mile away, the remains of which have been left as a monument.

Joining several thousand who were already there, they linked hands and sang protest songs for hours, including "We Shall Overcome" in English. Many of them wore white headbands and patches sewn into their clothes. On them were the slogans "Make Peace Without Weapons" and "Swords into Plowshares."

The next day eighty of them were taken in for questioning by the security police. Three were found to be children of East German Party officials. Occurring where they did, these events are at least as significant a sign of the times as anything that has happened in the United States or Western Europe. As Pleitgen observed, "given the difficulty of organizing anything like this here, getting 5,000[7] people to come to Dresden is the equivalent of getting 300,000 people to come to Bonn."[8]

They are also a sign that, contrary to claims by some of our critics, our protests are not "just what the Soviet authorities want to hear." Perhaps they would like to hear about just enough activity on our part to support a superficial "detente" and limited arms control. That would permit the two superpowers either to divide up the world into mutually agreed upon "spheres of influence" or to act out their rivalry with less damage to their domestic economies. But the Soviet rulers cannot be happy about activities in the West that stir up responses of the kind that took place in Dresden. The people who want to keep hearing about a militant, expanding Western movement for peace and justice are those within the Soviet bloc who oppose militarism and injustice in their own countries. They would like encouragement to believe that the peoples of the world can break down destructive rivalries by acting where they live and reaching out to one another across the artificial barriers that have made us enemies for too long.

Only a handful of American papers reported what happened in Dresden. Those that did buried the story in their inside pages and did none of the follow-up on-the-spot reporting that would have given it some impact. The fact that the unhappy East German authorities felt the sentiment was too strong and shared by too many to permit them to crack down in their usual manner may have had something to do with these failures of the American media. This made the story more "newsworthy," but not in the eyes of those who decide such matters. They prefer to tell us about the unsuccessful resistance activities of a few heroic and relatively isolated figures, preferably pro-Western or right-wing. But the Dresden Five Thousand were speaking to us about deep and broad sentiments that coincide with the sentiments of our own radical and anti-war forces.

Other Signs of the Times

Our knowledge of other, similar activities is fragmentary and uneven at best. We need to improve our methods of finding out about such things. But we do know that 10,000 teenagers gathered at a church-sponsored religious event in Eisenbach, East Germany, four months after the Dresden demonstrations, and that many of them wore the forbidden swords-into-plowshares emblem. The mood of the youth and the sponsoring clergy was such that the attending clergy announced that they would continue to wear the emblem, despite the ban. According to other clergymen, a dozen patchwearers a day are arrested in East Berlin alone. Some are released after the offending patches have been forcibly removed from their clothing; others suffer more severe penalties. We also know that Hungarian Catholic priests have been suspended for advocating the right of conscientious objection to military service, and that six thousand East German draftees and registrants have signed petitions asking for the right to perfom "social peace service" as an alternative to disserving the world in the armed forces.

We know that a group of Soviet peace activists organized in June 1982 a Group for the Establishment of Mutual Trust Between the U.S. and the U.S.S.R.[9] They called for a "four-sided dialogue" among the governments *and people* of the United States and the Soviet Union. Eleven of the members who held a clandestine press conference with Western reporters to announce formation of the group were quickly arrested and detained. In July two members of the group were arrested "to prevent any contact with 200 Scandinavians who staged a closely controlled peace march through several Soviet cities."[10] Still another member was arrested in August, to prevent a planned meeting with a group of visiting American activists, and placed in a psychiatric hospital for a month.

Despite these and other harassments, members of the group tried to hold another press conference on November first. They were forcibly prevented from holding it, but managed to get word out that "related cells have been formed in Novosibirsk, Leningrad and Odessa." They also said that they have received private messages of support from more than a thousand other Russians. The *New York Times* comments, somewhat disparagingly, that "this unofficial group remains a speck in contrast to the 80 million members claimed by the officially sanctioned Soviet Peace Committee."[11] But we would be foolish to underestimate the importance of this speck. Meanwhile, peace and disarmament slogans keep appearing on public walls in Moscow.

We also know that a total of more than a million Romanians marched in different cities in the autumn of 1982 for *bi-lateral, East-West disarmament.*[12] A story in the *Japan Times* (December 7, 1982) says:

> Romanian President and Communist Party leader Nicolas Ceausescu Saturday urged the United States and the Soviet Union to...reduce their nuclear arms in Europe. Speaking at the end of an anti-war mass rally of more than 300,000 Romanians marking a month of peace marches, Ceausecu said, "This biggest demonstration for peace and disarmament ever held in Romania is in support of all similar movements and mainfestations in Europe." [S]ince early November...a total of about 1.7 million people have taken part, the Agerpress news agency said.

If these activites took place in the former Soviet satellite of Romania, whose Communist Party still maintains "fraternal" membership in the Communist International, there must be millions in the Soviet Union and in countries whose governments are more rigidly pro-Soviet who are waiting for an appropriate time to come out of the closet with similar sentiments.

Meanwhile news of new activities keeps coming in, delayed in its arrival and ignored or barely mentioned by the American media. After completing the first draft of this chapter, I received, from France, the text of a letter signed by "hundreds of East German women" and sent to East German premier Erich Nonecker. It was in response to a new military service law that was passed on March 25, 1982. The text was published in the West German weekly, *Der Spiegel* on December 6, 1982. Some of the sentiments sound as if they could have been written by participants in the Womens Pentagon Action in this country. Here are a few excerpts.

> Among us are women both with and without children, Catholic and Lutheran, and women without any church affiliation...We women want to break the vicious cycle of violence and refuse to have anything to do with violence as a means of solving conflicts.
>
> We women see military service for women not as an expression of equal rights but as something that is opposed to our feminine consciousness. We do not see equality as standing side by side with the men who take up arms but rather beside those who have realized that fighting against the abstract enemy means the destruction of human life, which we reject.
>
> We women see readiness for military service as a threatening gesture that stands in the way of moral and military disarmament and which smothers the voice of human reason and replaces it with military obedience.
>
> We women do not want to have to stand one day in the ranks of the National People's Army and defend a country that would become uninhabitable, even after a conventional war in Europe that would probably end in a nuclear catastrophe.
>
> We women believe that humanity stands today on the brink of an abyss and that the piling up of more arms is insane and can only lead to a catastrophe.[13]

I have also come across references to further stirrings in Hungary. A report from an international peace conference in Athens, Greece in December, 1982 says in passing:

Although Romania and Yugoslovia were represented, organizers of the conference were disappointed that people from the newly established Peace Group for Dialogue in Hungary could not attend because they were denied visas.....However, a paper on "Possibilities for the Denuclearization of Hungary," written by Budapest peace activists, was circulated and discussed. Hungary is not believed to have nuclear weapons on its territory, but it has delivery systems, partly under Soviet supervision.[14]

One is reminded of the U.S. denial of visas to more than a hundred delegates from Japan, Canada and other countries to international activities in New York on and around June 12, 1982, during the U.N. Special Session on Disarmament. The irrelevant claim was that they were pro-Soviet, but this was not even true of many of them.[46]

International Viewpoint reprints an interview from an Austrian monthly (*Gegenstimmung*) with a Hungarian peace activist, Istvan Szent-Ivanyi. Here, again, are a few excerpts:

Q. So, an independent peace movement has been formed recently in Hungary as well?
A. The attempts to build one...go back perhaps a year. Before that there were groups of Catholic believers who had been opposing military service for ten years already. This movement functioned in a very conspiratorial fashion, and embraced perhaps two to three hundred young people. Those of them who refused the draft were sentenced to two to three years in prison. The opposition peace movement first made its views public in September 1981.

Szent-Ivanyi then discusses the attempts of the Communist Youth Organization, KISZ, to join and coopt two independent peace groups and the groups' adventures resisting these efforts. He concludes this section.

A group of high school students formed the Anti-Nuclear Campaign-Hungary. They planned a peace

march for March 9 [1982] with their own slogans and placards, directed against U.S. and Soviet armaments...
After this demonstration, [which was infiltrated and therefore had minimal attendance by independents] the Anti-Nuclear Committee decided not to work with the KISZ anymore but to organize its own actions...So they printed their own leaflets, increased the number of their activists to 120 and planned to publish their own journal, which they were stopped from doing.
You run into Anti-Nuclear·Committee activists all the time in the parks and street corners working to recruit to their group.

He also discusses a group of "sculptors and artists that formed a peace committee in March. They are planning a big peace exhibition in Budapest." He talks about "a peace group in Szeged at the university" and still another Catholic group who "are committed to peace on religious grounds and oppose all forms of violence." He says that

In our group there has been a lot of discussion about the question of draft resistance. But the more moderate members won with the argument that we should not let ourselves be divided right away over such a bone of contention but should confine ourselves in the beginning to the question of ending the arms race in the West and East.

If any of these events were publicized in the media that reach the bulk of Americans, they escaped my solicitous attention.

Where Do We Go From Here?

We shouldn't overestimate the present stage of pacifist revolt in any of these countries. Nor should we underestimate, in their case as ours, the internal and external difficulties they face. But there are many indications that everything we do here to develop a powerful, no-nonsense, non-cooptable anti-war movement that stands for peace through justice strikes a responsive chord.

The mass movements that have swept Western Europe and the United States are a good beginning. They have communicated a powerful message to our governments, more importantly to our fellow countrypeople and, perhaps most important of all, to the people of the countries against whom U.S. weapons are aimed. The importance of this kind of people-to-people communication is shown by the effect of the European protests in energizing the American movement, which was lagging until the Europeans led the way. In return, the American actions have sent a message of solidarity and hope back to the Europeans. Even more basic is the message that both movements are sending to the people in Soviet countries. The Europeans have the most direct contacts back and forth across the borders, particularly the Germans. But since the United States is key, the messages we send to our "enemies" by our actions are crucial, whether they are transmitted indirectly through our European counterparts or through the grapevine.

As we continue, we should realize that demanding a Nuclear Freeze was a good starting point but is not a good place to tarry for long. The Europeans do not want a freeze at the level of weapons already deployed by the two superpowers in Europe. Most of the protestors are asking for removal of the nuclear weapons currently deployed there by the United States and Soviet Union. They know that they are not safe so long as the existing arsenals are maintained. Similarly, the Japanese movement is now demanding removal of U.S. nuclear weapons from South Korea and the Philipines, and an end to the use of Japanese ports by U.S. ships carrying nuclear weapons. The Freeze makes sense only if it is viewed as a beginning stage in the development of a movement that makes these demands and adds a corresponding demand for the removal (abolition) of the nuclear weapons currently deployed in the United States and in its world-wide military installations. The people in the Soivet Union go to bed at night and wake up in the morning under the threat of these weapons. Our message to them will be a lot more convincing and more likely to encourage a powerful response when we attain this level of reality.

In a somewhat similar vein, it is right to call for multi-national disarmament, but not in such a way as to discourage unilateral beginnings. The United States does not have to wait for any other nation to disarm before it begins to disarm. We do not have to wait for the Soviet government to act before we demand that the United States act. Not just because the United States is one of the most powerful, aggressive, and therefore feared nations in the world. Not just because the sun never sets on its C.I.A. agents, Special Forces, corporate "vital interests" and nuclear weapons. But because for the United States to take a substantial unilateral step will do more than any other conceivable single act to stimulate popular pressures for multinational disarmament in other countries, including the Soviet Union.

I do not expect that we will achieve massive support for such a program right away. But those who understand the need for it should make our position clear. We can conduct educational campaigns along these lines while working cooperatively with those who are not yet convinced of the need to go that far.

It should not be so hard to prove the need. The reason so many people responded to the Freeze is that they know that the *present level* of weaponry threatens the continuation of life on earth. Anyone knowledgeable in these matters knows that the level twenty years ago was not safe. Millions of Americans and Russians would have perished in October 1962, when the Kennedy administration was on the verge of launching World War III. The Soviet Union, to its credit, backed down before the awesome reality. On that occasion, many people panicked for a few hours or days and then settled down to life as usual, though some did not and now play a vital role in today's disarmament movement. Now the threat is constant and it is even more unrealistic to ignore or forget it. When one finds oneself and one's companions at a dead-end on the edge of a precipice, the natural and correct thing to do is to cry out STOP! But the next necessary reaction is to *turn back, change directions, find an alternative path.*

We should think about an historical parallel with the movement against slavery. There was a time when opponents of slavery called for freezing slavery at its existing level. In the interests of what seemed to be political realism and influenced by the dependence of the Southern economy, *as currently organized*, on slavery, many concerned people said, let it continue in the

Southern states, but don't allow it in any new states. Who today would dare argue that slavery is "necessary" or acceptable anywhere?

Today it is just as relevant and urgent to move from a "freeze" position to an abolition position. It is necessary for safety. And it is necessary in order to purge society of the illusion that killing people in order to achieve economic or political ends is any more moral than making slaves of them.

The abolition of slavery was once considered utopian. Most people today think that the abolition of war is impractical. But as David McReynolds of the War Resisters League has written:

> The abolition of war is not utopian. It was utopian earlier in this century, but not now. As long as war could be waged and leave one side essentially intact, it was possible to wage war. But when the bomb was dropped on Hiroshima, it was war which became utopian, not disarmament.... The blunt fact is we don't know how to deal with international conflicts except by war—but we are going to have to learn.[15]

Notes

1. With thanks to the women's movement, I have paraphrased George Meredith's words to avoid his use of "man," "him," and "mankind" to refer to all of us, usages which violate the unity he obviously intended to affirm.
2. On May 28, 1945, Harry Hopkins, President Truman's special envoy to Moscow cabled Truman: "Japan is doomed and the Japanese know it. Peace feelers are being put out...and we should therefore consider together our joint attitudes [Soviet and American] and act in concert about the surrender of Japan."

The [James] *Forrestal Diaries* record in an entry dated July 13 [1945]: "The first real evidence of a Japanese desire to get out of the war came today through intercepted messages from Togo...to Sato, Jap [sic] ambassador to Moscow, instructing the latter to see Molotov if possible before his departure for the Big Three meeting...to lay before him the Emperor's strong desire to secure a termination of the war."

According to U.S. Strategic Bombing Survey No. 4, "Certainly prior to December 31, Japan would have surrendered, even if the atomic bombs had not been dropped, even if Russia had not entered the war, and even if no invasion had been planned or contemplated."

All three of the above are quoted in *The Free World Colossus,* David Horowitz, Hill and Wang, 1965. There are both older and more recent sources for the same basic information, but the American people overwhelmingly continue to believe the lie promoted at the time and now, that the bombs were dropped to save huge losses of American lives in a costly, inch-by-inch invasion of Japanese held islands and Japan itself.
3. Daniel Ellsberg lists 12 major, *documented* instances in his "Call to Mutiny," in *Protest and Survive,* E.P. Thompson and Dan Smith Editors, Monthly Review Press, 1982.
4. "Neither moralism nor fellow-travelling sentimentalism can be of any service in guiding the peace movement in its difficult relations with the Communist states. We are dealing, just as we are with the NATO states, with powerful entrenched military interests and with leaders who seek to advance their own objectives. The problem with the Communist rulers is that they are the ideological look-alikes of their opposite numbers in the West, thinking in the same terms of 'balance' and security through 'strength.'...The Western peace movement derives its strength precisely from its political independence, its 'unacceptable' demands upon both blocs.... We must make it clear that we find it intolerable that independent voices in the East are harassed or silenced; that we will not scurry around to [peace] conferences in Moscow or assemblies in Prague so long as that repression continues; that we intend to act as free citizens of a healed world and that we do not require permits from Zhukov [head of the Soviet Peace Committee]...to talk with citizens on the other side; and that, if it has to come to that, it is as easy to sit down in front of the Soviet Embassy as on Greenham Common." (E.P. Thompson, "END and the Soviet 'Peace Offensive'," *The Nation,* February 26, 1983.

5. Quoted from ETC, a Stockholm weekly, in *International Viewpoint*, May 1982, Montreuil, France.

6. *Mother Jones*, September-October 1982.

7. James Bergeron in *The Vermont Cynic*, University of Vermont. Bergeron is a U.S. Army volunteer (1980) who was "deeply affected" by the massive anti-militarist protests in West Germany in 1981. In November, he attended one of the rallies in uniform, was arrested, held under house arrest for two months, to keep his "cancerous ideas" from spreading, and then mustered out with what the Army calls a "less than honorbale discharge."

8. Reporting this story from West Germany, the *New York Times* said 4,000, but when Hochschild went to Dresden to investigate, he was told that there were five to six thousand. *Mother Jones, Ibid.*

9. *New York Times*, June 5, 1982.

10. *New York Times*, Nov. 2, 1982.

11. *Ibid.*

12. This information was brought to my attention by Japanese anti-nuclear activists when I was in Japan on the forthieth anniversary of the Japanese attack on Pearl Harbor to take part in mass protests organized around the slogan "No More Pearl Harbors; No More Hiroshimas."

13. *International Viewpoint*, 10 January 1983.

14. *In These Times,* Mike Jendrzejczyk.

15 "Beyond the Freeze, Toward Abolition," David McReynolds; War Resisters League, 339 Lafayette Street, New York, N.Y. 10012.

9
AFTERWORD
By Michael Albert &
David Dellinger

The contributors to *Beyond Survival* deal with many political, personal, economic and cultural relationships that have produced and now sustain the nuclear threat. Their analyses can contribute to the growth of a movement that will be capable of achieving peace and liberation. But for the most part our contributors do not discuss the day-to-day workings of the groups and organizations that might make up such a movement, or the ways in which such groups and organizations can interact positively with each other.

Accordingly, we thought it would be useful to include an Afterword addressing how anti-nuclear groups can embody alternative attitudes and relationships that will allow them to contribute to the emergence of a new type of society that draws on the latent skills, creative energies and combined insights of all its members.

In writing this Afterword we especially kept in mind two of the lessons that flow from *Beyond Survival*. One is the necessity to develop mutually beneficial relationships between those whose present dominating concern is to deal exclusively with the nuclear danger and those whose life experience has also led them to break compellingly with some other dehumanizing aspects of the present society.

The second lesson concerns the relationship of anti-nuclear activists with those who still see no grounds for hope in any alternative to the militarization of society. The Afterword discusses the need for imaginative efforts by anti-nuclear individuals and groups not only to reach out to new constituencies and address this type of despair, but also, despite wide-ranging differences, to achieve an internal solidarity that can inspire others.

Adding to the demands of the anti-nuclear movement will require some painful soul-searching by many newly concerned supporters of the freeze. It will meet principled resistances by sincere advocates of a single-issue approach. And it will have to contend with the usual attempts by less principled supporters of the status quo to limit the movement to a more superficial analysis and program. A realistic assessment is suggested in two thoughtful articles in *Win* magazine's special issue "Directions for Disarmament," November, 1982. After saying that "freeze supporters should avoid criticizing more far-reaching disarmament efforts," Mark Niedergan writes that on the other hand progressives should realize the danger that they will "scare off new activists by appearing 'too radical'." Still, he continues, "it is the responsibility of a leader to stimulate and challenge those who are listening."

Carl Conetta writes:

> The task of progressives is not to rebuke popular critiques of nuclear weapons but to *enrich* them; to form, in a sense, a bridge between popular conceptions and a more comprehensive analysis...The challenge that faces the disarmament movement is to develop a strategy that can navigate between isolation and cooptation.

Conetta also accurately points out that:

> As most of us can testify, the break with the conservative "status quo" begins with regard to one or a few issues we find personally compelling—like U.S. intervention in El Salvador or the threat of nuclear war. When new activists are met at the entry point to a movement with an explicit or implicit *demand* [emphasis added] for political consensus that departs too widely from their current orientation they will find it difficult to participate in that movement. This is particularly tragic because...[o]nly the accumulation of personal experience in political struggle is rich enough, individualized enough and compelling enough to lay the basis for a "clean break" [with "establishment ideology"].

Through political activity, activists come into new relations with existing power structures...and begin to feel the need for a more comprehensive and critical perspective. It becomes a special responsibility of progressives to nurture the type of political context which invites the "demobilized" sections of the public into activism.

With these insights in mind, we would like to summarize some lessons from *Beyond Survival* concerning the internal functioning of a sound local disarmament organization and the uses and limitations of coalition building.

The Organization as Microcosm

As was pointed out in a number of contributions, how we organize and conduct ourselves in our own organizations will critically affect how well we reach out to new audiences to expand our movement. Like the members of any movement, those who seek disarmament must pay close attention to the internal strength and cohesiveness of their groups lest a weakness in these areas becomes their Achilles heel.

One of the frequent failures of social movements is a lack of attention to analysis and strategy and to the effort that is needed to be sure all members participate effectively in their elaboration and application. Yet a movement that ignores analysis and strategy is destined to errors of ignorance, while a movement that depends on a single individual or small group to act as its "intellect" is doomed to be undemocratic and squander the potential creativity of most of its members. Internal education should be pursued as a high priority. Arguments that members are too busy organizing may be countered by the observation that increasing the political and psychological awarenesses of those who are engaged in outreach is itself a critical component of good organizing.

"Business" has a way of crowding out discussions of the personal and political problems that inevitably accompany movement activism. But regular sessions for sharing ideas and experiences concerning goals, strategy, and personal problems in a non-emergency atmosphere are crucial for consciousness-raising and for feeding the creative energies and political vision of good organizers. They help everyone gain the perspective and confidence essential to democratic participation and simultaneously provide a context for addressing short-term problems. Rather than have only a few leaders develop original ideas among themselves, *as many people as possible should be involved.*

Diversity of Culture and Consciousness

Another problem common to social movements is a tendency to become in-grown and clubbish. Habits take over and diversity of ideas and methods disappears. What should be a creative, flexible program geared to change in light of new lessons and circumstances becomes rote. One useful way to improve a group's grasp on diverse ideas and feelings is to incorporate within it avenues through which people with differing perspectives can make their views known. The most familiar vehicle for this is the movement caucus, a subgroup identified by a shared background, set of experiences or commitment. Besides their other functions, caucuses of women, workers, Third World members, senior citizens, youth, lesbians and gays or just people with a minority opinion on an important issue can organize particular programs that prove enlightening and improve the group's knowledge, program, social relations and cohesiveness. Indeed for disarmament groups to place active value on the creation of women's, workers' and minority caucuses would in turn provide needed leadership regarding issues of gender, class and race and make it more likely that the movement's culture and style will respond to and communicate with members of all constituencies potentially in favor of disarmament—a central issue addressed by most of our contributors.

One of the major themes of *Beyond Survival* is that racist, sexist, classist and ageist attitudes all help provide the psychological and institutional context that encourages militaristic responses to international disputes. Sexual objectification, toleration of violence against women and the denigration of various categories of people at home and abroad to subhuman status all contribute to making our culture numb to the inhumanity of arms production and war. Similarly, the production of arms is propelled not only by venal foreign policy considerations but also by structural pressures of a capitalist economy that require vast governmental spending on projects which must neither conflict with existing power relationships nor compete with private industry. So, even to pursue its *own* priority concern effectively, the disarmament movement needs to address issues of imperialism, labor, race, gender and the economy directly. It can best do so with the help and active participation of the prime victims of society's failings in these areas, and caucuses are one means to assure that their voices will speak and be heard.

Internal Solidarity

Sometimes, ironically, movements and progressive organizations become lonely places to operate. Mutual support is absent as each individual deals with tasks, feelings, worries, or hopes in relative isolation. The alienation is little different, in such circumstances, than that felt in "establishment institutions," but the personal pain is often greater because expectations are higher and defenses are down. Encourging and assisting "affinity groups" that bring together a small group of people with complementary but diverse attitudes and levels of experience can provide valuable means for consciousness raising and for the bonding that is indispensible to a successful resistance movement. Affinity groups can help reduce the alienation felt by new members in an unfamiliar setting by familiarizing them with the histories and experiences that have disappeared down the "memory hole" of the dominant culture and by reassuring them that their fears and failings are not private, but part of a process that everyone goes through. On the other hand, affinity groups can also help veterans who may be scarred by their experiences and mired in the past, sorely in need of the fresh perspectives and new ideas that come from having been born or activated in a later period. Most current affinity groups have been formed as tactical support groups for civil disobedience demonstrations, though they often live on to fulfill the roles described above. Why not form them with the broader aims in mind in the first place?

Democratic Self-Management

Finally, and in the spirit of the foregoing suggestions, it is critical to stress the importance of constant attention to maintaining internal democracy, avoiding debilitating divisions of labor and promoting the dispersal and rotation of empowering responsibilities. The Student Non-Violent Coordinating Committee, the most successful organizing group in the Southern civil-rights movement, used to say that the only successful organizer is one who does not make herself or himself indispensable. Within six months she or he ought to be able to leave without significantly reducing the morale or effectiveness of the group. If leaders have special experience or skills, they should recognize the importance of teaching the skills and communicating the experiences and of not monopolizing positions of responsibility or public visibility. The quickest thinking or more vocal participants should help create a setting that encourages less vocal members to speak out and should listen carefuly to what they have to say. Their insights may be more accurate or profound than those who speak more easily, or they may provide a missing link in the group's thinking. And while the most experienced activists have a special responsibility due to their accumulated confidence and skills, achieving these goals must be the responsibility of everyone in the group. Everyone should shun excessive reliance on a single leader or group of leaders and should help those in leadership roles to develop egalitarian attitudes and practices. The internal structure of the disarmament movement will dramatically affect the morale and creativity of its members. It will influence their understanding of alternative structures and relationships that can foster self-management in place of the hierarchical inequalities in power and decision-making that now exist in the larger society. How we handle these matters will influence our ability to affect local and national policies in the coming decades.

Coalition Building

Through the experiences of the past two decades, many activists have come to feel that our society is plagued by an interlocking network of oppressions requiring a variety of autonomous movements. But practice has shown that to be fully effective these movements must cooperate and entwine. After reading about these experiences in this volume or experiencing the lessons they evince first hand in movement practice, it is apparent that attaining a freeze, rolling back arms, or diminishing the prosects of nuclear war are all in part dependent on parallel successes of labor, anti-imperialist, women's, anti-racist and other movements. Likewise, it is not so difficult to discern, for example, that women's efforts to overcome the debilitating effects of sexism (or Third World community efforts to overcome racism) are partly dependent upon parallel successes in altering military, economic, and racial (or sexual) social relations. But it is something else entirely to bring diverse movements with different priority focuses into communication with one another—to cooperate, to learn from one another, and ultimately to provide assistance and sustenance to one another. This is the essential task of "coalition-building."

Criteria for A Successful Coalition

A successful coalition unites disparate movements and organizations while respecting the integrity, focuses and agendas of each. It energizes and empowers people by letting them know that, contrary to the impression they might get from the media and government, there are thousands, probably millions, who share their anger at the status quo and have somewhat similar dreams and visions of better ways for human beings to relate to each other and solve our problems. Such a coalition allows each participating group to benefit from contact with others, learning lessons about new strategies and tactics, learning about the linkages of social problems, and the power of unified responses. Every participant group's strength, intellectually and at demonstrations, is enhanced by its ties to and knowledge of other organizations and their experiences.

Besides the pressures on the government and the message of hope that gets through to the public at coalition demonstations most of the participants are encouraged to speak and act more bravely back where they came from. Many are stimulated to engage in more advanced resistance activities that may have been learned from one or another of the groups that made up the coalition: sit-ins, blockades, draft resistance, tax refusal, defections and other principled activities by G.I. s, etc.

Coalitions have two distinctive functions that set them apart from single-focus disarmament organizations. If either predominates over the other, a coalition does not live up to its maximum potential. The first function is to unite a range of politically, culturally, and geographically diverse organizations and individuals in common actions expressive of their areas of *agreement*. The aim is to create a powerful voice to press for universally desired changes in the most massive possible way. The second function is to give voice and visibility to the *differing* programs, analyses, cultures (and sometimes tactics) of the diverse parties within the coalition—publicly, through the events it sponsors, and privately, through the interchanges that take place internally as members work together planning and organizing demonstrations, hammering out areas of agreement, and hopefully respectfully discussing areas of disagreement. The aim is a percolation of insights and broadening of the political awareness of all participants. The successful coalition is the one that accomplishes each of the functions in a way which simultaneously helps to accomplish the other. Coalitions which see the functions as opposed and seek to accomplish one at the expense of the other usually fail at both and don't last long.

The Least-Common-Denominator Approach

People who stress the outreach function to the relative neglect of the political development function usually advocate a least-common-denominator approach. The theory is that a coalition can be strongest and reach furthest by giving voice only to the things all members agree on. At first glance this appears to be a sound idea. By submerging the controversial aims and means of each group, we present a united front and achieve a focussed impact. No one is embarrassed by speakers who go beyond agreed topics, nor by tactical options that not everyone wishes to promote. The coalition's relationships with the public are thereby safeguarded and enhanced, both with newly concerned people whom it attracts to a demonstration for the first time, and also with those who do not attend but will form their impressions from the media which will have a harder time playing up the radicals, "freaks," and "ne'er-do-wells" and their "outlandish" slogans, to the neglect of the central areas of agreement. Finally, the coalition itself can function smoothly, efficiently and without the painful encounters that often accompany attention to anything other than *already shared* points of agreement. All the controversial aims of each particular movement which a part of every other movement might disagree with are left unspoken—at least at committee meetings—thus avoiding unnecessary friction, resignations, and perhaps even dissolution of the coalition.

In practice, however, almost none of it works this way. Instead of being strengthened by being honed to a single sharp point, the least-common-denominator coalition is robbed of its richness and diversity—and so is the public that comes into direct or indirect contact with it. The movement loses its ability to provide a challenging selection of ideas. It sacrifices many of the stimuli to private and public growth that are so necessary to changing the moral and political atmosphere of the country. Contrary to least-common-denominator expectations, the public is also divided and diverse in the experiences and insights that move it. It is not a monolithic, reactionary or apathetic whole that needs to be talked down to because it is incapable of serious thought or attention to more than one simple idea. A coalition should not approach potential recruits in the manner of the TV shows that present pablum rather than solid food. When coalitions take this approach, they often succeed in attracting a temporarily huge audience and in stirring its emotions in a simplistic context that caricatures reality. But the allegiances of audiences aroused in this way are tenuous and through no fault of their own, their understanding is likely to be shallow. They tend to be passive, subject to being wooed away by some other simplistic program or turned in a different direction by some "scare" or "scandal" invented by the government. As Eugene Debs said years ago: "I would not be a Moses to lead you into the promised land, because if I could lead you into it, someone else could lead you out of it."

Some of the subjects and views excluded by the least-common-denominator approach to forming a disarmament coalition would indeed worry some potential participants, perhaps even keep them away at the beginning. But inclusion of these ideas in a way that doesn't coerce every movement participant to accept them but does compel everyone to recognize their existence and assess their merit would have many counter-balancing virtues. It would challenge participants and public alike with new ideas and possibilities. It would attract important new constituencies, adding their strengths and simultaneously opening them to important linkages between their area of compelling concern and the struggle for disarmament. And it would enrich the political awareness and agendas of disarma-ment activists as well. Many prestigious leaders of the anti-bomb movement wanted to exclude any mention of U.S. interventions in Vietnam during the early stages of that war, but public concern with Vietnam soon outstripped its concern with the bomb. And of course it was in Vietnam that the bomb was almost used, and probably would have been used except for the *combined* strengths of the anti-Vietnam-war and anti-bomb movements. To overlook the lesson of this example is a kind of a-historicism the movement can ill afford.

Yet contemporary advocates of the least common denomin-ator approach have succeeded in eliminating such issues as unemployment, the militarization of the economy, sexism and racism from the advance calls to some anti-nuclear demonstra-tions. Even the issue of El Salvador and other Central Ameican interventions has often been excluded, ostensibly in order to reach mainstream America with the most critical concern of the day, and the one they are most likely to respond to, disarmament. The folly of this type of thinking, however well-motivated, has been amply argued in many contributions to this book. By this unneccessary narrowing, causes of the arms race are ignored, factors contributing to public acceptance of government nuclear policies are misunderstood, conflicts that could grow into a nuclear holocaust are left to fester unopposed. Moreover, in the long run, we deny ourselves access to so many constituencies and reduce our own credibility and wisdom by such an amount that we wind up demobilizing and de-energizing more people than an enriched political perspective might have initially scared off.

As if these failings of the least-common-denominator approach were not enough, its most determined advocates often turn out not to be advocating a genuine least-common-denominator orientation at all. Rather, what they really seek is acceptance of the most timid and conservative position within the coalition, which is the one they themselves hold. They give up nothing, but ask those who are less tied to the status quo, and who trust the government less and an alert informed people more, to give up a great deal. But, as E.P. Thompson of the English Campaign for Nuclear Disarmament and the Committee for European Nuclear Disarmament has written:

> The "defense" establishments of both sides are alarmed by the spontaneity and lack of deference of the movement. They see it as "destabilizing." They seek to constrain it within traditional political forms and categories, and to confine all the turbulent waters of popular demonstrations into a stagnant lake of secretive negotiations about "balance," conducted with due propriety by the proper and authorized personnel of the rival establishments. If this was to happen then the chance of a third way to peace would be lost. That is why the peace movement must continue to influence the political process, but from outside its forms and independent of its controls. It must remain autonomous and non-aligned.[3]

When the conservative position does turn out to be a least-common-denominator of sorts, it is a position that can be coopted fairly easily by the government, with an assist from the media. For example, to the extent that the Ban-the-Bomb movement of the late Fifties and early Sixties excluded fundamental criticism of U.S. foreign policy and the economic and racist views that underlie it, limiting discussions to the harmful effects of fallout made it easier for the government to dismantle the movement by agreeing to underground rather than overground testing. In the case of the Vietnam war, the effort for years was to exclude anti-imperialist analyses and calls for bringing the troops home in favor of more conventional calls for peace negotiations. No one could seriously object to peace negotiations, so, in a sense, it was a lowest common denominator approach. But in isolation this formulation would have lent credence to the "wrong war at the wrong time" position that the government eventually settled on (for a time) as a rationale for leaving Vietnam while continuing the drives and policies that have led to our present peril.

Ironically, if the cautious advocates of a simplistic call for negotiations had succeeded in excluding a direct demand to bring the troops home, they would have weakened the movement's outreach to a sizeable public not commonly involved at the time in anti-war activities: the G.I. s and their friends and families, who ultimately played a major role in ending the war. And the same observation applies to their attempts to exclude support for draft resisters and "deserters." Not only does the least common denominator approach risk cooptation, it even fails to reach out to the broadest possible audiences. Perhaps, therefore, the real motivation for the least common denominator approach has less to do with movement dynamics and more to do with appealing for media coverage and the good will of "experts" and "professionals." For it is undeniable that many of *these* constituencies *do* welcome any narrowing of movement ideas and constraining of tactical options. And, in a sense, the blessing of these powerful people does give the movement (and certain of its leaders) a temporary visibility and legitimacy. But at what cost?

It is important to win the most honest and wide-ranging media coverage we can and we should be as accommodating as our principles allow. But to appeal to media representatives by making our movements correspond to *their images of what we should be* is to sacrifice our aims in an effort to publicize them. To strive for "respectability" is to forget that this honor is bestowed by the institutions and individuals who enact the policies we oppose. They do not *give* it to their opponents for being successful, but only for becoming unsuccessful. We can gain respectability by appealing to their norms and values, what *they* admire, and by forgetting why we sought to be heard in the first place. Or, on the other hand, we can gain the eyes and ears of the media by being so insightful and effective that we cannot be ignored.

Finally, internal cohesiveness and development of trust are not necessarily advanced by leaving unspoken the controversial aims or emphases of each segment of a coalition that some other segment might disagree with. The problem is that the undiscussed commitments of each group are usually no less important to their view of *themselves* than the concerns which become the basis of the coalition's overt functioning. Without the opportunity to air diverse viewpoints and collectively work out their relationship to coalition work, people develop hidden agendas that crop up in devious ways at inopportune moments. Soon people scheme to introduce the forbidden subjects or gain a camouflaged advantage for their favored positions. Others react by trying to exclude people they disagree with from important comittees or press conferences where they might "say the wrong thing." After a while everyone begins to assume the worst: that their fellow coalitionists can't be trusted; that they have entered the coalition not to engage in a truly cooperative effort but to coopt energies and constituencies without in any way altering their own attitudes and aims. "And if they're doing that, we will have to also."

Such coalitions are very fragile. The issues that are put under the table rarely stay there, but when they do surface, since there is no means for handling them, there is apt to be a confrontation rather than respectful dialogue. After a while, the tenuous coalition is taken over by a single or a few tendencies, or suffers from the resignations of people who have been disillusioned by the coalition's failure to deal with different outlooks in an open, mature fashion. Not realizing that coalition work can be inspiring and enlightening, a living model of the possibilities of combining unity and heterogeneity, the much sought after "new faces" in whose name the coalition was pressured to adopt its least-common-denominator approach may be the first to be disillusioned—not just with that particular coalition but with the entire organized movement.

The Maximalist Coalition

The second common approach to coalition-building reverses the error of the least-common-denominator adherents. It emphasizes the need to combine diverse insights in order to attain a comprehensive politics but carries this out in a manner that prevents it from reaching a wide audience, rather than vice versa. Holding high the slogan that "we have got to get together to defeat the common enemy," these coalitionists try to hammer out a comprehensive maximalist program of agreement—the well-known laundry list of society's injustices. All the planks of every movement's self-definition must become planks of the whole coalition's definition. Every member of each movement is confronted with a call to adopt all the focuses and priorities of all the other movements. In essence, rather than a coalition, these coalitionists seek to create a "super-movement" embodying the program of all the "sub-movements" they want to amalgamate.

The problem is that there is no real basis or reason to pursue this level of agreement. Efforts to create the new, all-embracing "coalition" progress for a while because people are hungry for the strengths they hope will come from uniting the entire left. Everyone hopes that this time it will work, and fears that if it doesn't it will discourage potential activists by showing that leftists "can't get it together." But attrition gradually sets in and the effort dissolves or becomes a front for a few groups who dominate it but claim that it represents a far wider spectrum of participants than it does.

The reality is that progressives indeed cannot get it together in this monolithic way and would in any case suffer severe losses if they did make a go of it. There are different views about how to organize, what focuses to address, what tactics to employ. And there are different attitudes toward how movements should be structured and how different movements should work together or, on the other hand, function autonomously. We need autonomous movements with different focuses to extend everyone's understandings of *particular* oppressions and the appropriate strategies for dealing with them. We need specialized autonomous movements each of which can explore its specific area of injustice and congenially encompass those particular elements of the society most affected by it. To submerge the anti-war, women's, rank-and-file worker's, and anti-racist movements in a super-movement which effectively eliminates each as a separate entity would guarantee an overall diminution of creativity in each of these critical constituencies and in the coalitions through which they work. It would reduce the ability to reach out to hesitant and often justifiably mistrustful people who share the same oppression. And, as history has amply demonstrated, it would make it more likely that the leadership of Third World, women, and rank-and-file working people will be tokenized as the "super-movement" comes under sway of more highly-educated, more confident, or especially better connected and subsidized white males.

Autonomy Within Solidarity

Ironically, the least-common-denominator and maximalist approaches converge in their results. Both limit outreach, genuine cross fertilization and the kinds of creativity that arise from combining freedom to pursue one's own special concerns with participation in a coalition with others who are similarly pursuing theirs. Clearly we need coalitions that are more than the bare intersection of their parts but don't put excessive pressures or restraints on their member groups. A vital coalition should force its member organizations and movements to understand linkages and develop more holistic political analyses—but slowly, at a pace governed by their actual experiences.

A workable coalition of this kind must accept the legitimacy of discussion of *all* the issues and approaches important to *all* of its member organizations. It will develop opportunities to do this that don't unduly prolong its policy-making and business meetings: internal educational sessions, public forums and teach-ins, a wide range of presentations at demonstrations, even multi-level demonstrations, with sufficient separation in place and time to make clear who is doing what. It won't impose any type of monolithic conformity or allegiance, either to a cautious least-common-denominator or to a shopping list of demands that includes every complaint and proposed solution by every aggrieved member organization. Not everyone accepts everything put forward by everyone but everyone admits that no one has all the answers and that all the attempts the member movements are making deserve critical appraisal and respectful expression of whatever agreements or differences may follow. Solidarity and autonomy are both priorities and not mutually exclusive.

This type of coalition would agree to a set of aims that all member movements *would* actively and visibly support. It would have both national and local offices, and at-large as well as organizational members. Indeed, it seems to us that many existing organizations would join such a coalition. Moreover, we believe that there are also thousands of people who would be more likely to become active for the first time (or again) as at-large coalition members rather than as members of any one of the coalition's member organizations. What would be most attractive is the multiplicity of focuses and the overarching *agreement to disagree* while being mutually respectful about all members' orientations.

The disarmament movement has a special responsibility and need to spearhead the effort to create and sustain this type of coalition. Its responsibility stems from two related facts. First, not everyone is a woman, Third Worlder, rank-and-file worker, welfare recipient, etc., but everyone will be a victim of nuclear war if it comes. Second, of all progressive movements, the movement for disarmament has the greatest access to fiscal, material, and media resources (though the warning about our relations to the media mentioned above and in Chomsky's essay should be kept in mind.)

The disarmament movement's special *need* arises from the reality that while nuclear war may threaten to extinguish all life, this dire eventuality is rather abstract and of the future compared to losing a job, a limb in an industrial accident, a welfare check, or an education, or being beaten up or otherwise mistreated as a woman, gay person, or black. There are limits to the daily reminders of the dangers of nuclear war and their ability to propel people to act in a sustained manner. In fact, there is a considerable psychological pressure not to keep facing up to the problem and not to continue acting so as to avoid the fear and insecurity that accompanies awareness. The result, as several contributors to *Beyond Survival* point out, is that while disarmament sentiment can sweep the country and swell to immense proportions in a very short span, it can fade away almost as quickly for long periods of time. To gain strength and continuity it needs to gain roots that tie it more closely to people's daily experiences. This is most apt to occur if disarmament work becomes closely associated with the other important social movements of our time with which it is logically linked.

To make this effort is not artificial or arbitrary. As we struggle for survival for ourselves and our fellows, for our children and their children's children, it is only sensible to examine and challenge the superstitions and practices that have placed all human life in jeopardy. As we do so, we become more and more closely linked with these other movements. Step by step we come to realize that in order to win the struggle for survival we must aim at much more than survival.